MISTER

MORGEN

MISTER

MORGEN

IGOR HOFBAUER

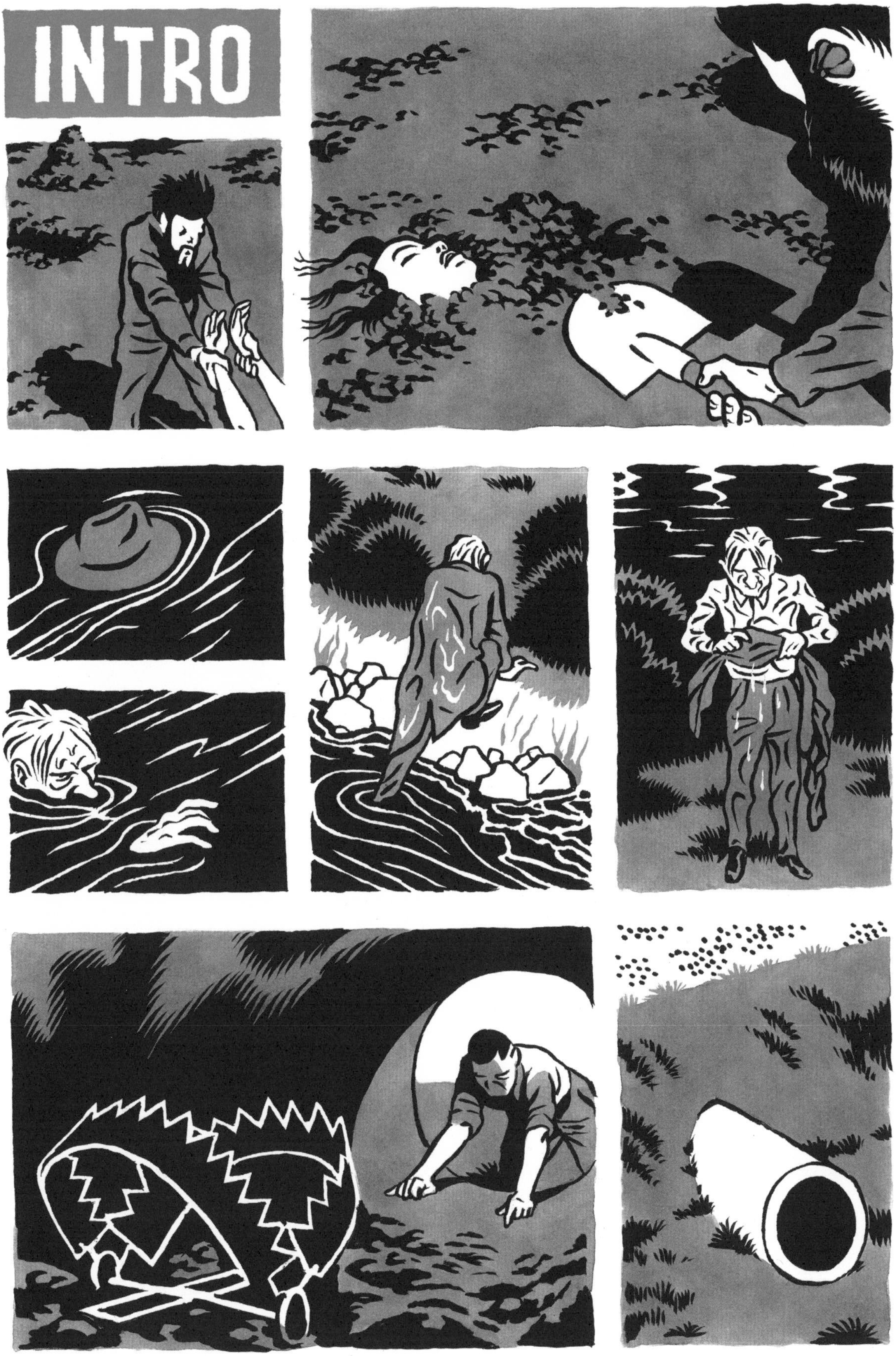
INTRO

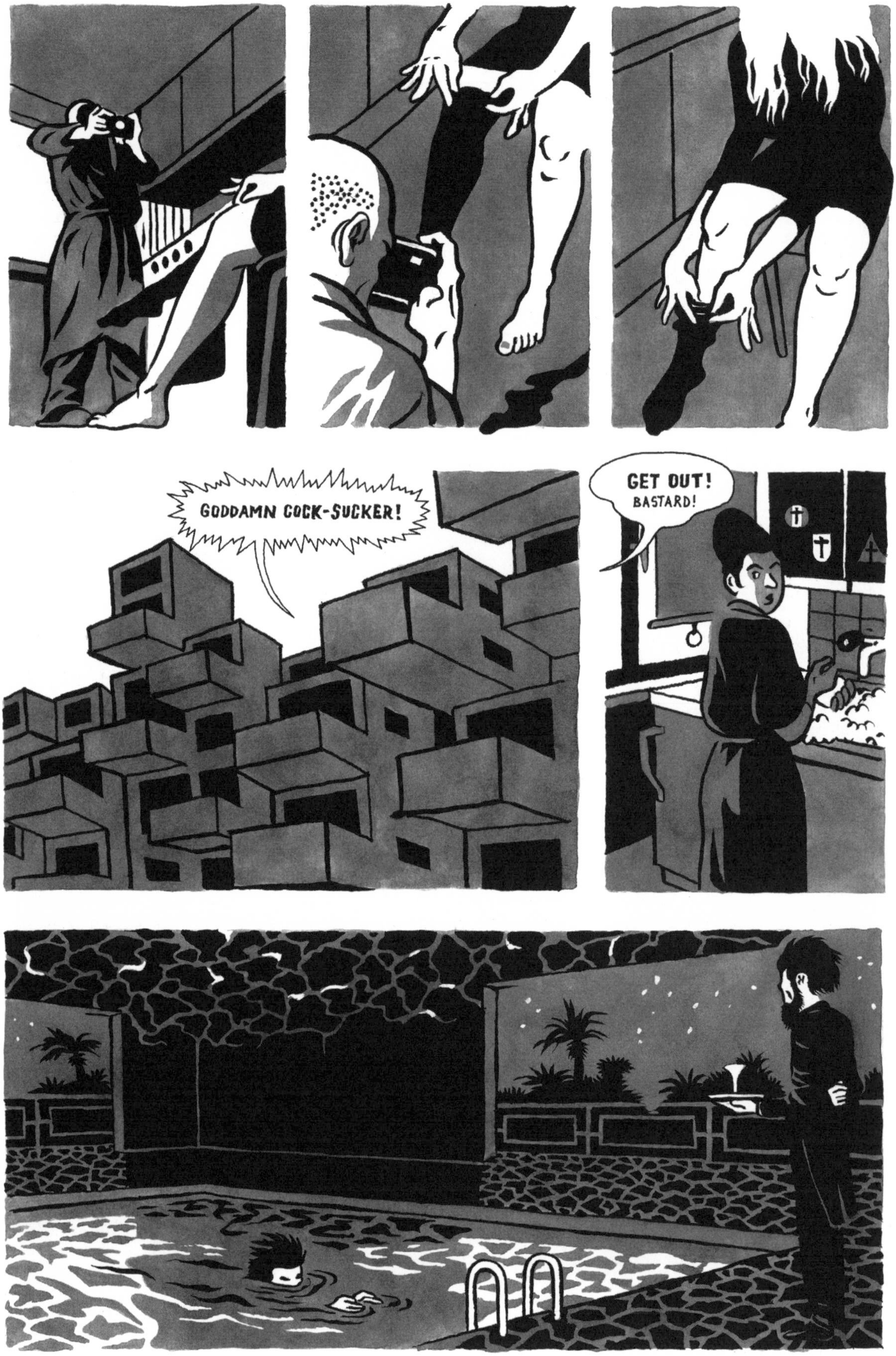
GODDAMN COCK-SUCKER!
GET OUT! BASTARD!

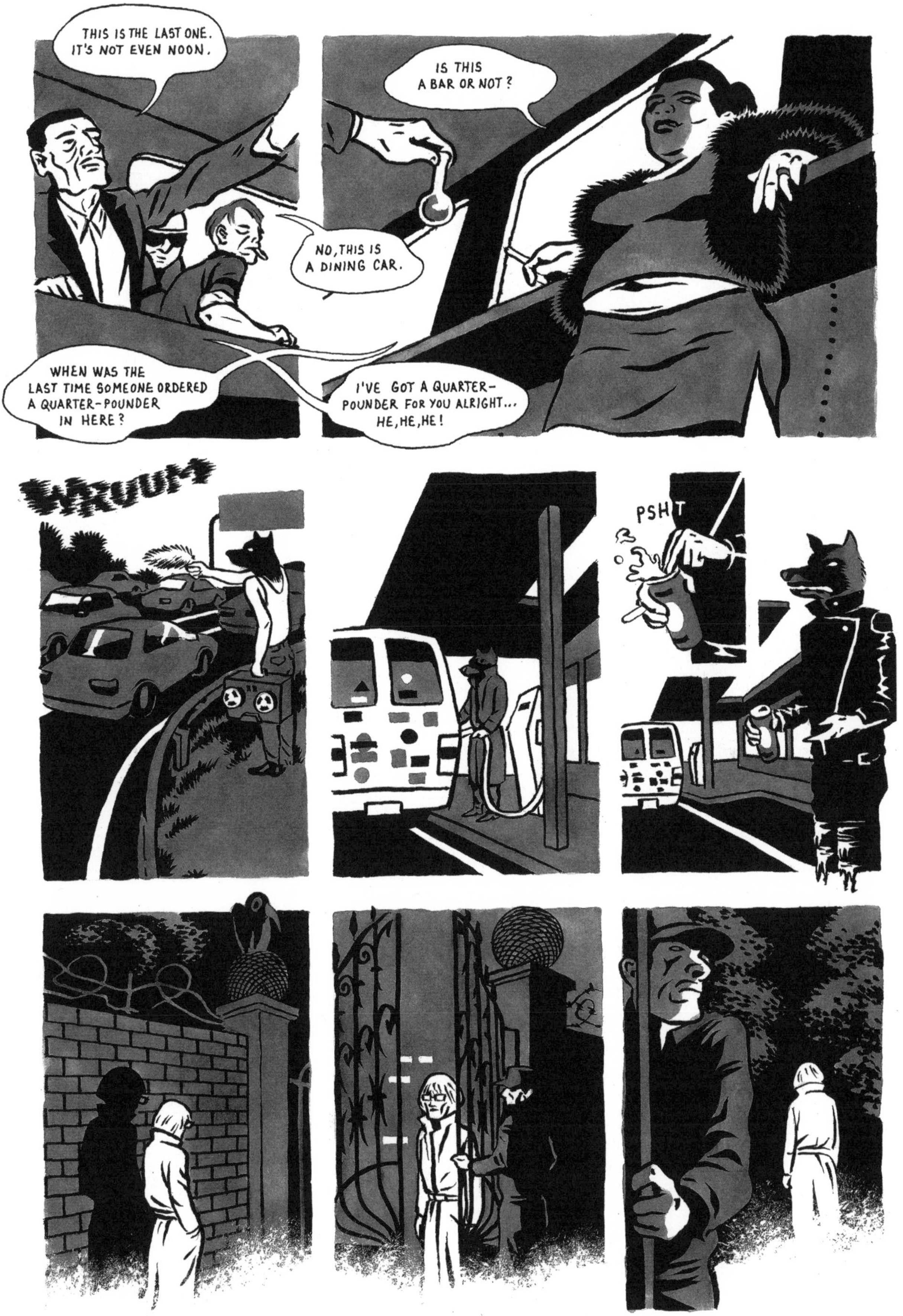

THIS IS THE LAST ONE. IT'S NOT EVEN NOON.
IS THIS A BAR OR NOT?
NO, THIS IS A DINING CAR.
WHEN WAS THE LAST TIME SOMEONE ORDERED A QUARTER-POUNDER IN HERE?
I'VE GOT A QUARTER-POUNDER FOR YOU ALRIGHT... HE, HE, HE!
WRUUM
PSHT

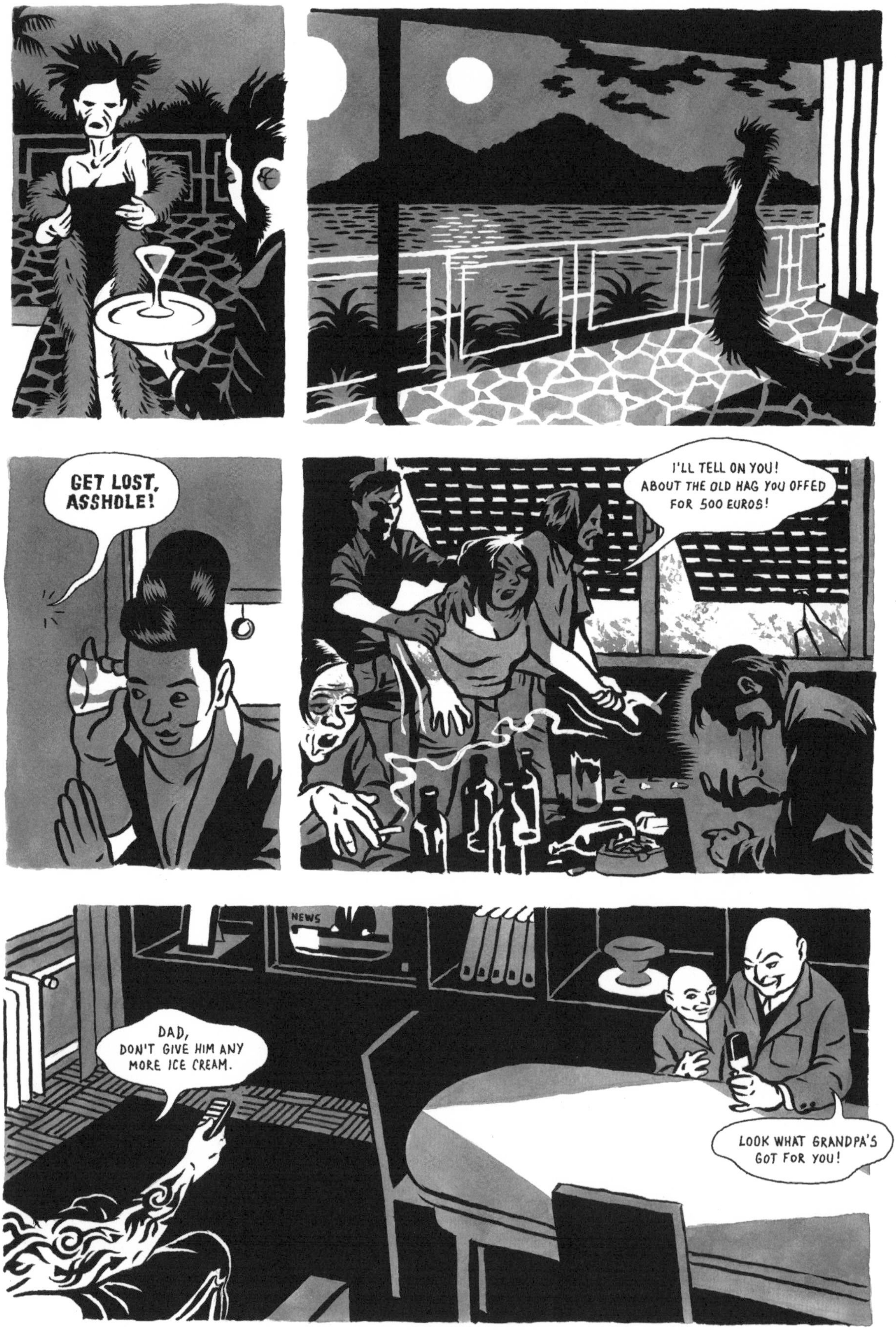
GET LOST, ASSHOLE!
I'LL TELL ON YOU! ABOUT THE OLD HAG YOU OFFED FOR 500 EUROS!
DAD, DON'T GIVE HIM ANY MORE ICE CREAM.
LOOK WHAT GRANDPA'S GOT FOR YOU!
NEWS

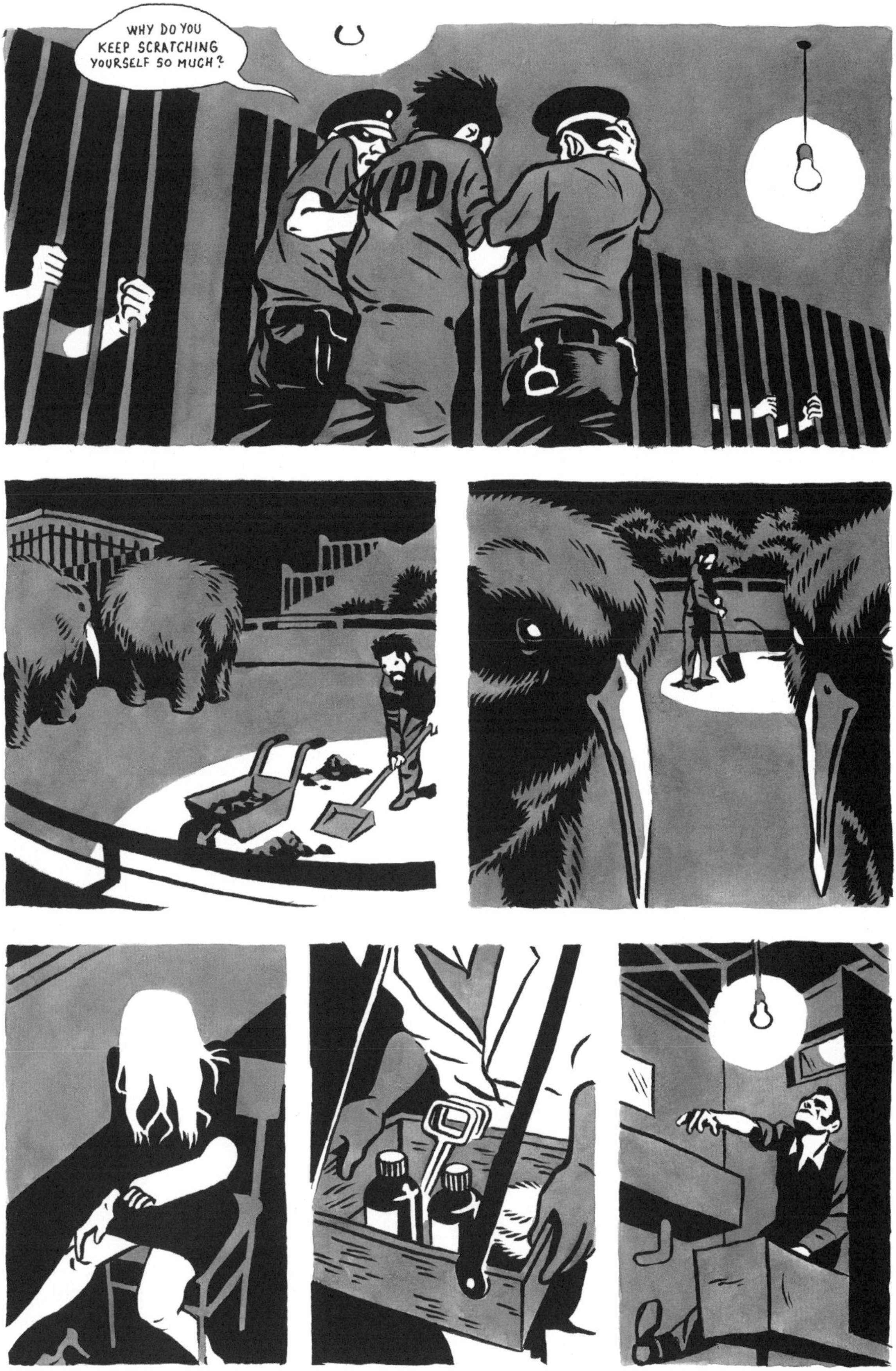
WHY DO YOU KEEP SCRATCHING YOURSELF SO MUCH?
NPD

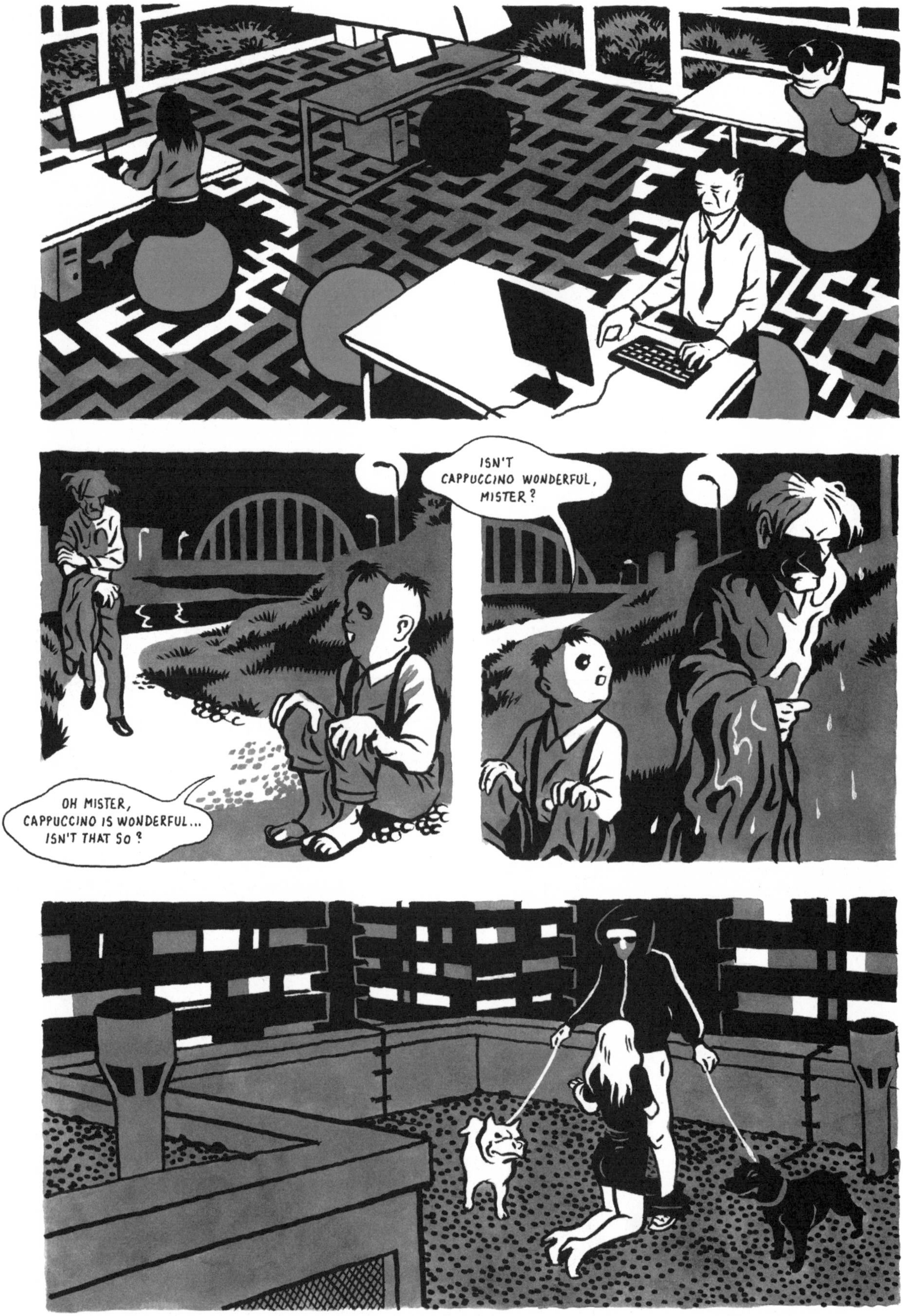
OH MISTER, CAPPUCCINO IS WONDERFUL... ISN'T THAT SO?
ISN'T CAPPUCCINO WONDERFUL, MISTER?

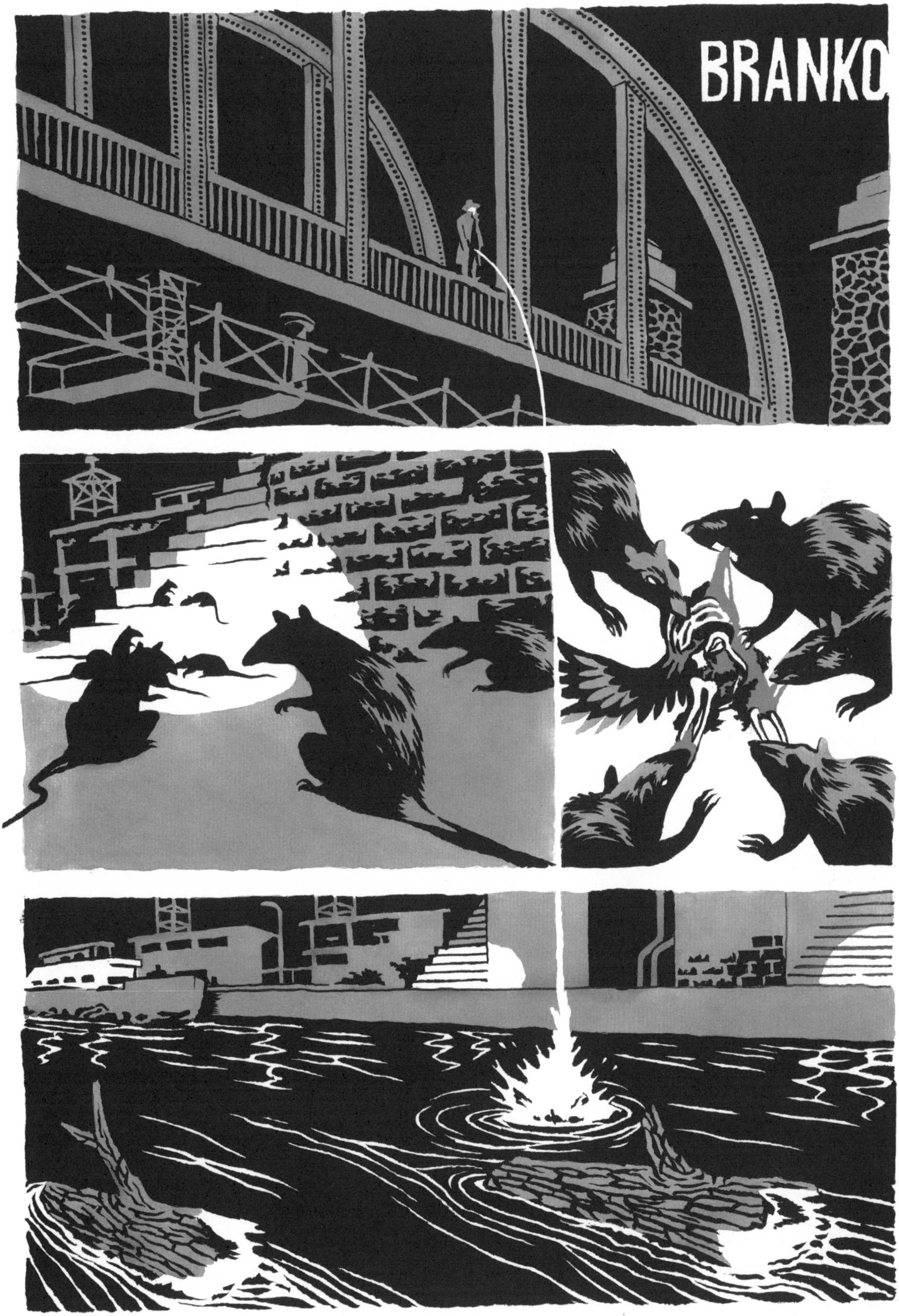
BRANKO

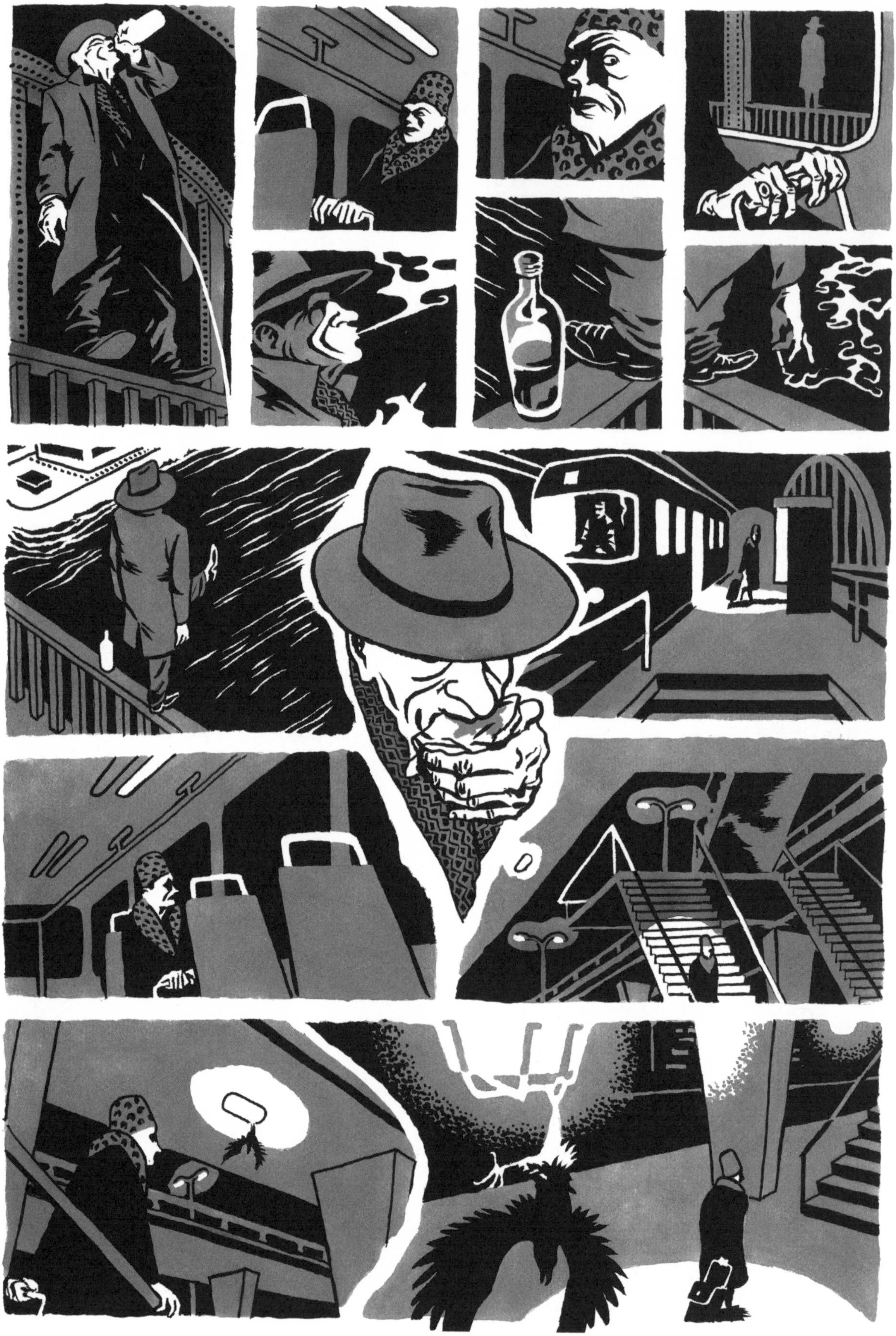

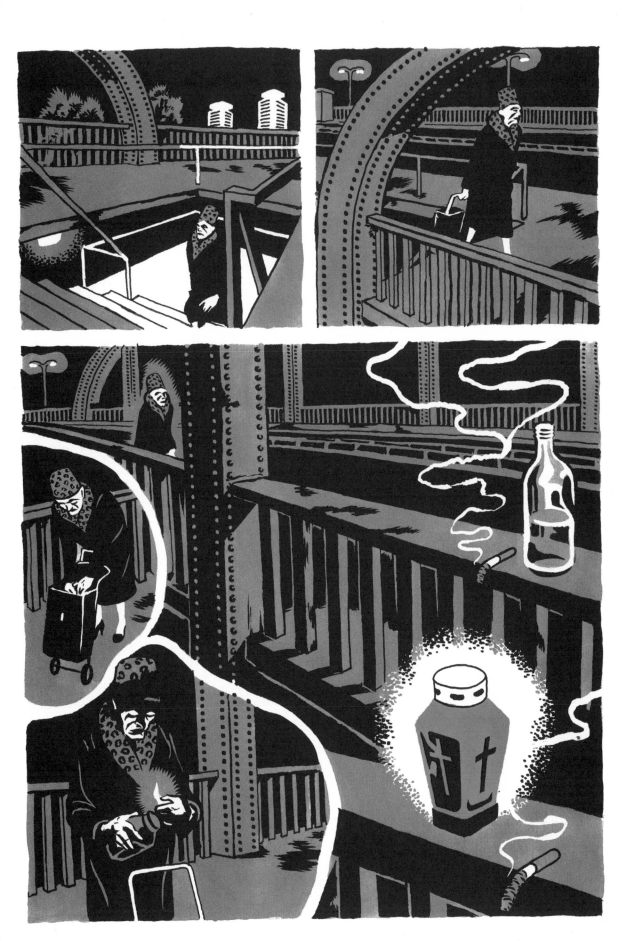

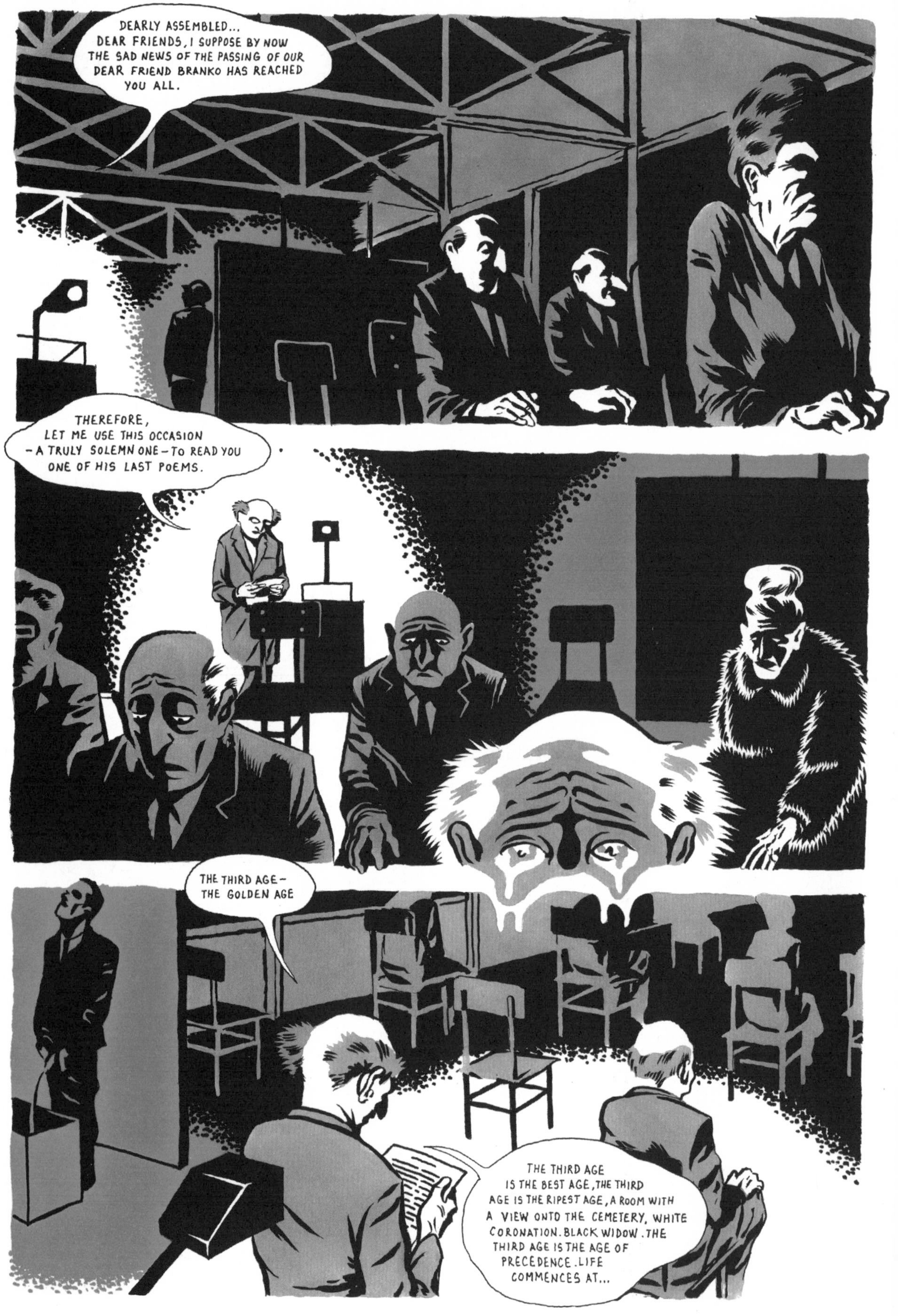
DEARLY ASSEMBLED... DEAR FRIENDS, I SUPPOSE BY NOW THE SAD NEWS OF THE PASSING OF OUR DEAR FRIEND BRANKO HAS REACHED YOU ALL.
THEREFORE, LET ME USE THIS OCCASION – A TRULY SOLEMN ONE – TO READ YOU ONE OF HIS LAST POEMS.
THE THIRD AGE – THE GOLDEN AGE
THE THIRD AGE IS THE BEST AGE, THE THIRD AGE IS THE RIPEST AGE, A ROOM WITH A VIEW ONTO THE CEMETERY, WHITE CORONATION. BLACK WIDOW. THE THIRD AGE IS THE AGE OF PRECEDENCE. LIFE COMMENCES AT...

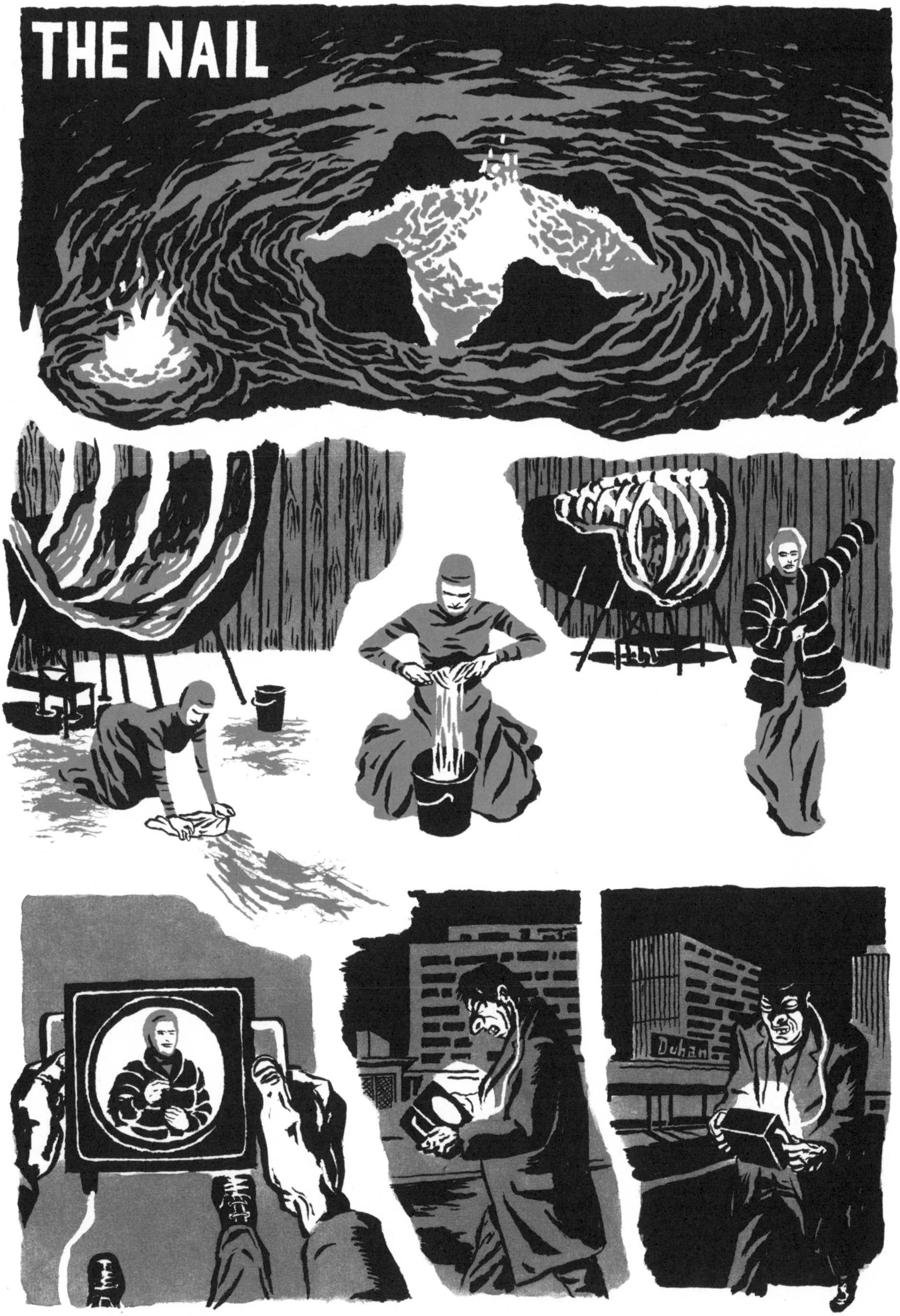
THE NAIL
Duhan

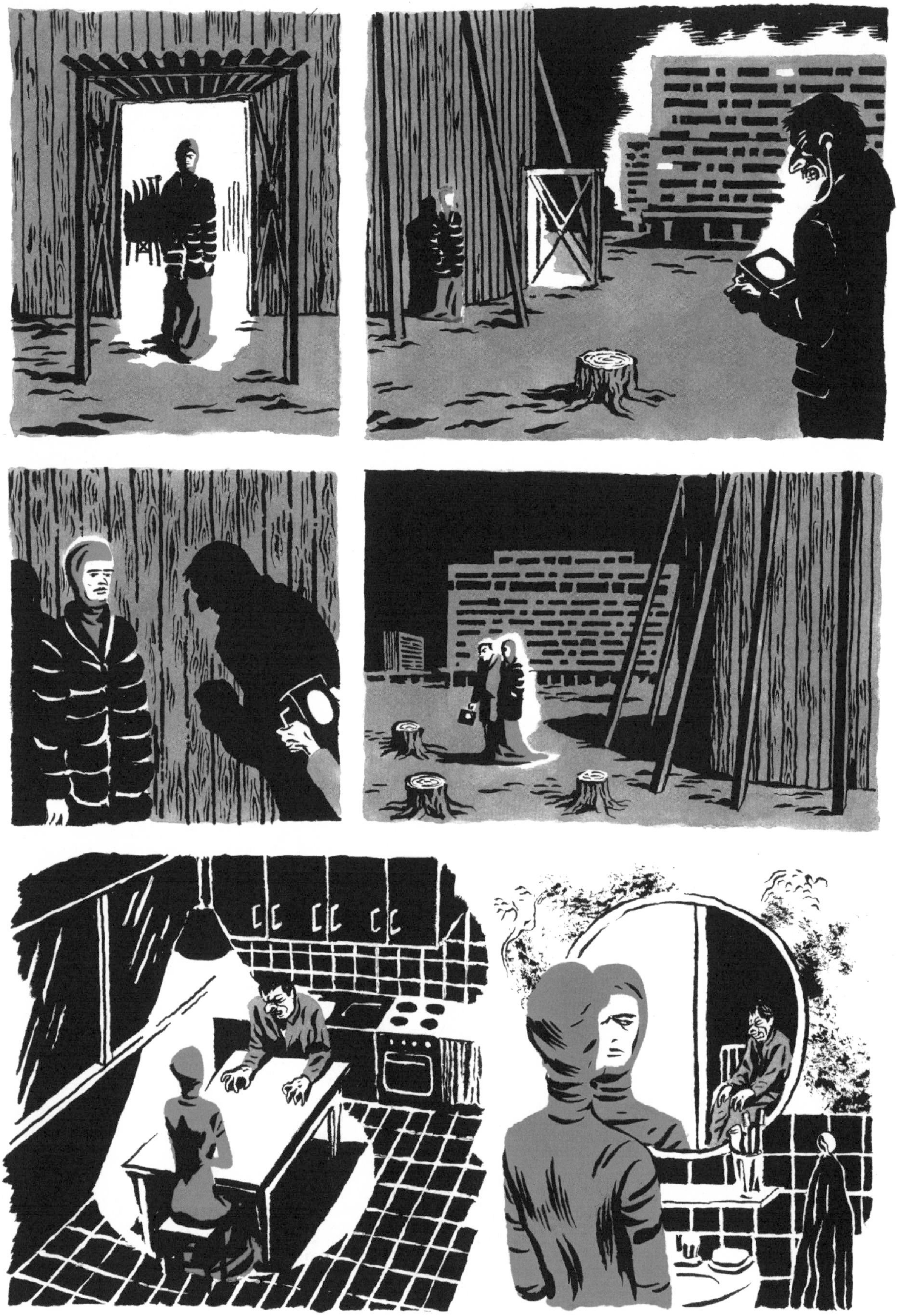

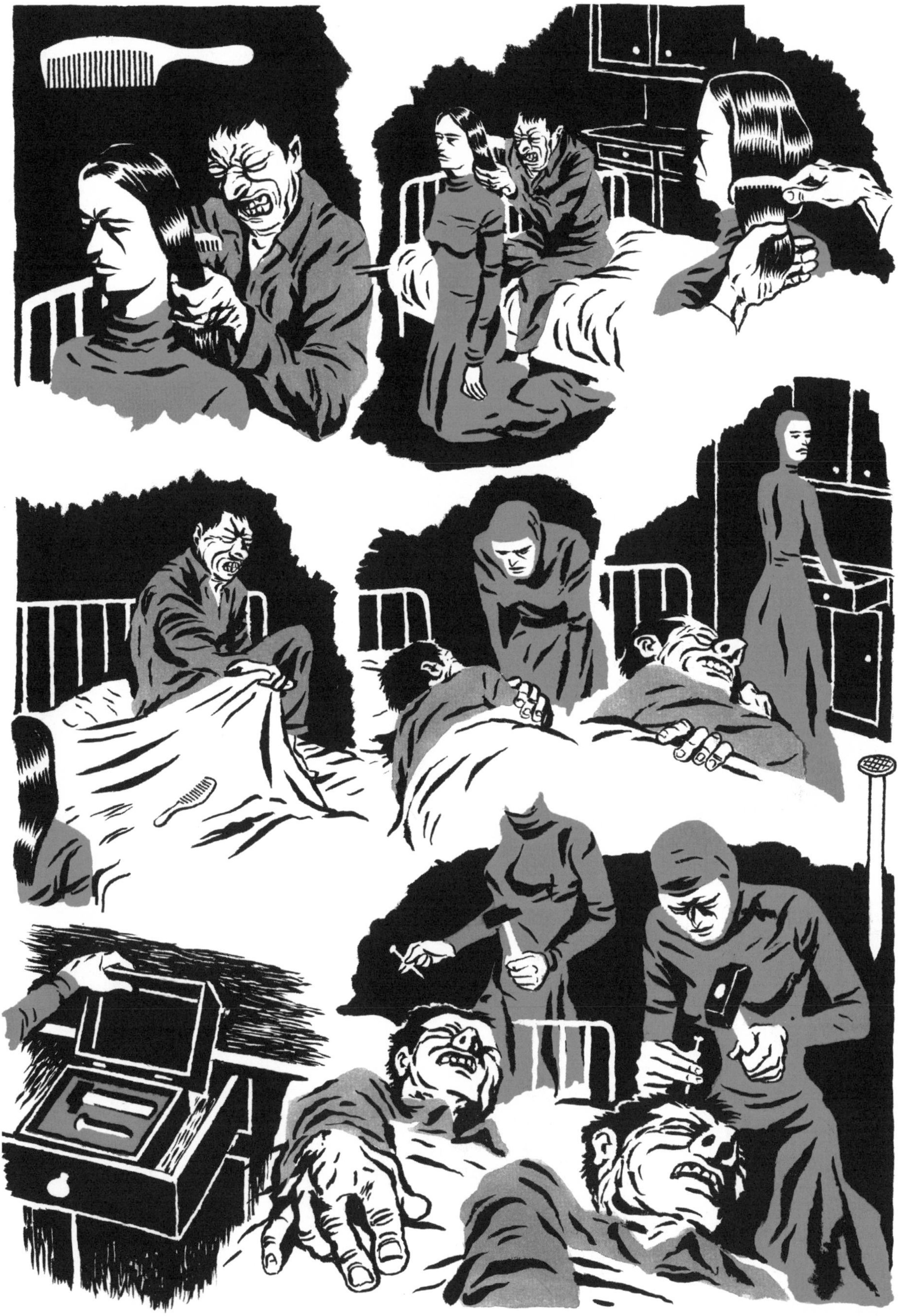

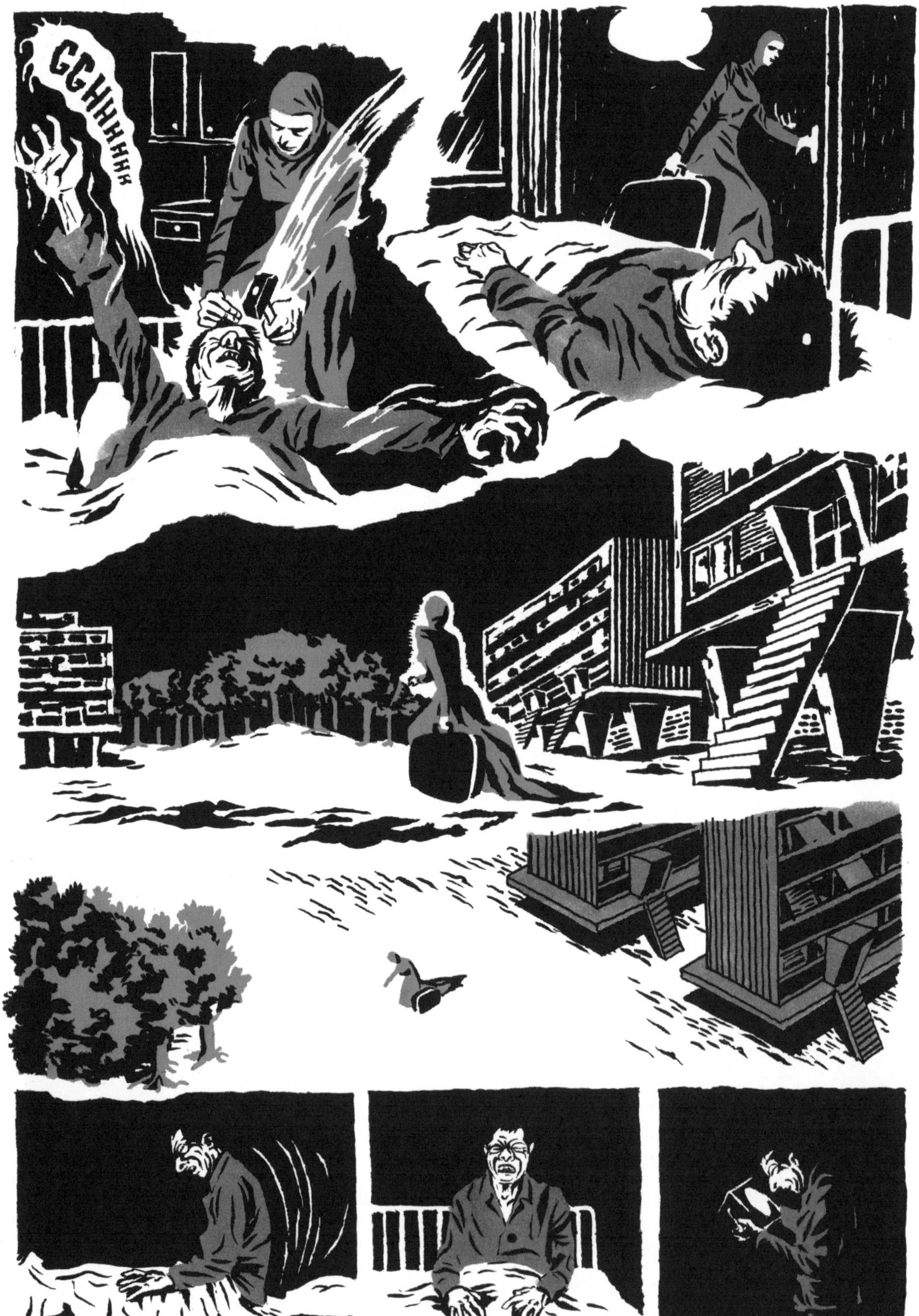
GGHHHHHHK

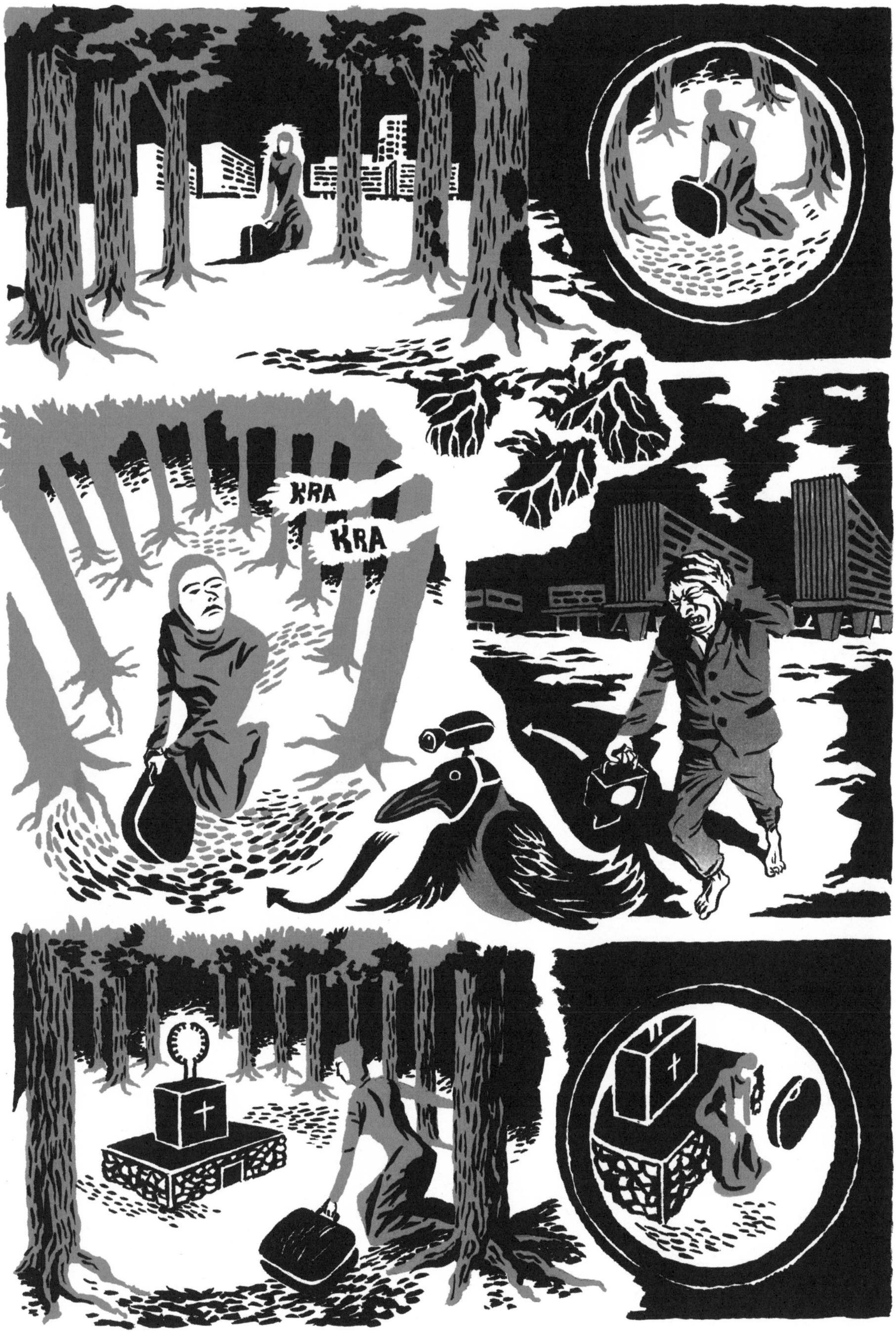
KRA
KRA

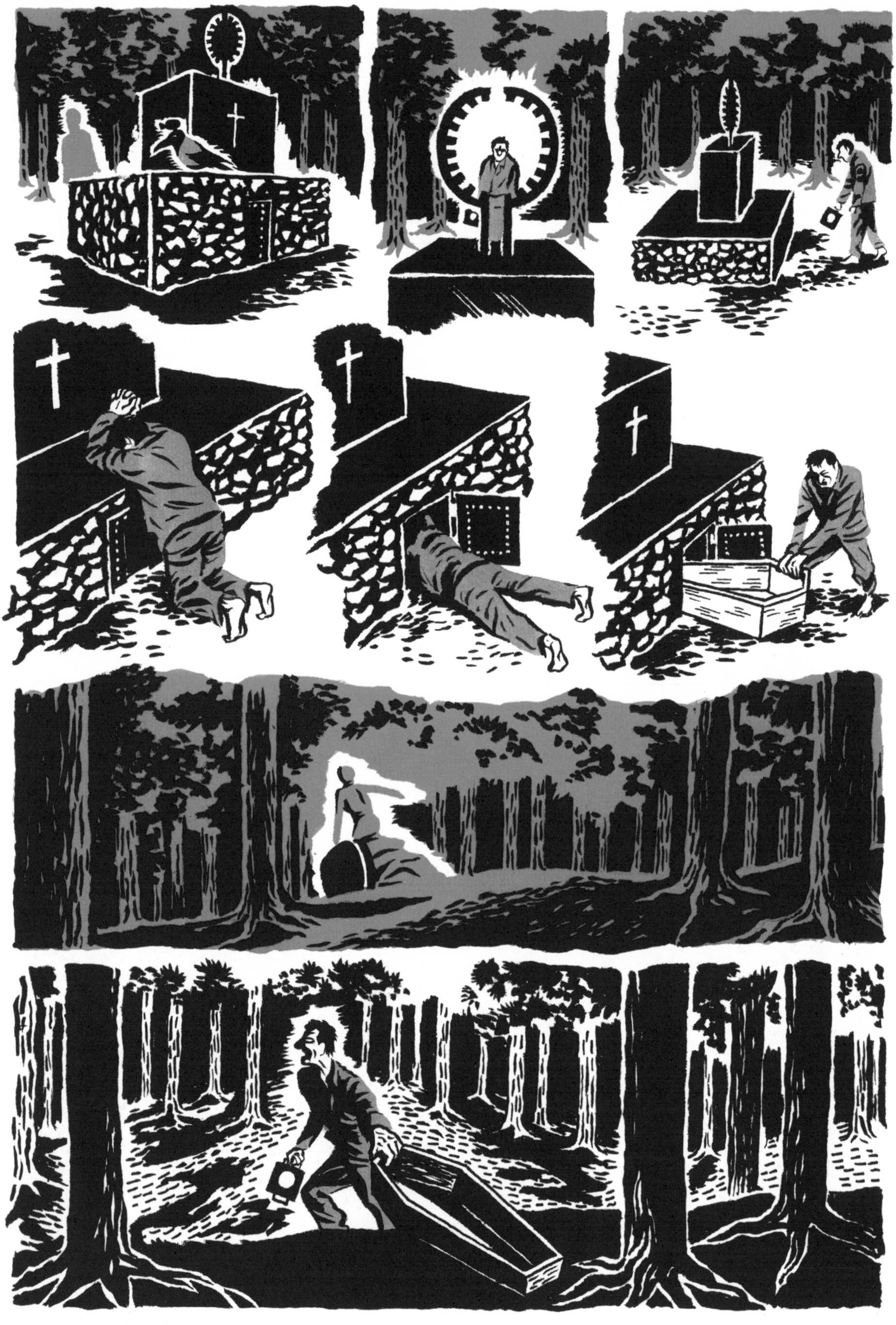

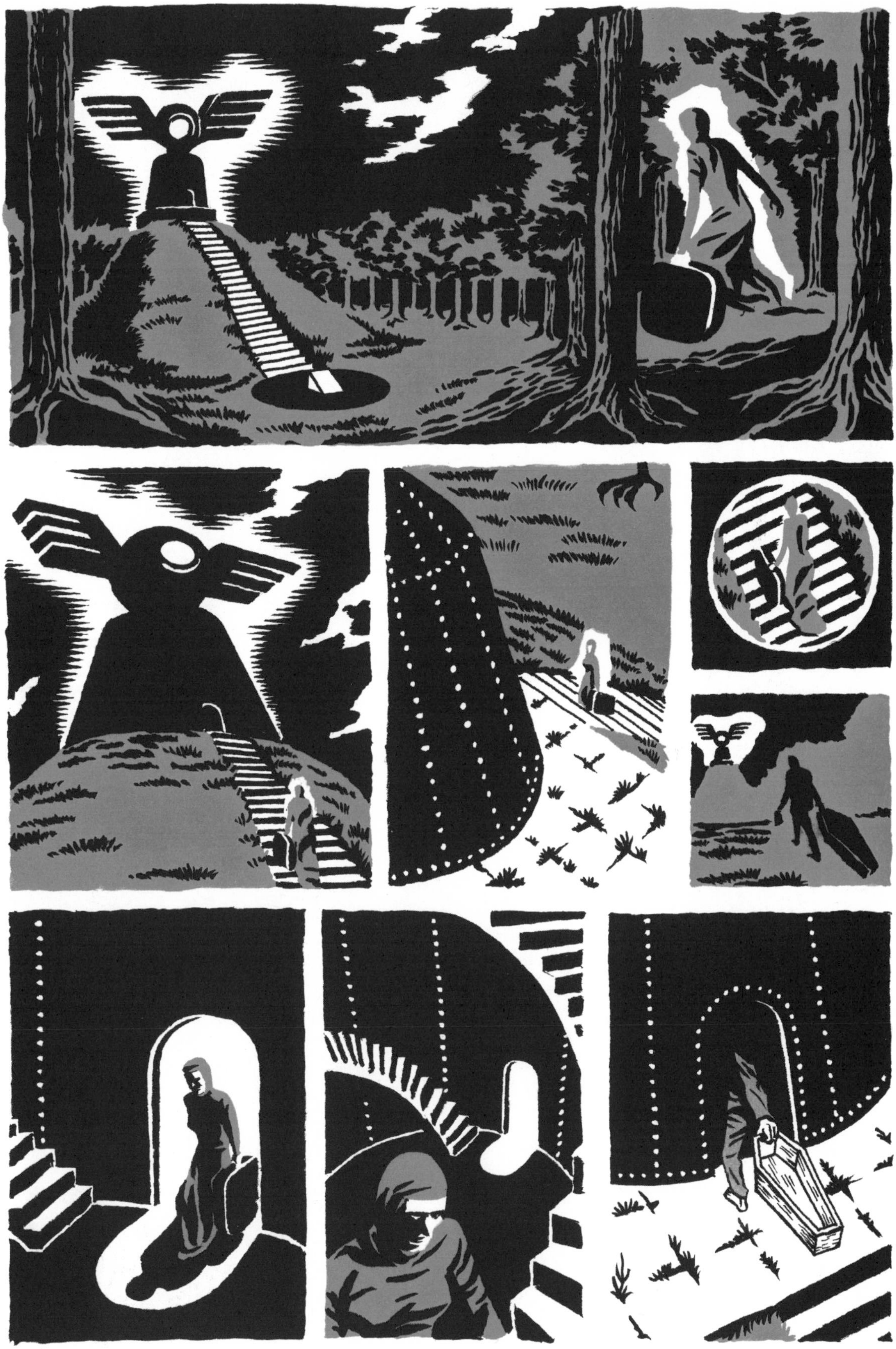

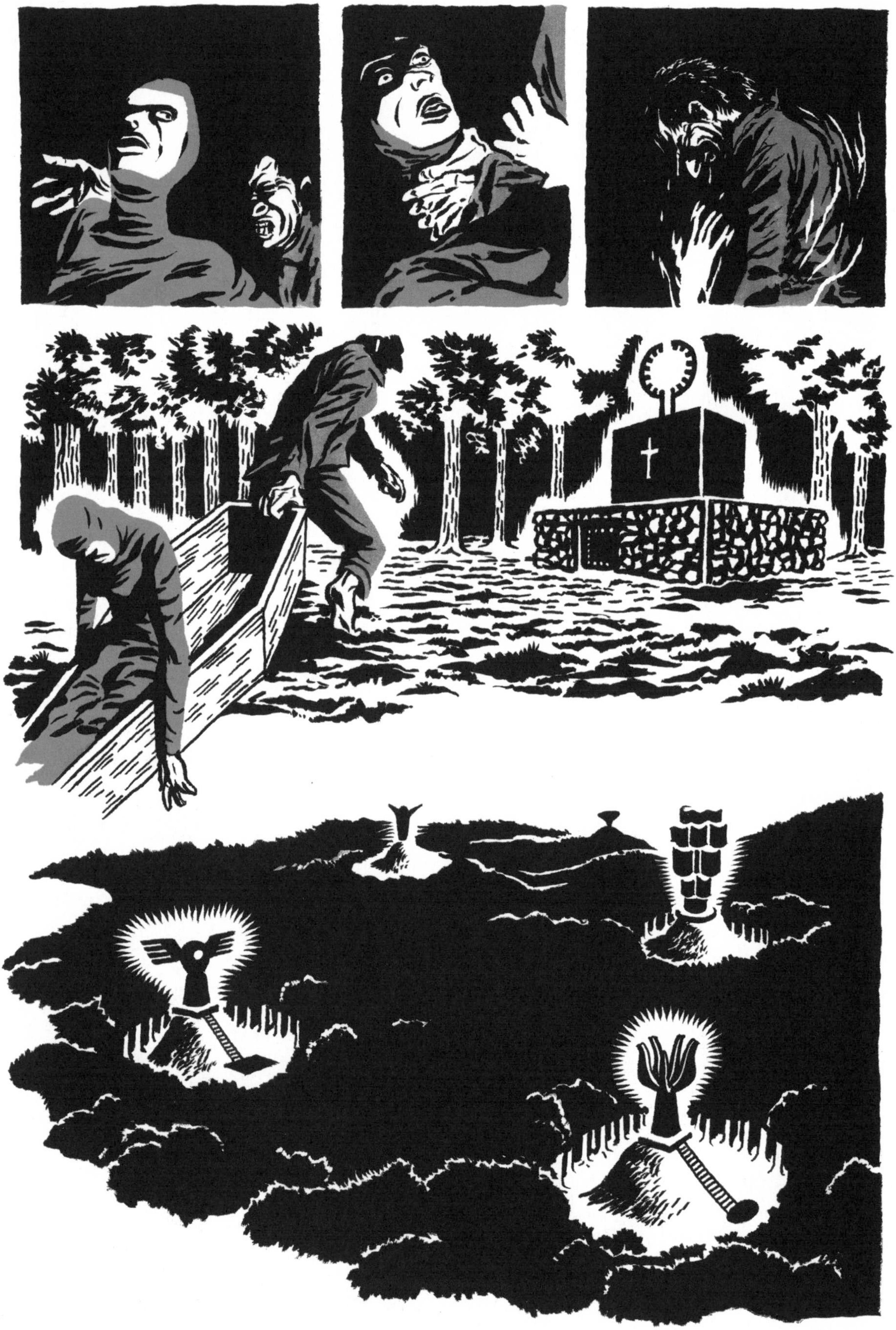

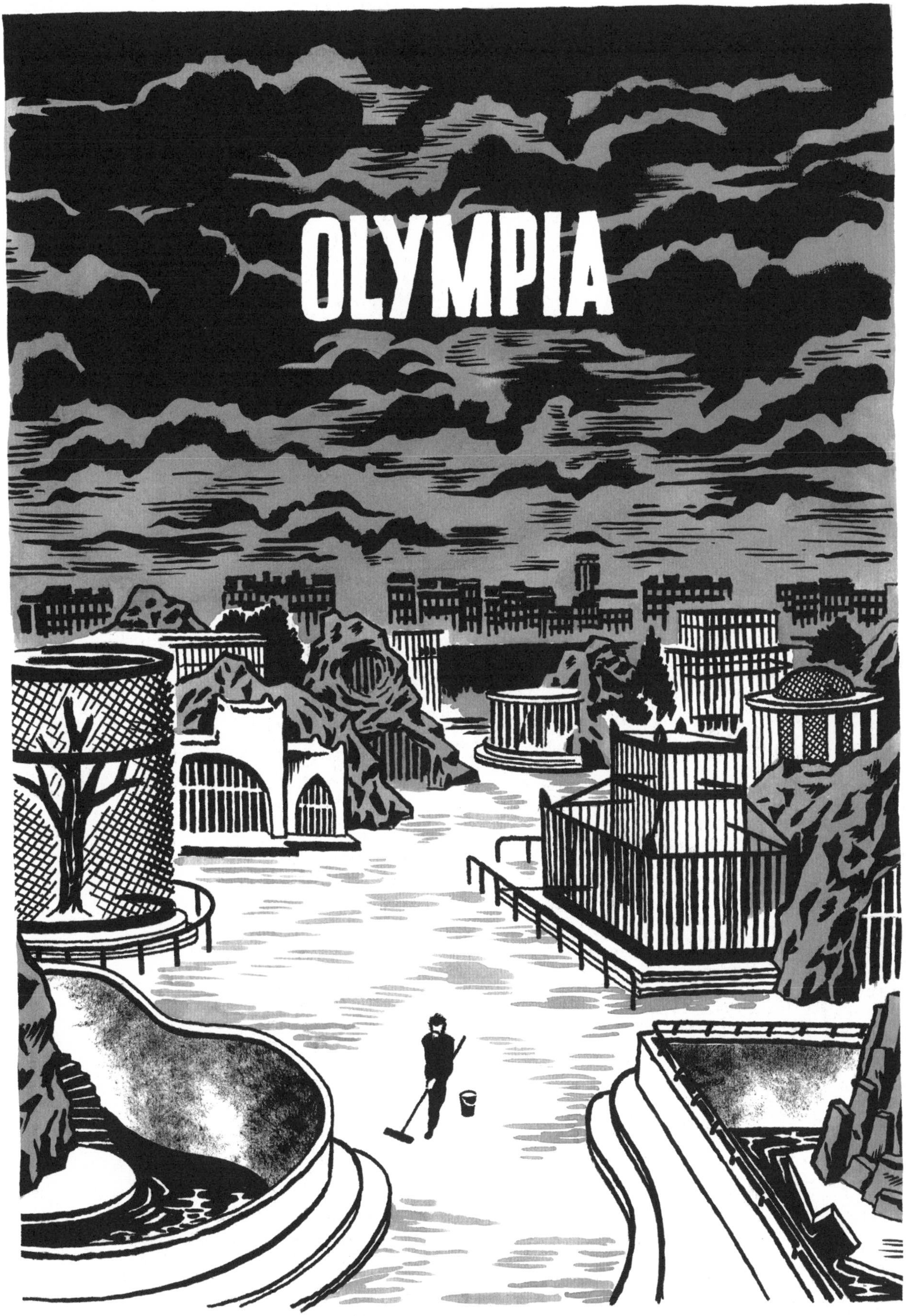
OLYMPIA

THAT DAY, LIKE ANY OTHER DAY AFTER THE VISITORS ARE GONE, I BEGAN CLEANING THEIR WASTE. THAT'S WHEN HE SHOWED UP.

HE WAS THE TYPE THAT, ONCE YOU'VE SEEN HIS BACKSIDE — YOU JUST KNEW WHAT THE FRONT WOULD LOOK LIKE.

EXCUSE ME...

I'VE BEEN TOLD THAT YOU COULD SHOW ME THE WAY TO LADY OLYMPIA'S RESIDENCE.

I AM WELL AWARE THAT MY APPEARANCE SCARES PEOPLE BUT STILL, IT DIDN'T SEEM TO HAVE THAT EFFECT ON HIM.

LISTEN, YOUNG MAN, FIRSTLY, WE ARE CLOSED. SECONDLY, THE LADY DOES NOT RECEIVE VISITORS ANYMORE. YOU MIGHT AS WELL FORGET ABOUT IT.

IF YOU WOULD LET ME SEE HER AT LEAST. YOU SEE, I AM WORKING ON A STORY ABOUT THE STARS OF YESTERDAY.

AH, DOES ANYONE HAVE THE SLIGHEST INTEREST IN THOSE DAYS ANYMORE?

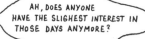

NOT MANY DO, I MUST ADMIT. STILL, THERE IS A HANDFUL OF ENTHUSIASTS. I FOR INSTANCE, POSSESS ALL HER RECORDINGS AND, TO BE HONEST, AM VERY CURIOUS TO SEE HOW SHE LOOKS NOW.

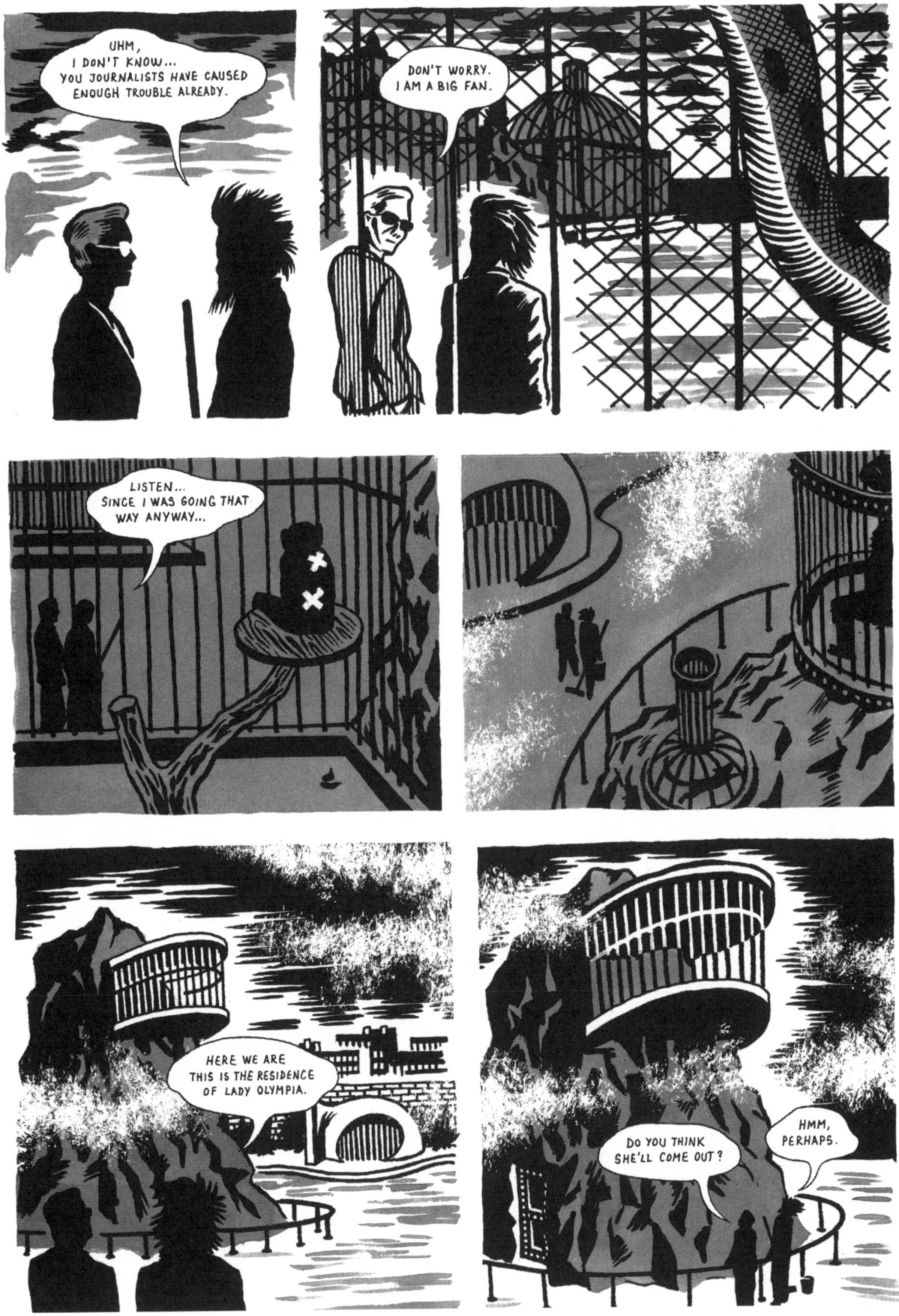
UHM, I DON'T KNOW... YOU JOURNALISTS HAVE CAUSED ENOUGH TROUBLE ALREADY.
DON'T WORRY. I AM A BIG FAN.
LISTEN... SINCE I WAS GOING THAT WAY ANYWAY...
HERE WE ARE THIS IS THE RESIDENCE OF LADY OLYMPIA.
DO YOU THINK SHE'LL COME OUT?
HMM, PERHAPS.

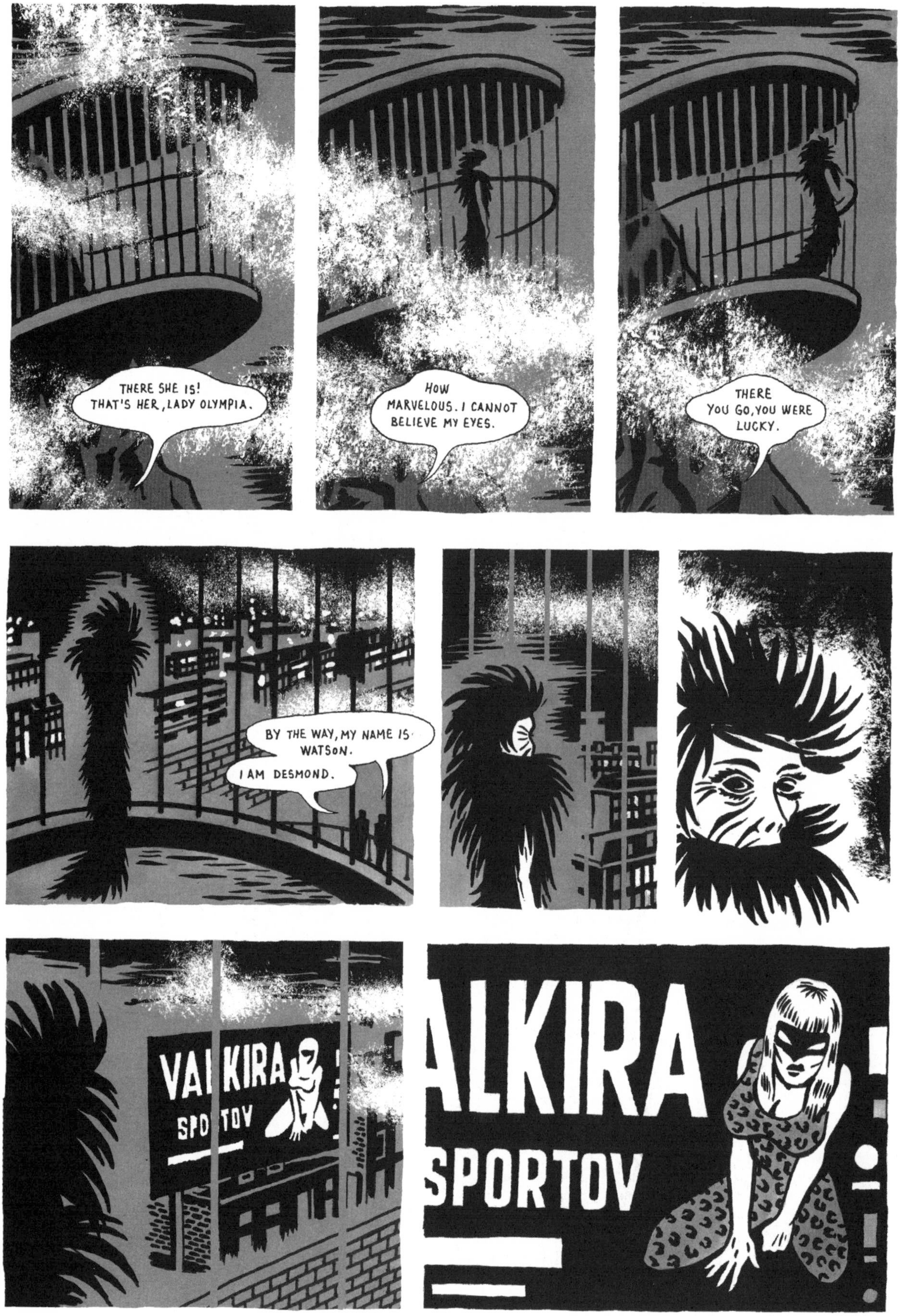
THERE SHE IS! THAT'S HER, LADY OLYMPIA.
HOW MARVELOUS. I CANNOT BELIEVE MY EYES.
THERE YOU GO, YOU WERE LUCKY.
BY THE WAY, MY NAME IS WATSON.
I AM DESMOND.
VALKIRA
SPORTOV
ALKIRA
SPORTOV

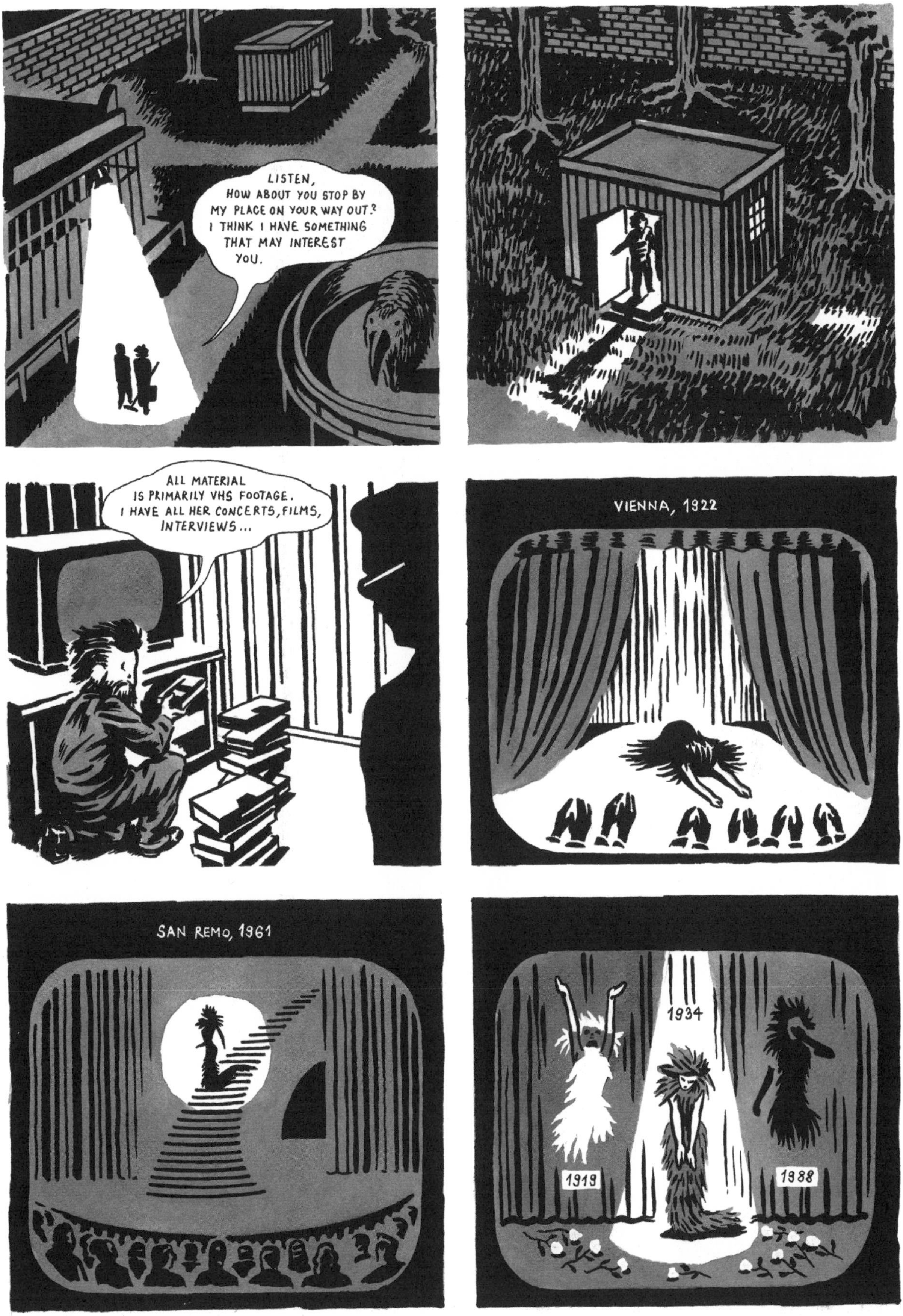
LISTEN,
HOW ABOUT YOU STOP BY MY PLACE ON YOUR WAY OUT? I THINK I HAVE SOMETHING THAT MAY INTEREST YOU.
ALL MATERIAL IS PRIMARILY VHS FOOTAGE. I HAVE ALL HER CONCERTS, FILMS, INTERVIEWS...
VIENNA, 1922
SAN REMO, 1961
1934
1919
1988

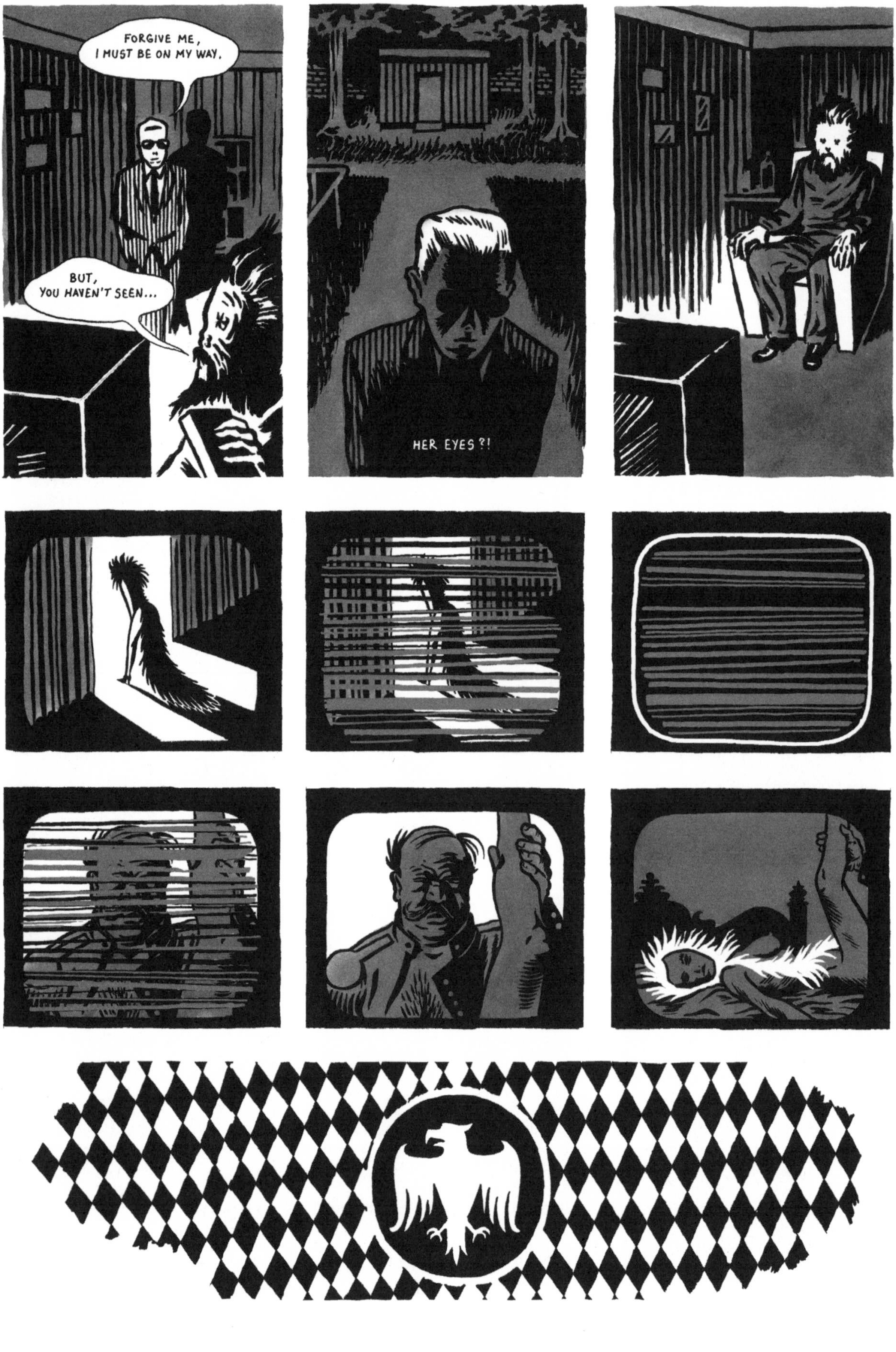
FORGIVE ME, I MUST BE ON MY WAY.
BUT, YOU HAVEN'T SEEN...
HER EYES?!

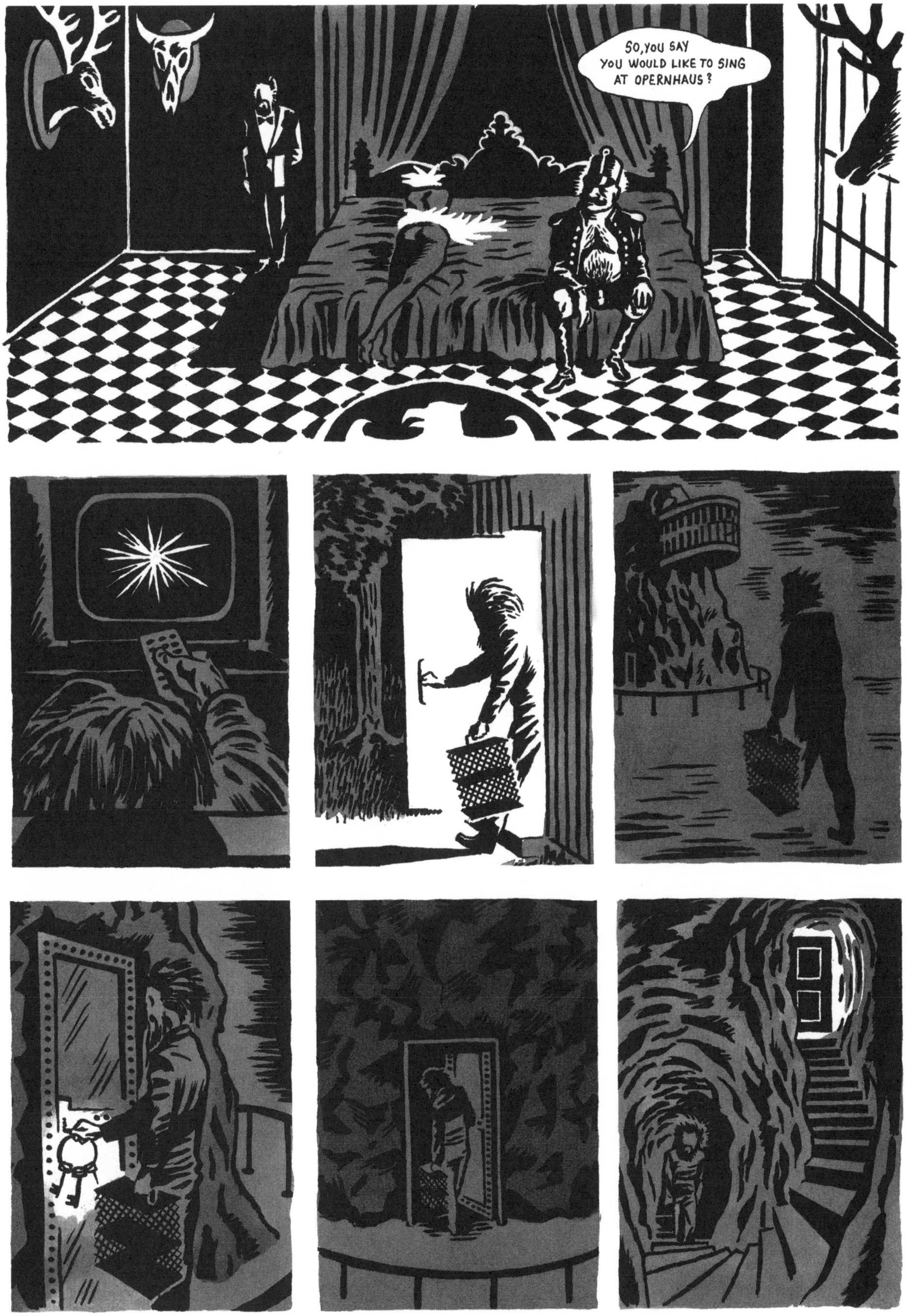
SO, YOU SAY
YOU WOULD LIKE TO SING
AT OPERNHAUS?

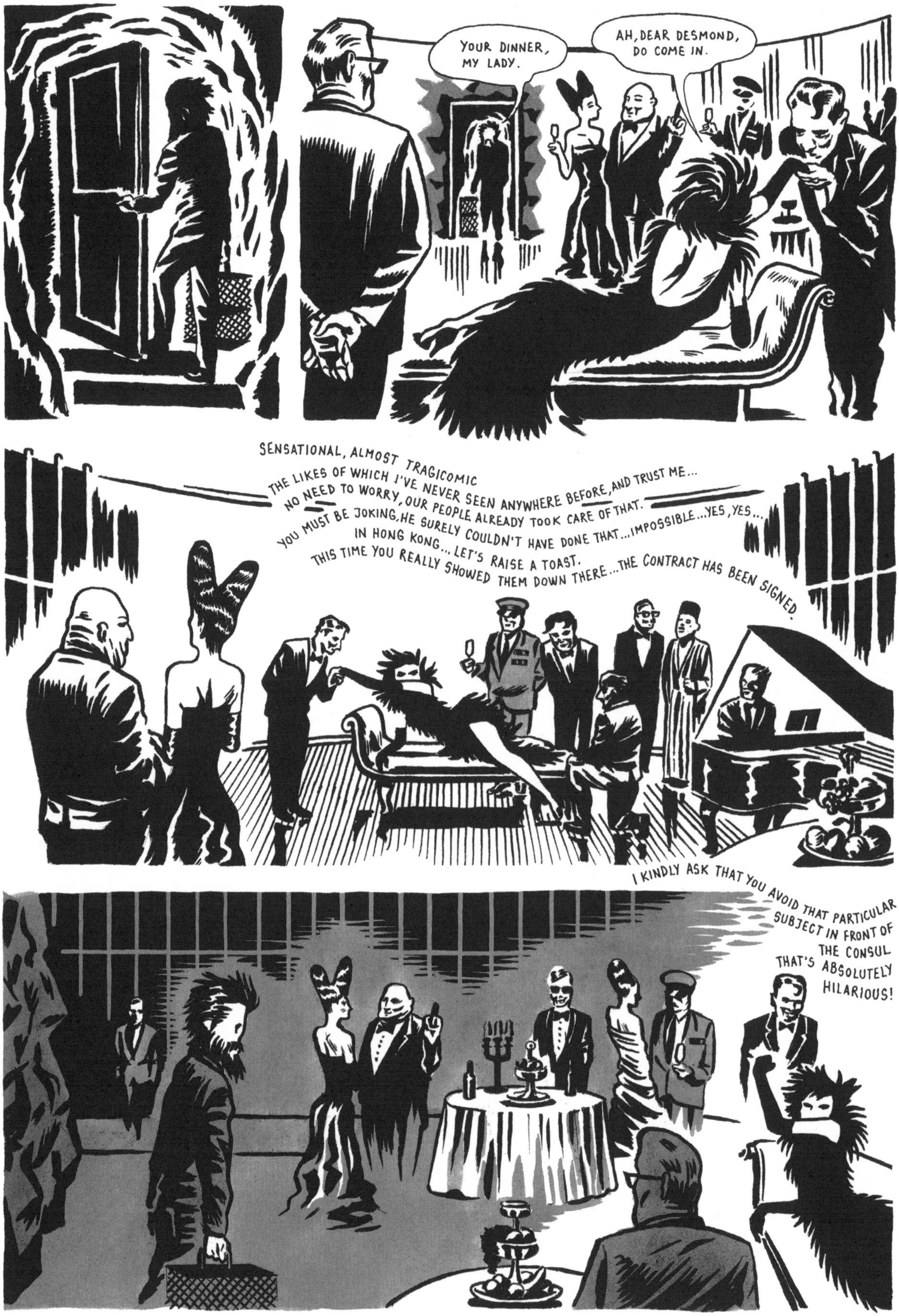
YOUR DINNER, MY LADY.
AH, DEAR DESMOND, DO COME IN.
SENSATIONAL, ALMOST TRAGICOMIC
THE LIKES OF WHICH I'VE NEVER SEEN ANYWHERE BEFORE, AND TRUST ME...
NO NEED TO WORRY, OUR PEOPLE ALREADY TOOK CARE OF THAT.
YOU MUST BE JOKING, HE SURELY COULDN'T HAVE DONE THAT... IMPOSSIBLE... YES, YES...
IN HONG KONG... LET'S RAISE A TOAST.
THIS TIME YOU REALLY SHOWED THEM DOWN THERE... THE CONTRACT HAS BEEN SIGNED.
I KINDLY ASK THAT YOU AVOID THAT PARTICULAR SUBJECT IN FRONT OF THE CONSUL
THAT'S ABSOLUTELY HILARIOUS!

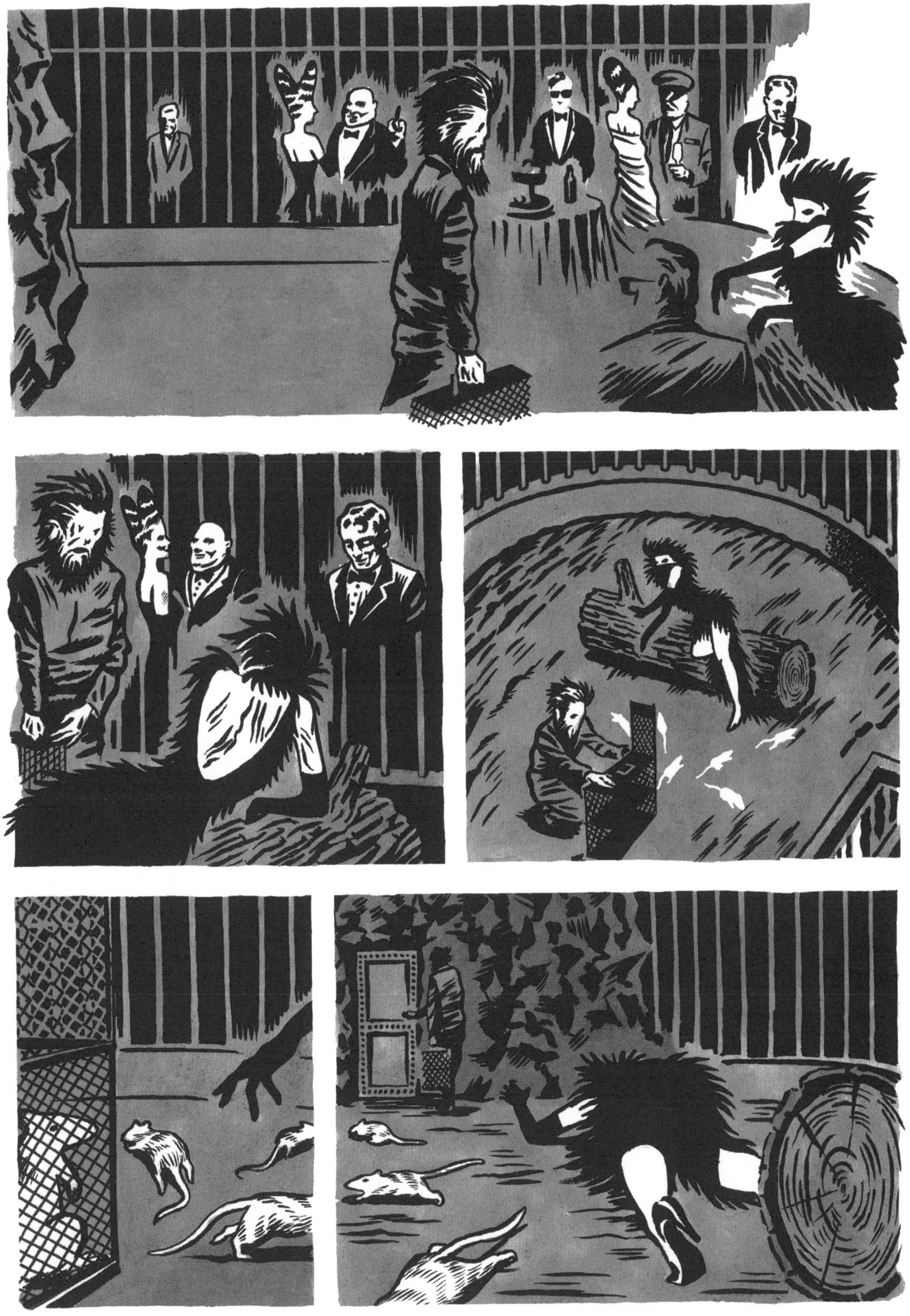

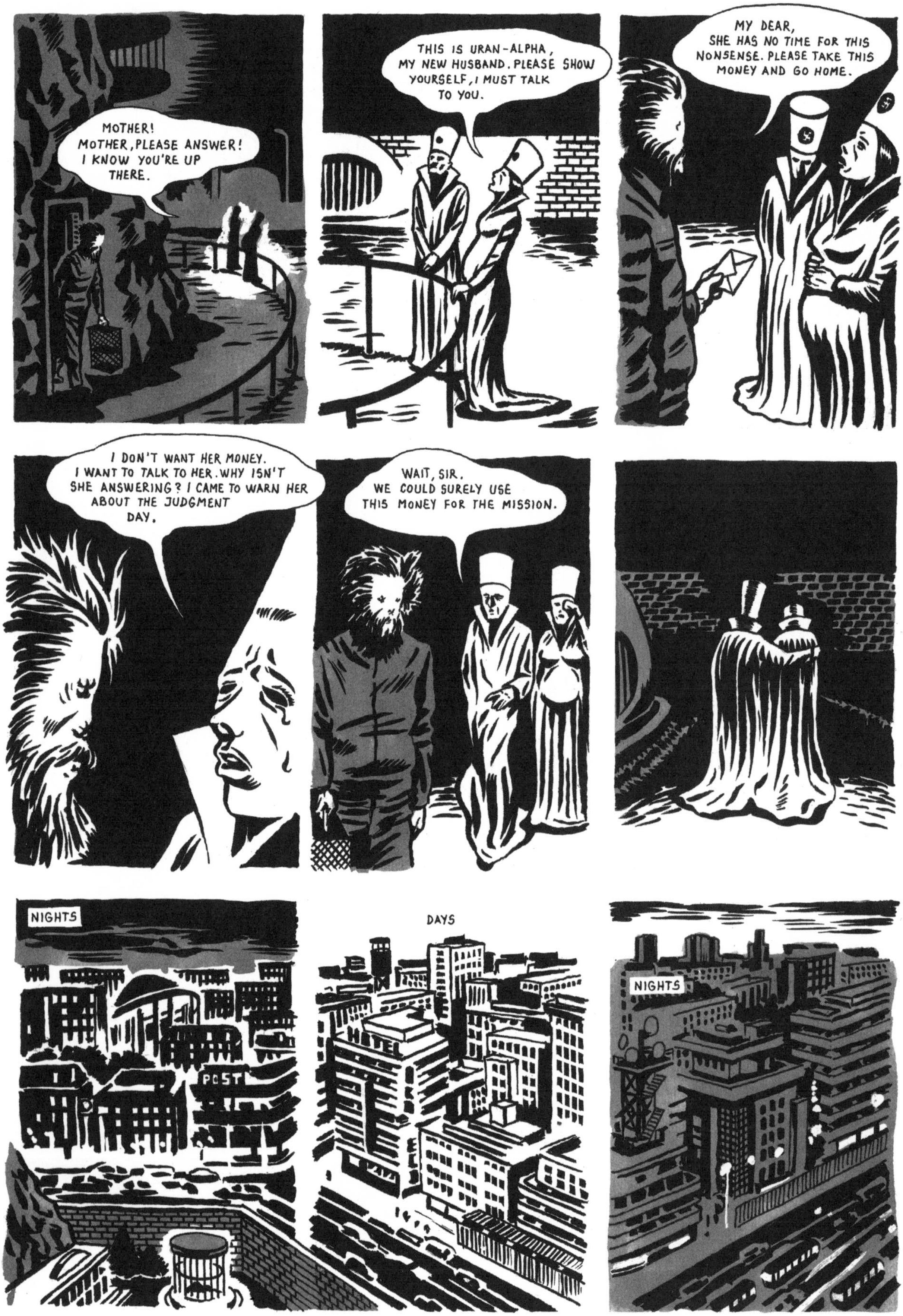
MOTHER! MOTHER, PLEASE ANSWER! I KNOW YOU'RE UP THERE.
THIS IS URAN-ALPHA, MY NEW HUSBAND. PLEASE SHOW YOURSELF, I MUST TALK TO YOU.
MY DEAR, SHE HAS NO TIME FOR THIS NONSENSE. PLEASE TAKE THIS MONEY AND GO HOME.
I DON'T WANT HER MONEY. I WANT TO TALK TO HER. WHY ISN'T SHE ANSWERING? I CAME TO WARN HER ABOUT THE JUDGMENT DAY.
WAIT, SIR. WE COULD SURELY USE THIS MONEY FOR THE MISSION.
NIGHTS
POST
DAYS
HOTEL
NIGHTS

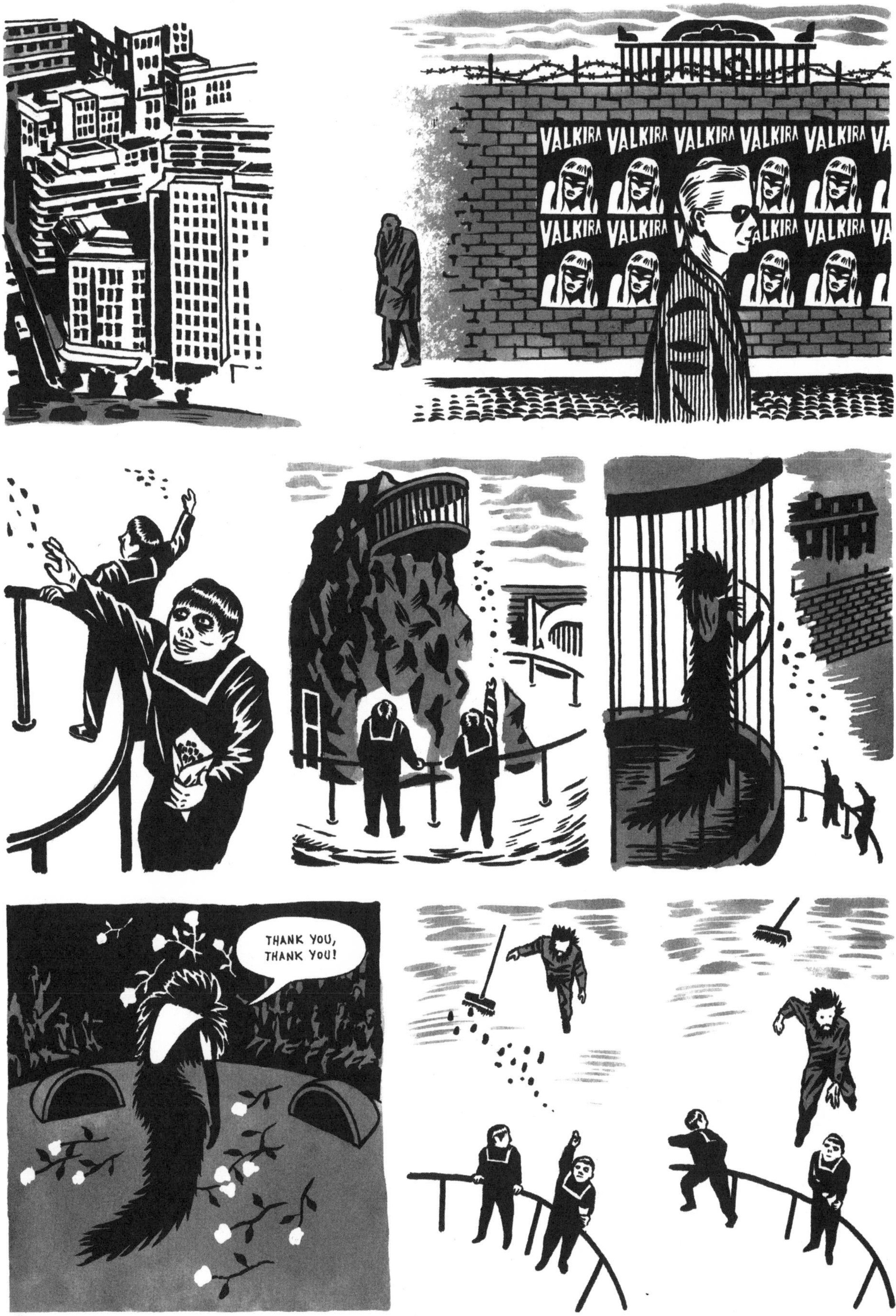
VALKIRA VALKIRA VALKIRA VALKIRA VALKIRA
THANK YOU, THANK YOU!

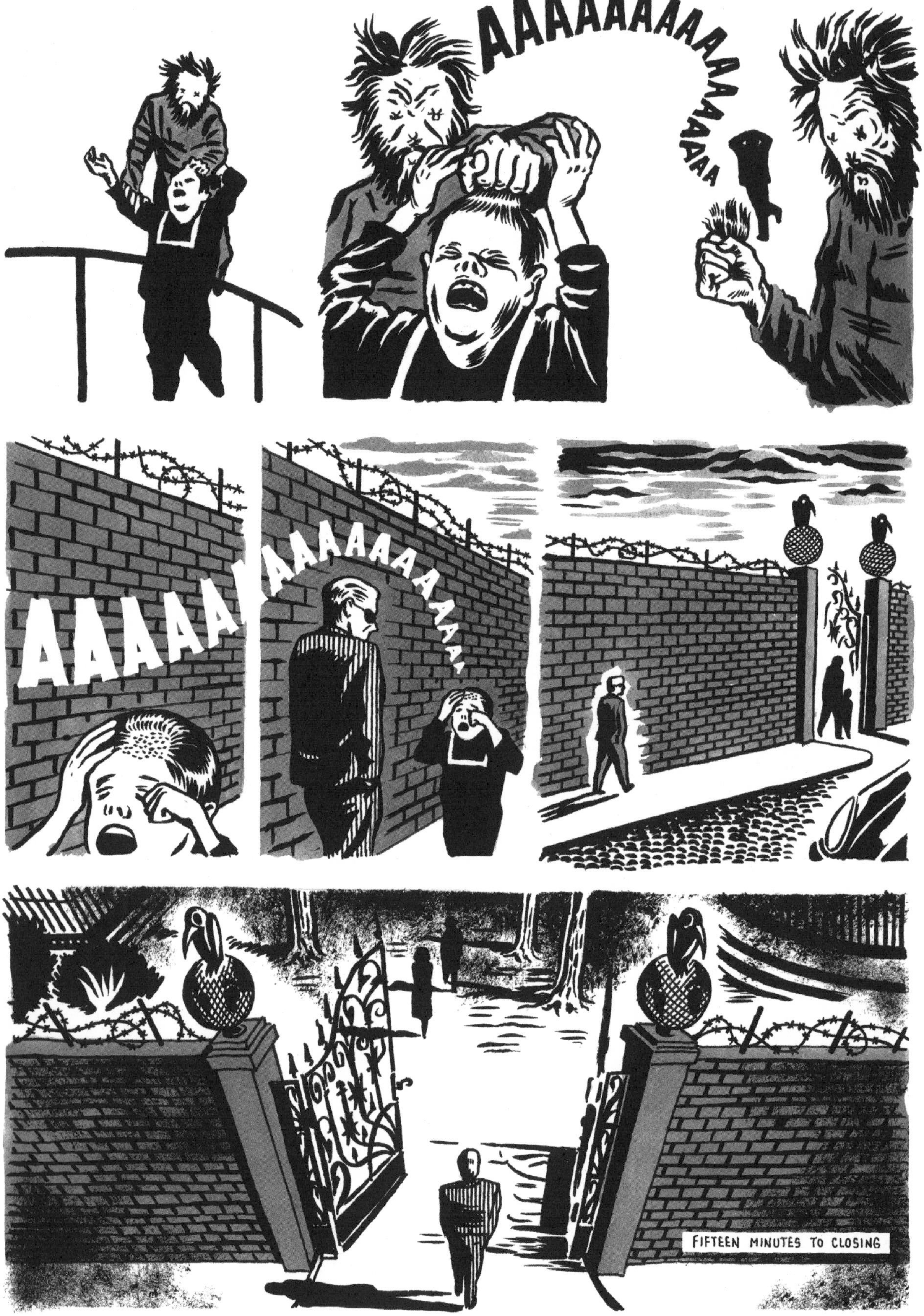
AAAAAAAAAAAAAAAAA
AAAAA
AAAAAAAAAAAA
FIFTEEN MINUTES TO CLOSING

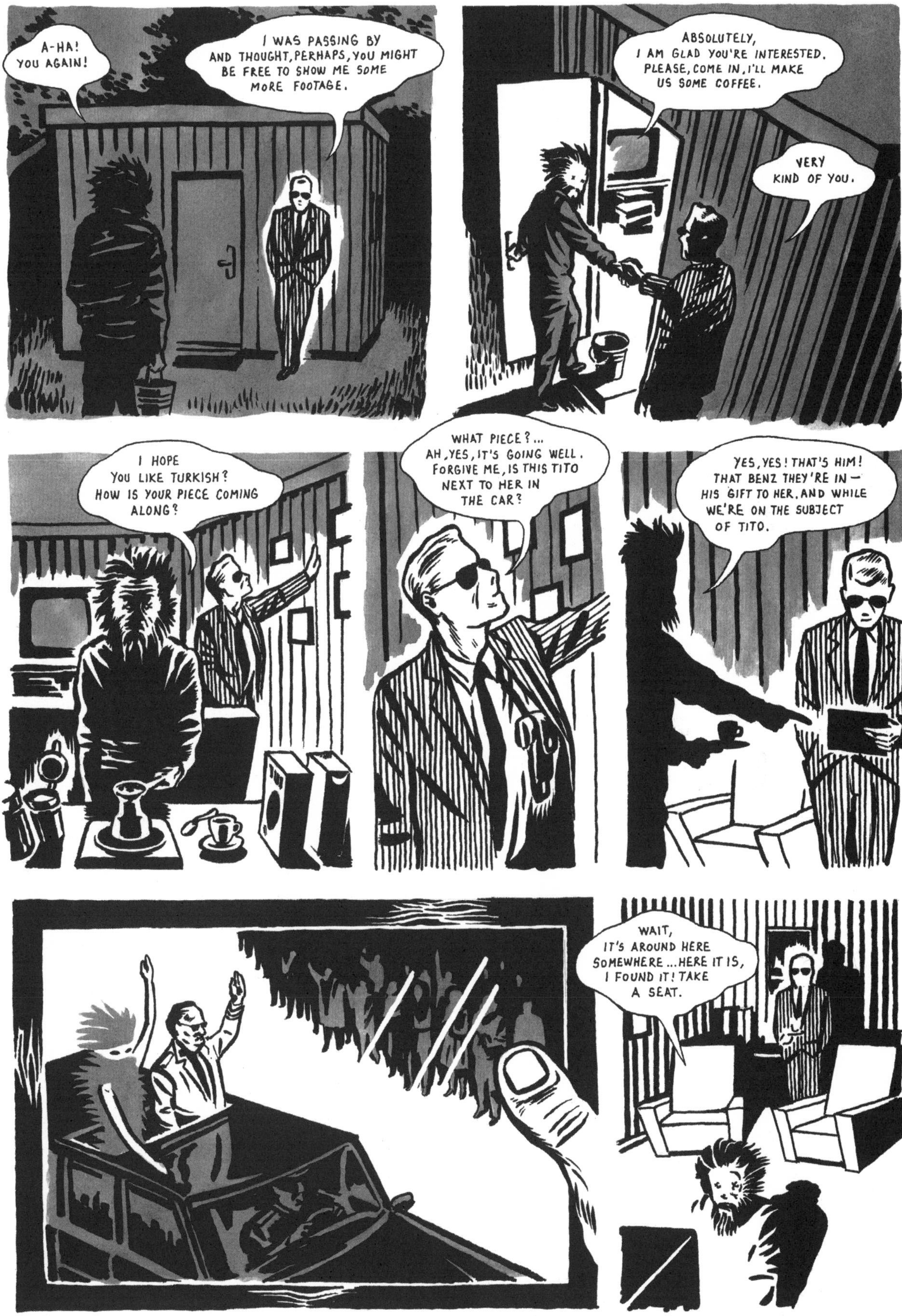
A-HA!
YOU AGAIN!
I WAS PASSING BY AND THOUGHT, PERHAPS, YOU MIGHT BE FREE TO SHOW ME SOME MORE FOOTAGE.
ABSOLUTELY, I AM GLAD YOU'RE INTERESTED. PLEASE, COME IN, I'LL MAKE US SOME COFFEE.
VERY KIND OF YOU.
I HOPE YOU LIKE TURKISH? HOW IS YOUR PIECE COMING ALONG?
WHAT PIECE?... AH, YES, IT'S GOING WELL. FORGIVE ME, IS THIS TITO NEXT TO HER IN THE CAR?
YES, YES! THAT'S HIM! THAT BENZ THEY'RE IN — HIS GIFT TO HER. AND WHILE WE'RE ON THE SUBJECT OF TITO.
WAIT, IT'S AROUND HERE SOMEWHERE ... HERE IT IS, I FOUND IT! TAKE A SEAT.

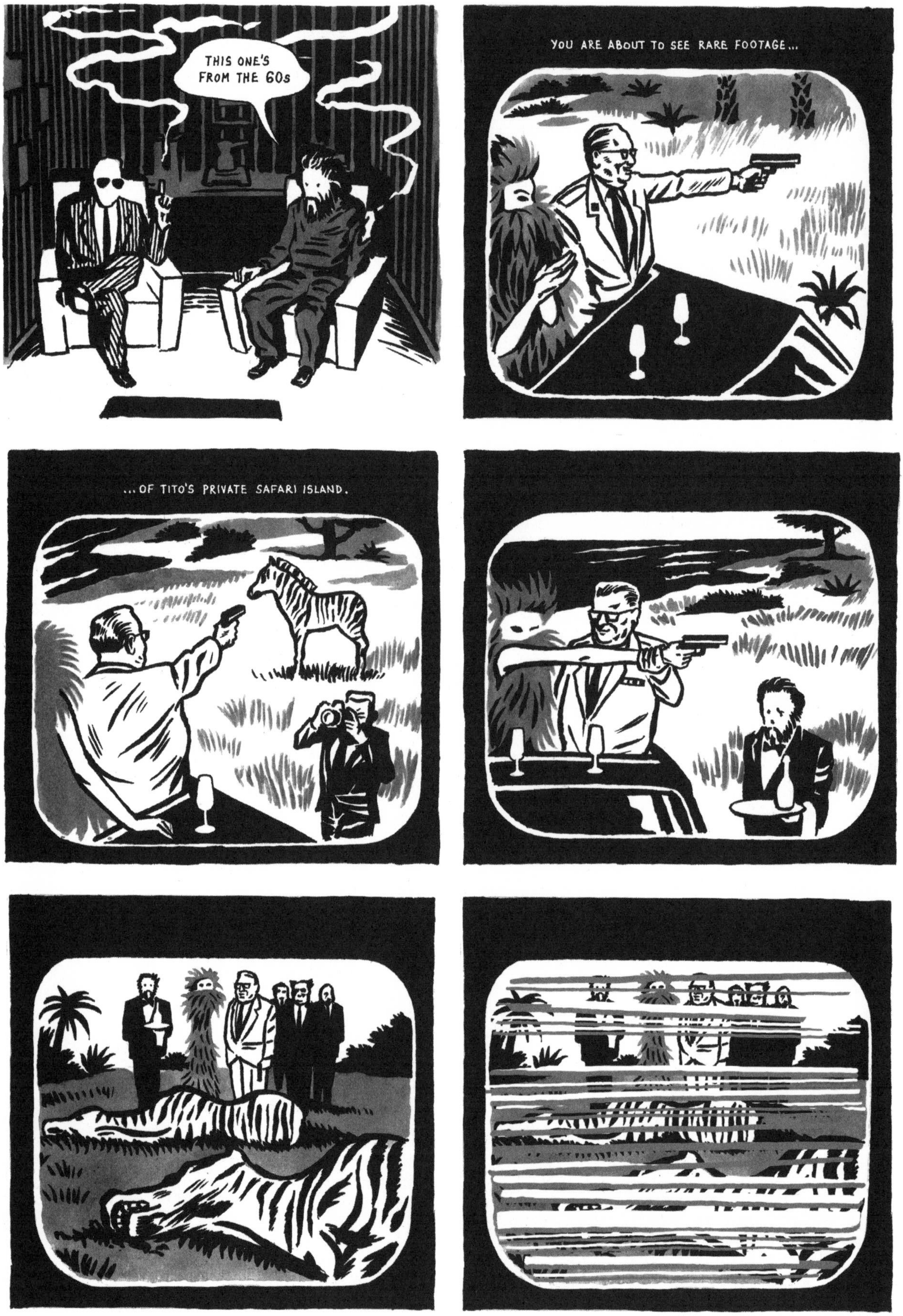
THIS ONE'S FROM THE 60s
YOU ARE ABOUT TO SEE RARE FOOTAGE...
...OF TITO'S PRIVATE SAFARI ISLAND.

THIS IS DIFFERENT, THE PRESENTATION OF THE MEDAL OF ACHIEVEMENT IN BUCHAREST.

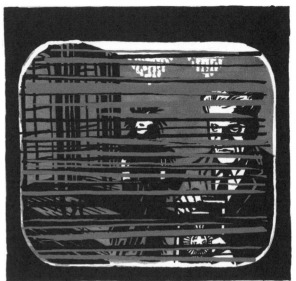

THIS IS HER LAST INTERVIEW IN NOVEMBER 1988.

WITH US IN THE STUDIO TONIGHT—A DISTINGUISHED GUEST SOME OF OUR OLDER VIEWERS ARE SURE TO REMEMBER.

PLEASE TELL US, WHAT IS YOUR OPINION ON TODAY'S STARS, LIKE VICKY, CAROLE ZANA, ULTRA...?

YOU KNOW HOW IT GOES— THEY VANISH AS SUDDENLY AS THEY APPEAR. I SERIOUSLY DON'T UNDERSTAND HOW PEOPLE MANAGE TO STAY ON TOP OF ALL THOSE NAMES.

HOW ABOUT VALKIRA? SHE'S REMAINED ON TOP FOR A WHILE NOW. DO YOU PREDICT A LENGTHY CAREER FOR HER, SUCH AS YOURS HAD BEEN?

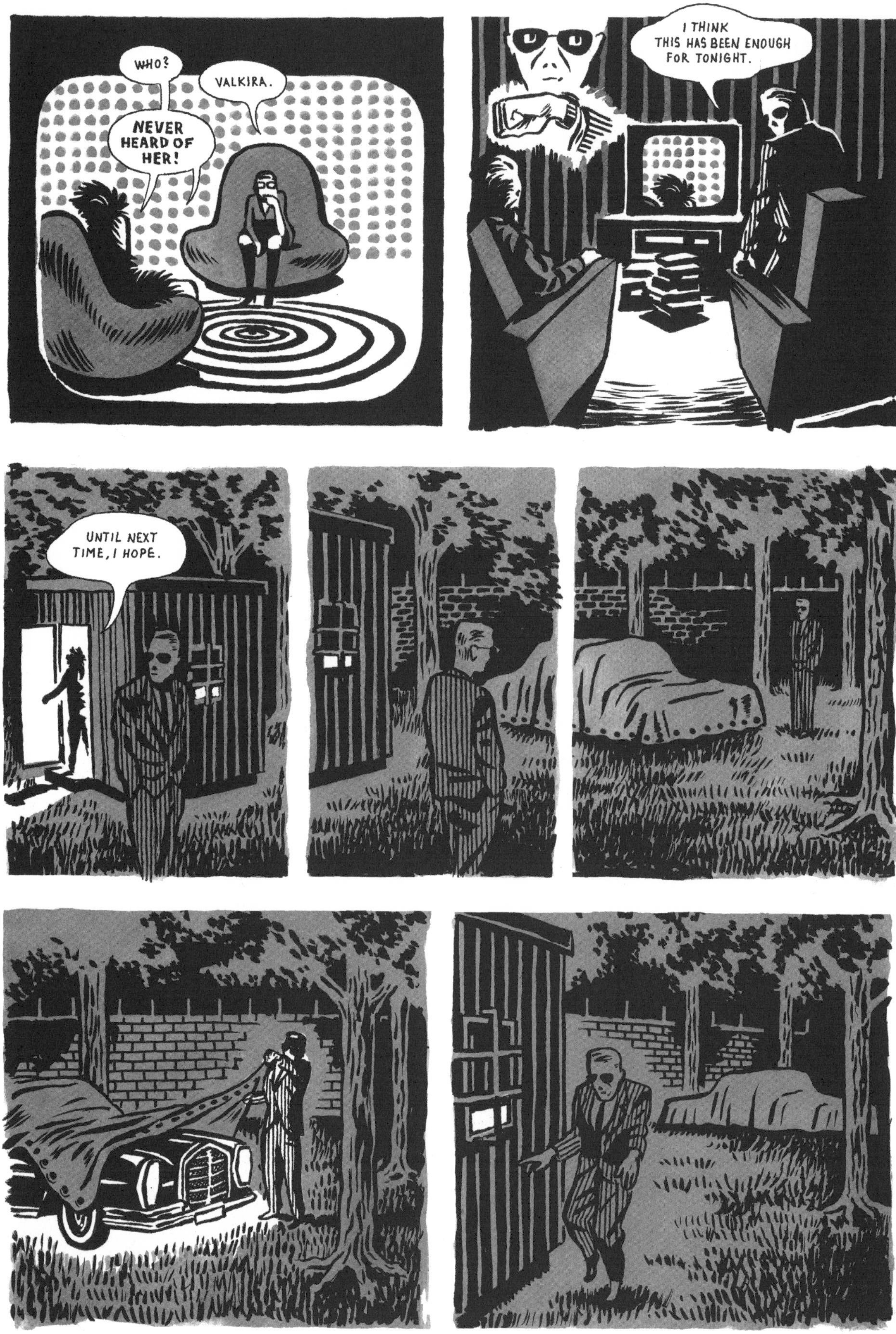
WHO?
VALKIRA.
NEVER HEARD OF HER!
I THINK THIS HAS BEEN ENOUGH FOR TONIGHT.
UNTIL NEXT TIME, I HOPE.

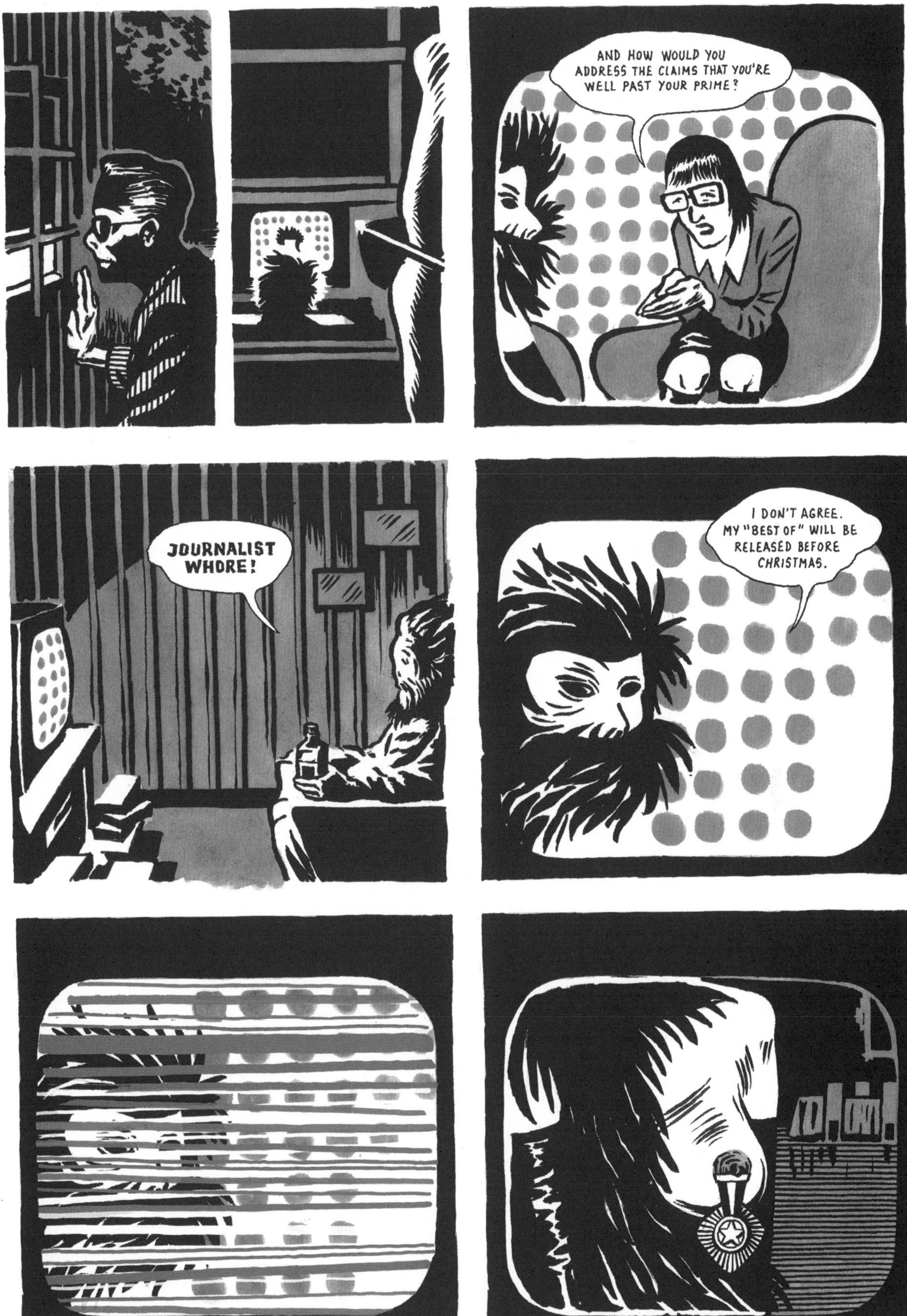
AND HOW WOULD YOU ADDRESS THE CLAIMS THAT YOU'RE WELL PAST YOUR PRIME?
JOURNALIST WHORE!
I DON'T AGREE. MY "BEST OF" WILL BE RELEASED BEFORE CHRISTMAS.

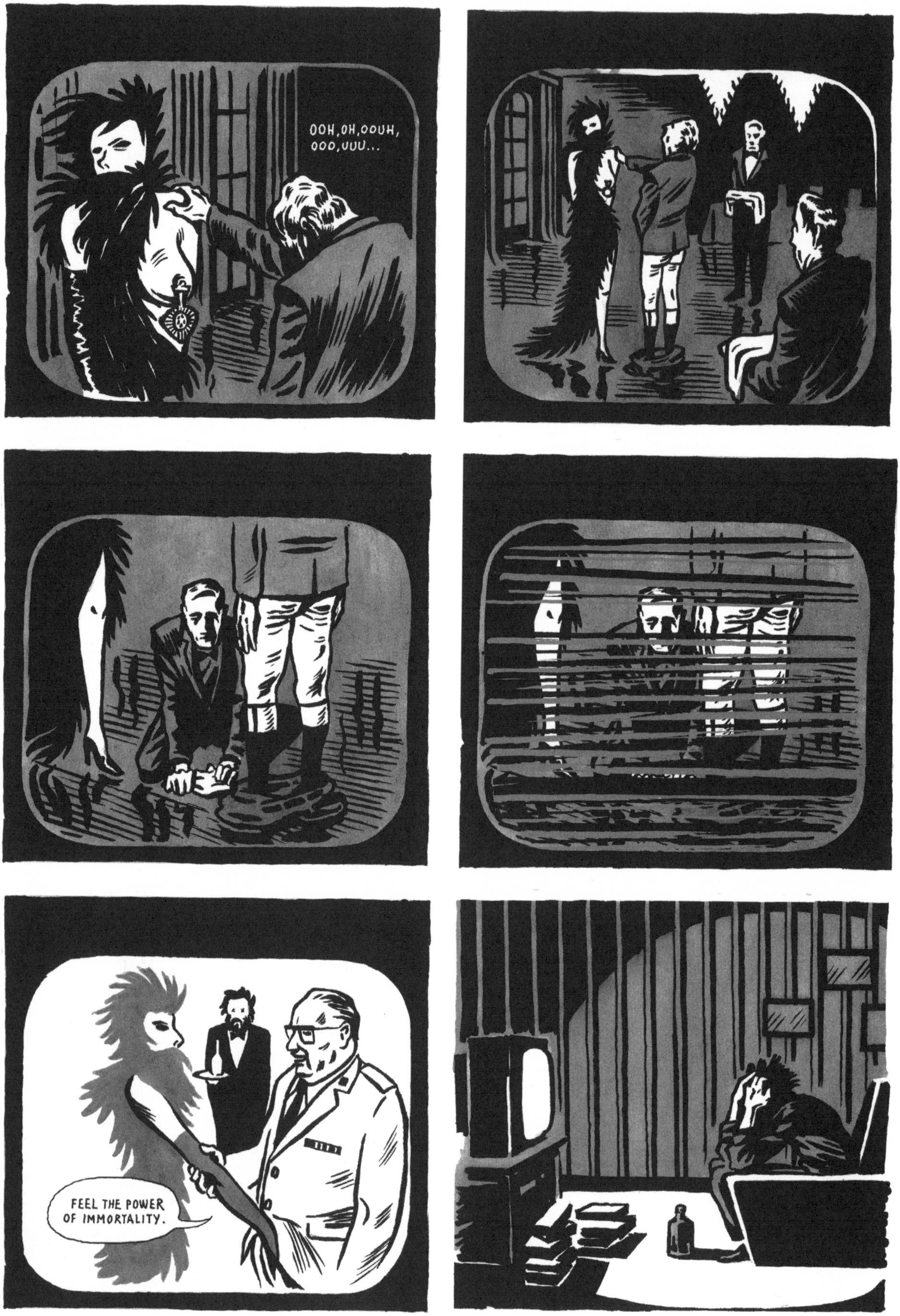
OOH, OH, OOUH, OOO, UUU...
FEEL THE POWER OF IMMORTALITY.

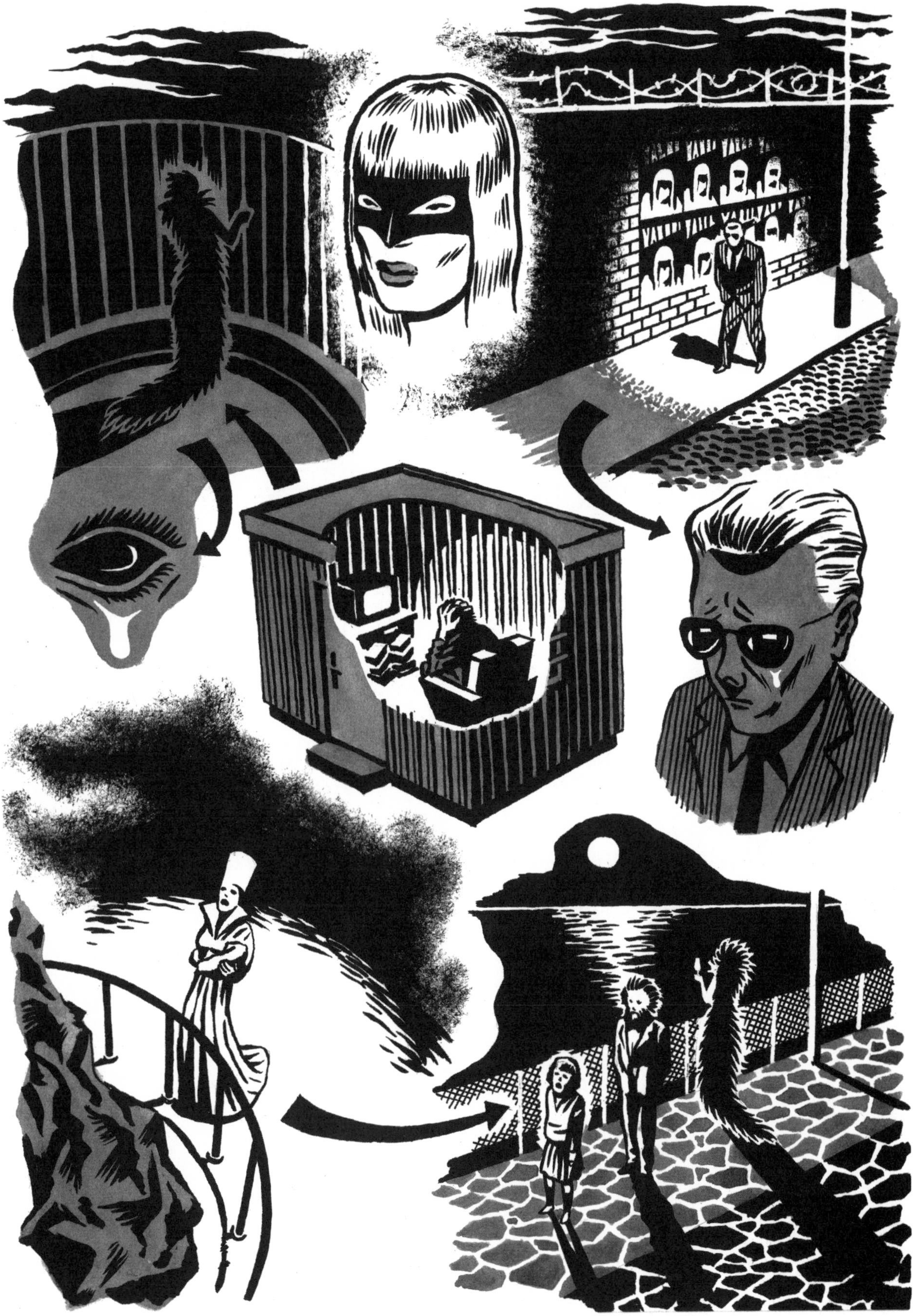

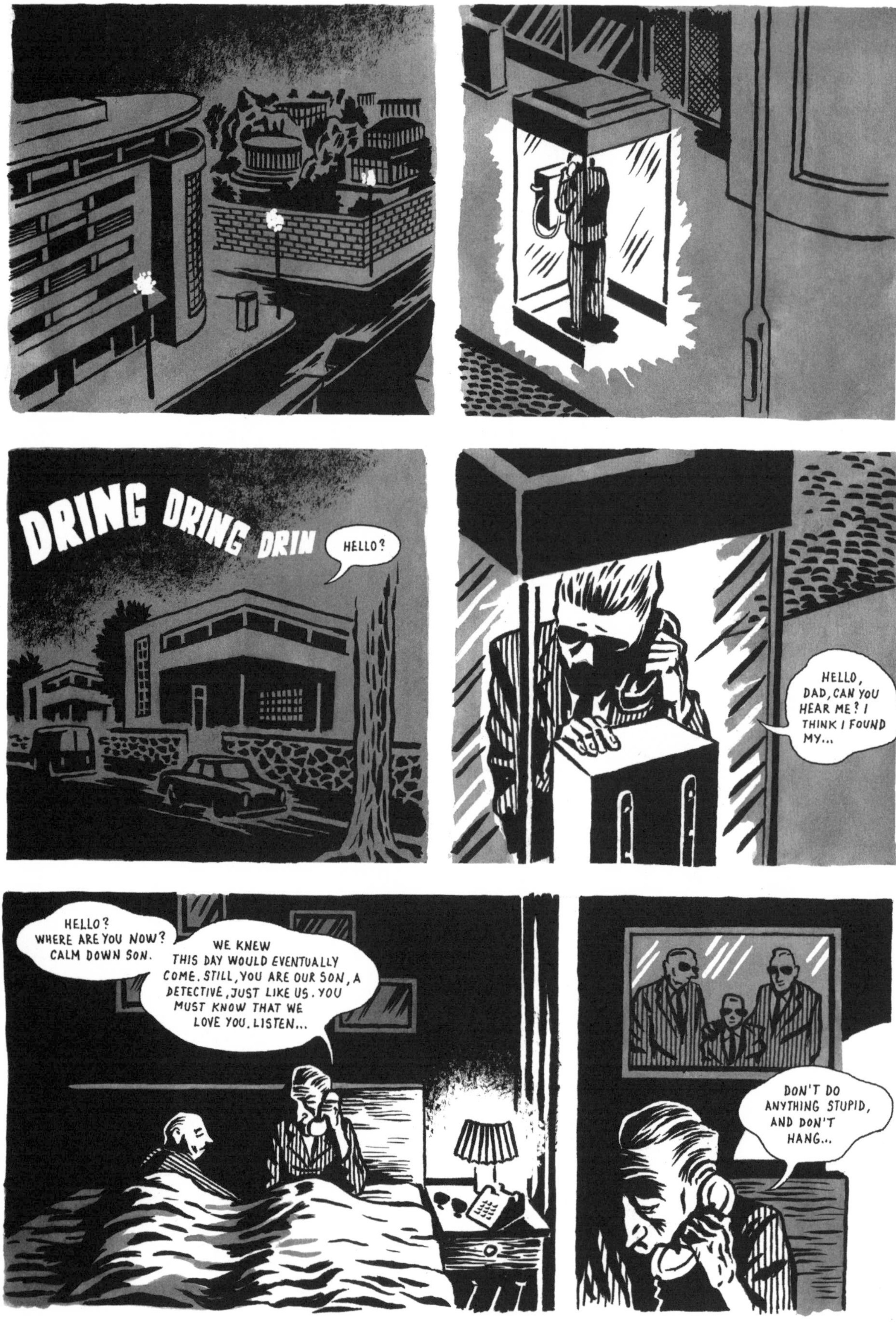
DRING DRING DRIN
HELLO?
HELLO, DAD, CAN YOU HEAR ME? I THINK I FOUND MY...
HELLO? WHERE ARE YOU NOW? CALM DOWN SON.
WE KNEW THIS DAY WOULD EVENTUALLY COME. STILL, YOU ARE OUR SON, A DETECTIVE, JUST LIKE US. YOU MUST KNOW THAT WE LOVE YOU. LISTEN...
DON'T DO ANYTHING STUPID, AND DON'T HANG...

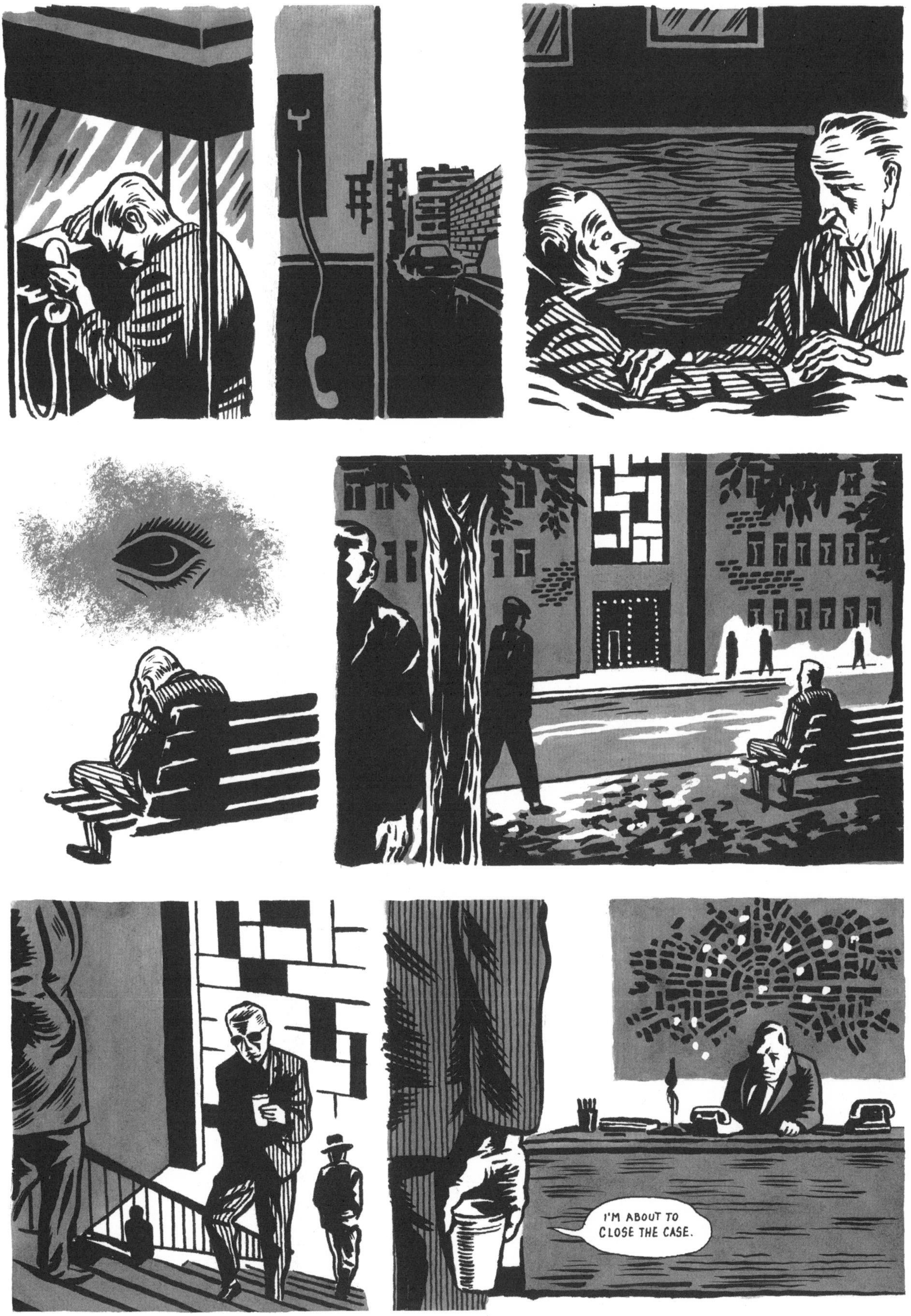
I'M ABOUT TO CLOSE THE CASE.

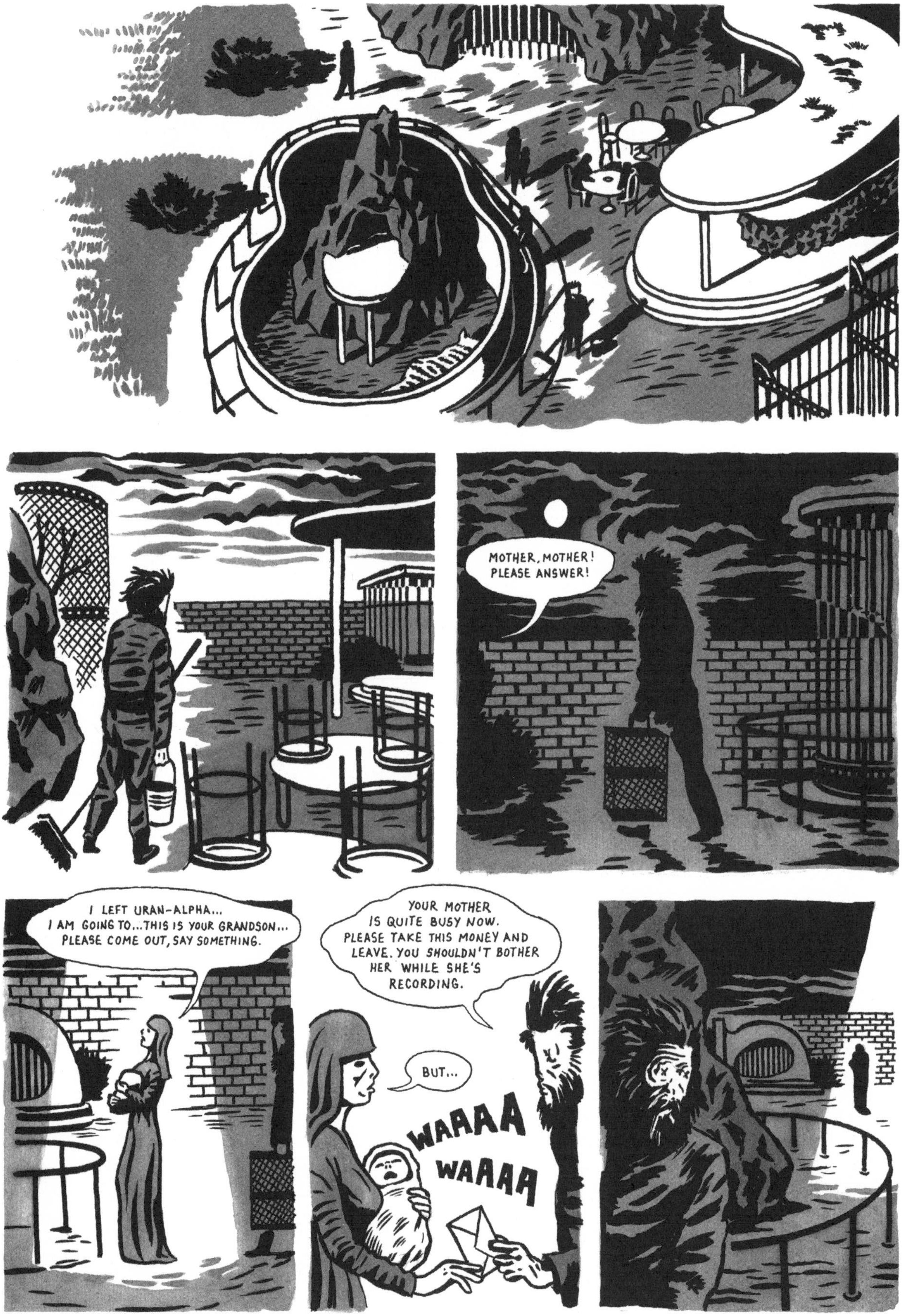
MOTHER, MOTHER!
PLEASE ANSWER!
I LEFT URAN-ALPHA... I AM GOING TO...THIS IS YOUR GRANDSON... PLEASE COME OUT, SAY SOMETHING.
YOUR MOTHER IS QUITE BUSY NOW. PLEASE TAKE THIS MONEY AND LEAVE. YOU SHOULDN'T BOTHER HER WHILE SHE'S RECORDING.
BUT...
WAAAA
WAAAA

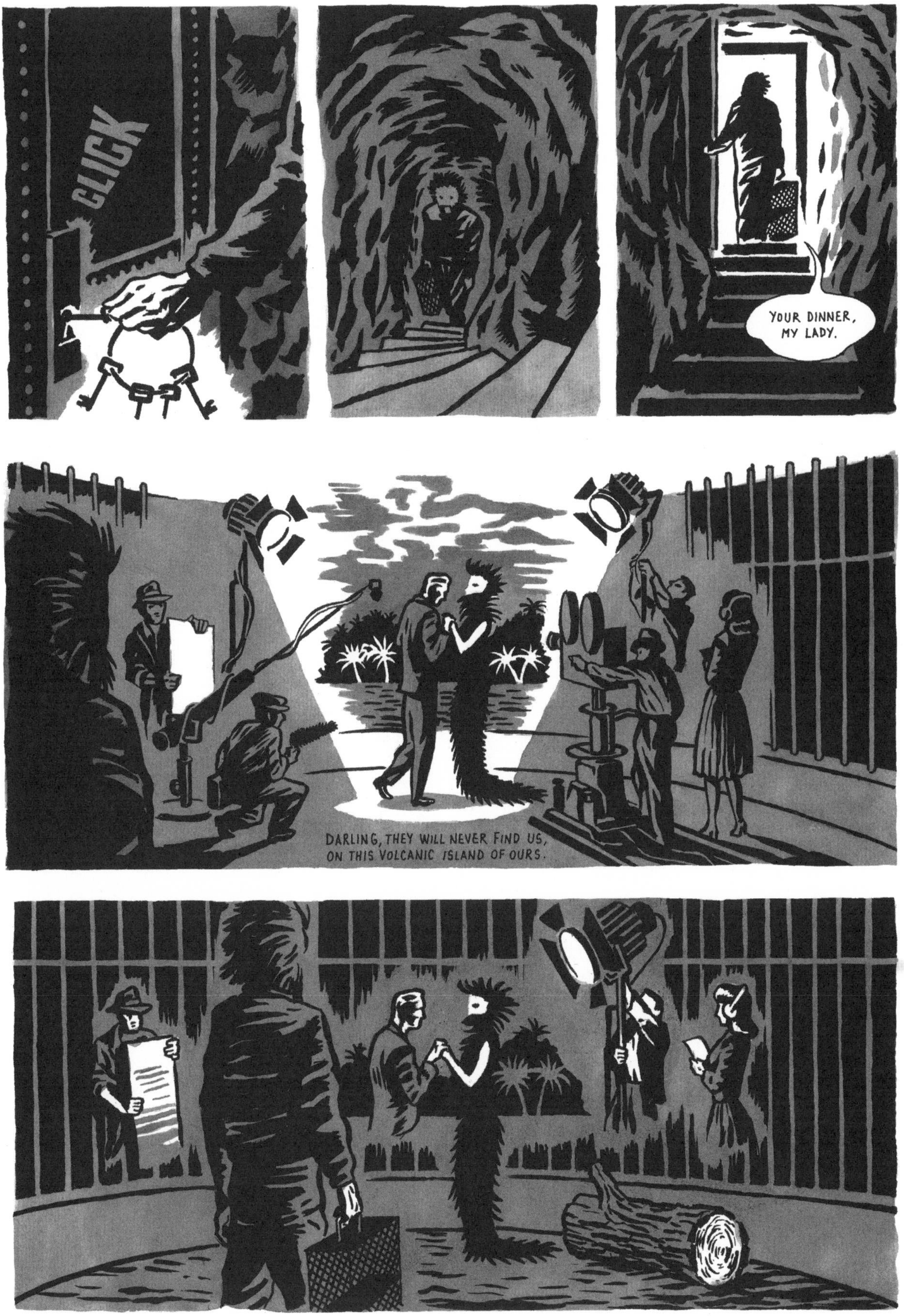
CLICK
YOUR DINNER, MY LADY.
DARLING, THEY WILL NEVER FIND US, ON THIS VOLCANIC ISLAND OF OURS.

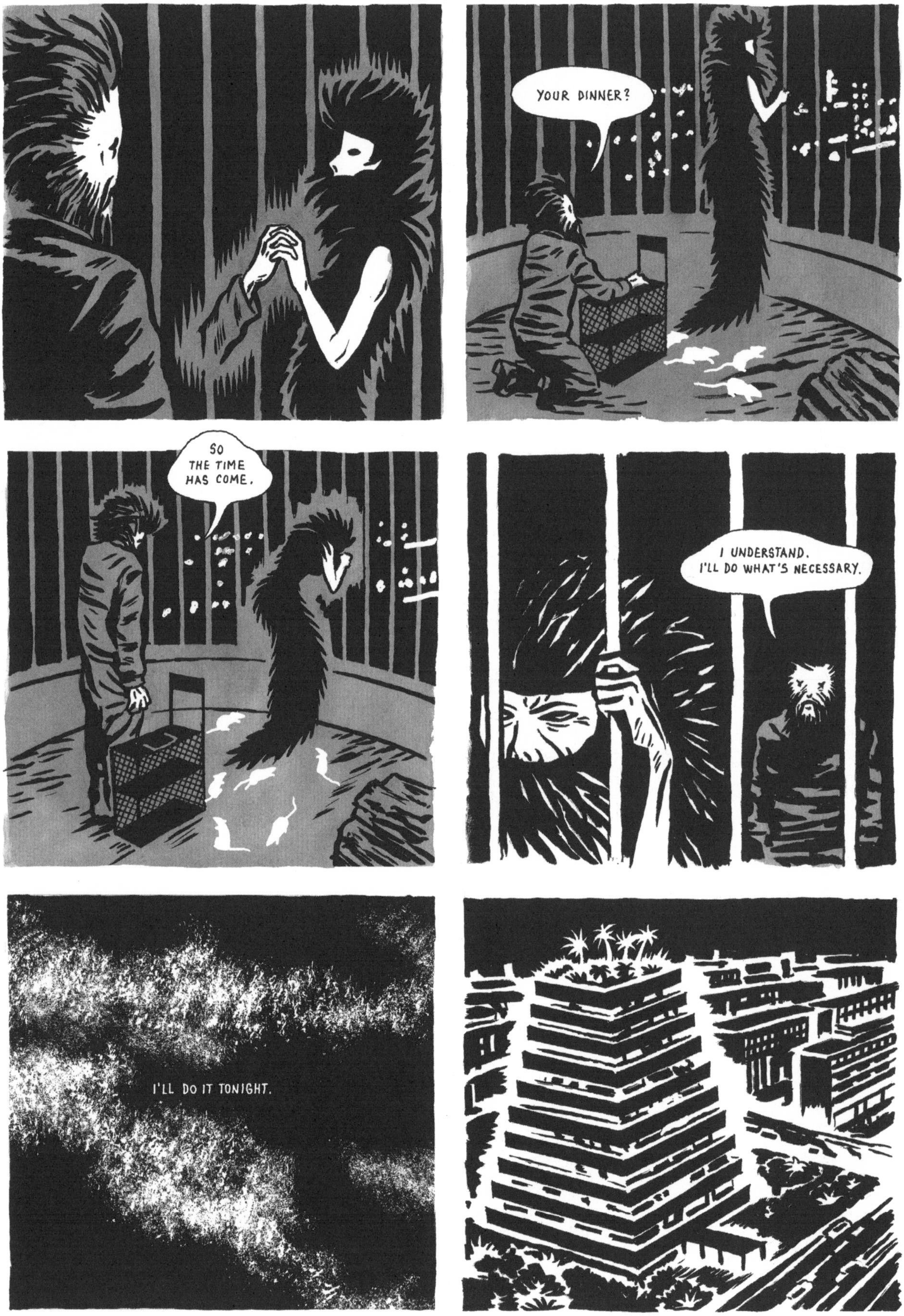
YOUR DINNER?
SO THE TIME HAS COME.
I UNDERSTAND. I'LL DO WHAT'S NECESSARY.
I'LL DO IT TONIGHT.

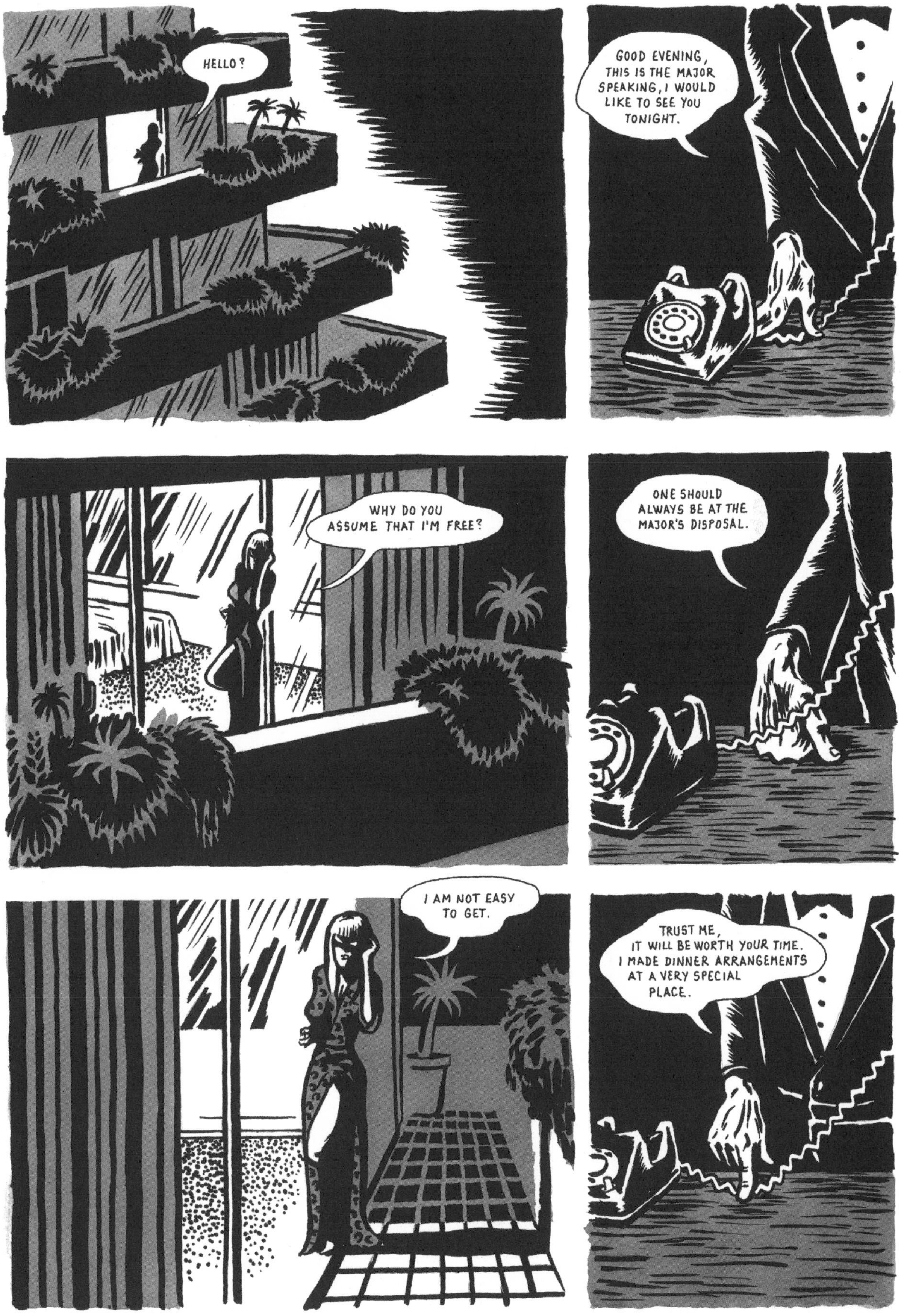
HELLO?
GOOD EVENING, THIS IS THE MAJOR SPEAKING, I WOULD LIKE TO SEE YOU TONIGHT.
WHY DO YOU ASSUME THAT I'M FREE?
ONE SHOULD ALWAYS BE AT THE MAJOR'S DISPOSAL.
I AM NOT EASY TO GET.
TRUST ME, IT WILL BE WORTH YOUR TIME. I MADE DINNER ARRANGEMENTS AT A VERY SPECIAL PLACE.

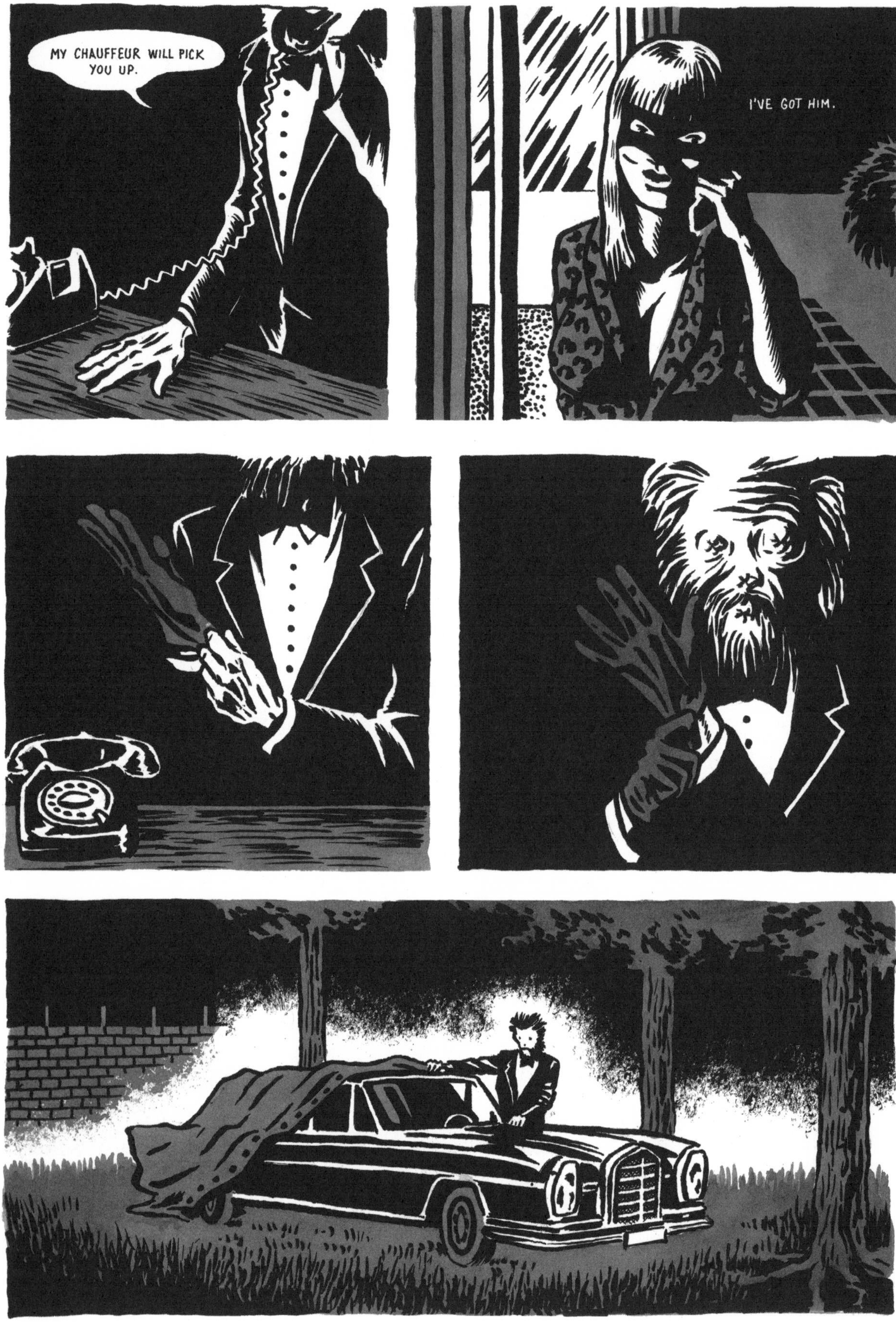
MY CHAUFFEUR WILL PICK YOU UP.
I'VE GOT HIM.

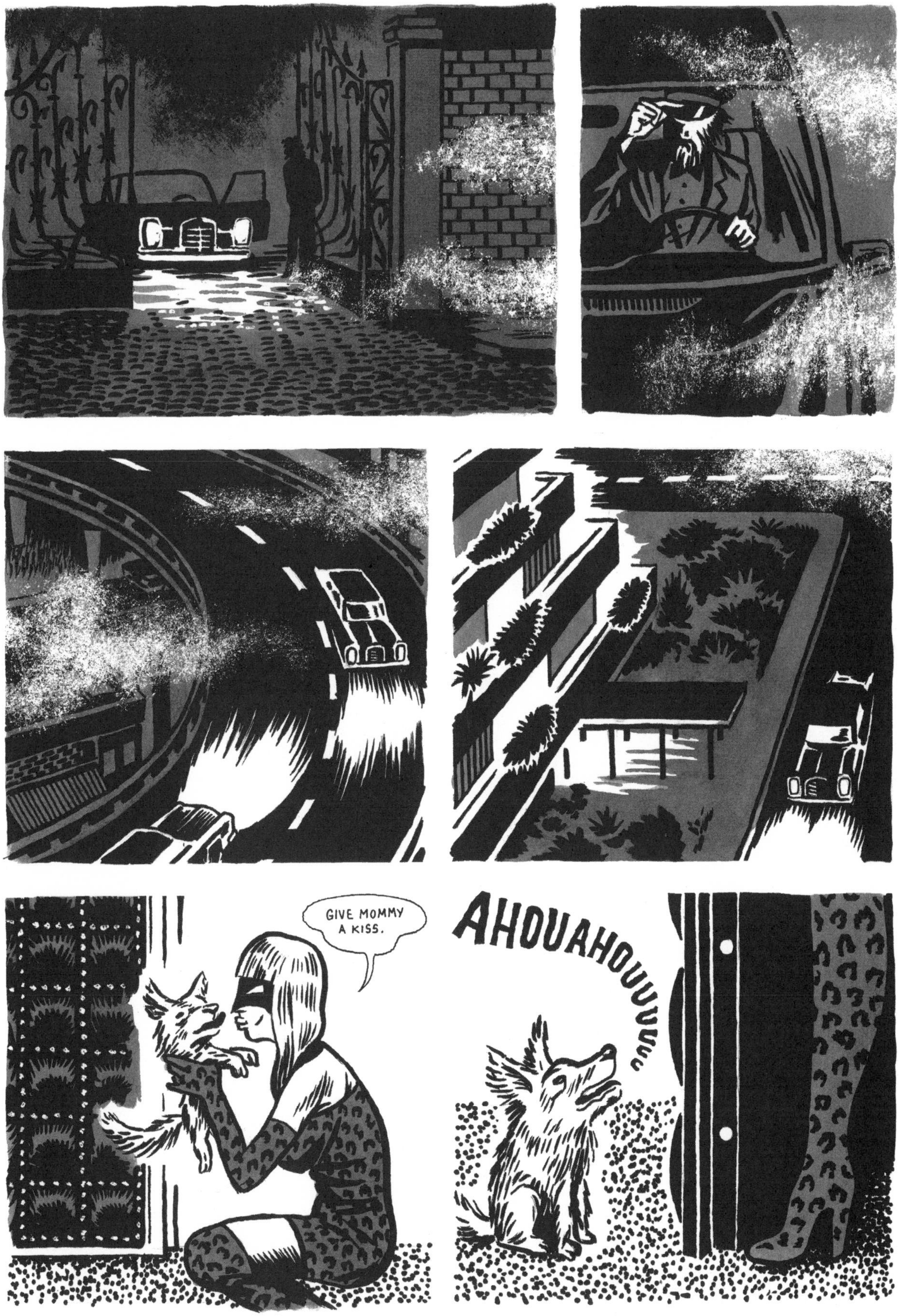
GIVE MOMMY A KISS.
AHOUAHOUUUUU...

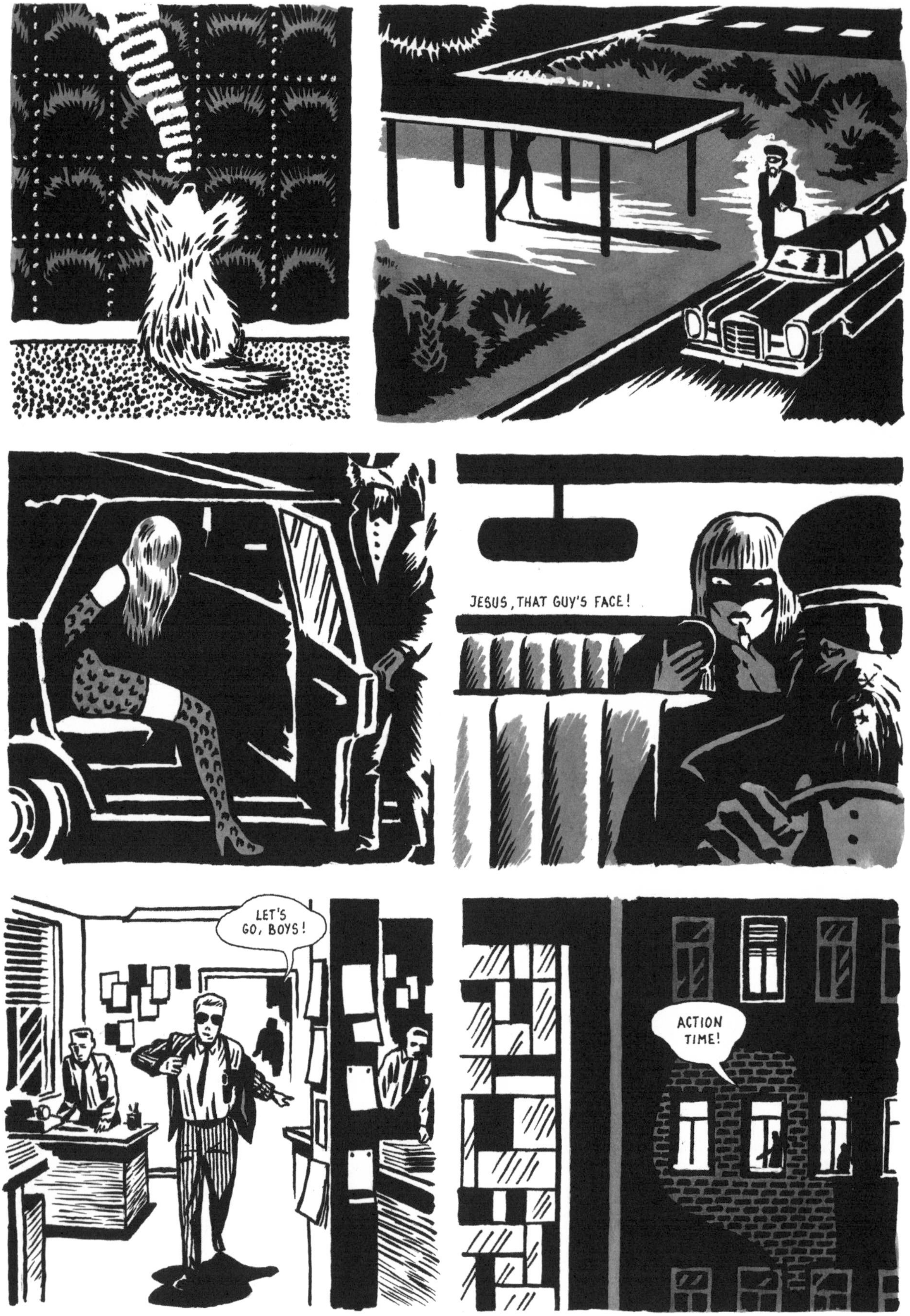
JESUS, THAT GUY'S FACE!
LET'S GO, BOYS!
ACTION TIME!

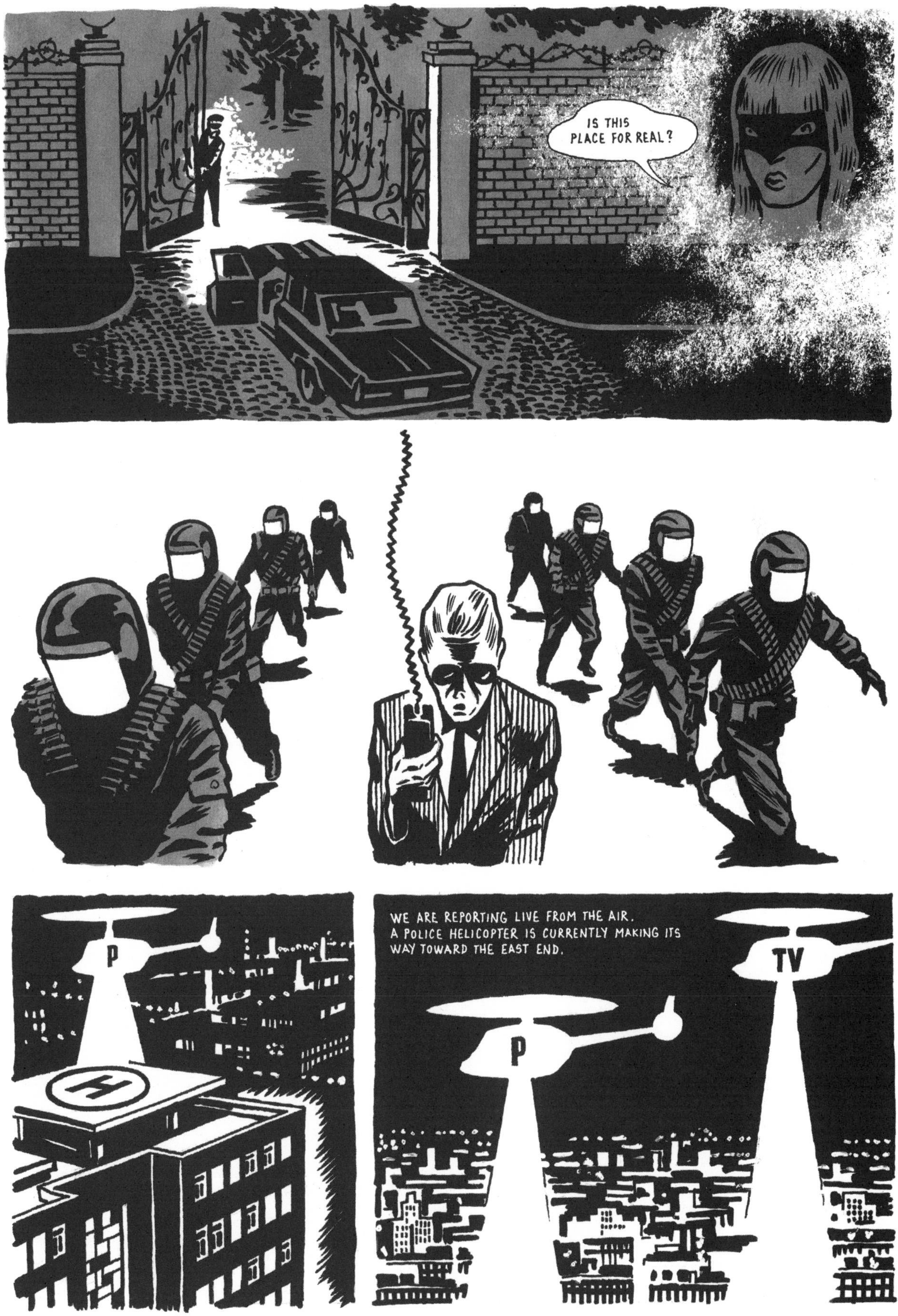
IS THIS PLACE FOR REAL?
P
H
WE ARE REPORTING LIVE FROM THE AIR. A POLICE HELICOPTER IS CURRENTLY MAKING ITS WAY TOWARD THE EAST END.
TV
P

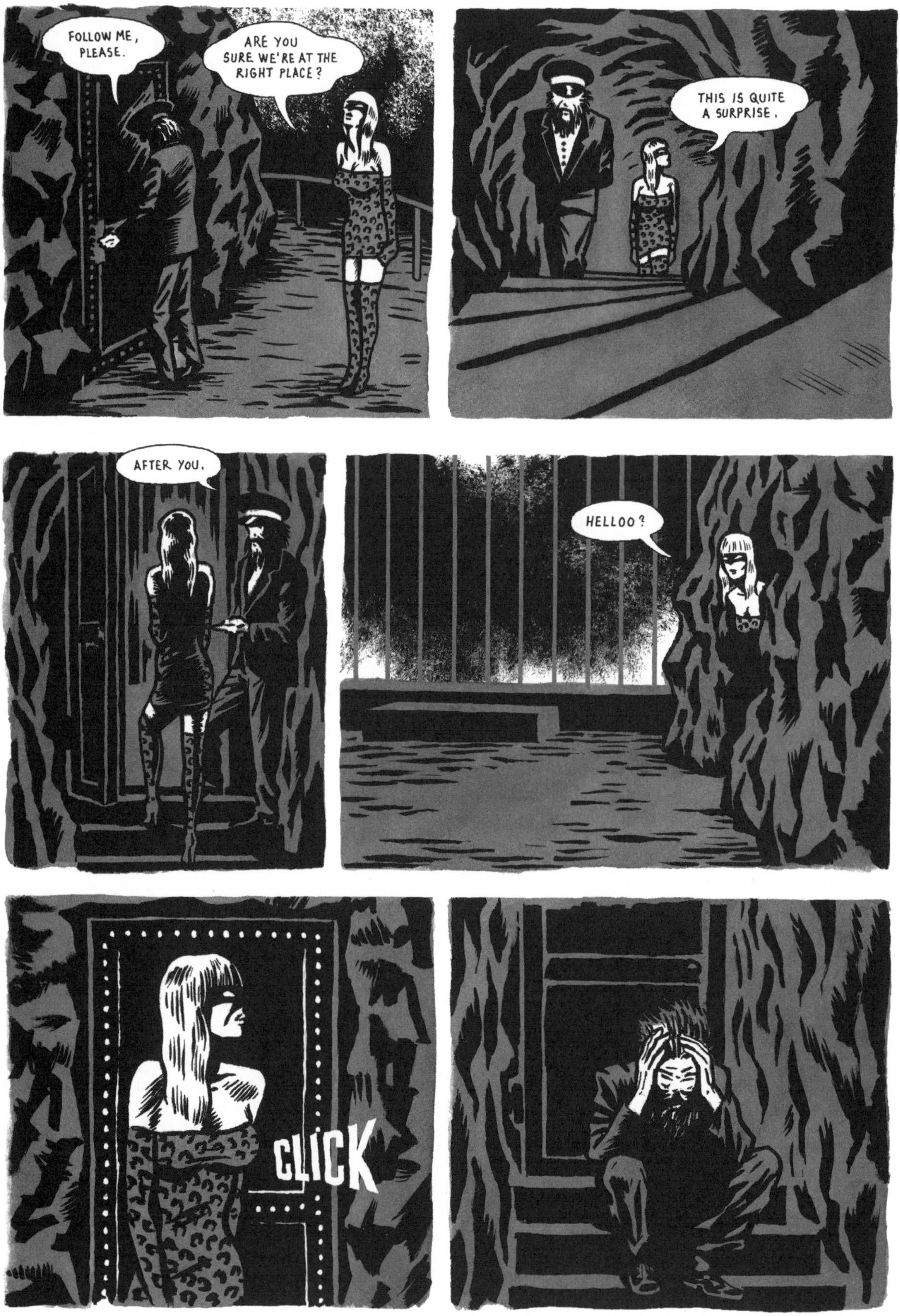
FOLLOW ME, PLEASE.
ARE YOU SURE WE'RE AT THE RIGHT PLACE?
THIS IS QUITE A SURPRISE.
AFTER YOU.
HELLOO?
CLICK

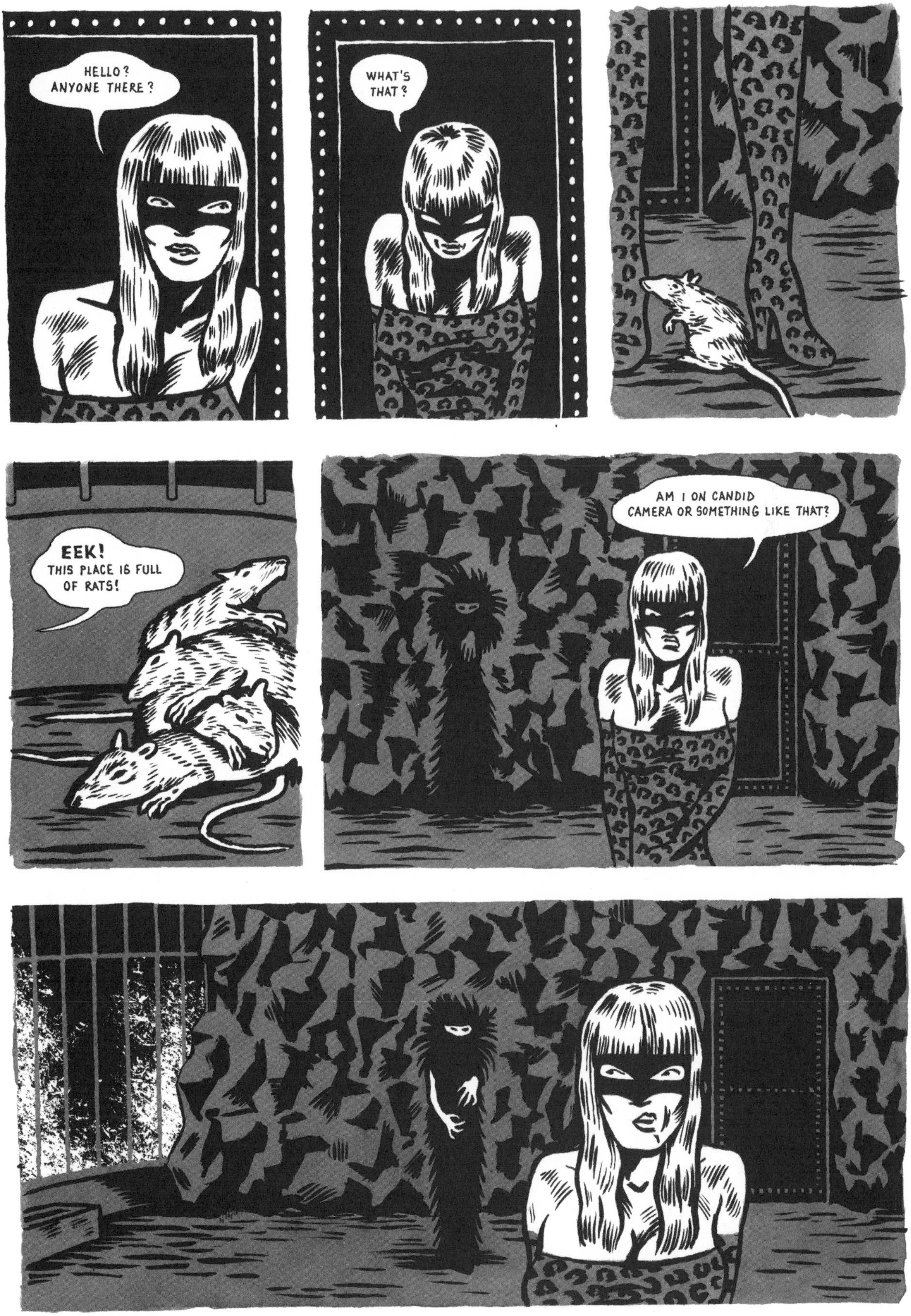
HELLO? ANYONE THERE?
WHAT'S THAT?
EEK! THIS PLACE IS FULL OF RATS!
AM I ON CANDID CAMERA OR SOMETHING LIKE THAT?

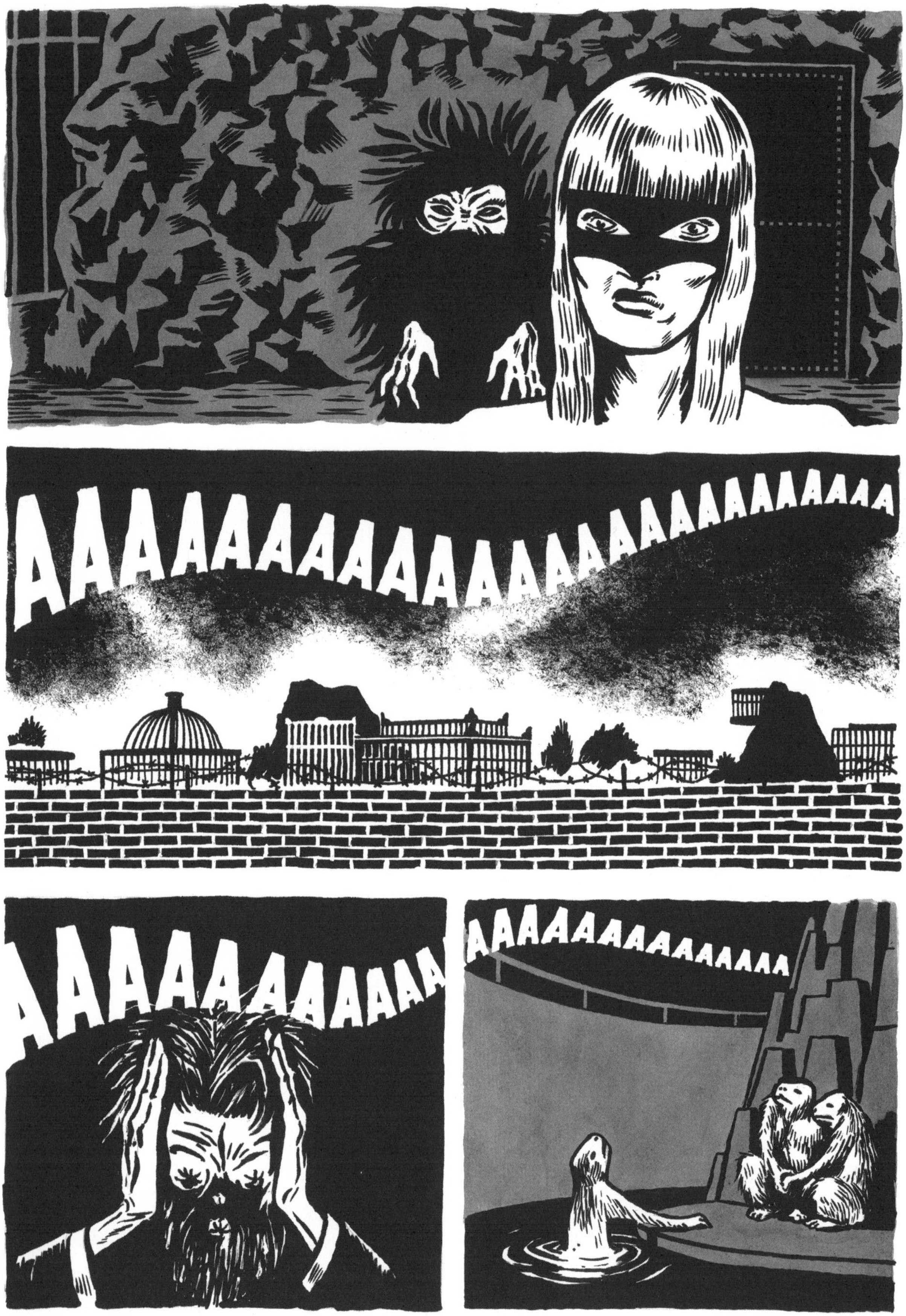
AAAAAAAAAAAAAAAAAAAAAAAAAA
AAAAAAAAAAAA
AAAAAAAAAAAAAAA

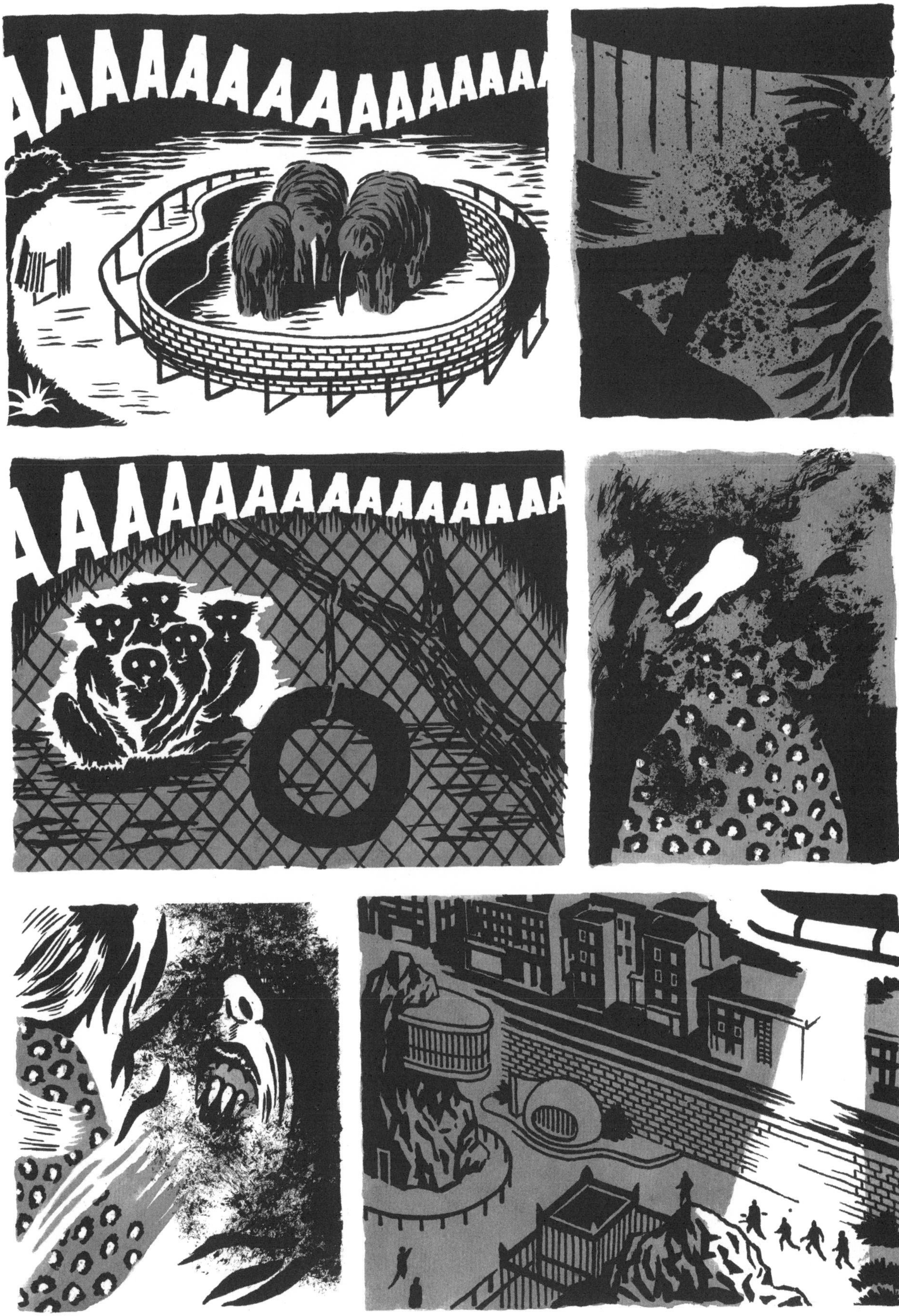
AAAAAAAAAAAAAAA
AAAAAAAAAAAAAAA

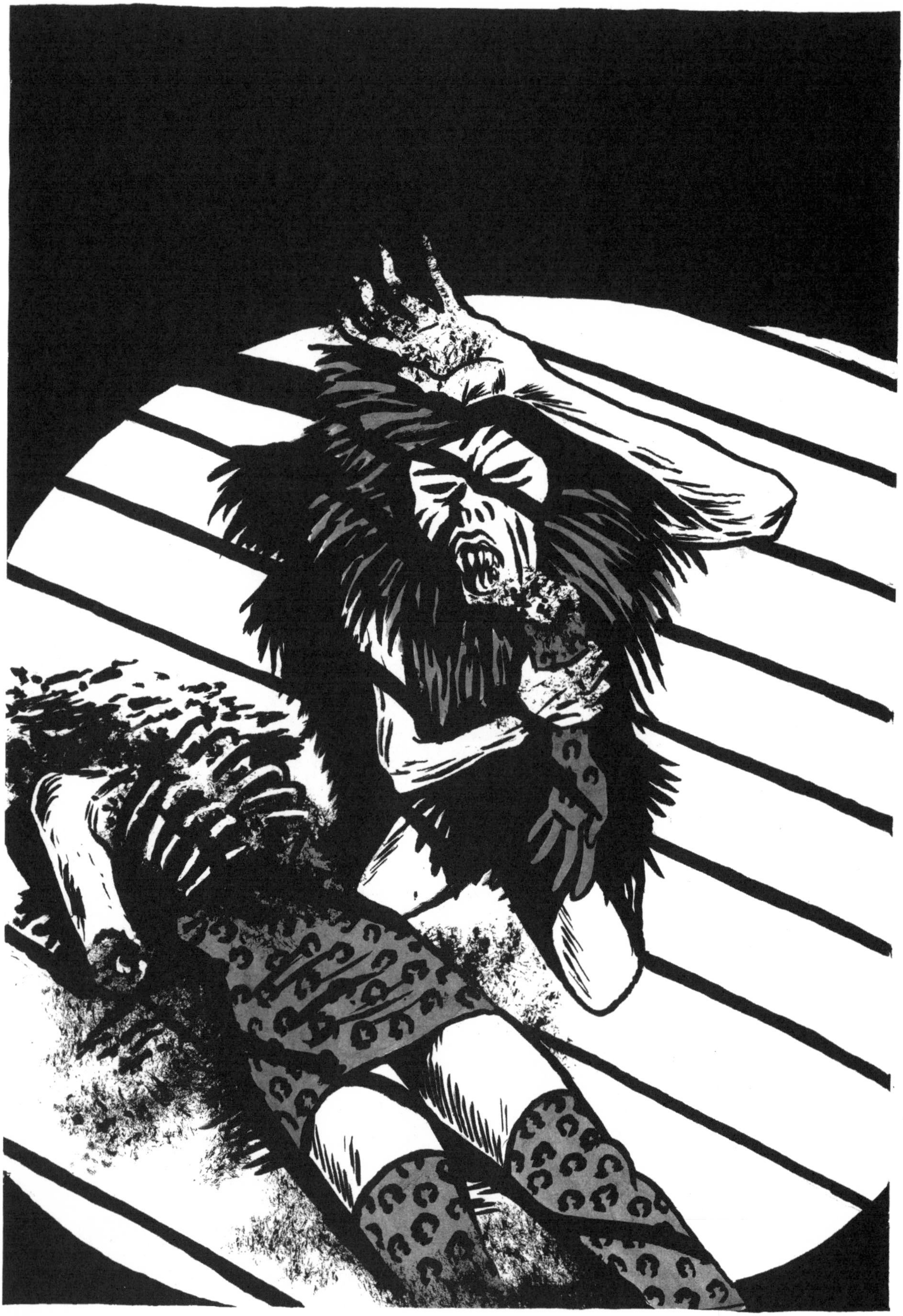

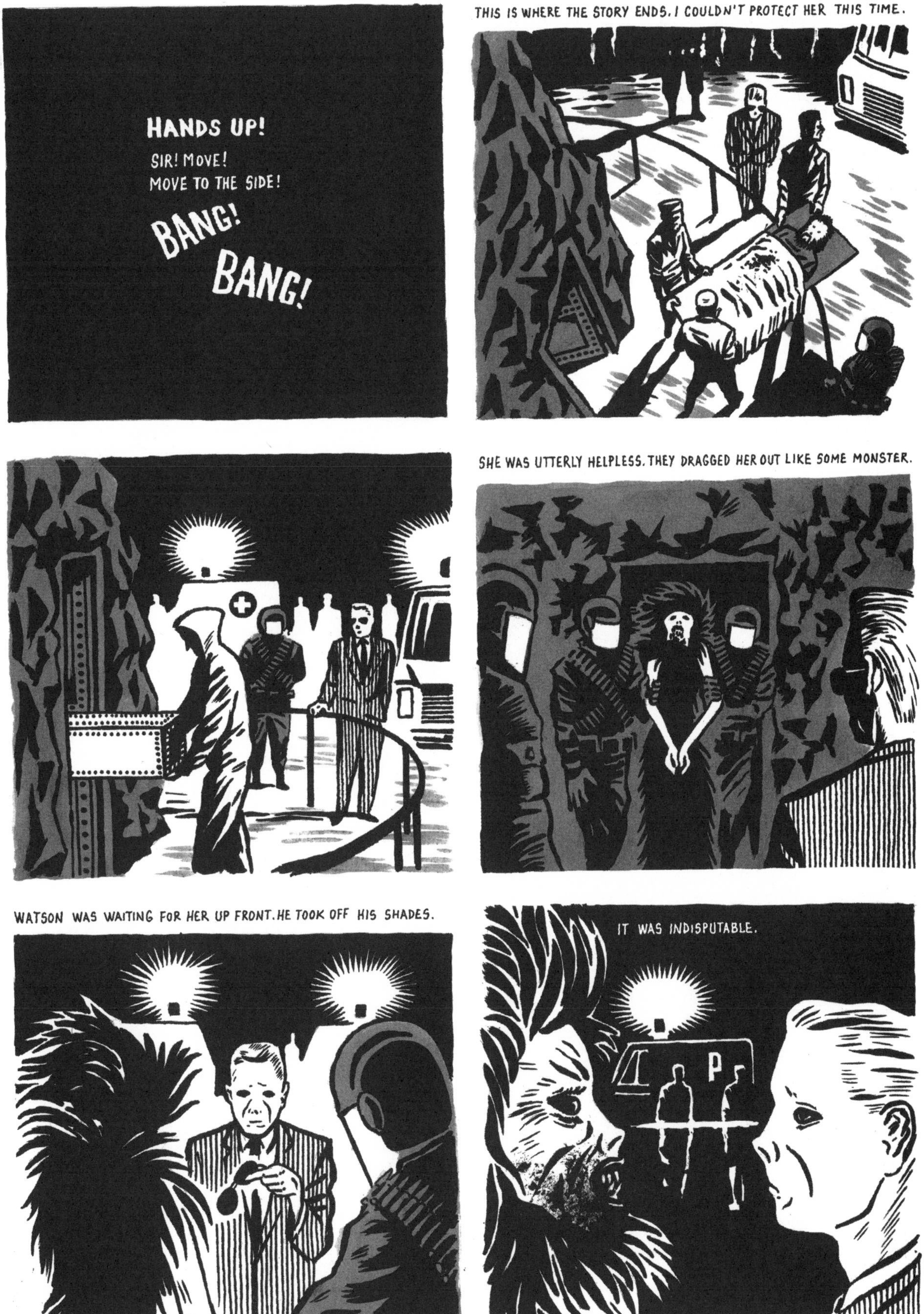
HANDS UP!
SIR! MOVE!
MOVE TO THE SIDE!
BANG!
BANG!
THIS IS WHERE THE STORY ENDS. I COULDN'T PROTECT HER THIS TIME.
SHE WAS UTTERLY HELPLESS. THEY DRAGGED HER OUT LIKE SOME MONSTER.
WATSON WAS WAITING FOR HER UP FRONT. HE TOOK OFF HIS SHADES.
IT WAS INDISPUTABLE.

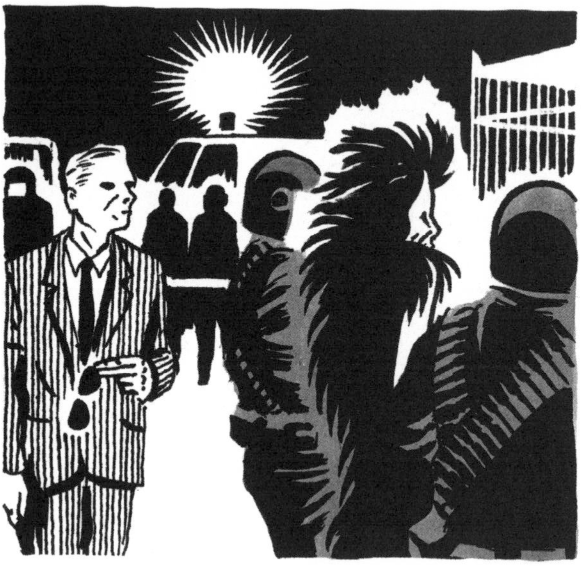

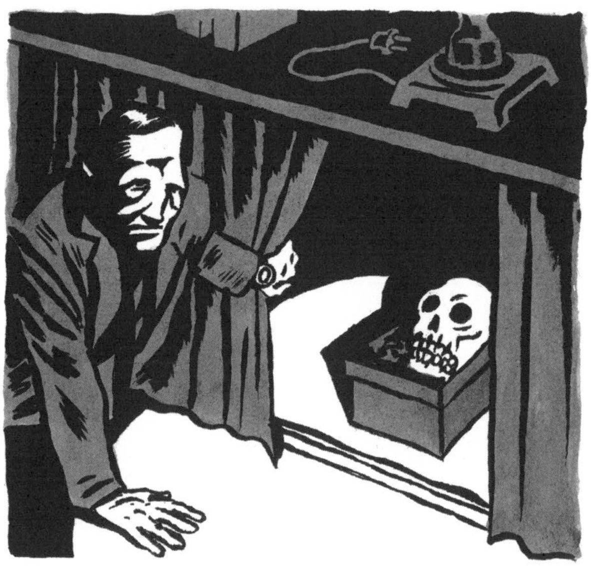

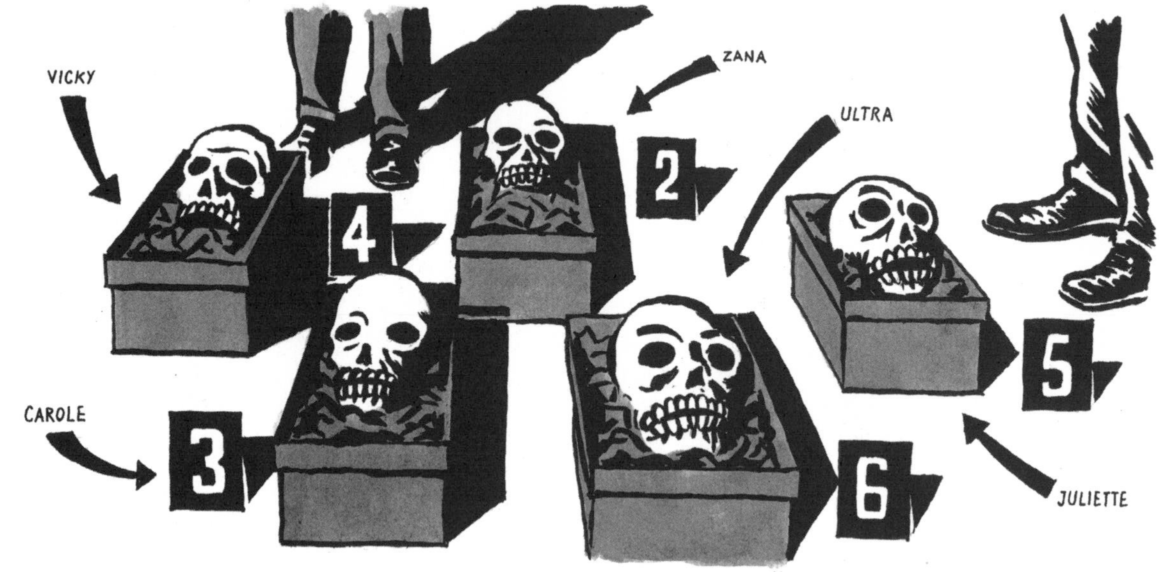
VICKY
ZANA
ULTRA
4
2
5
CAROLE
3
6
JULIETTE

HE SURE HAD ME FOOLED, AND I THOUGHT I WOULD NEVER SEE HIM AGAIN.

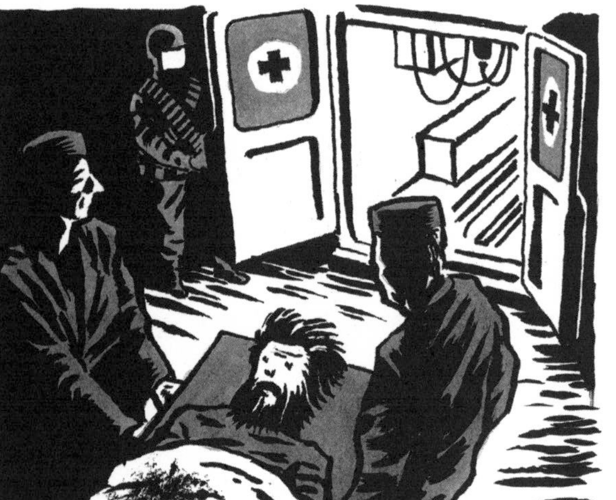

THAT SMALL BUNDLE I WAS ORDERED TO THROW IN THE RIVER.
I DISOBEYED THE ORDER, I COULDN'T DO IT.

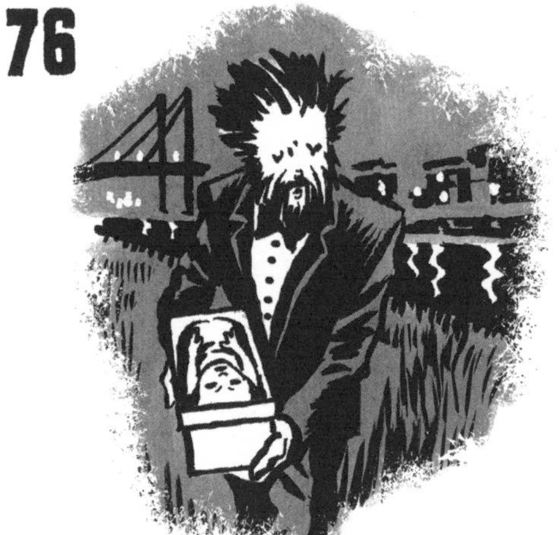
76

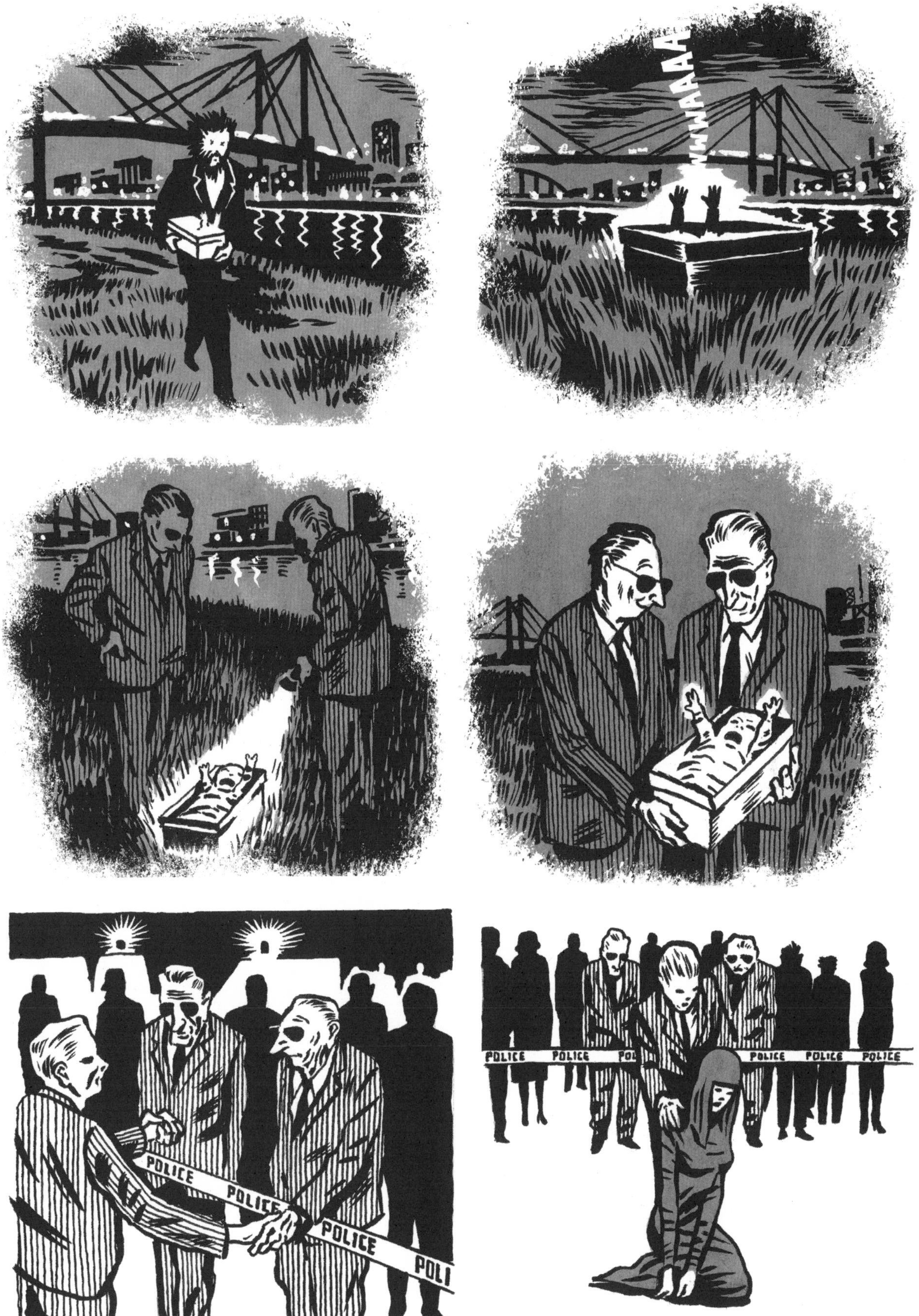
WWWAAAA
POLICE POLICE POLICE POLI
POLICE POLICE POL POLICE POLICE POLICE

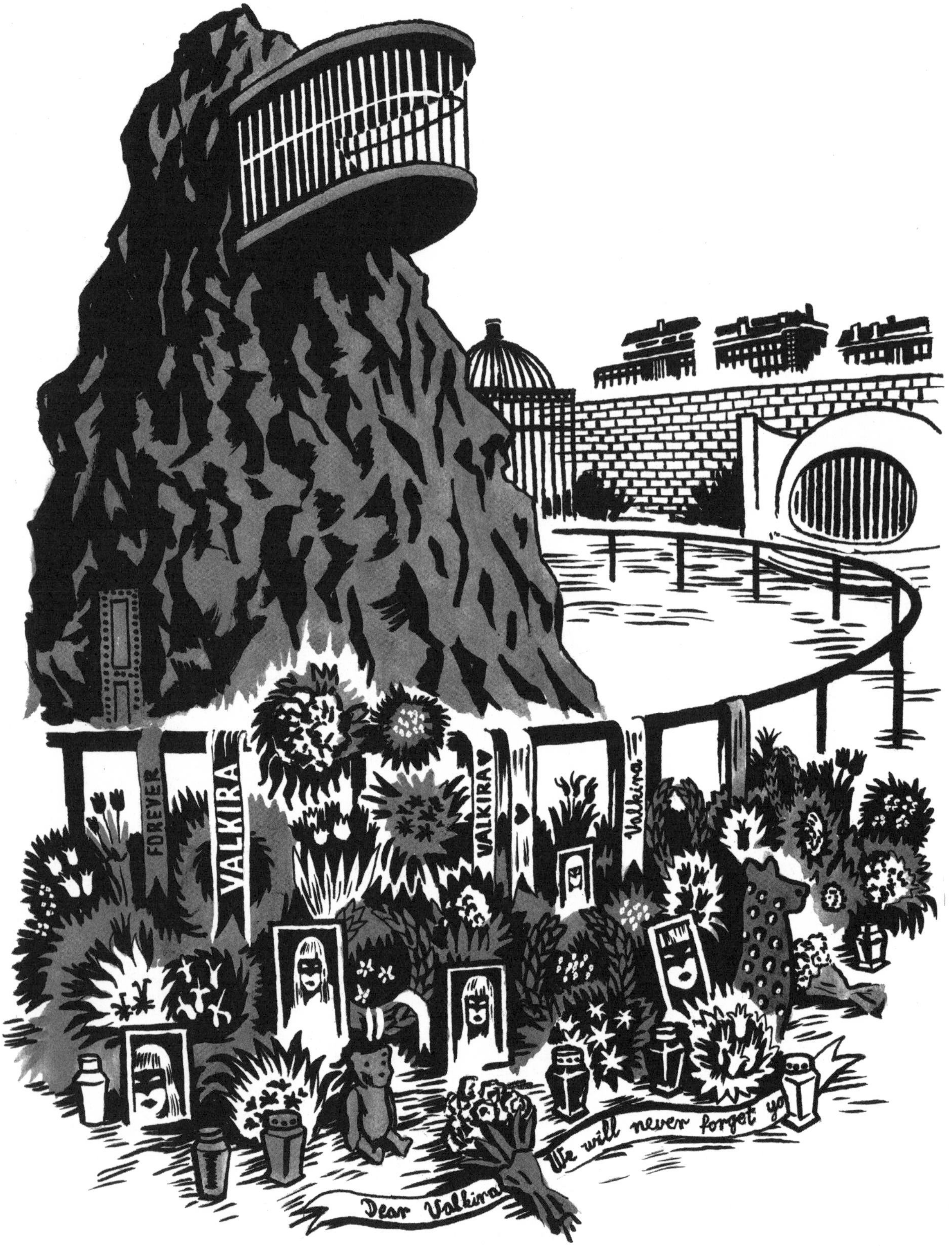

FOREVER
VALKIRA
VALKIRA
Valkira
Dear Valkira
We will never forget yo

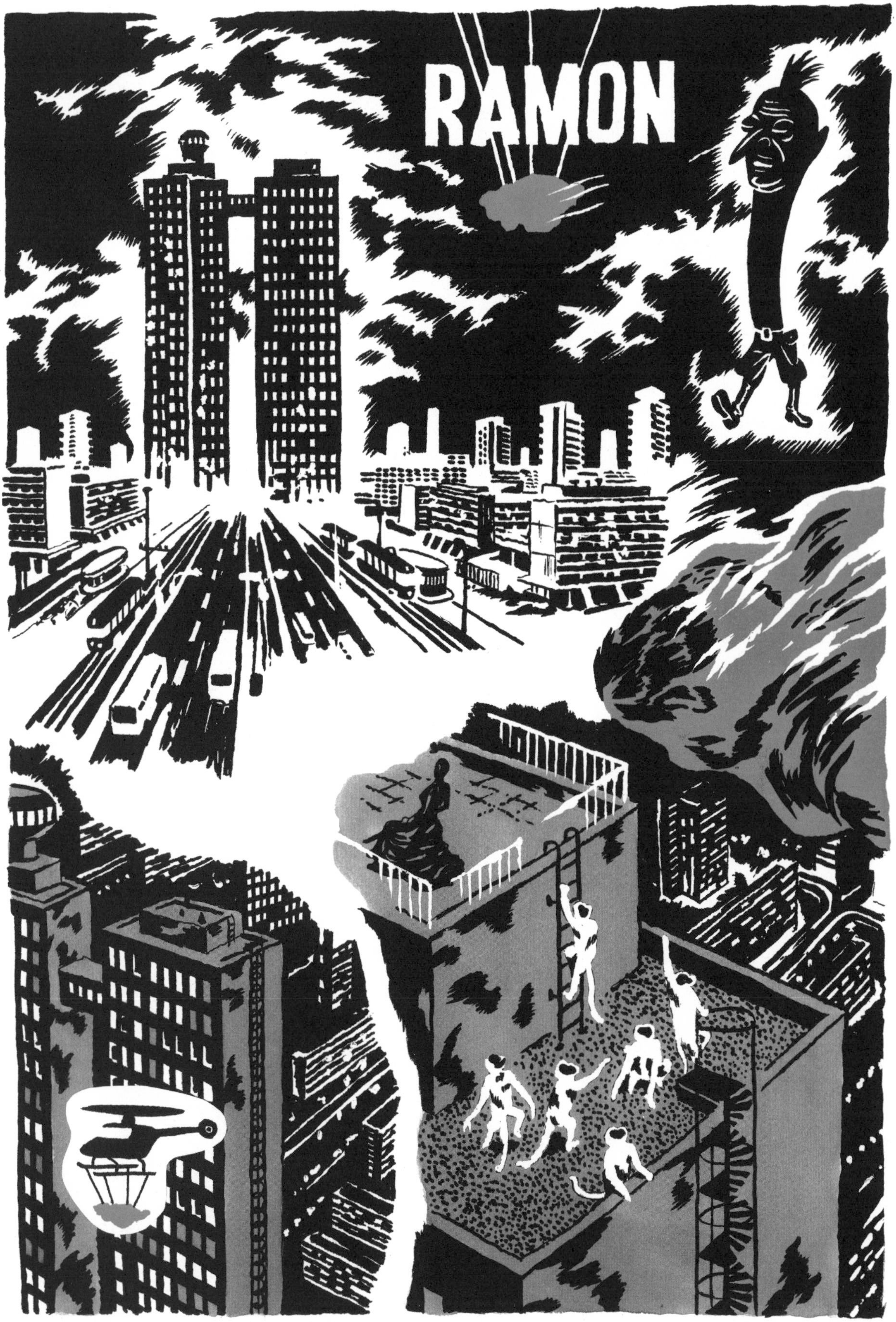
RAMON

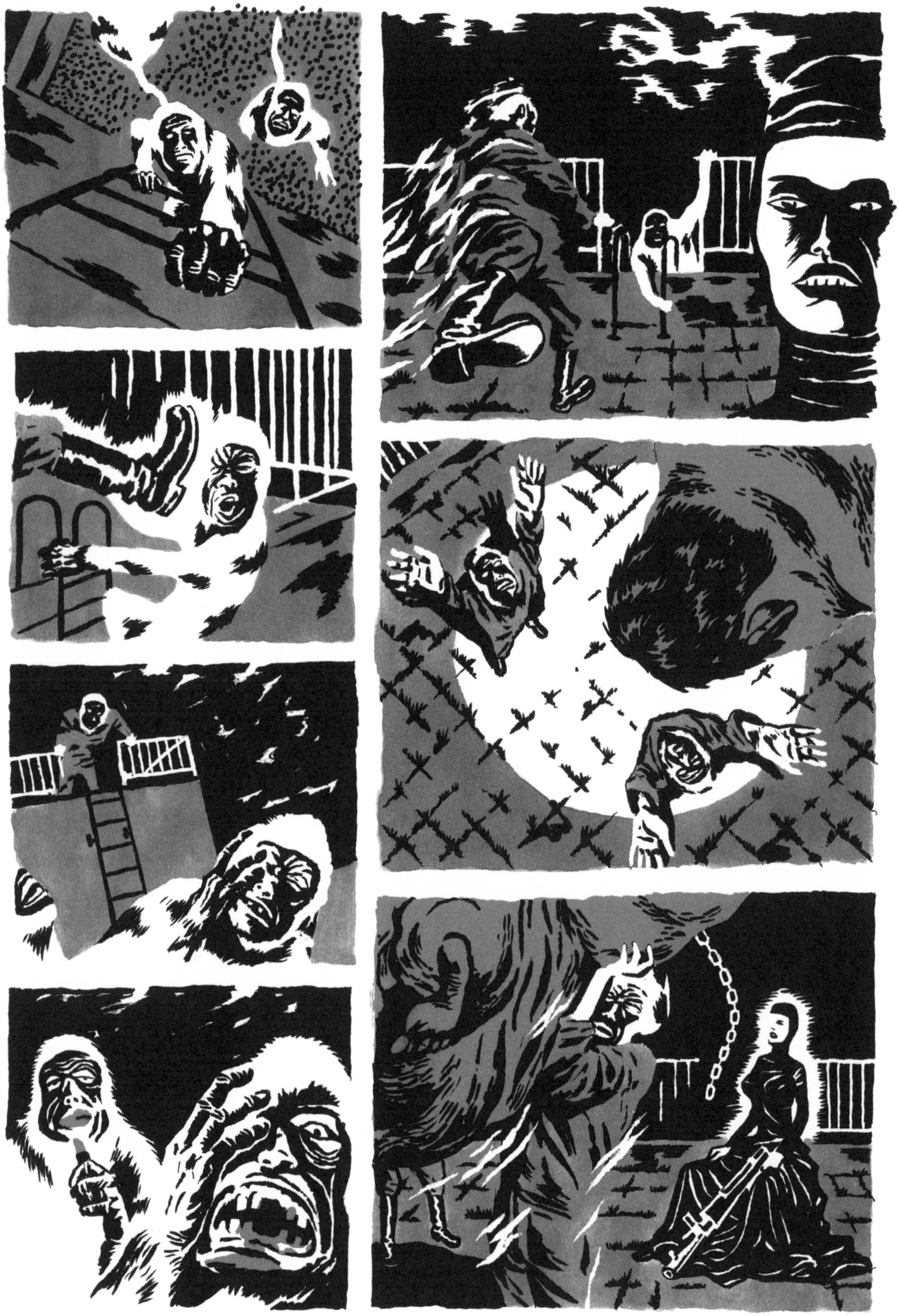

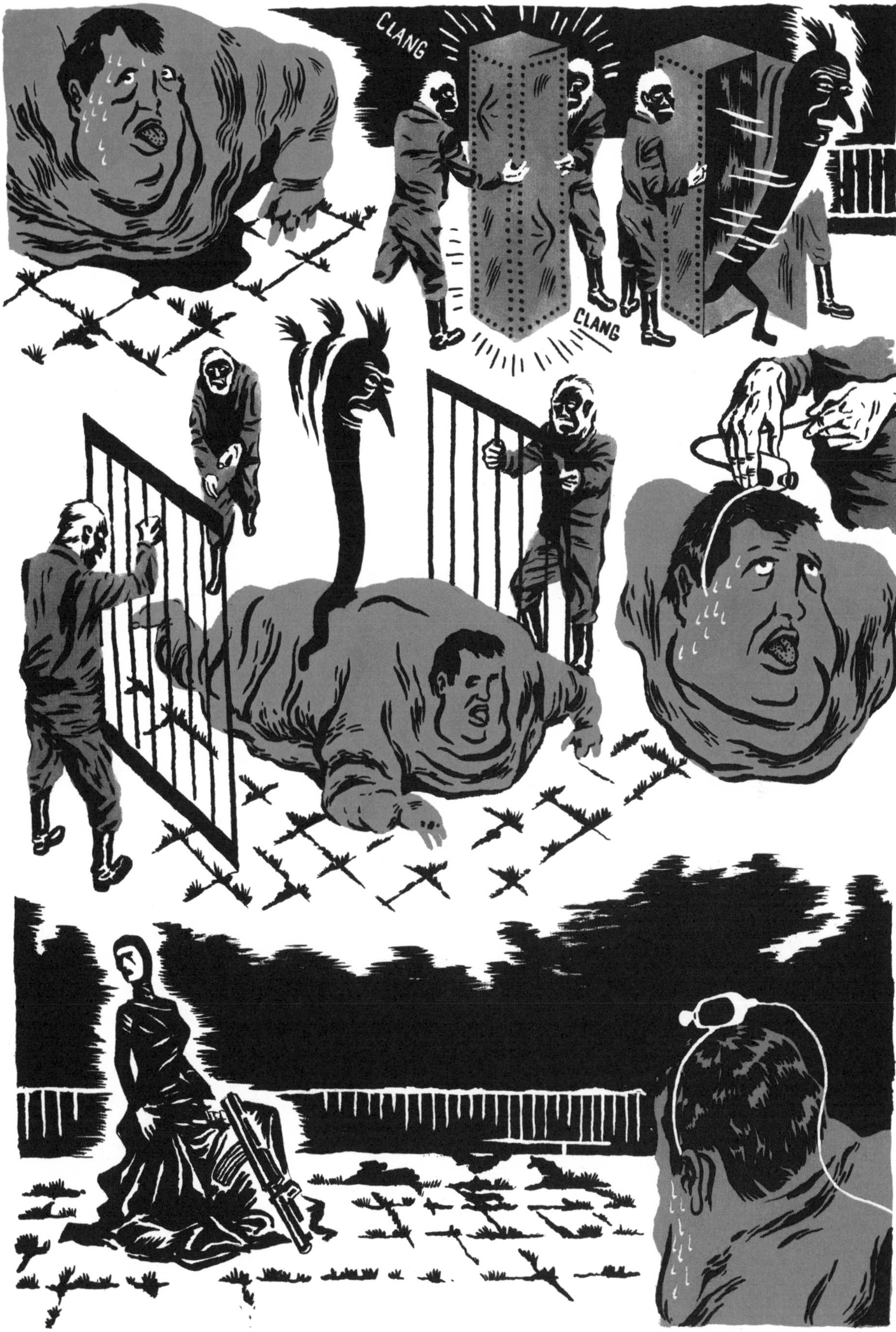
CLANG
CLANG

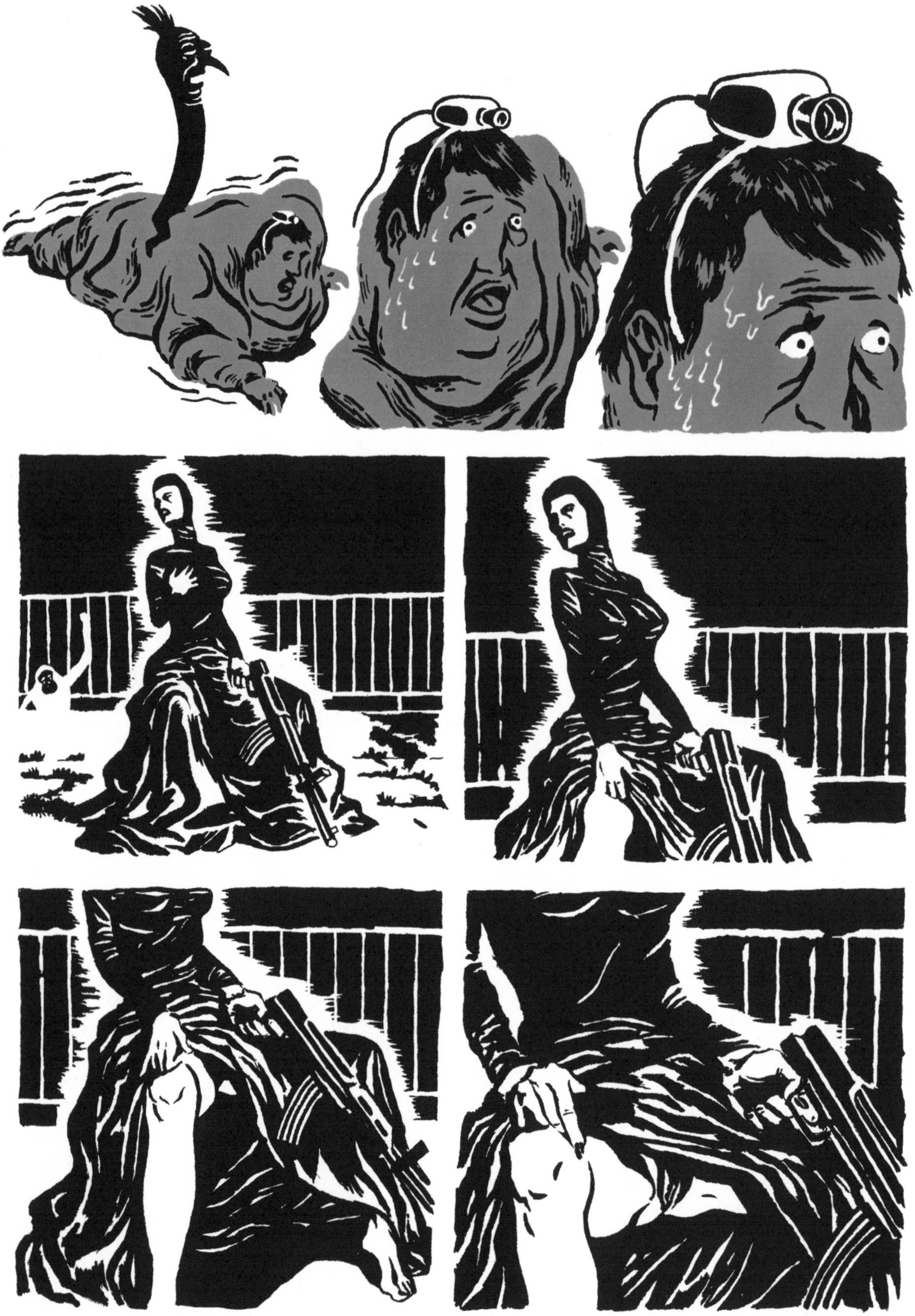

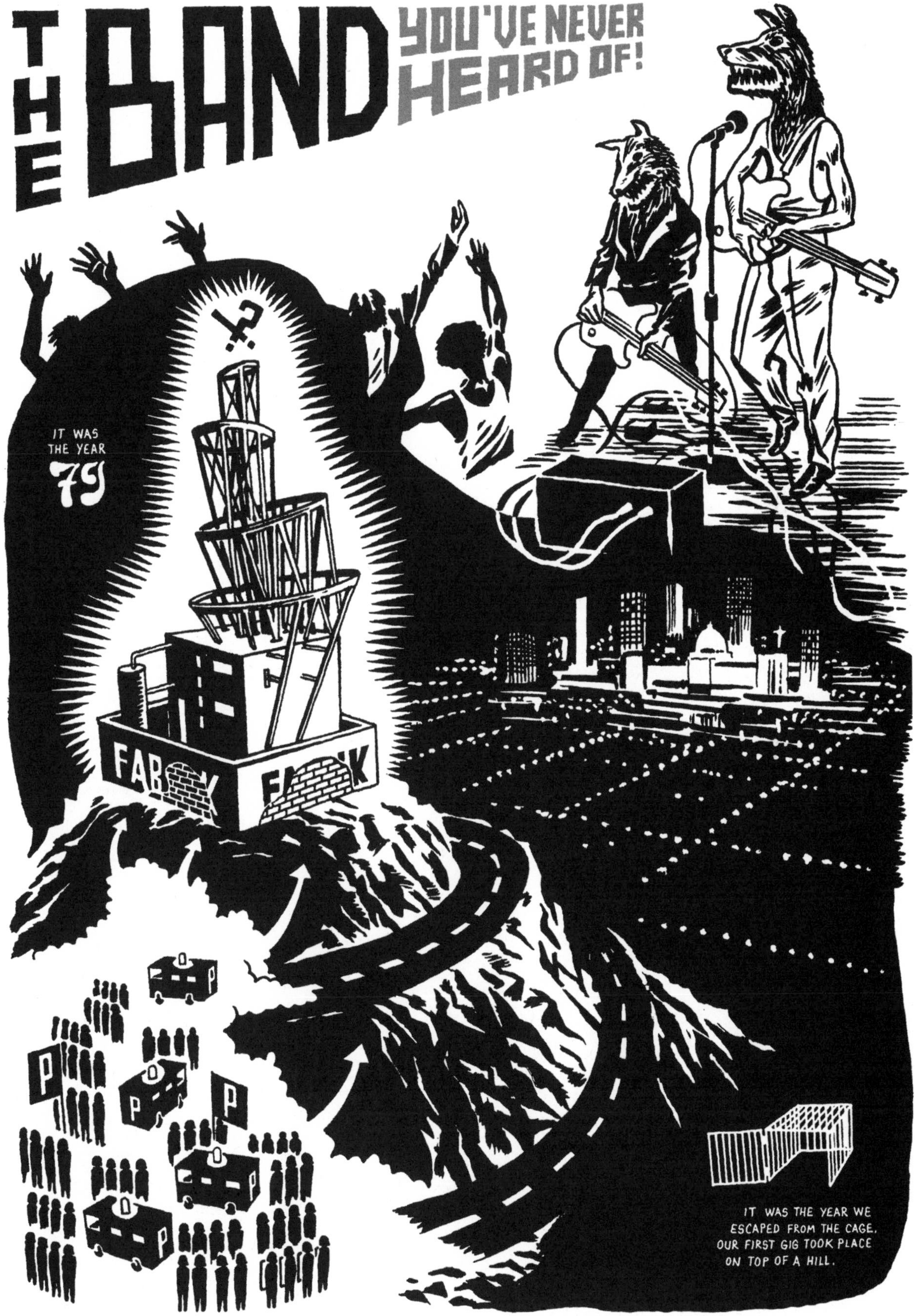
THE BAND YOU'VE NEVER HEARD OF!
IT WAS THE YEAR 79
IT WAS THE YEAR WE ESCAPED FROM THE CAGE. OUR FIRST GIG TOOK PLACE ON TOP OF A HILL.

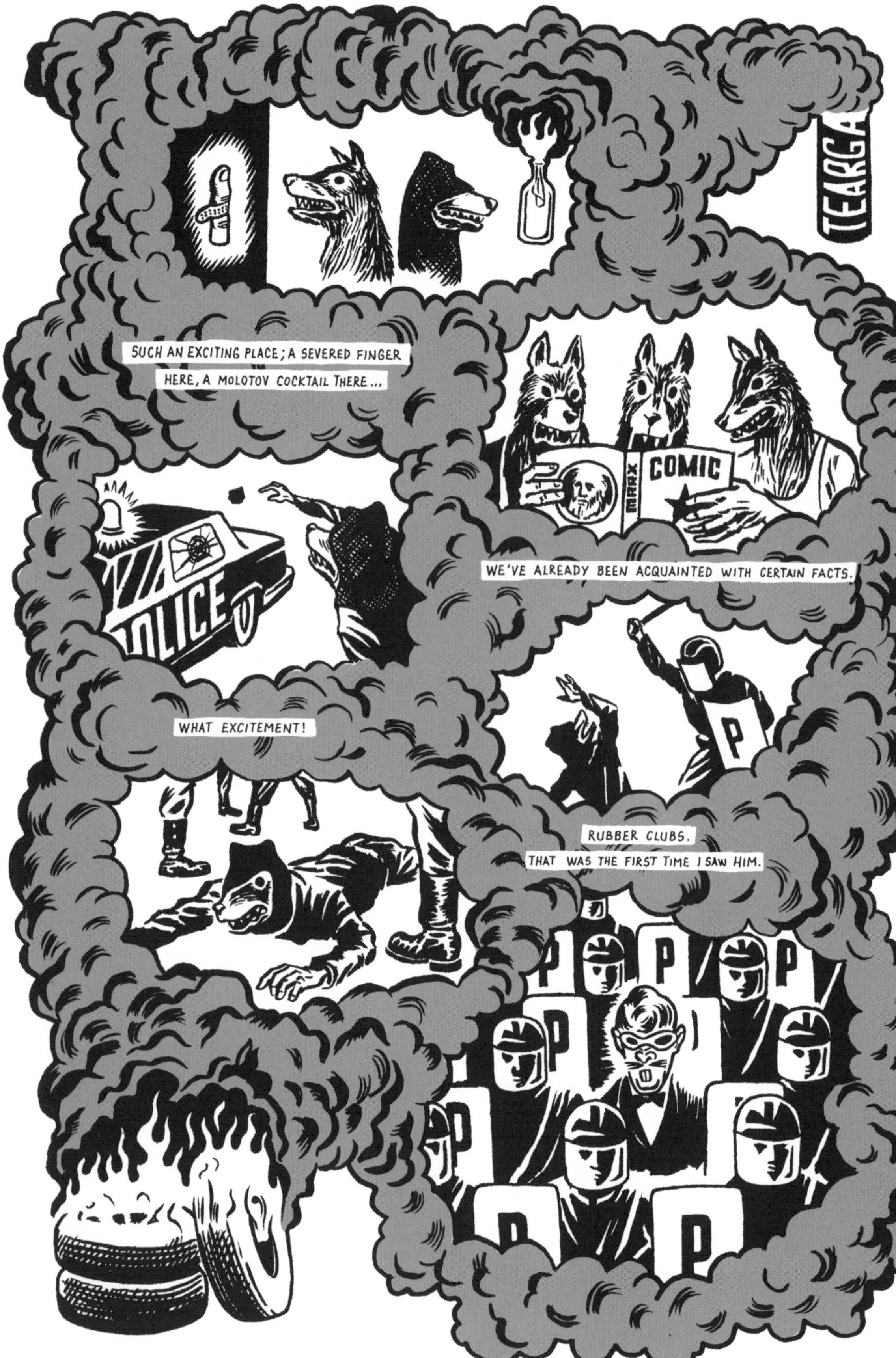
TEARGA
SUCH AN EXCITING PLACE; A SEVERED FINGER HERE, A MOLOTOV COCKTAIL THERE...
MARX
COMIC
WE'VE ALREADY BEEN ACQUAINTED WITH CERTAIN FACTS.
OLICE
WHAT EXCITEMENT!
P
RUBBER CLUBS.
THAT WAS THE FIRST TIME I SAW HIM.

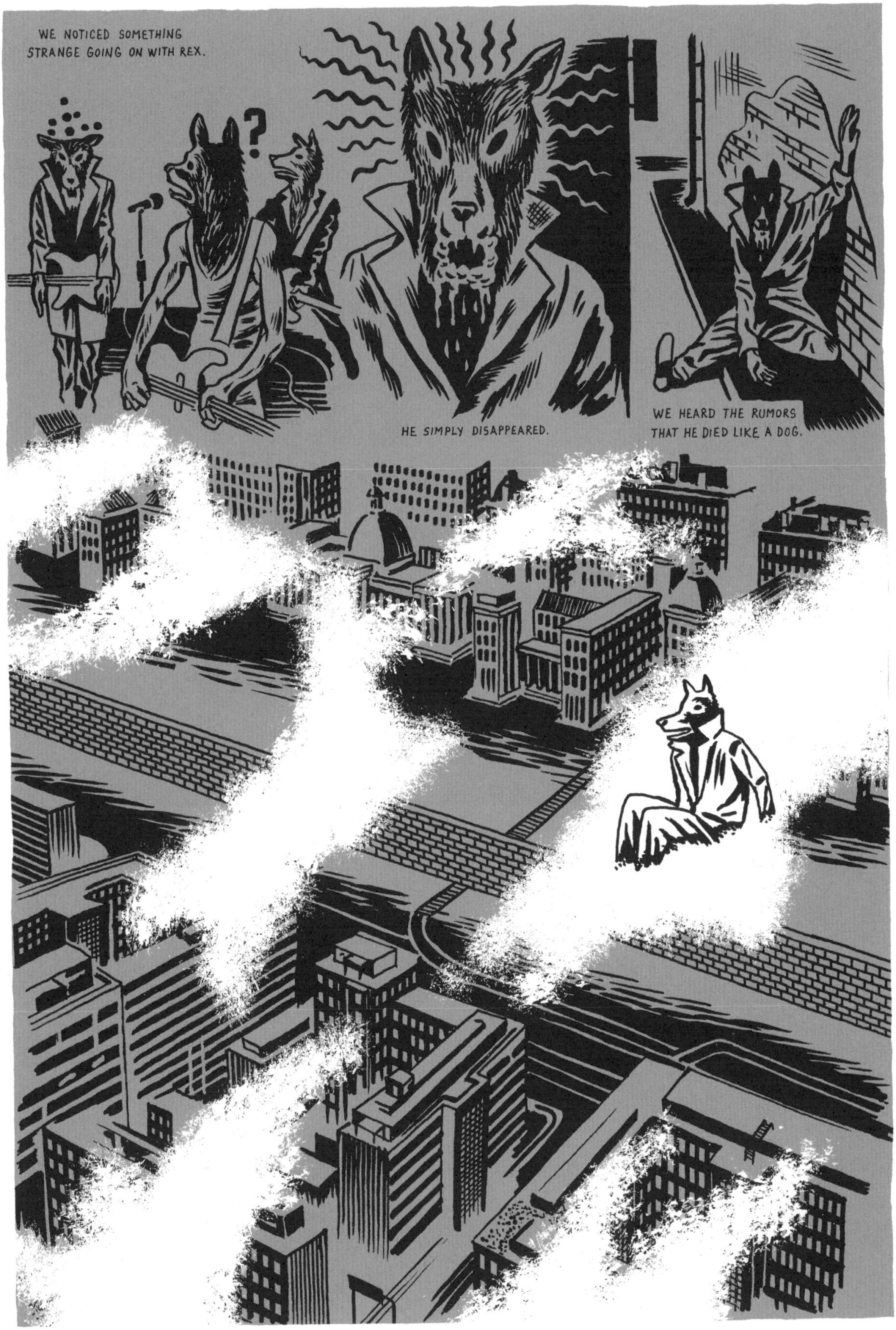
WE NOTICED SOMETHING
STRANGE GOING ON WITH REX.
?
HE SIMPLY DISAPPEARED.
WE HEARD THE RUMORS
THAT HE DIED LIKE A DOG.

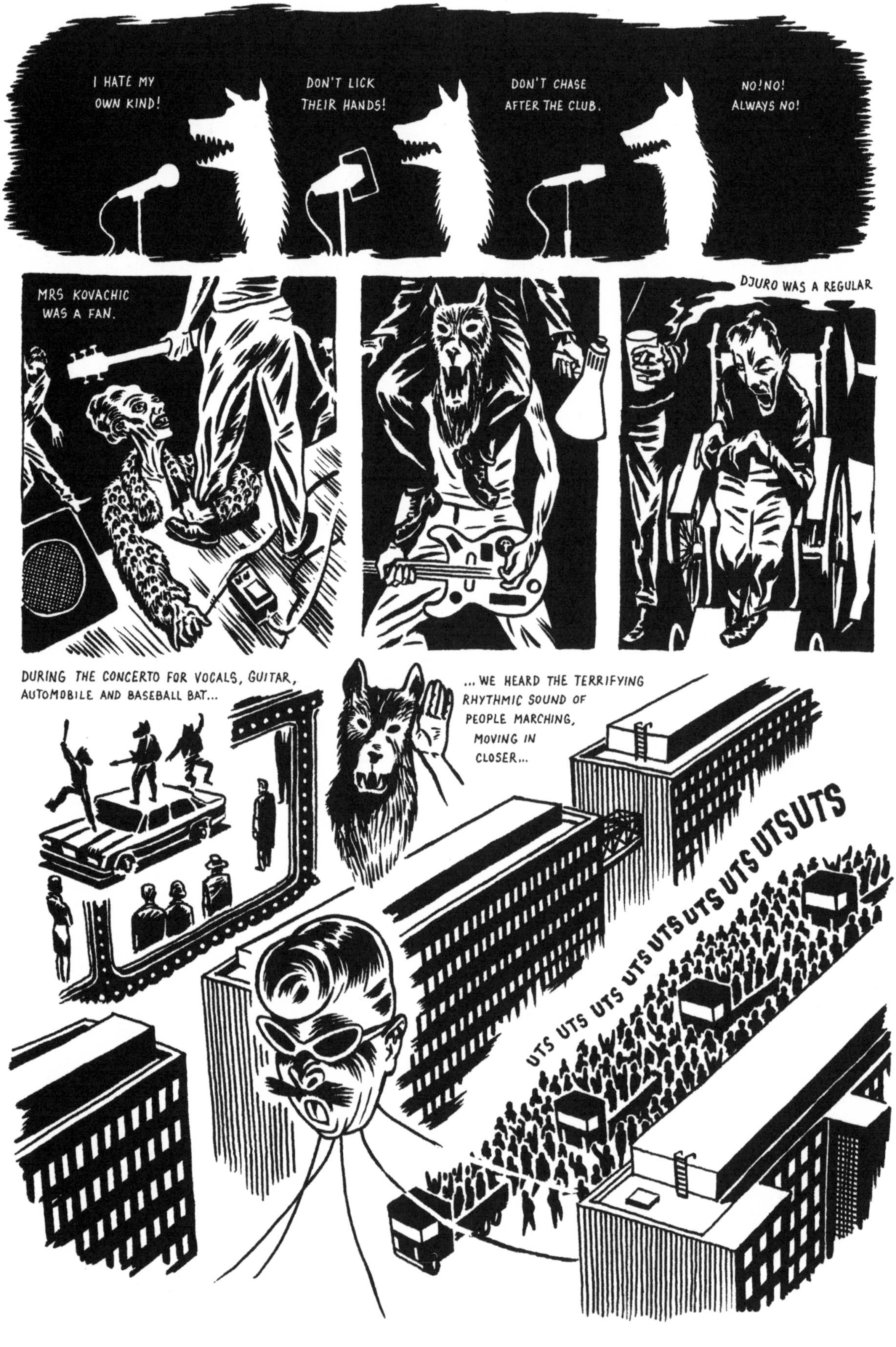
I HATE MY OWN KIND!
DON'T LICK THEIR HANDS!
DON'T CHASE AFTER THE CLUB.
NO! NO! ALWAYS NO!
MRS KOVACHIC WAS A FAN.
DJURO WAS A REGULAR
DURING THE CONCERTO FOR VOCALS, GUITAR, AUTOMOBILE AND BASEBALL BAT...
... WE HEARD THE TERRIFYING RHYTHMIC SOUND OF PEOPLE MARCHING, MOVING IN CLOSER...
UTS UTS UTS UTS UTS UTS UTS UTS UTS UTS UTS UTS UTS

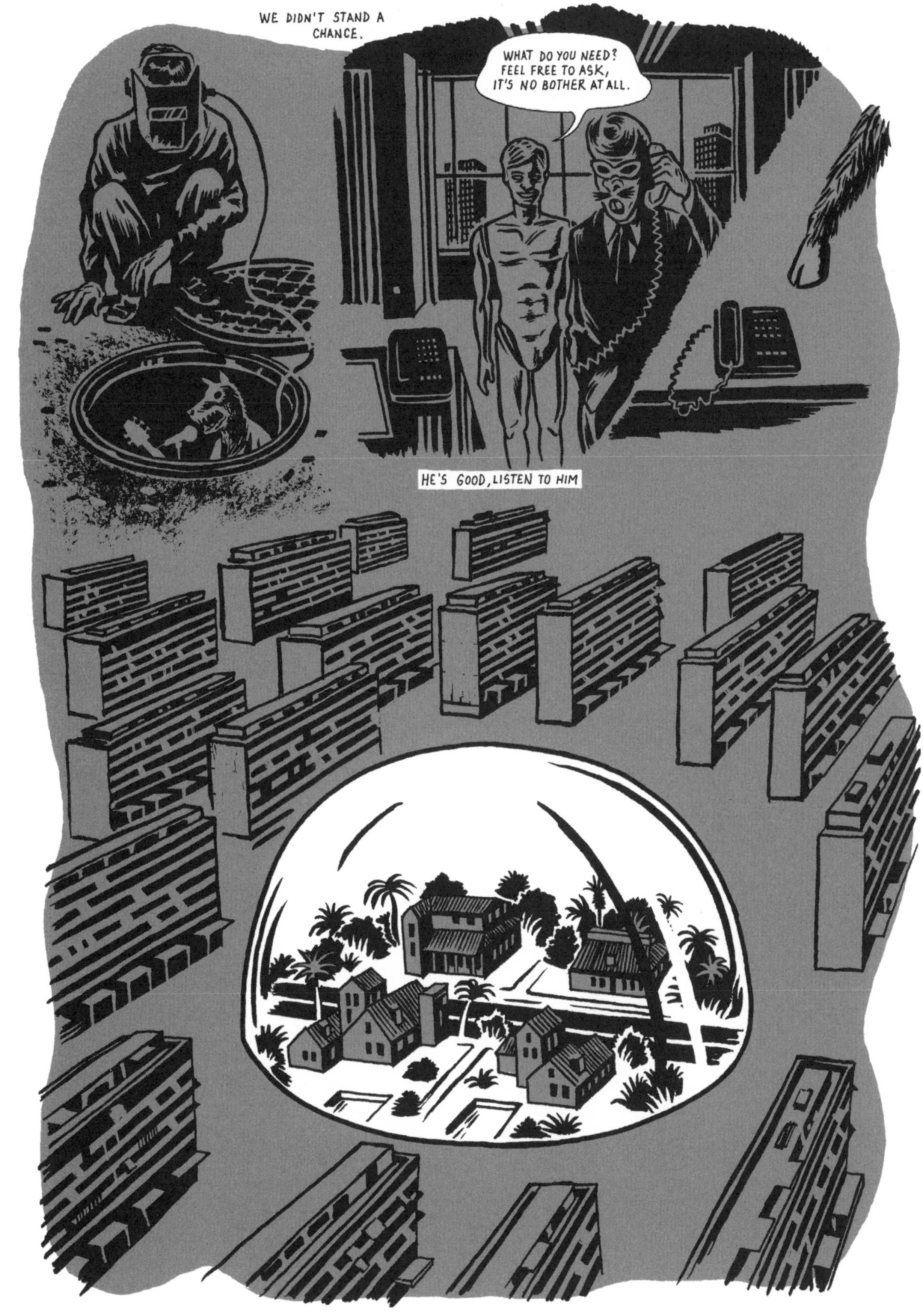

WE DIDN'T STAND A CHANCE.
WHAT DO YOU NEED? FEEL FREE TO ASK, IT'S NO BOTHER AT ALL.
HE'S GOOD, LISTEN TO HIM

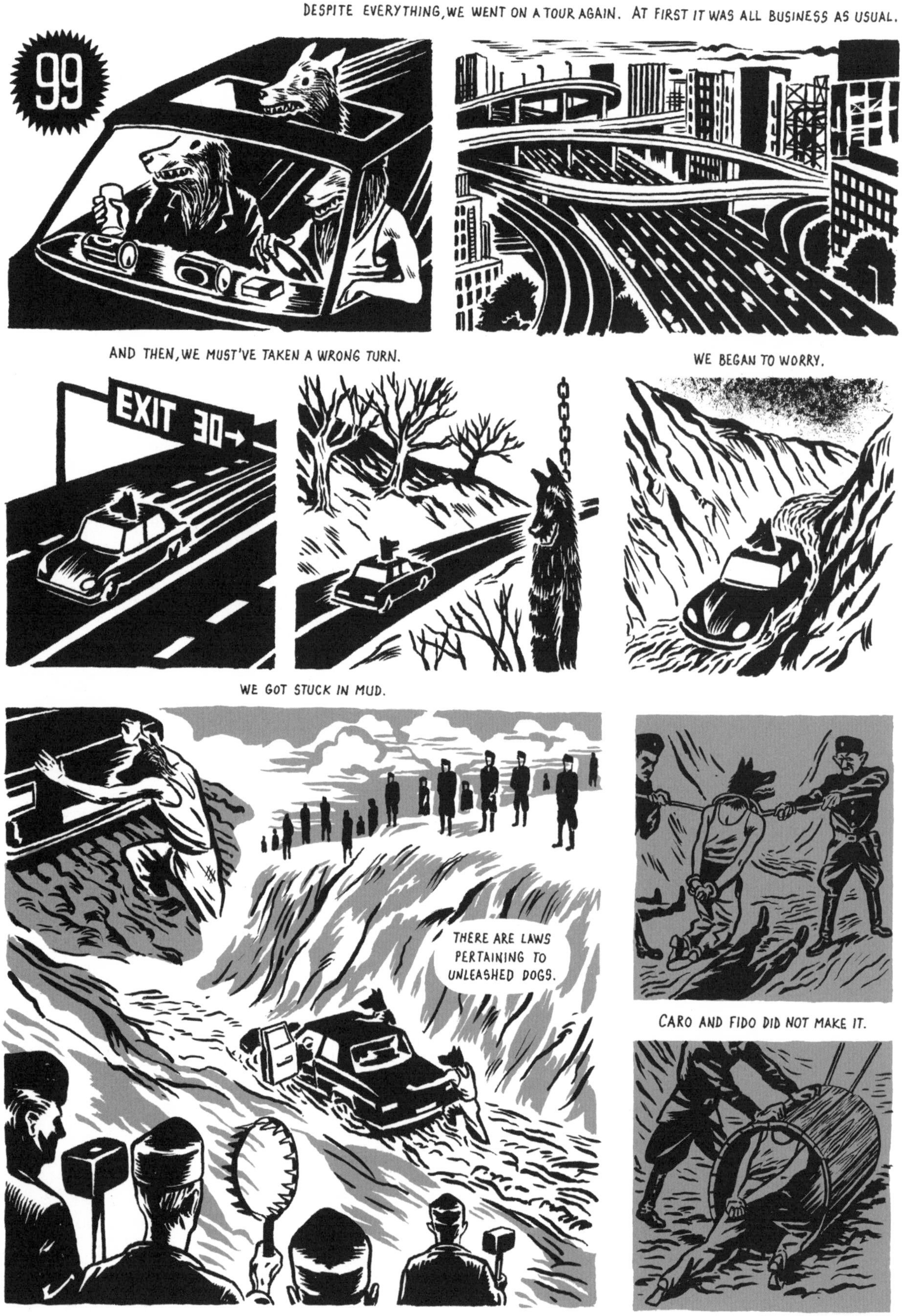
DESPITE EVERYTHING, WE WENT ON A TOUR AGAIN. AT FIRST IT WAS ALL BUSINESS AS USUAL.
99
AND THEN, WE MUST'VE TAKEN A WRONG TURN.
EXIT 30→
WE BEGAN TO WORRY.
WE GOT STUCK IN MUD.
THERE ARE LAWS PERTAINING TO UNLEASHED DOGS.
CARO AND FIDO DID NOT MAKE IT.

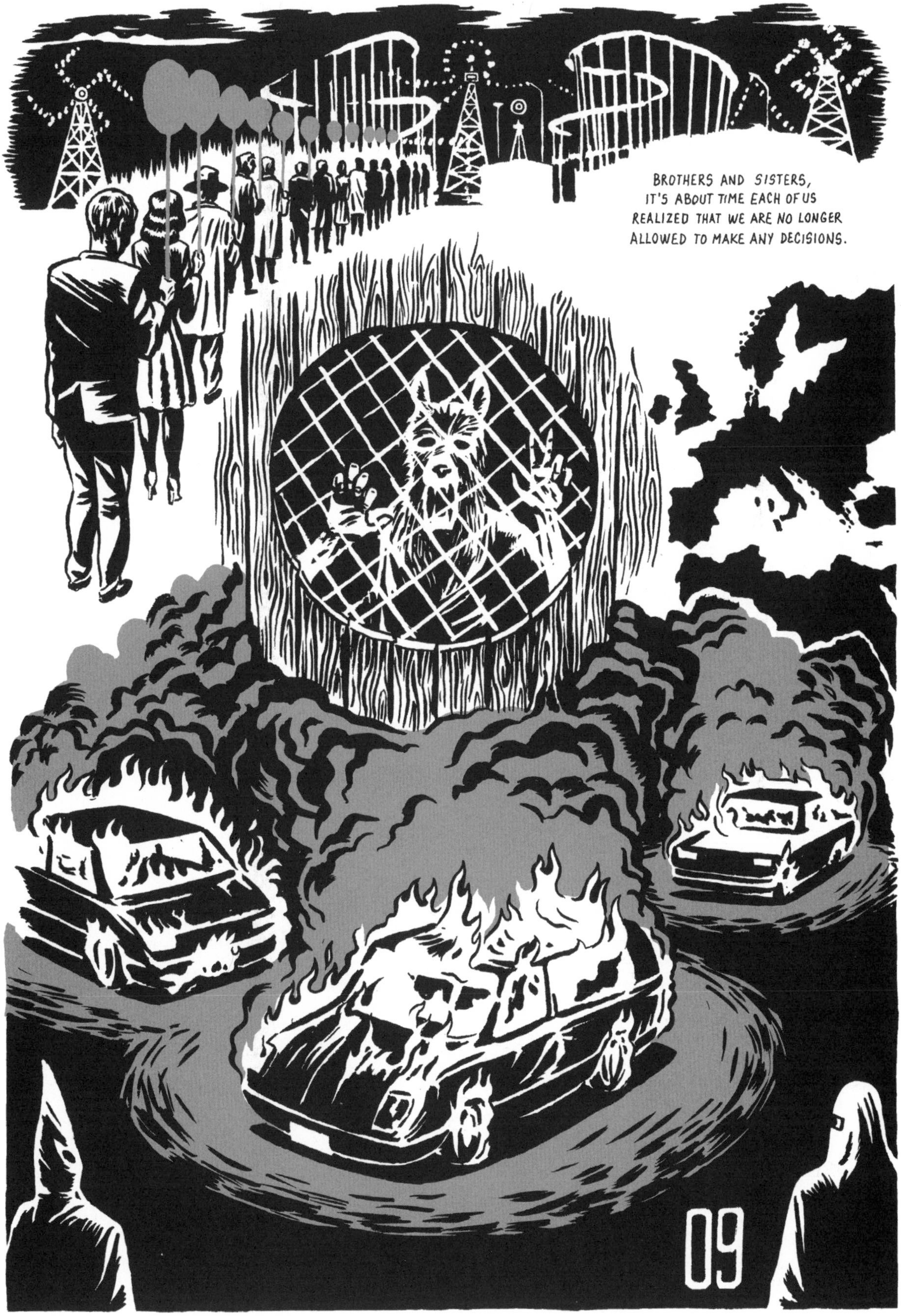
BROTHERS AND SISTERS,
IT'S ABOUT TIME EACH OF US
REALIZED THAT WE ARE NO LONGER
ALLOWED TO MAKE ANY DECISIONS.
09

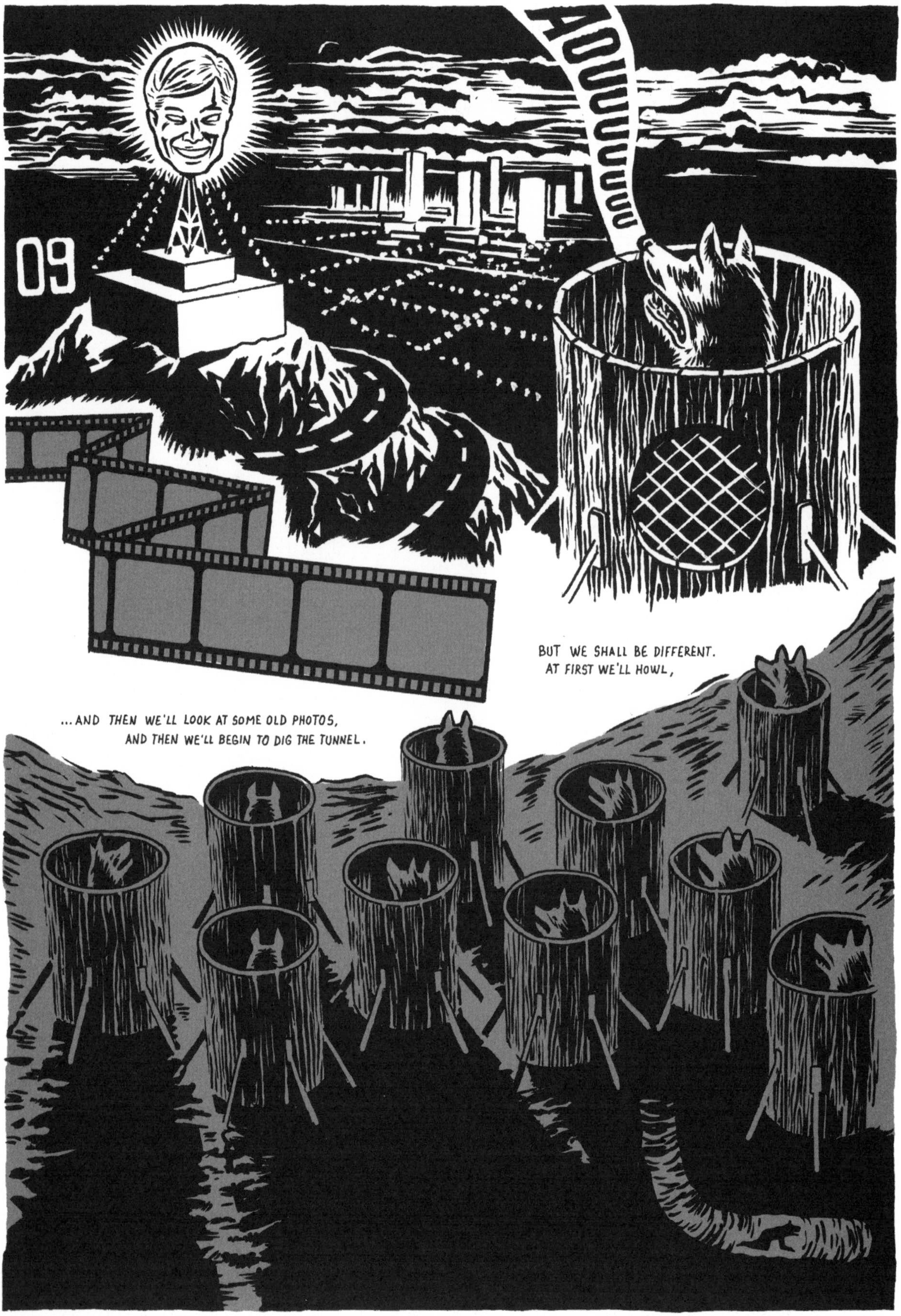
09
AOUUUUUUU
BUT WE SHALL BE DIFFERENT.
AT FIRST WE'LL HOWL,
...AND THEN WE'LL LOOK AT SOME OLD PHOTOS,
AND THEN WE'LL BEGIN TO DIG THE TUNNEL.

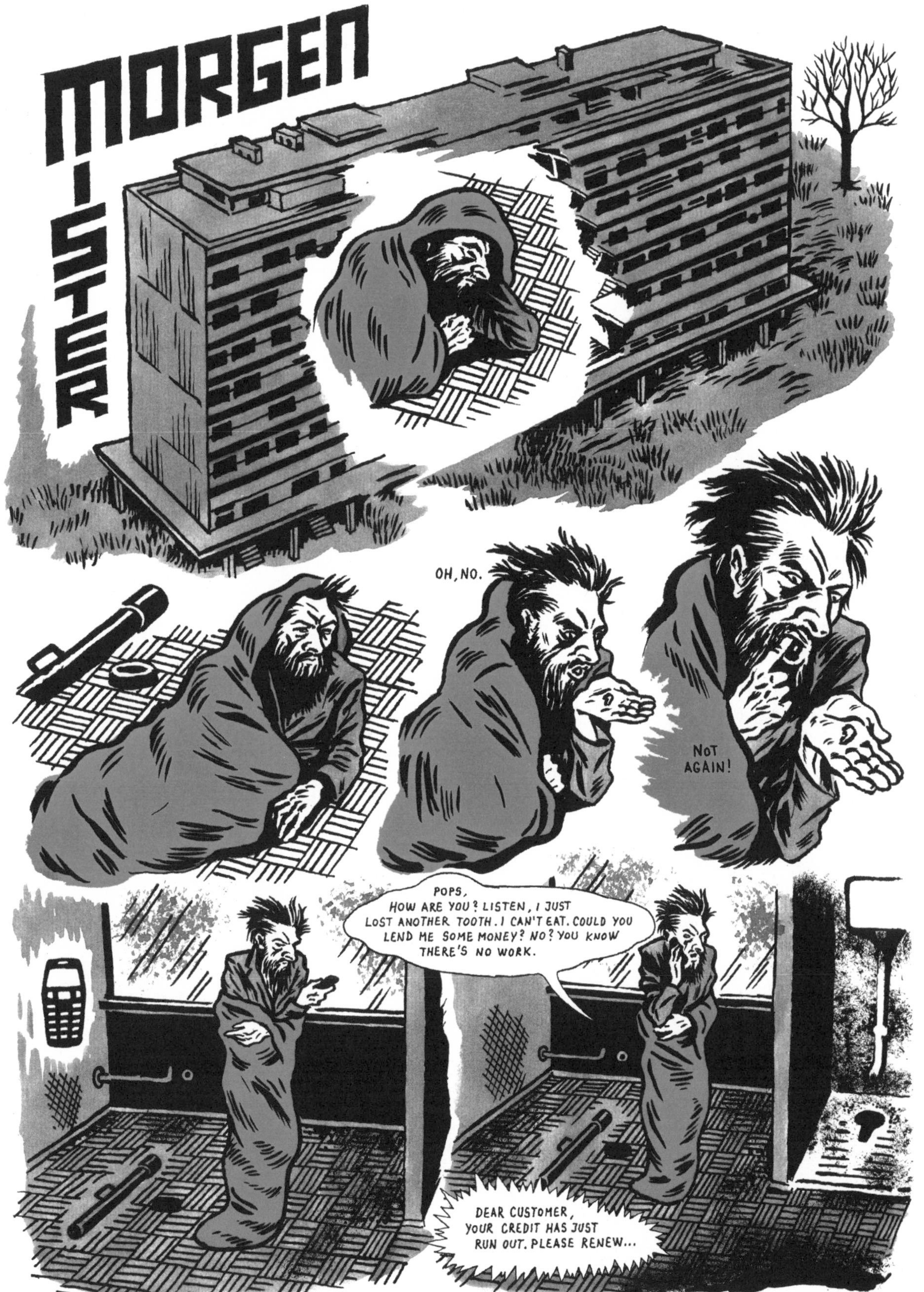
MORGEN
MISTER
OH, NO.
NOT AGAIN!
POPS, HOW ARE YOU? LISTEN, I JUST LOST ANOTHER TOOTH. I CAN'T EAT. COULD YOU LEND ME SOME MONEY? NO? YOU KNOW THERE'S NO WORK.
DEAR CUSTOMER, YOUR CREDIT HAS JUST RUN OUT. PLEASE RENEW...

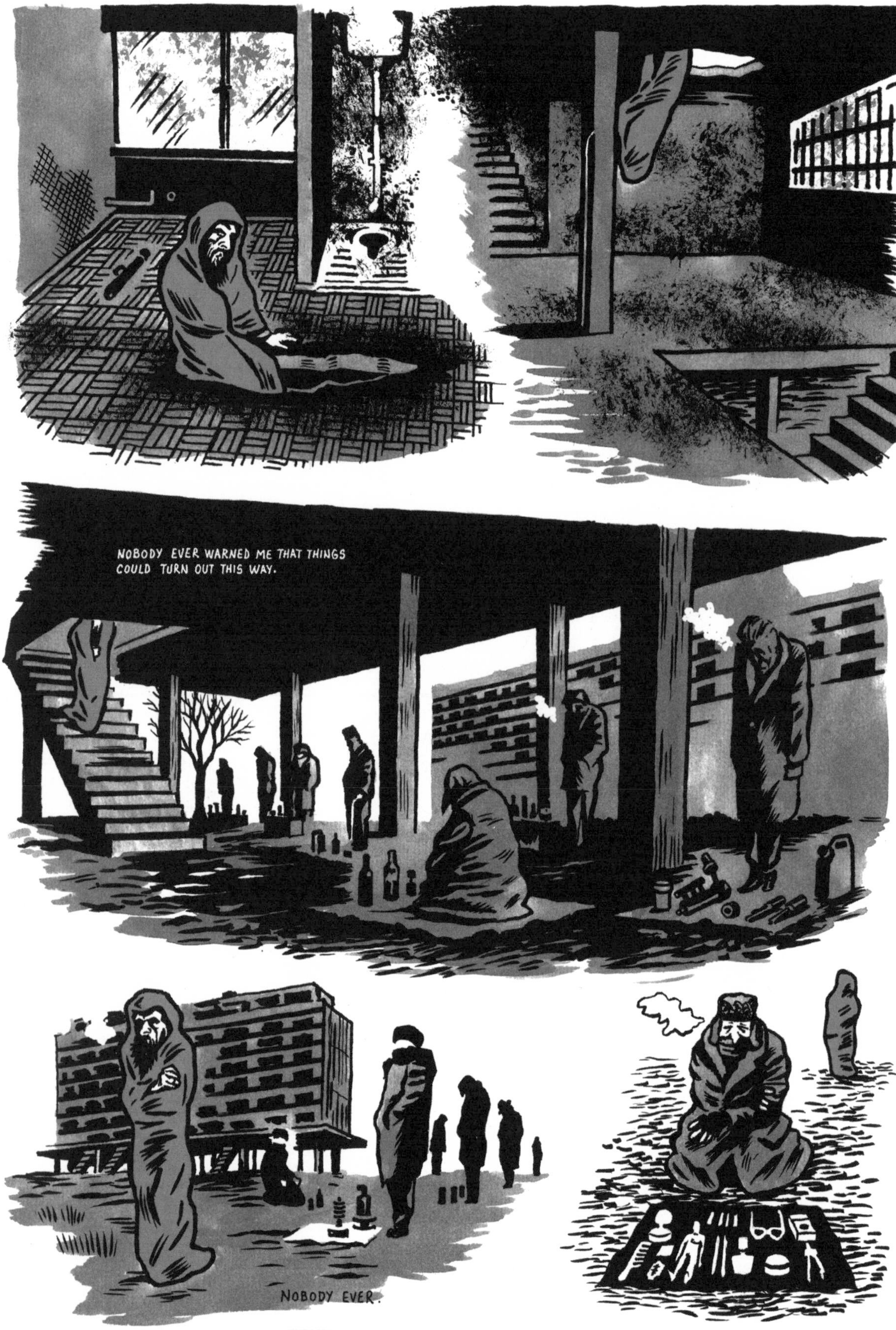
NOBODY EVER WARNED ME THAT THINGS
COULD TURN OUT THIS WAY.
NOBODY EVER.

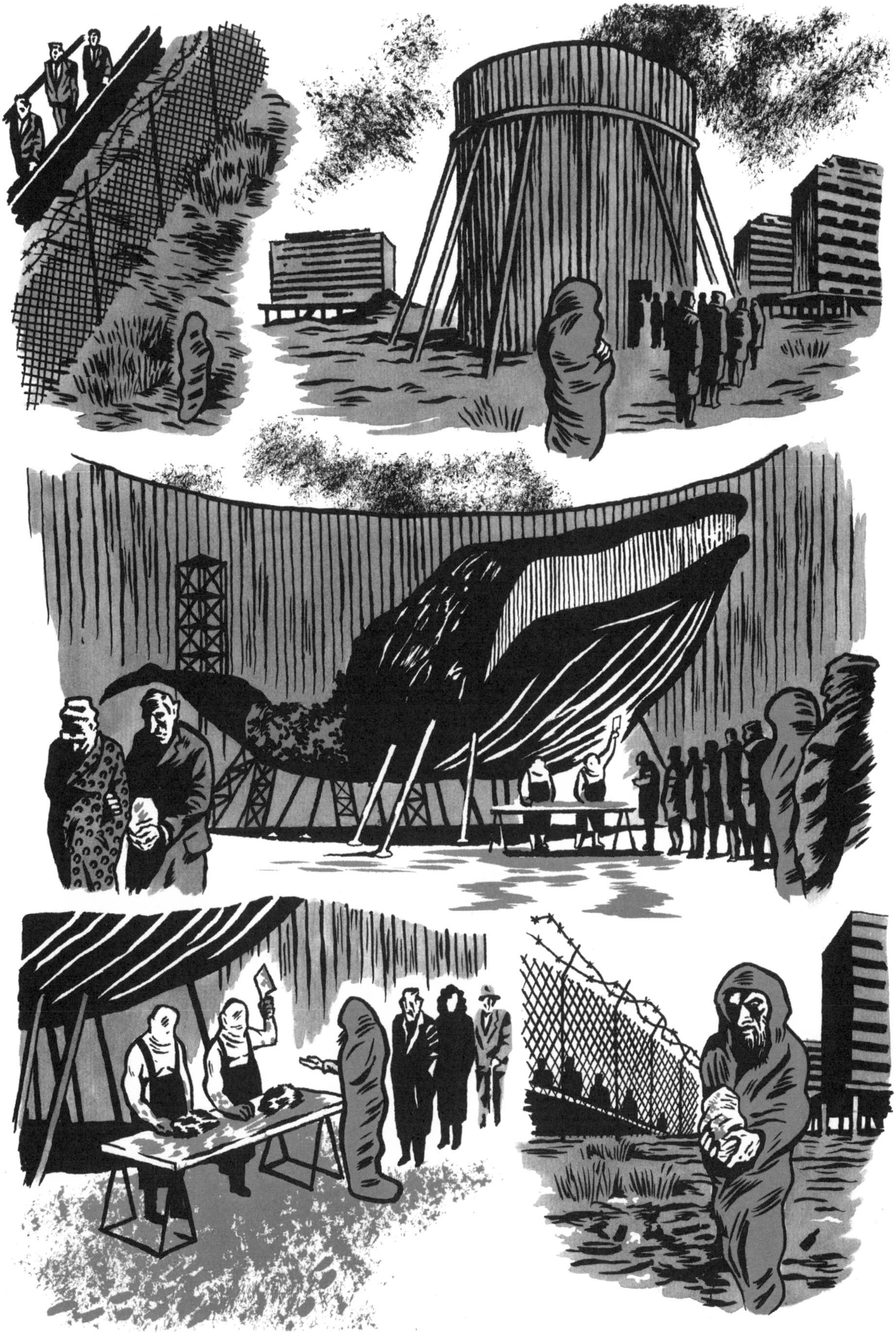

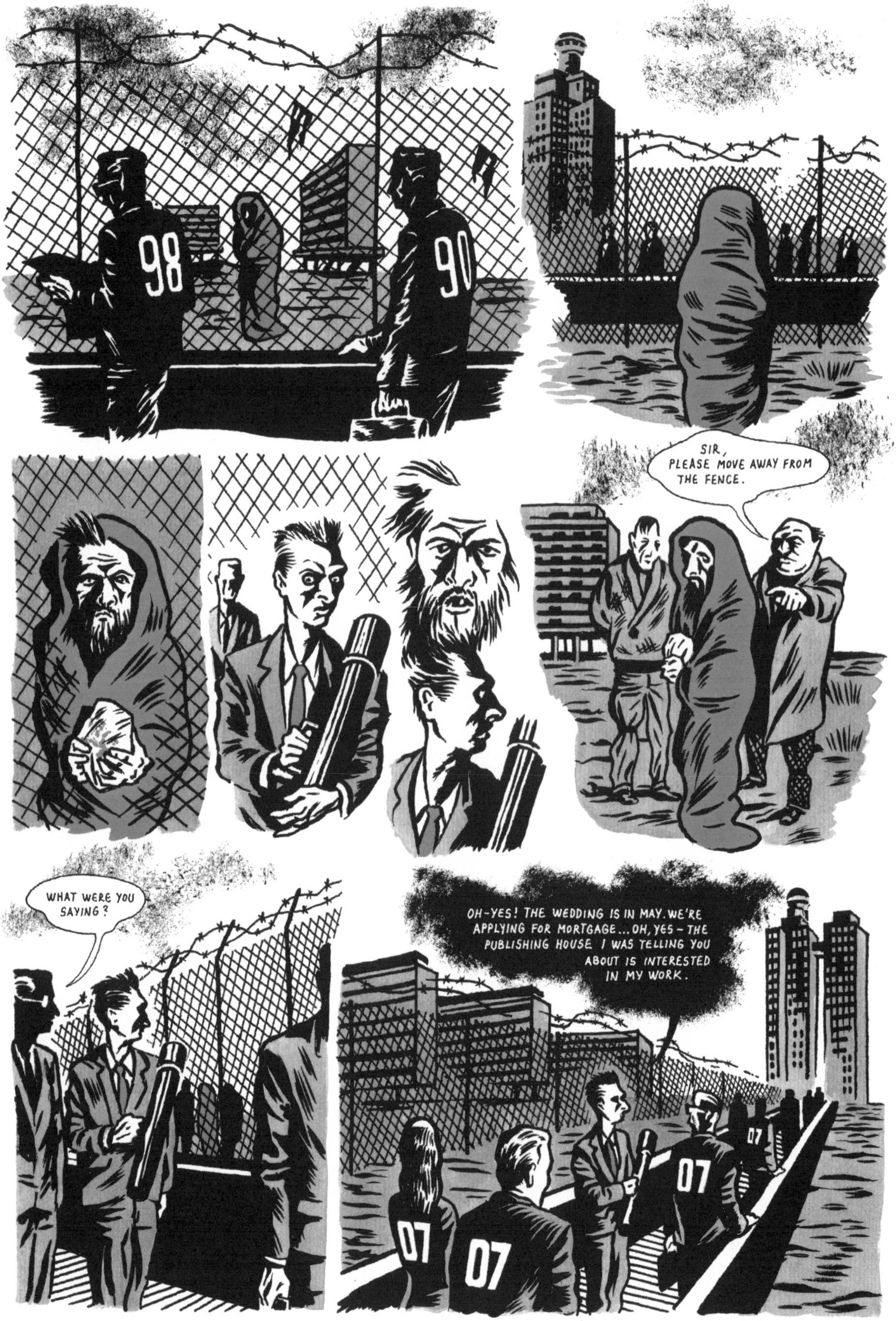
98
90
SIR, PLEASE MOVE AWAY FROM THE FENCE.
WHAT WERE YOU SAYING?
OH-YES! THE WEDDING IS IN MAY. WE'RE APPLYING FOR MORTGAGE... OH, YES - THE PUBLISHING HOUSE I WAS TELLING YOU ABOUT IS INTERESTED IN MY WORK.
07
07
07
07

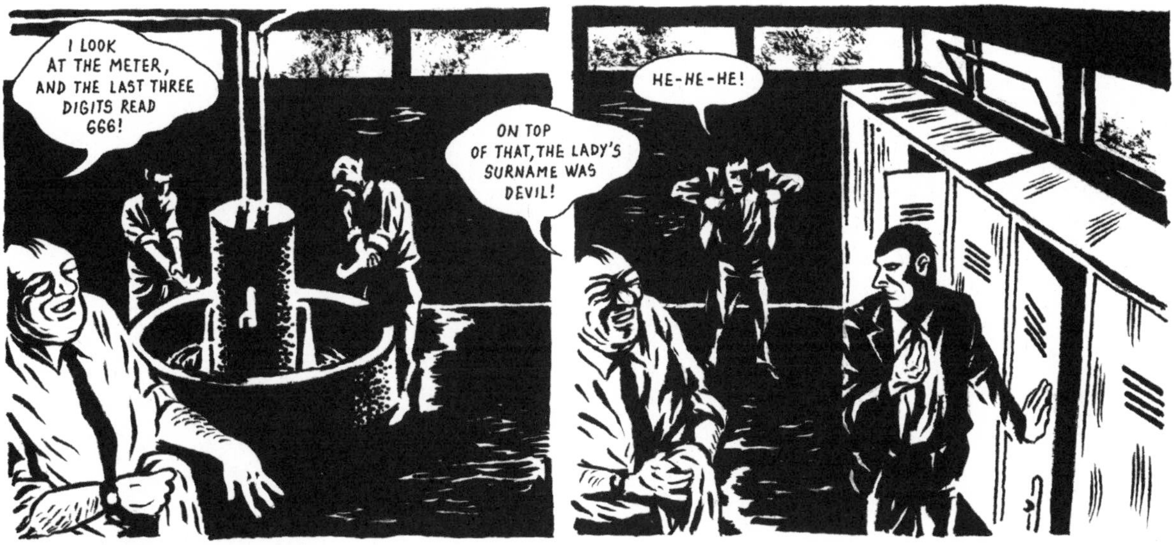
I LOOK AT THE METER, AND THE LAST THREE DIGITS READ 666!
ON TOP OF THAT, THE LADY'S SURNAME WAS DEVIL!
HE-HE-HE!

DANILO

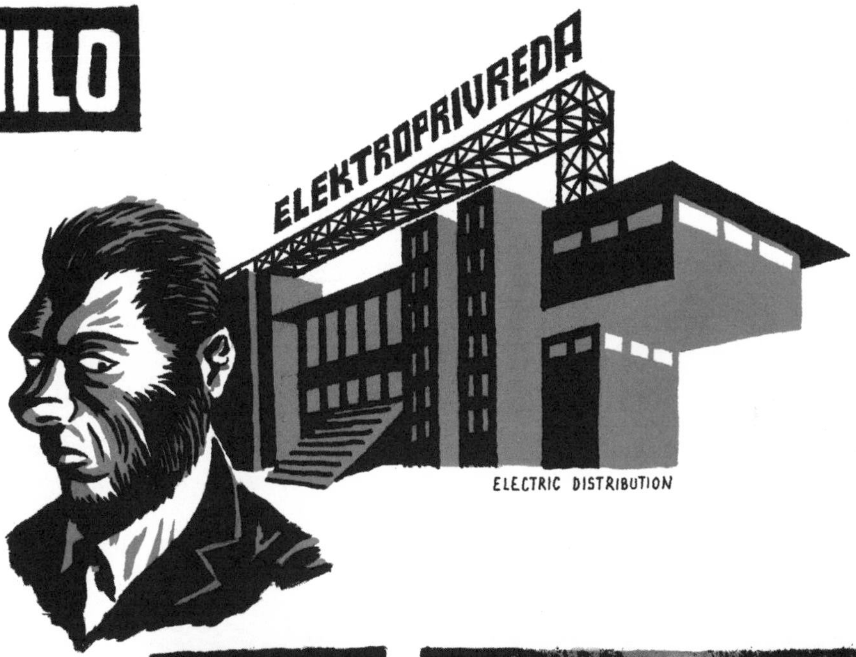
ELEKTROPRIVREDA
ELECTRIC DISTRIBUTION

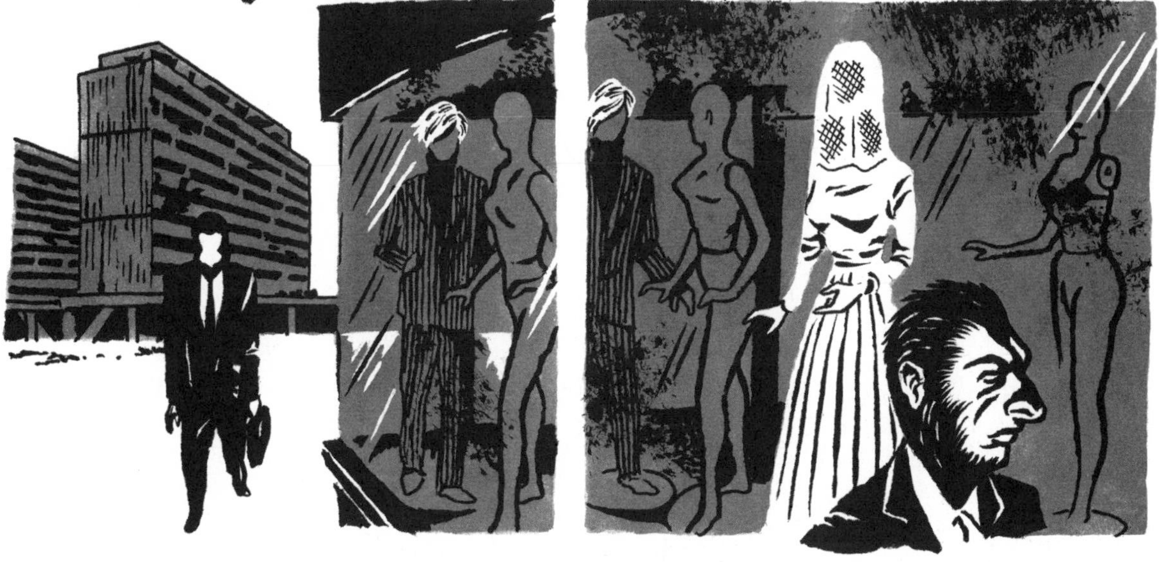

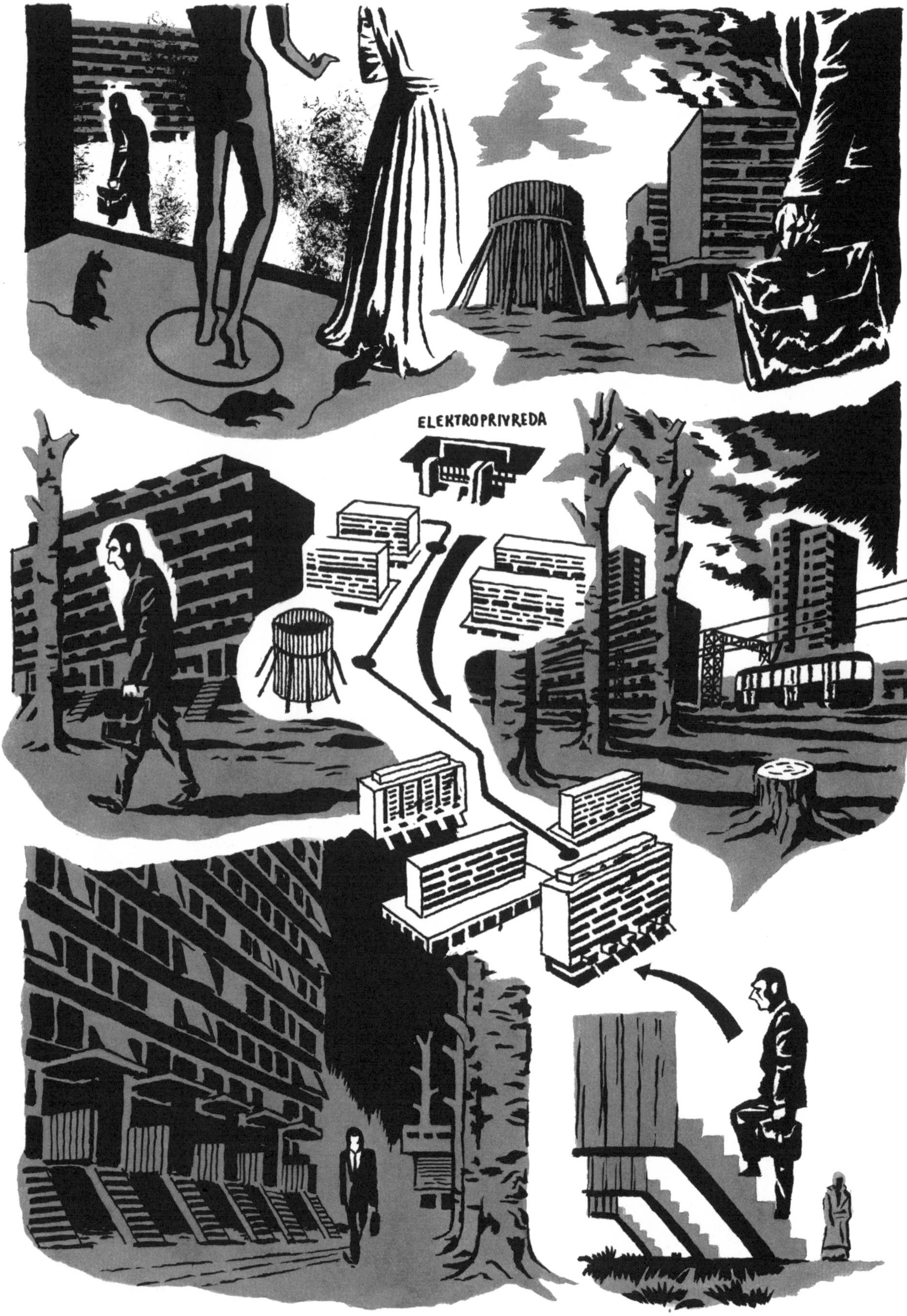
ELEKTROPRIVREDA

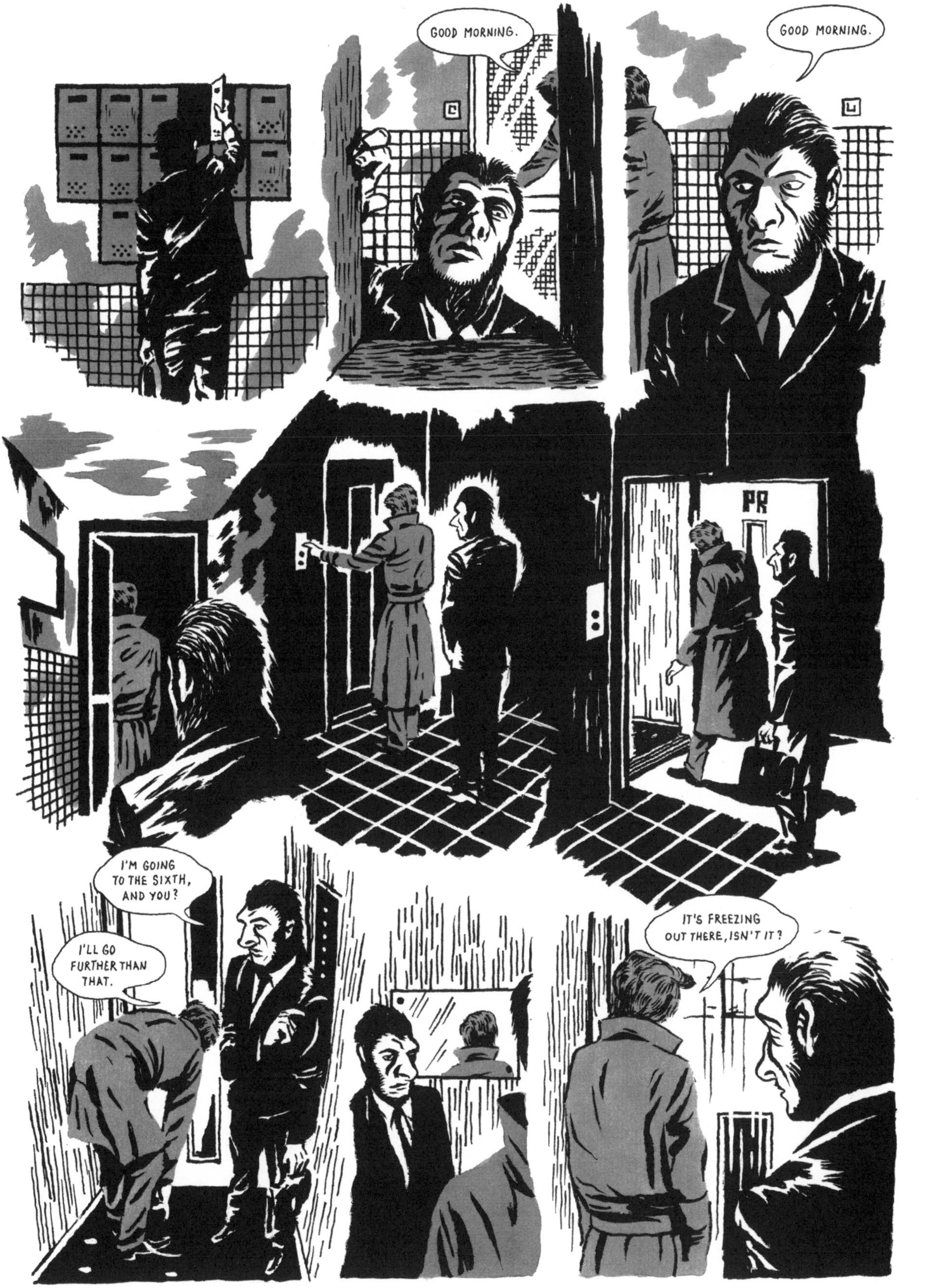
GOOD MORNING.
GOOD MORNING.
I'M GOING TO THE SIXTH, AND YOU?
I'LL GO FURTHER THAN THAT.
IT'S FREEZING OUT THERE, ISN'T IT?

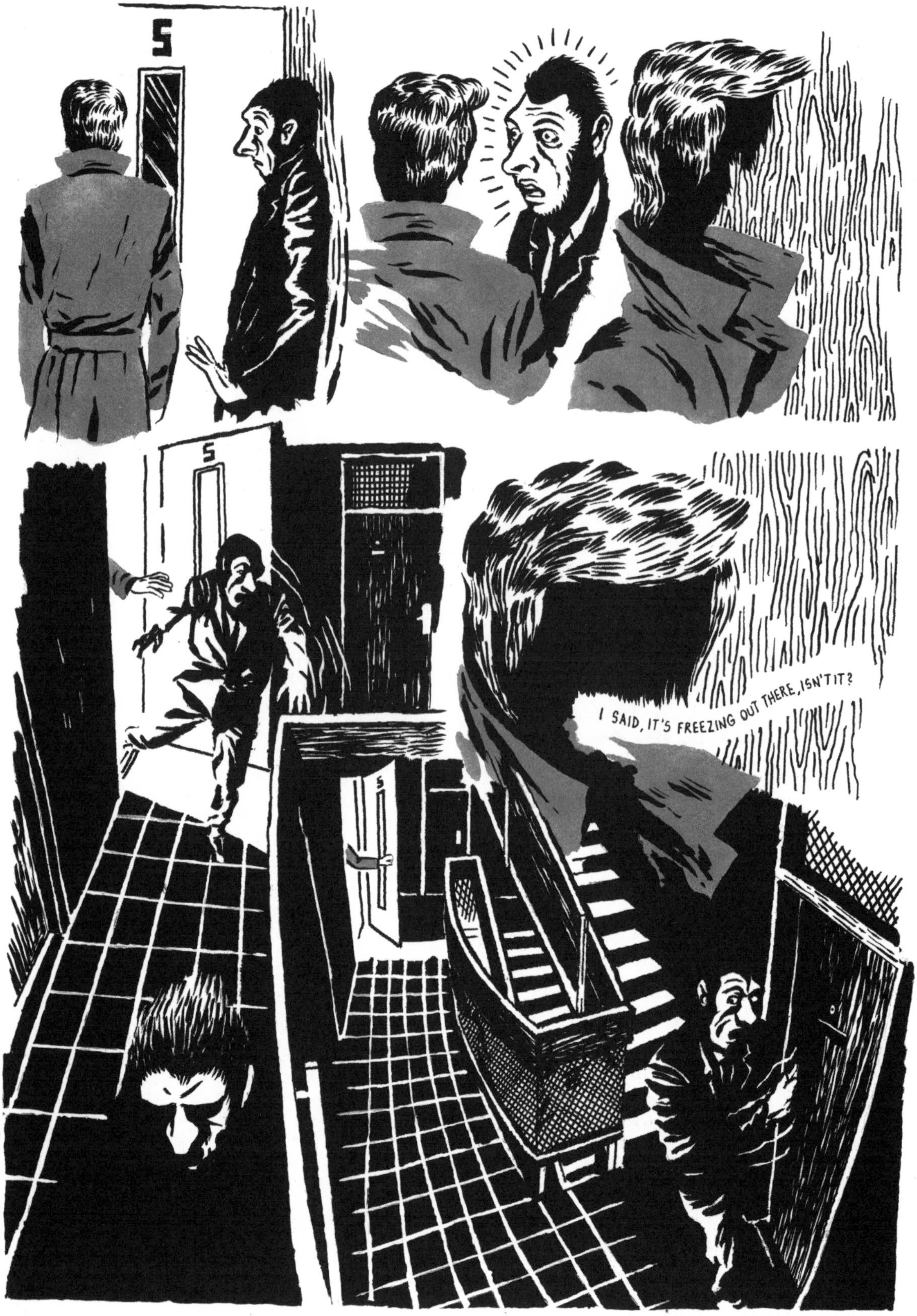
I SAID, IT'S FREEZING OUT THERE, ISN'T IT?

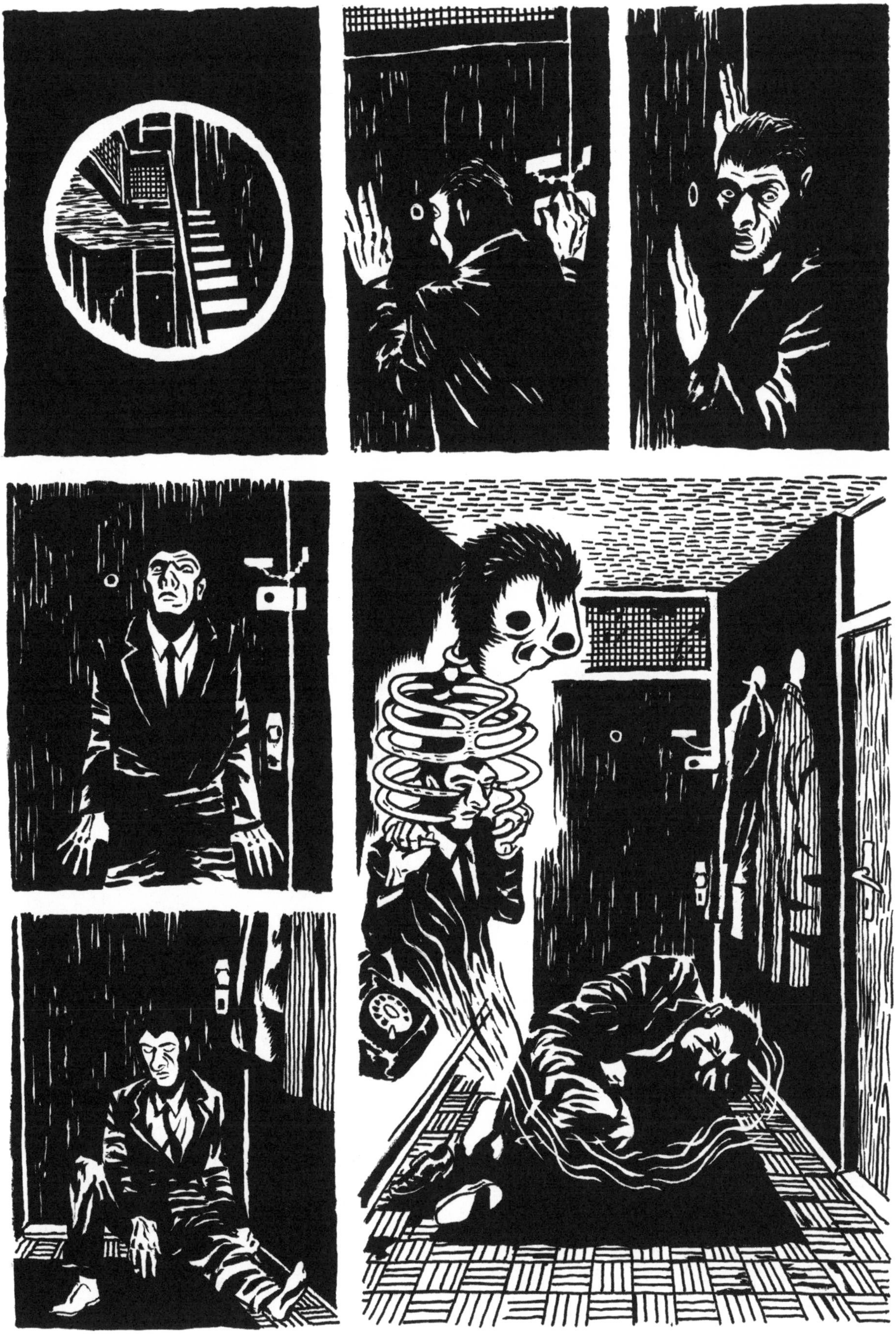

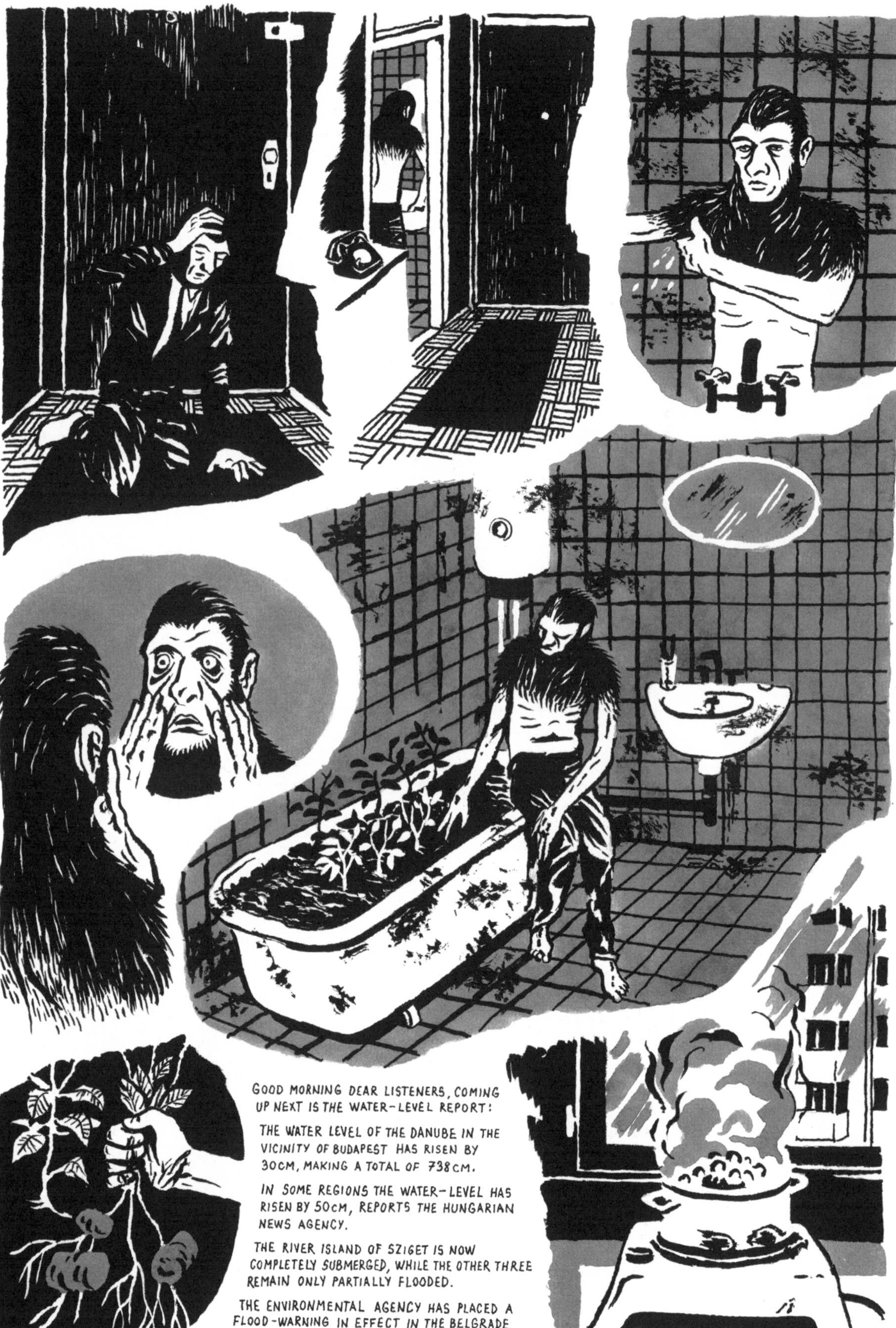
GOOD MORNING DEAR LISTENERS, COMING UP NEXT IS THE WATER-LEVEL REPORT:
THE WATER LEVEL OF THE DANUBE IN THE VICINITY OF BUDAPEST HAS RISEN BY 30CM, MAKING A TOTAL OF 738CM.
IN SOME REGIONS THE WATER-LEVEL HAS RISEN BY 50CM, REPORTS THE HUNGARIAN NEWS AGENCY.
THE RIVER ISLAND OF SZIGET IS NOW COMPLETELY SUBMERGED, WHILE THE OTHER THREE REMAIN ONLY PARTIALLY FLOODED.
THE ENVIRONMENTAL AGENCY HAS PLACED A FLOOD-WARNING IN EFFECT IN THE BELGRADE AREA FOR WEDNESDAY.

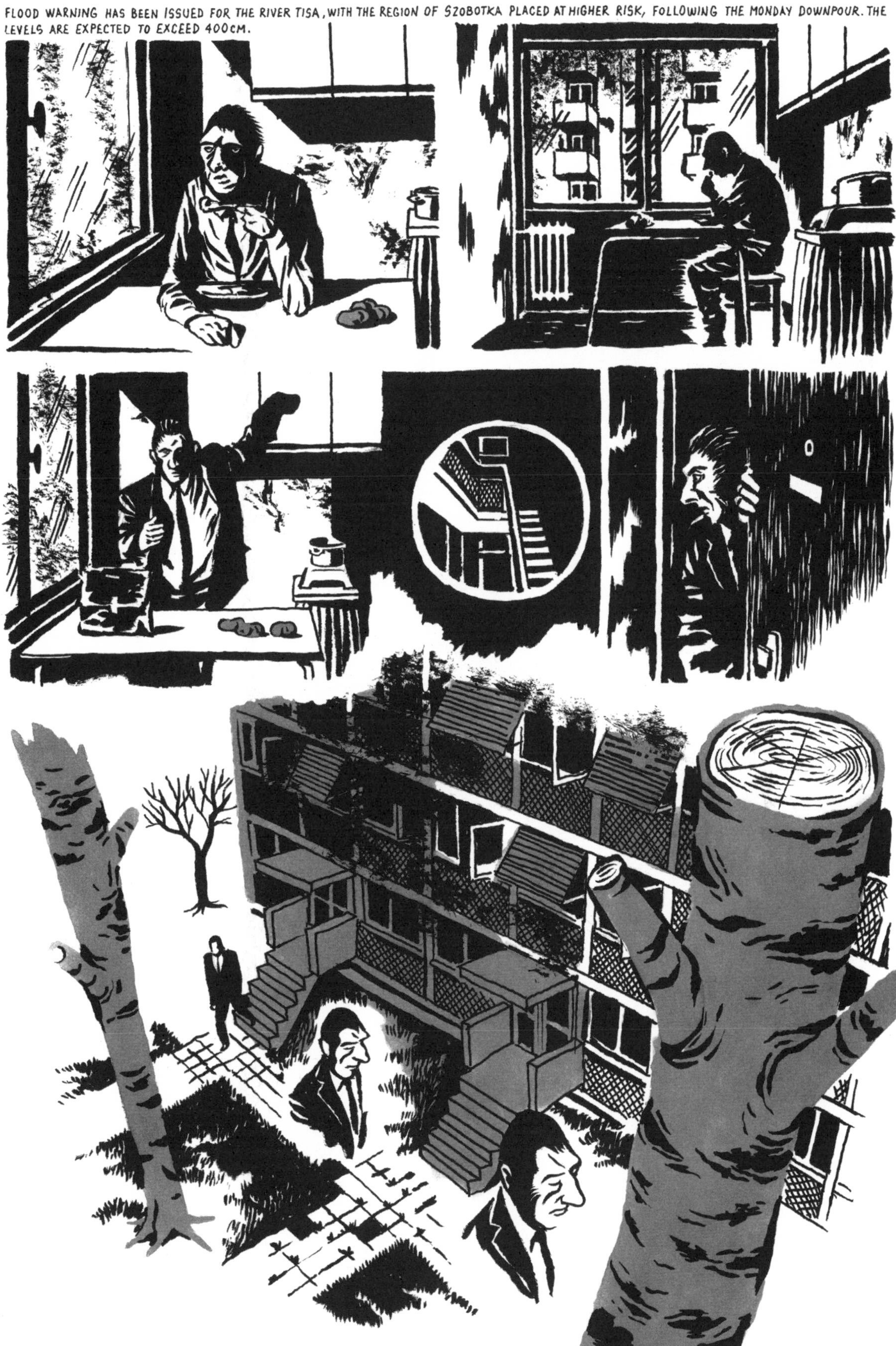
FLOOD WARNING HAS BEEN ISSUED FOR THE RIVER TISA, WITH THE REGION OF SZOBOTKA PLACED AT HIGHER RISK, FOLLOWING THE MONDAY DOWNPOUR. THE LEVELS ARE EXPECTED TO EXCEED 400CM.

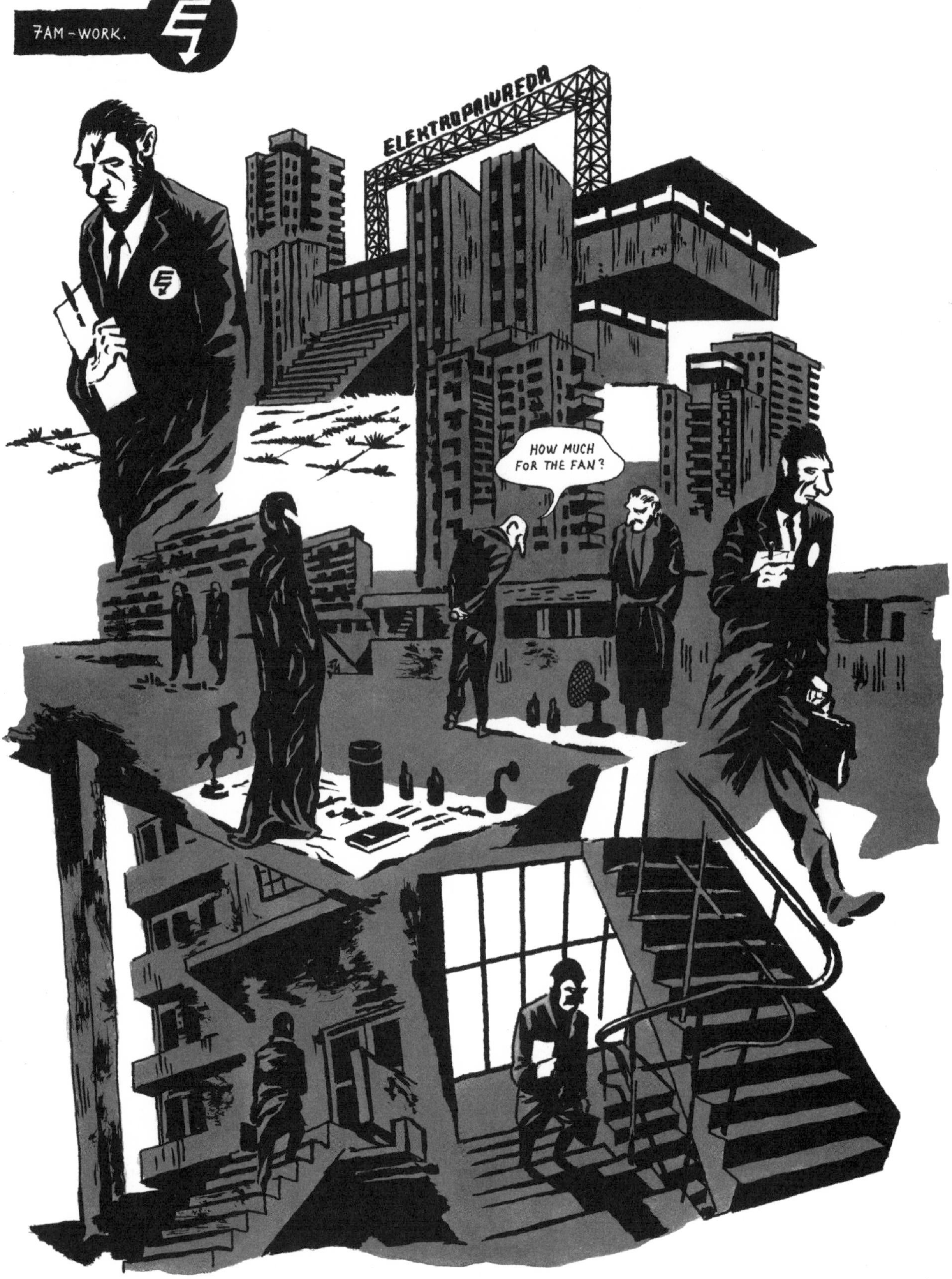
7AM–WORK.
ELEKTROPRIVREDA
HOW MUCH FOR THE FAN?

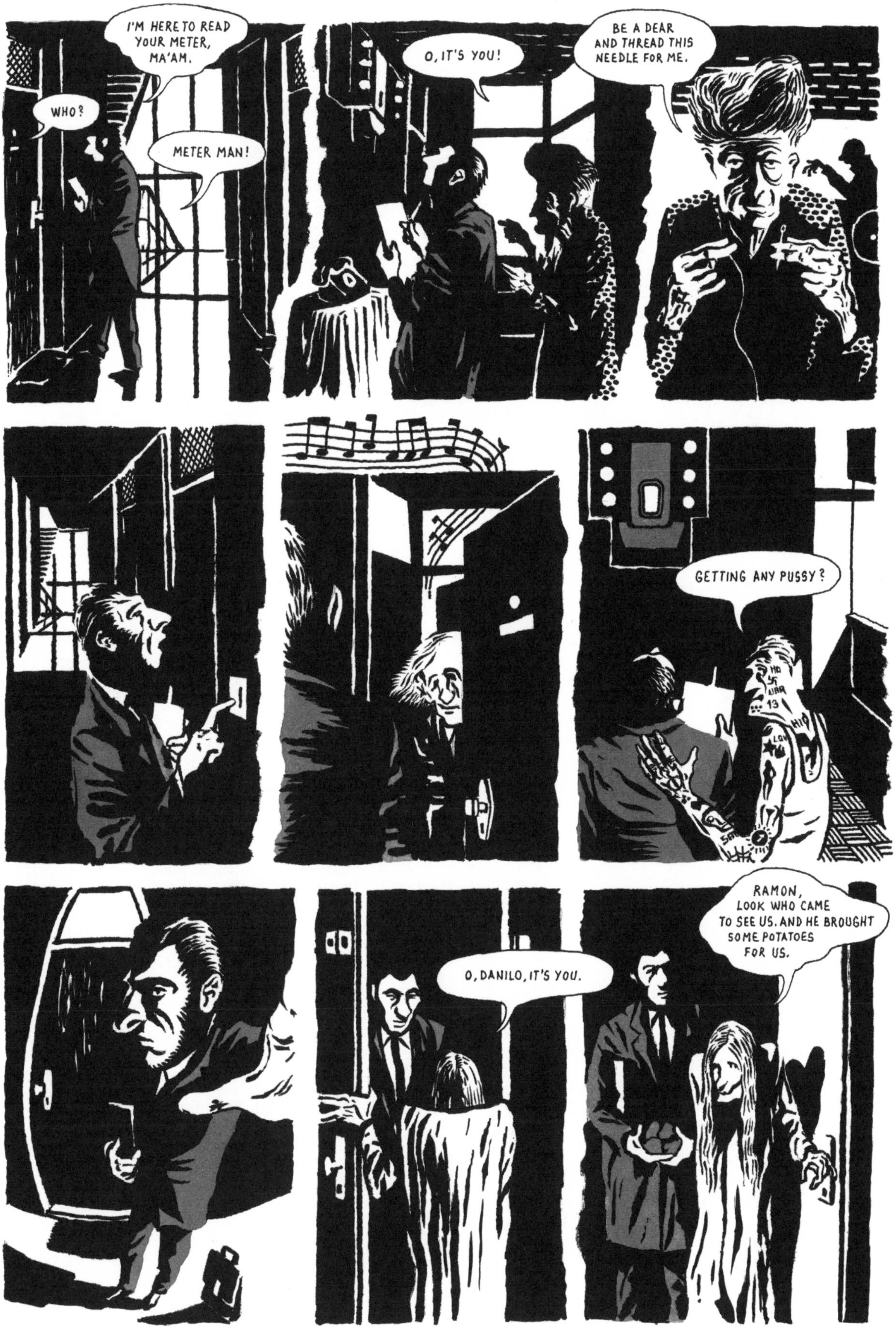
WHO?
I'M HERE TO READ YOUR METER, MA'AM.
METER MAN!
O, IT'S YOU!
BE A DEAR AND THREAD THIS NEEDLE FOR ME.
GETTING ANY PUSSY?
O, DANILO, IT'S YOU.
RAMON, LOOK WHO CAME TO SEE US. AND HE BROUGHT SOME POTATOES FOR US.

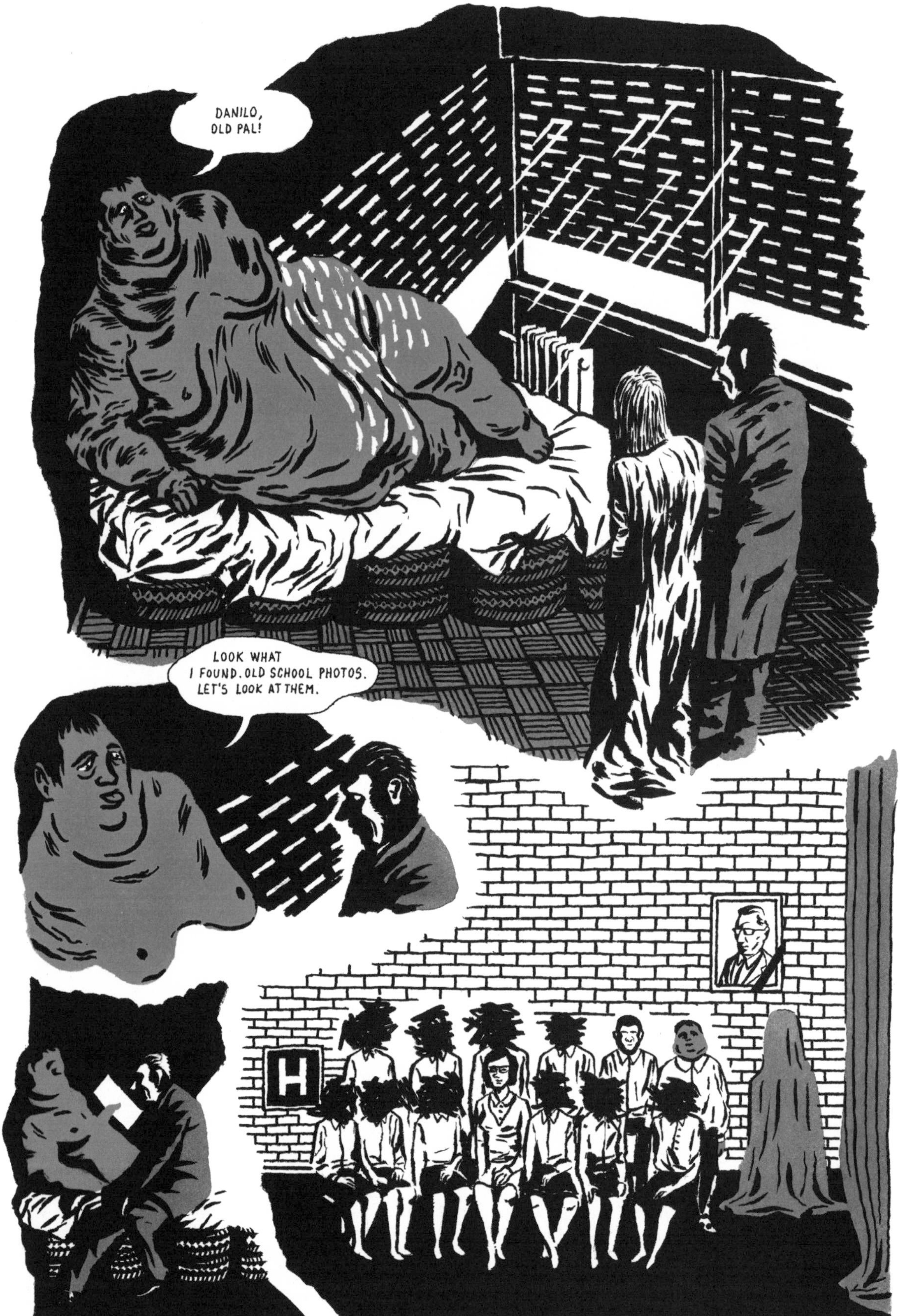
DANILO, OLD PAL!
LOOK WHAT I FOUND. OLD SCHOOL PHOTOS. LET'S LOOK AT THEM.
H

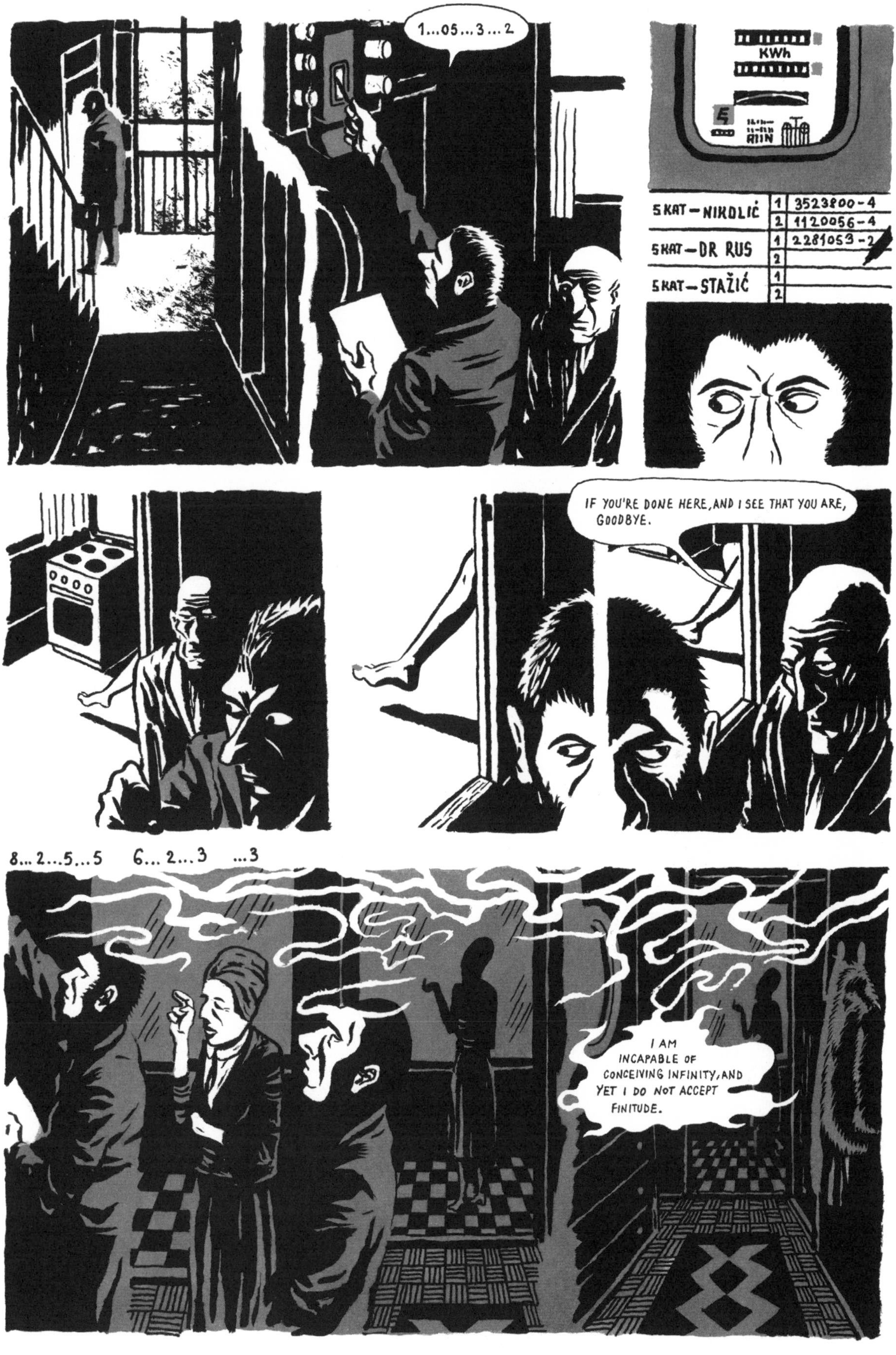
1…05…3…2
KWh
5 KAT – NIKOLIĆ 1 3523800-4
2 1120056-4
5 KAT – DR RUS 1 2281053-2
2
5 KAT – STAŽIĆ 1
2
IF YOU'RE DONE HERE, AND I SEE THAT YOU ARE, GOODBYE.
8…2…5…5 6…2…3 …3
I AM INCAPABLE OF CONCEIVING INFINITY, AND YET I DO NOT ACCEPT FINITUDE.

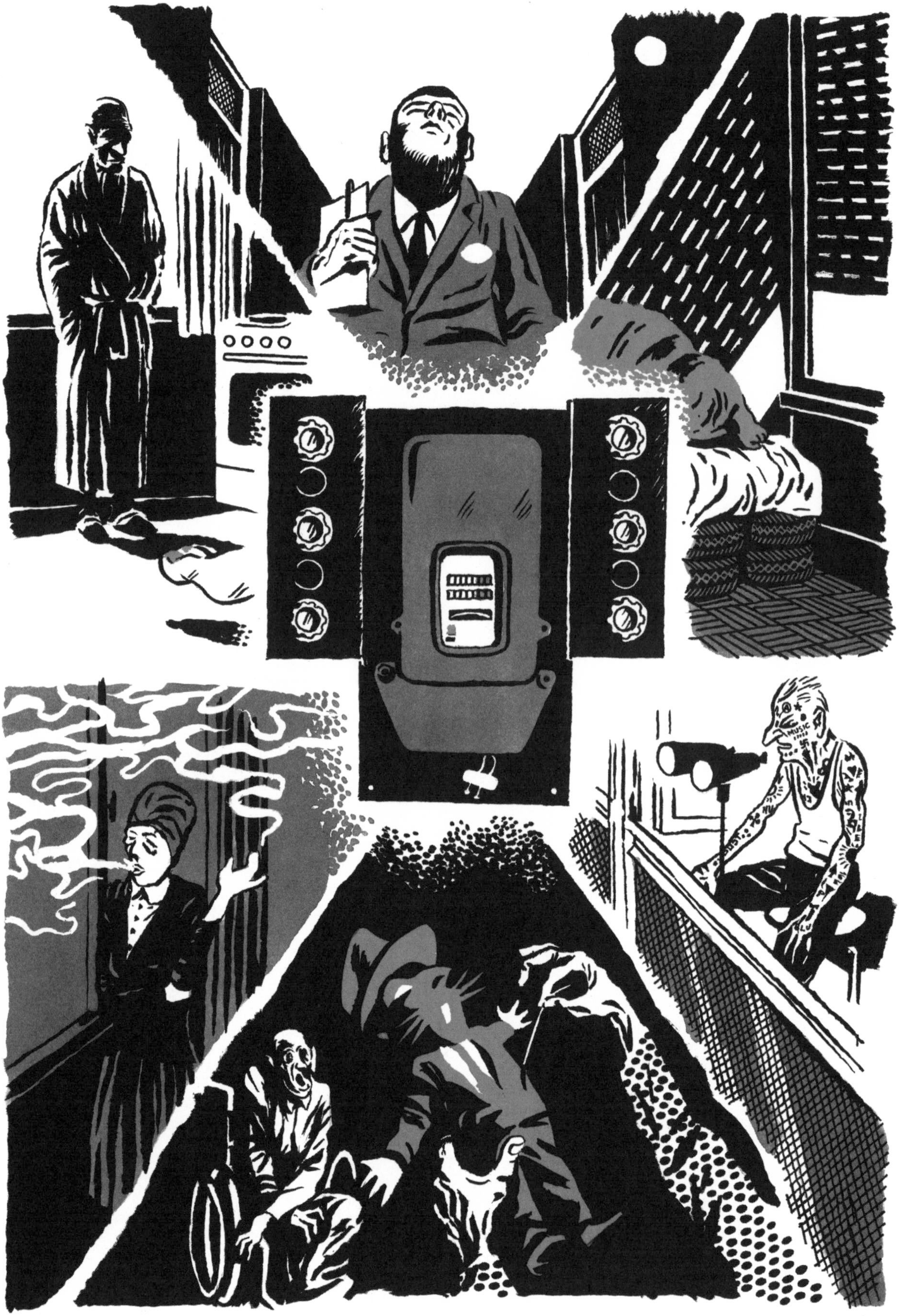

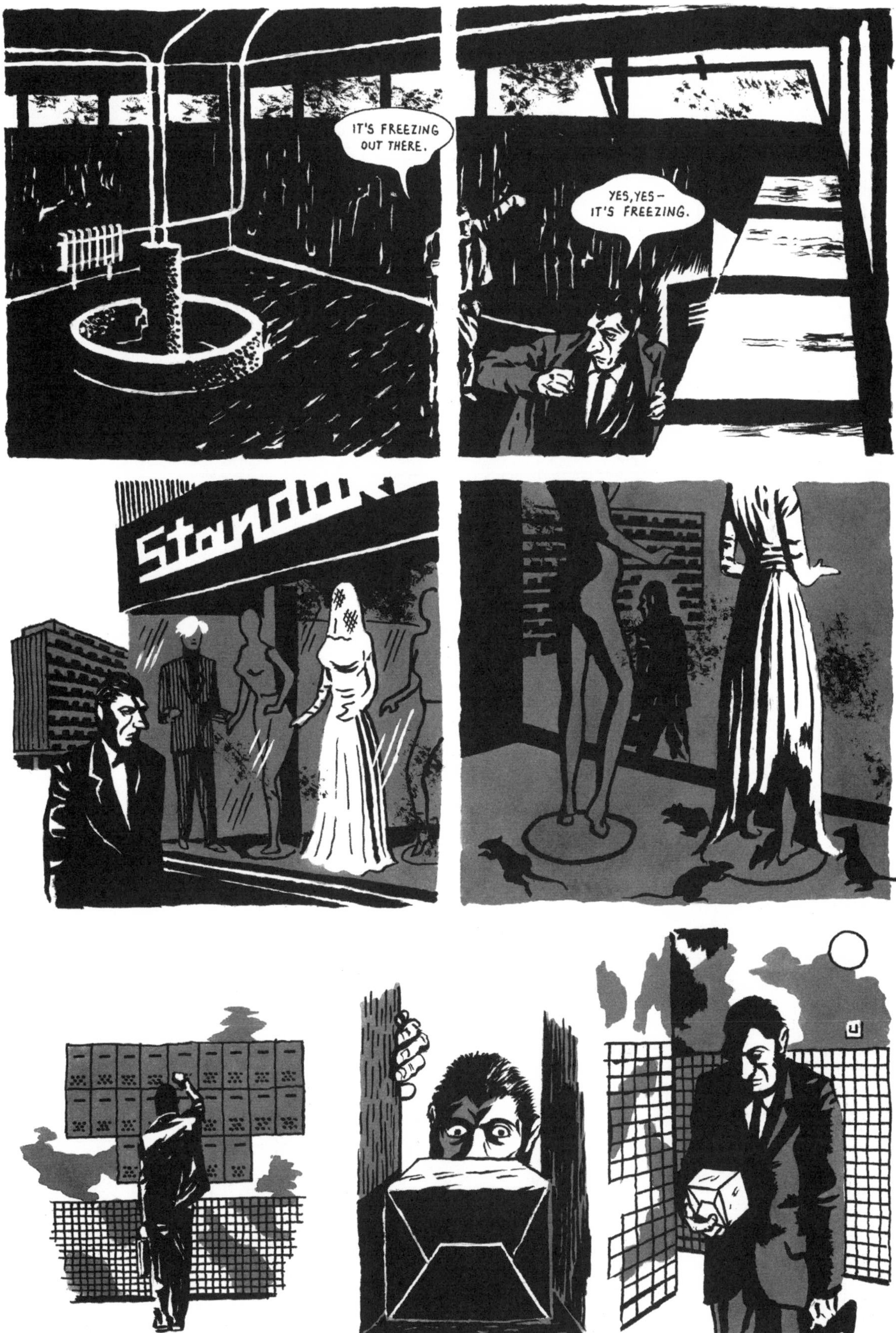
IT'S FREEZING OUT THERE.
YES, YES— IT'S FREEZING.

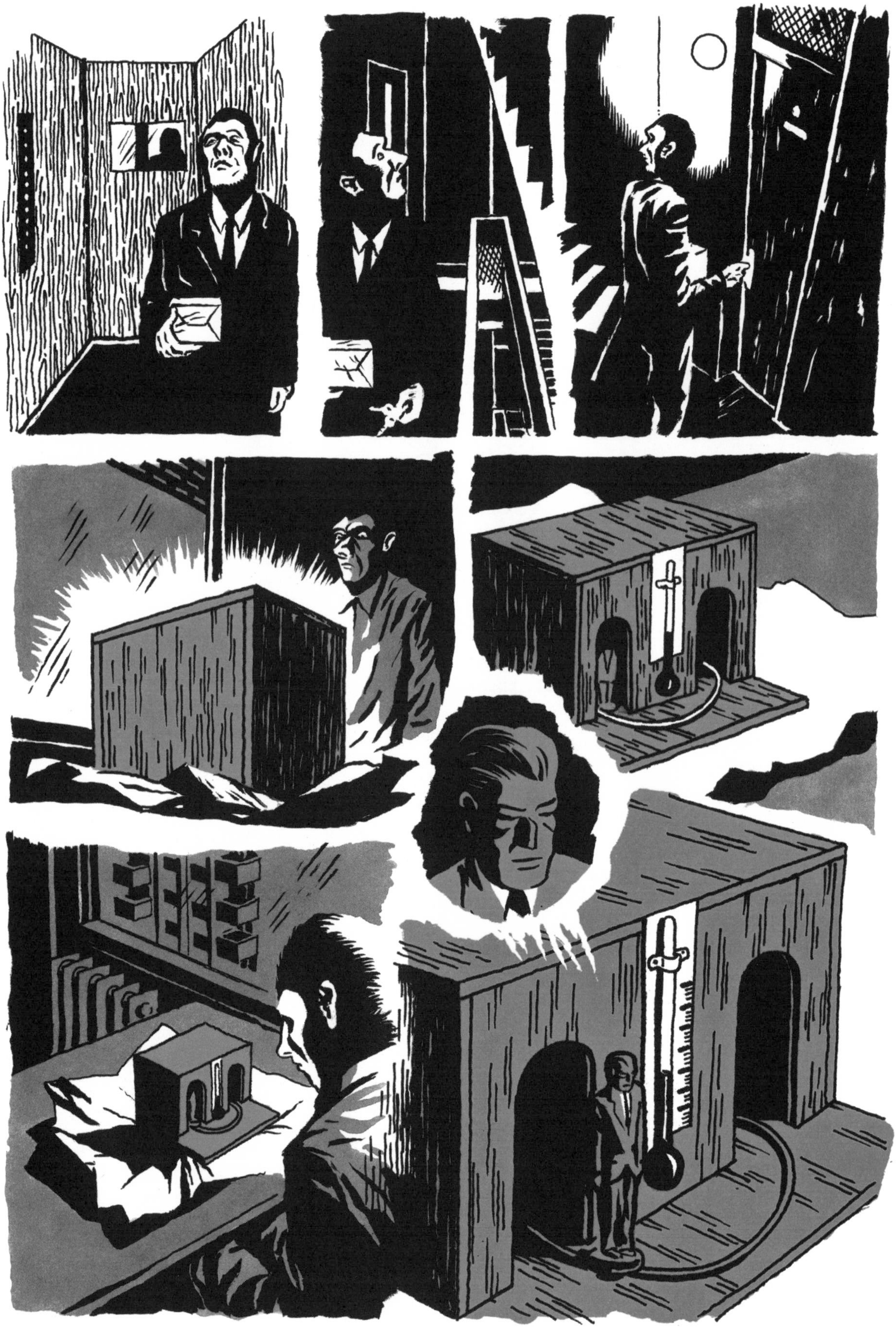

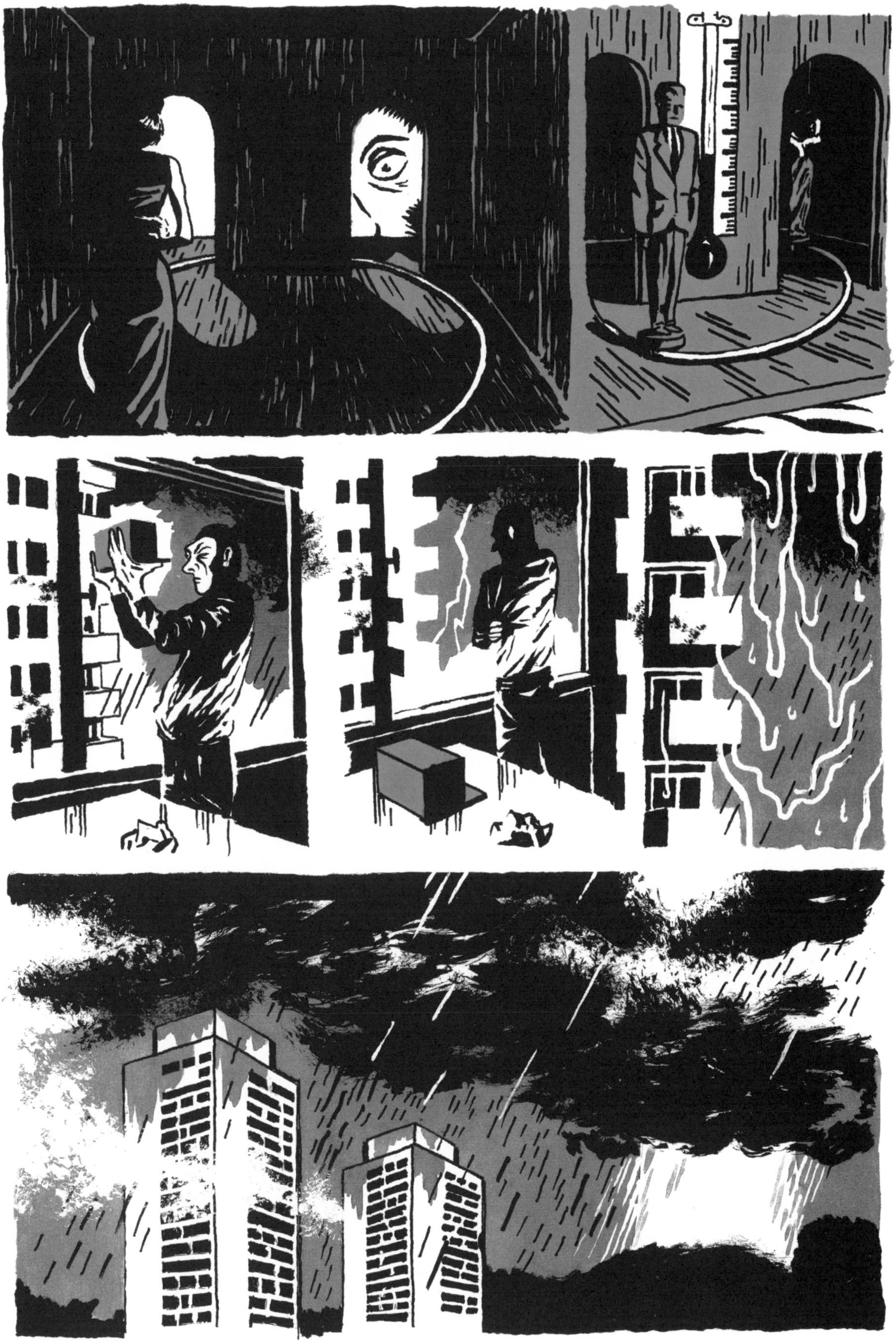

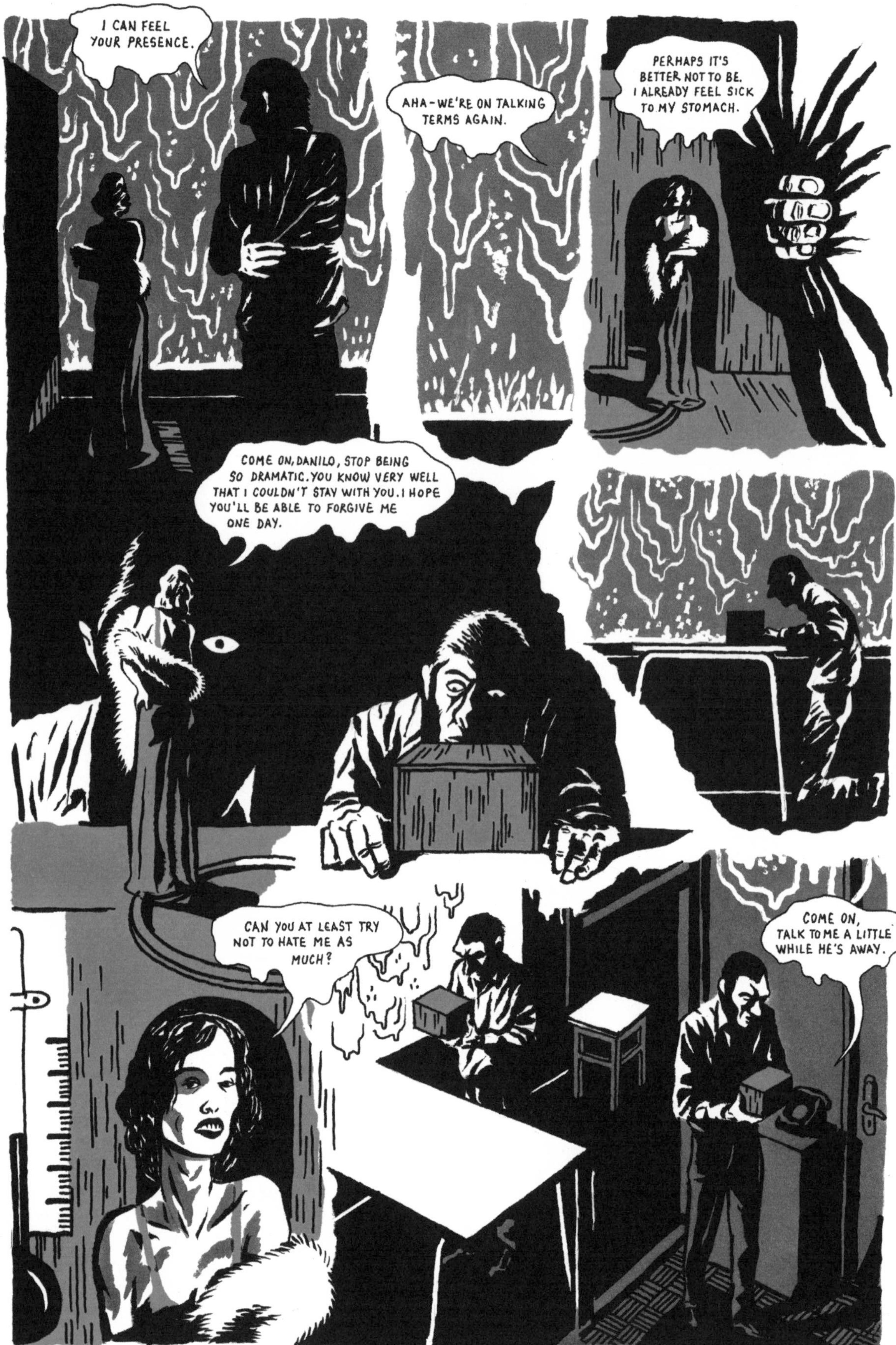
I CAN FEEL YOUR PRESENCE.
AHA - WE'RE ON TALKING TERMS AGAIN.
PERHAPS IT'S BETTER NOT TO BE. I ALREADY FEEL SICK TO MY STOMACH.
COME ON, DANILO, STOP BEING SO DRAMATIC. YOU KNOW VERY WELL THAT I COULDN'T STAY WITH YOU. I HOPE YOU'LL BE ABLE TO FORGIVE ME ONE DAY.
CAN YOU AT LEAST TRY NOT TO HATE ME AS MUCH?
COME ON, TALK TO ME A LITTLE WHILE HE'S AWAY.

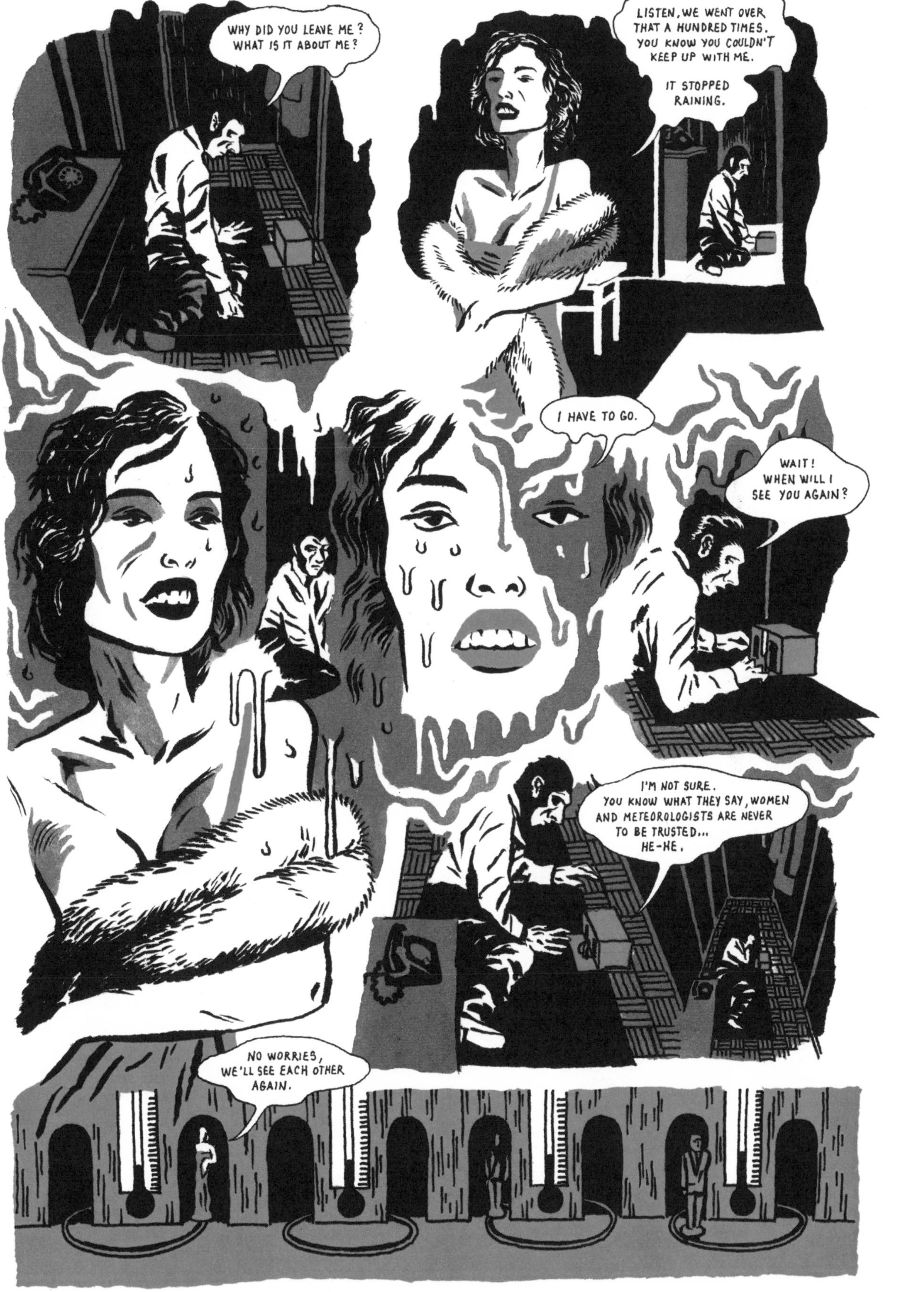
WHY DID YOU LEAVE ME? WHAT IS IT ABOUT ME?
LISTEN, WE WENT OVER THAT A HUNDRED TIMES. YOU KNOW YOU COULDN'T KEEP UP WITH ME.
IT STOPPED RAINING.
I HAVE TO GO.
WAIT! WHEN WILL I SEE YOU AGAIN?
I'M NOT SURE. YOU KNOW WHAT THEY SAY, WOMEN AND METEOROLOGISTS ARE NEVER TO BE TRUSTED... HE-HE.
NO WORRIES, WE'LL SEE EACH OTHER AGAIN.

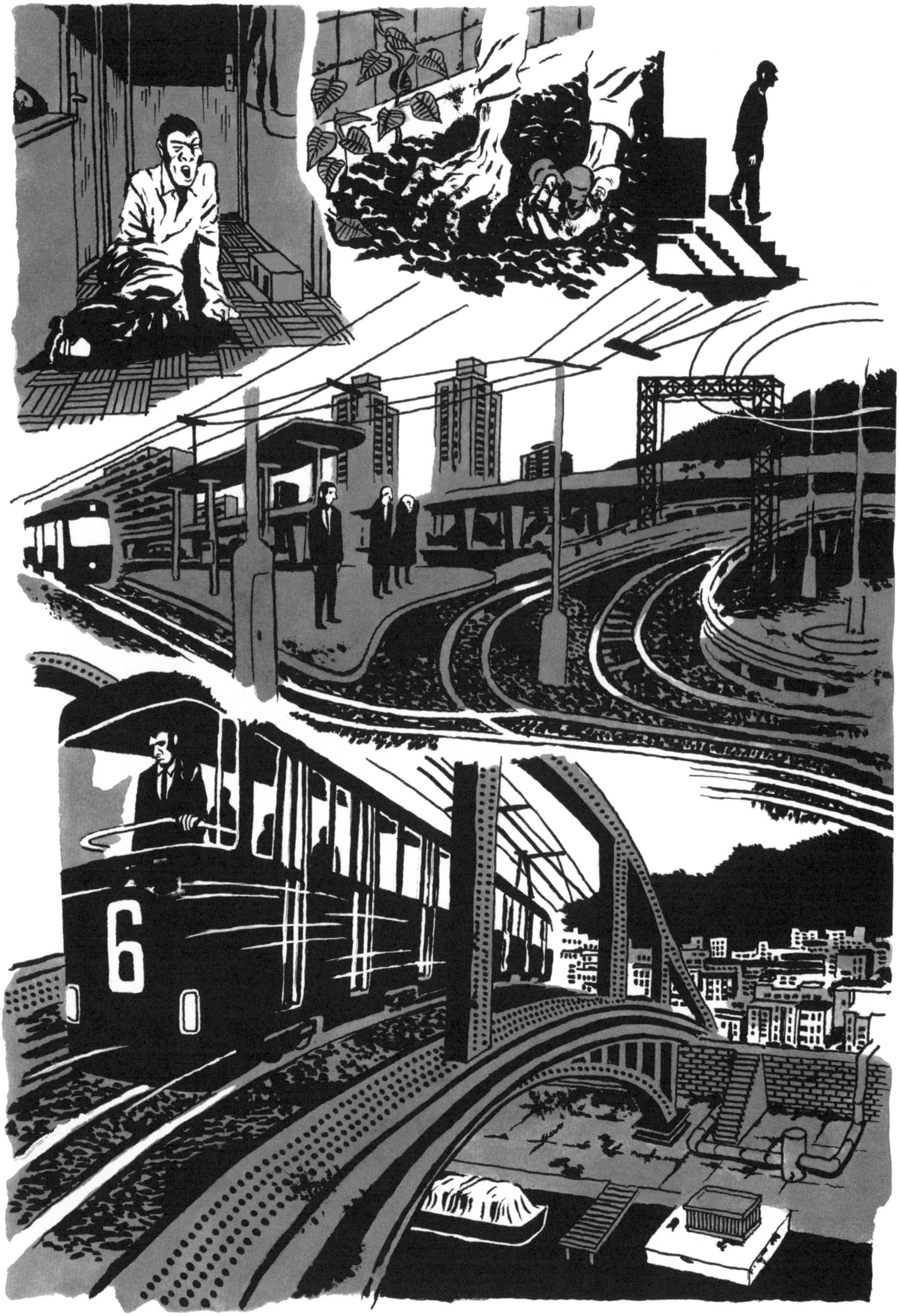
6

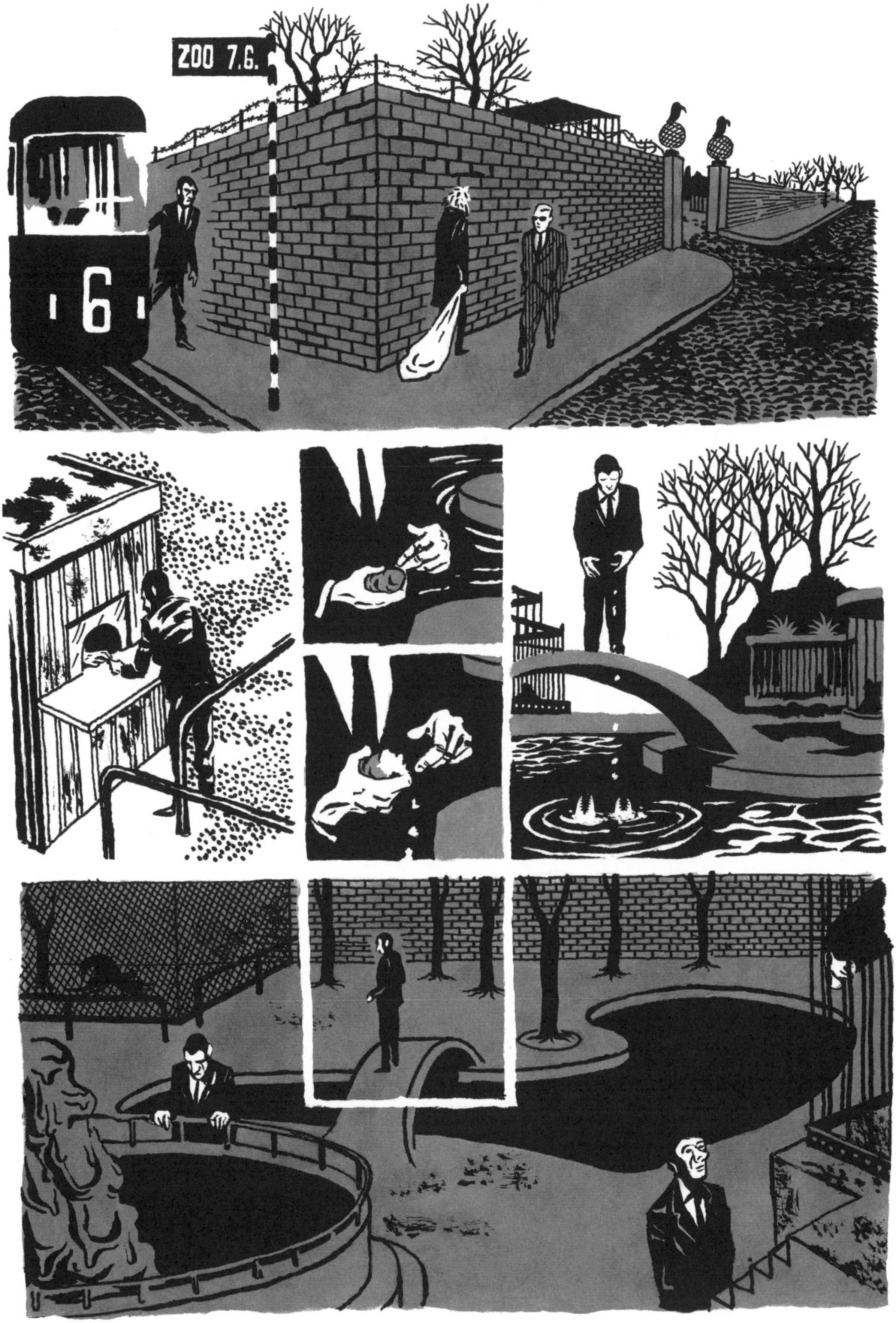
ZOO 7.G.
6

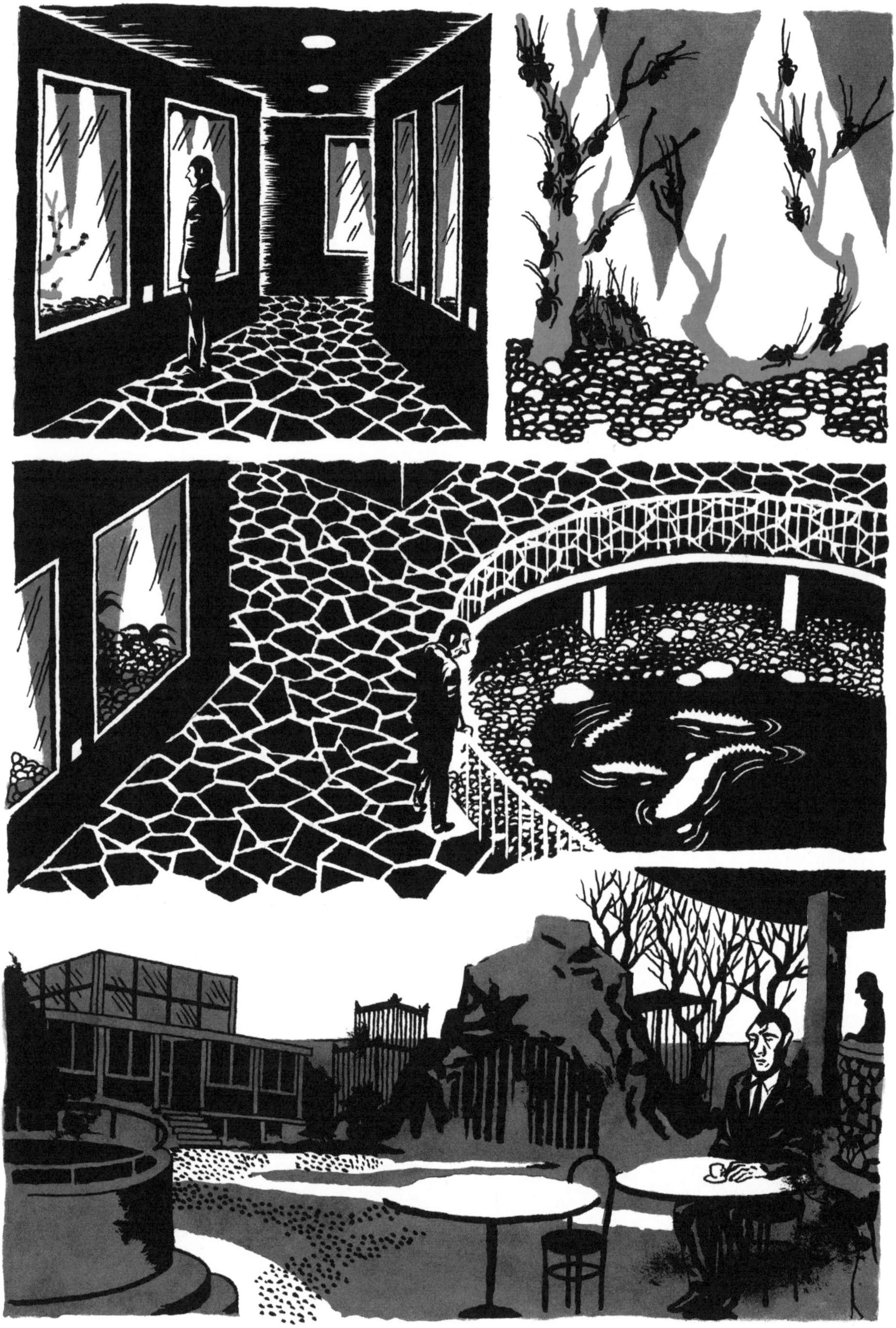

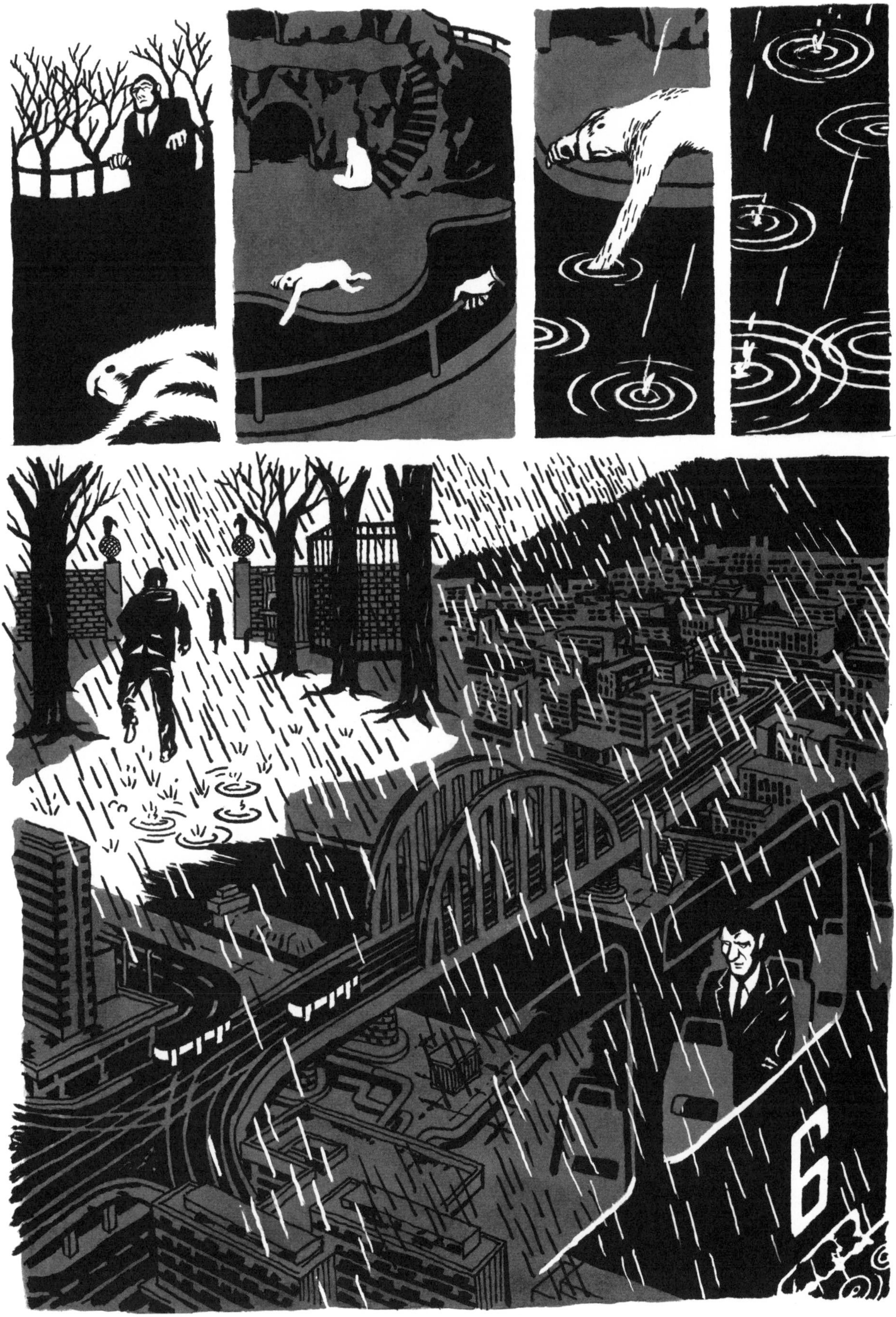
6

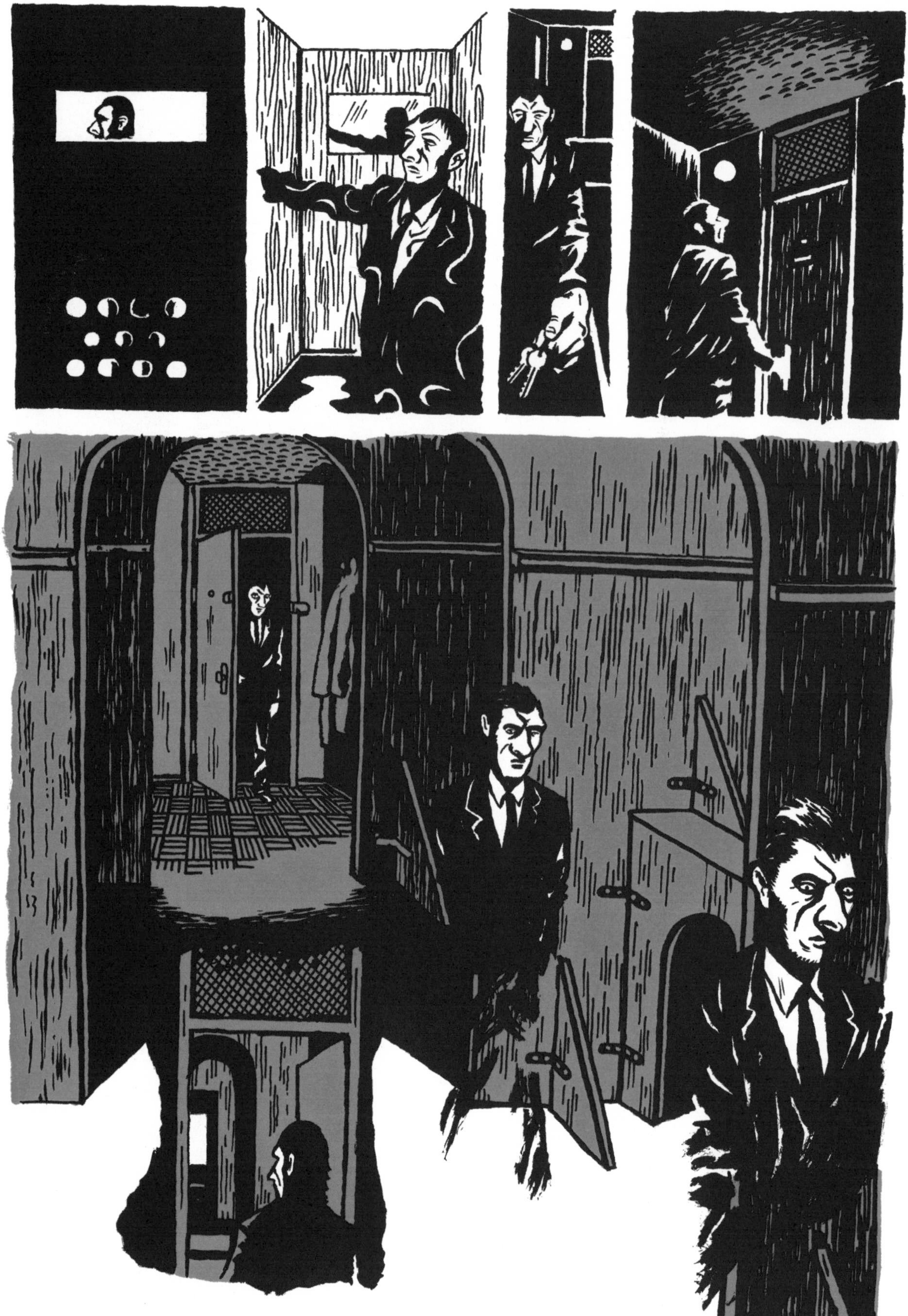

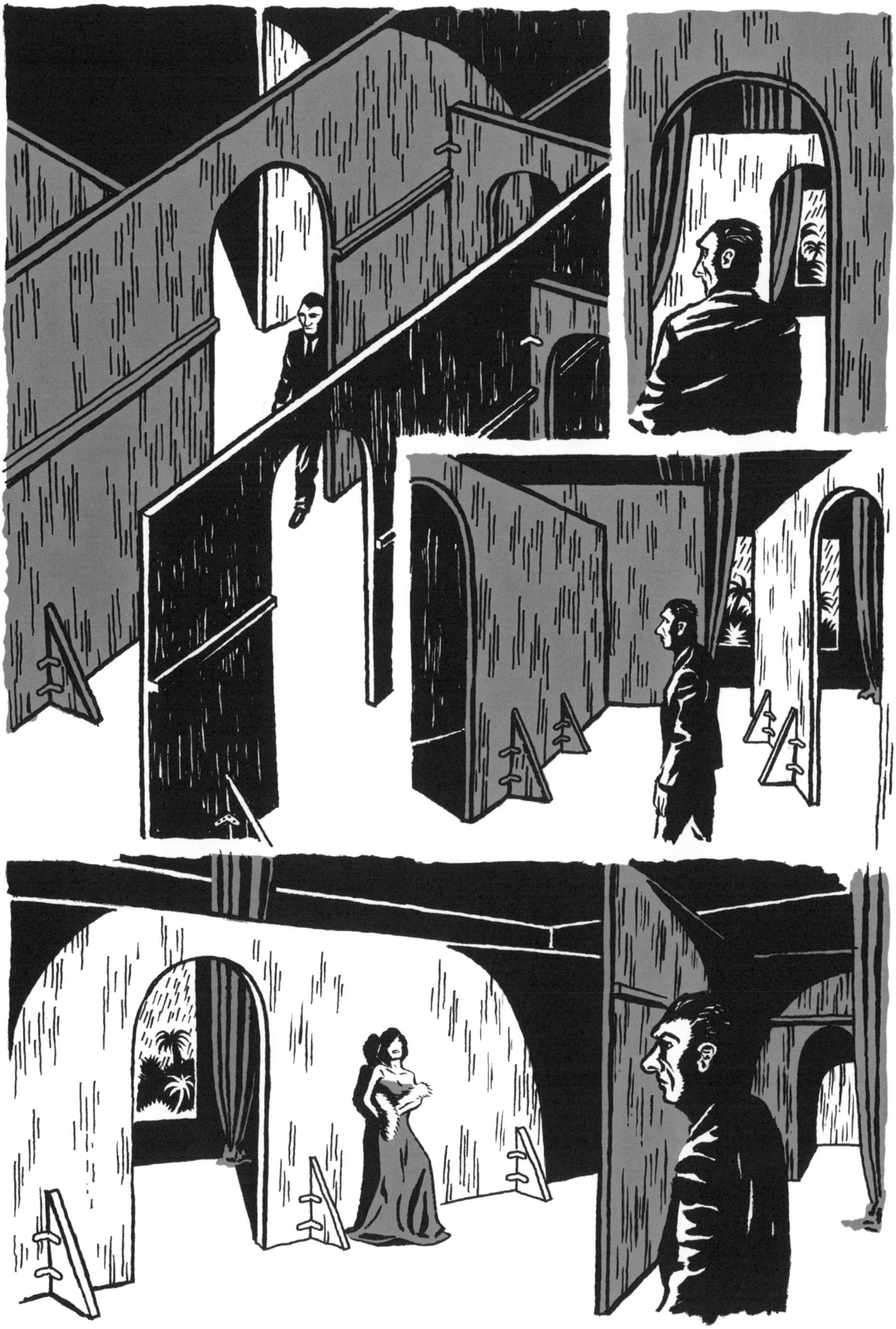

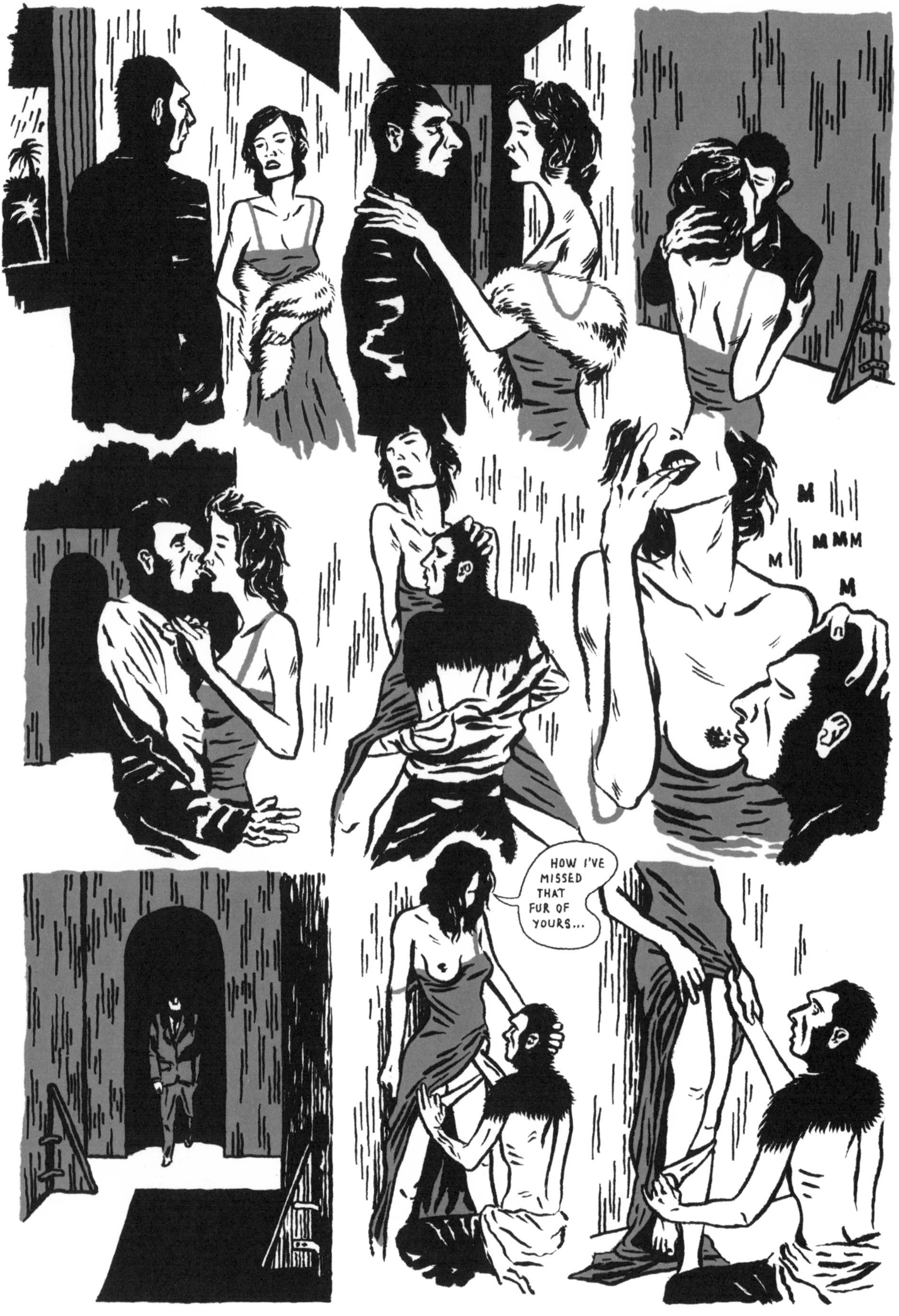
M
MMM
M
M
HOW I'VE MISSED THAT FUR OF YOURS...

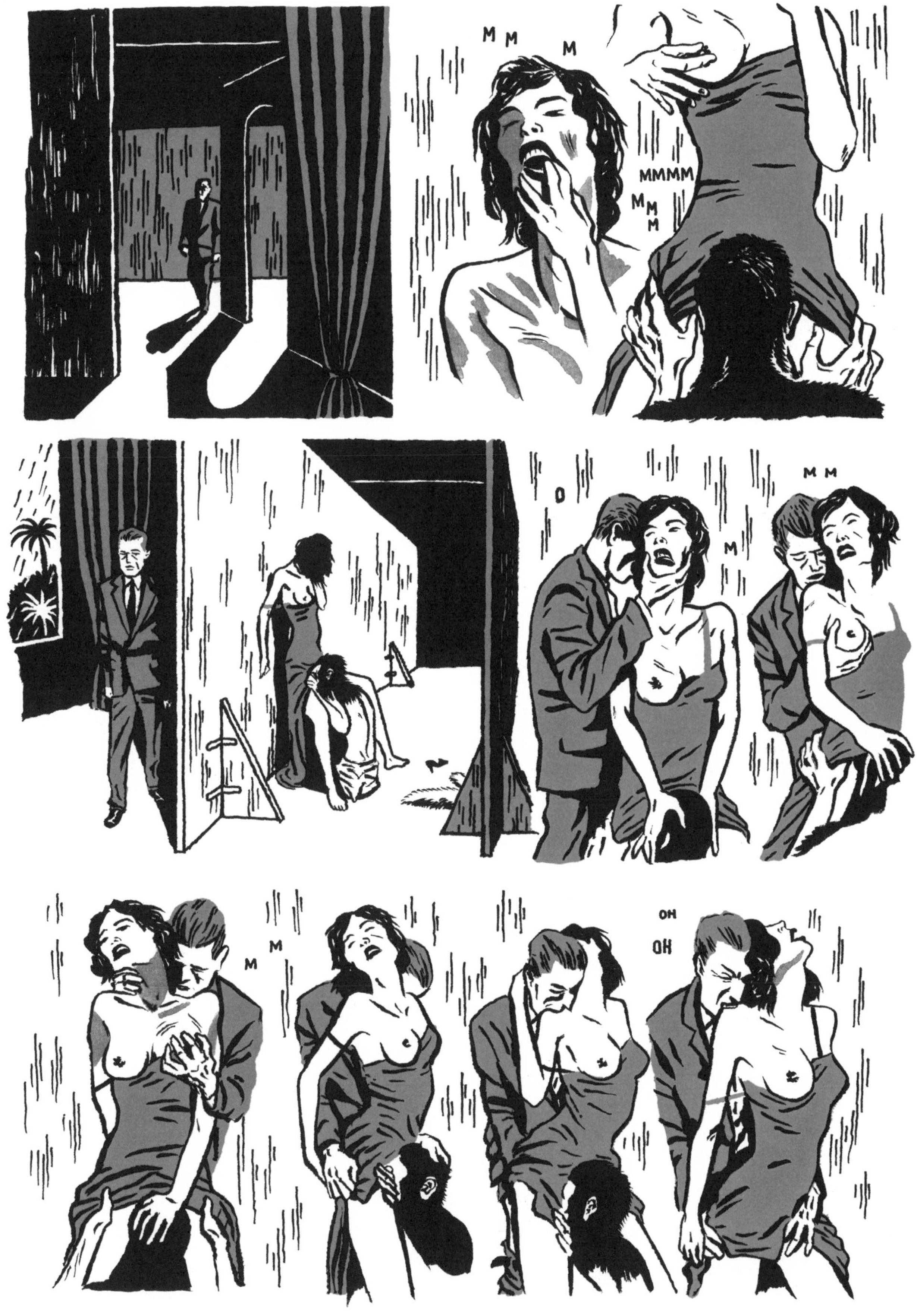
M M M
MMMM
M M M
O
M M
M
M M
OH
OH

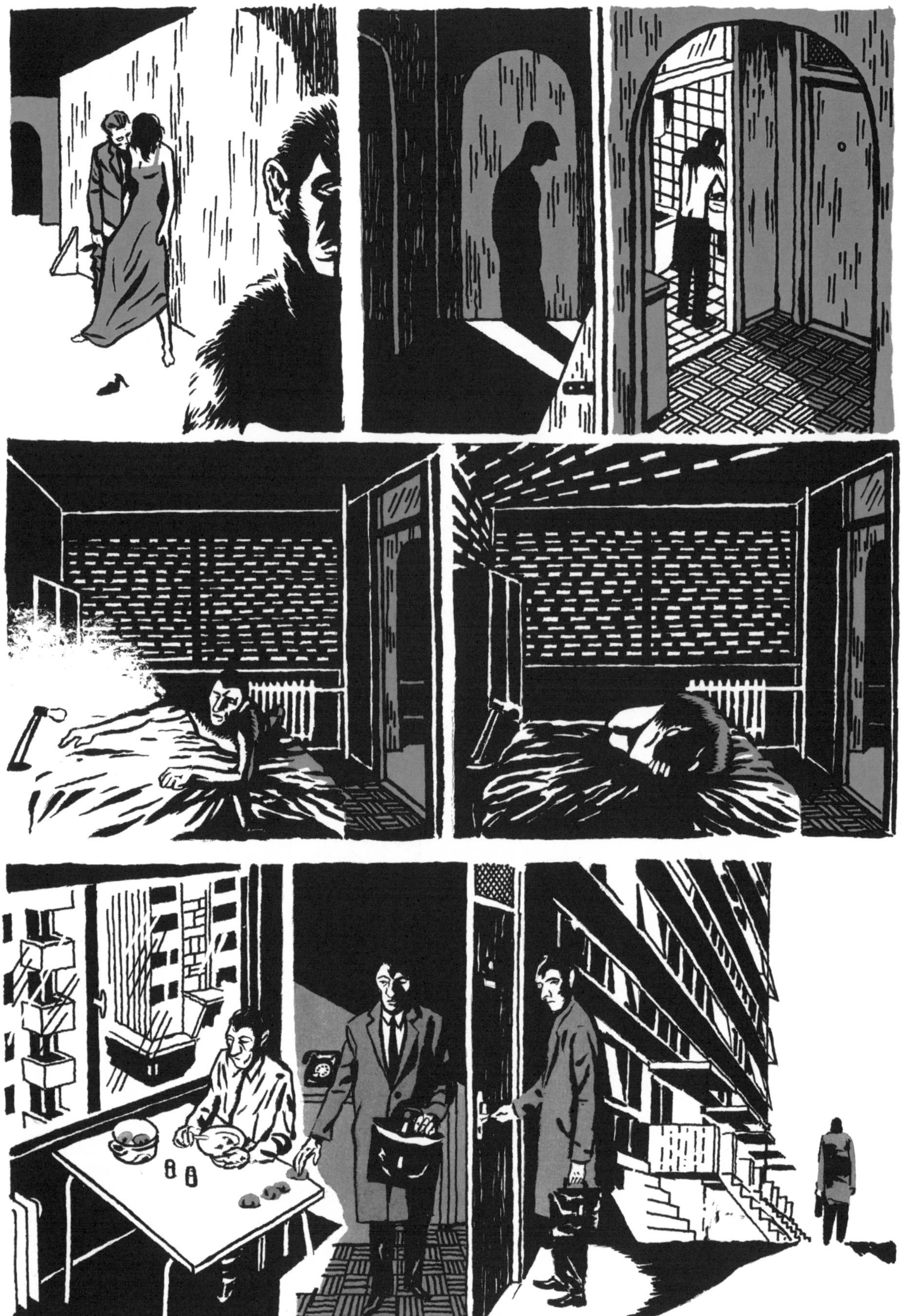

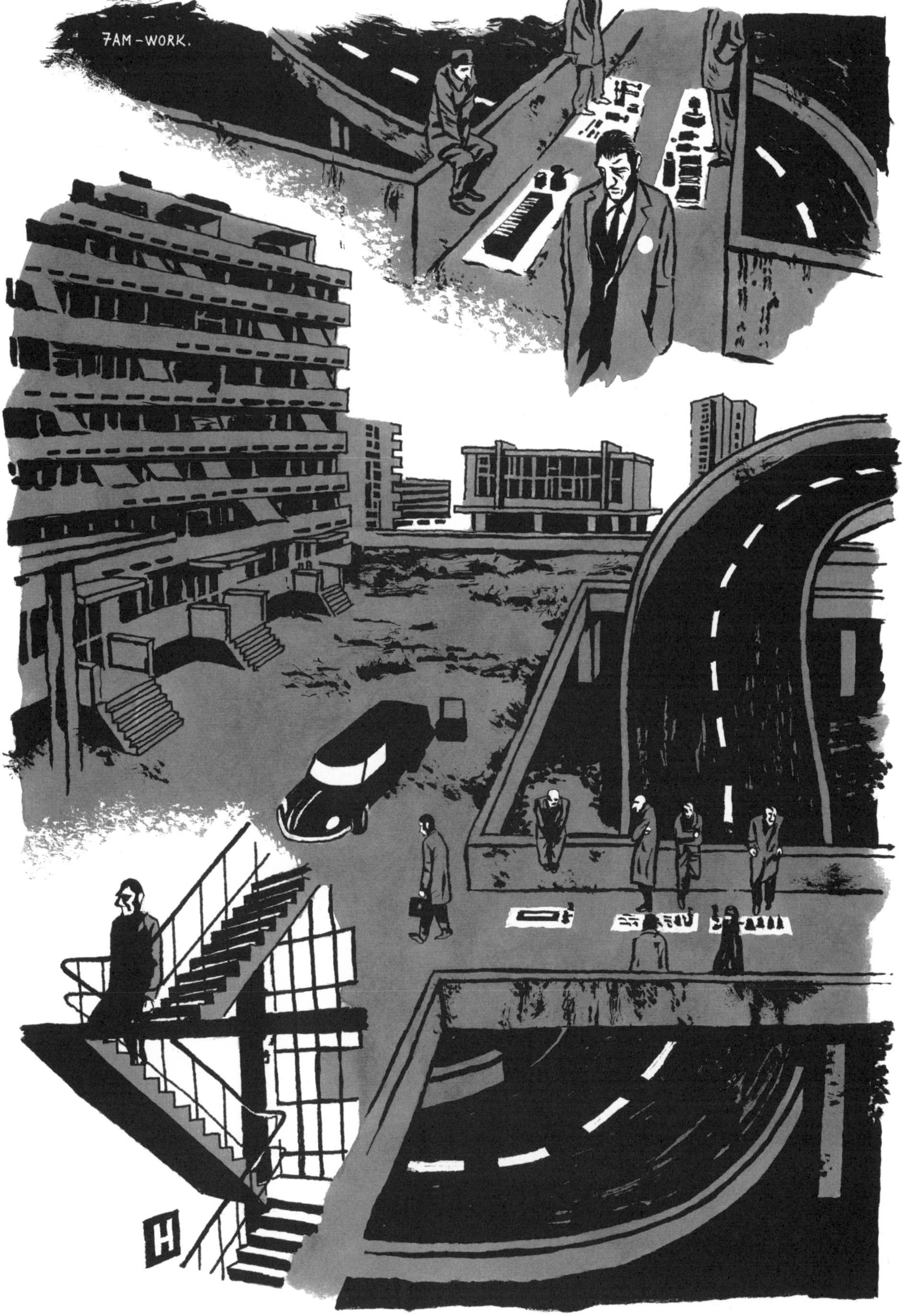
7AM - WORK.

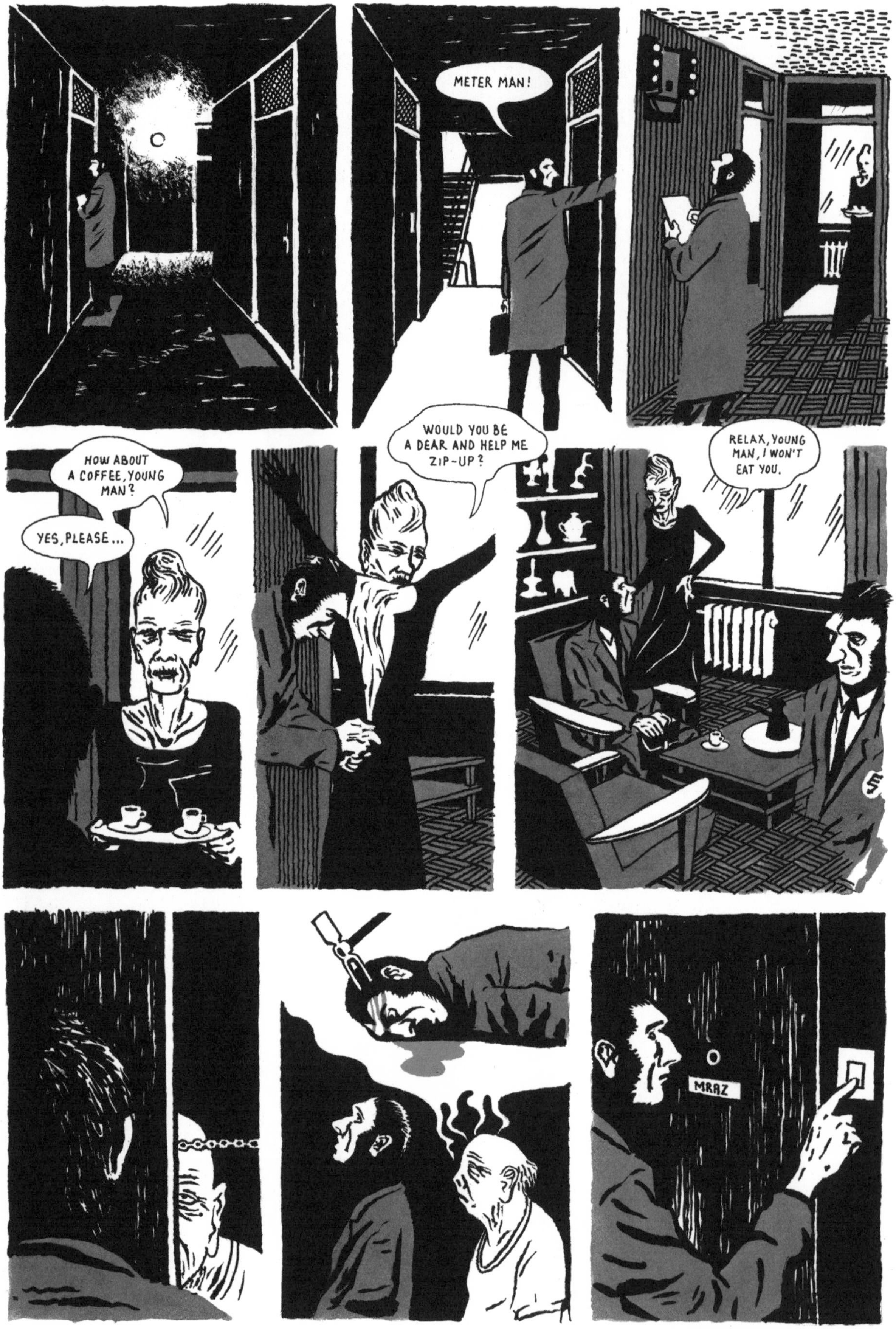
METER MAN!
HOW ABOUT A COFFEE, YOUNG MAN?
YES, PLEASE...
WOULD YOU BE A DEAR AND HELP ME ZIP-UP?
RELAX, YOUNG MAN, I WON'T EAT YOU.
MRAZ

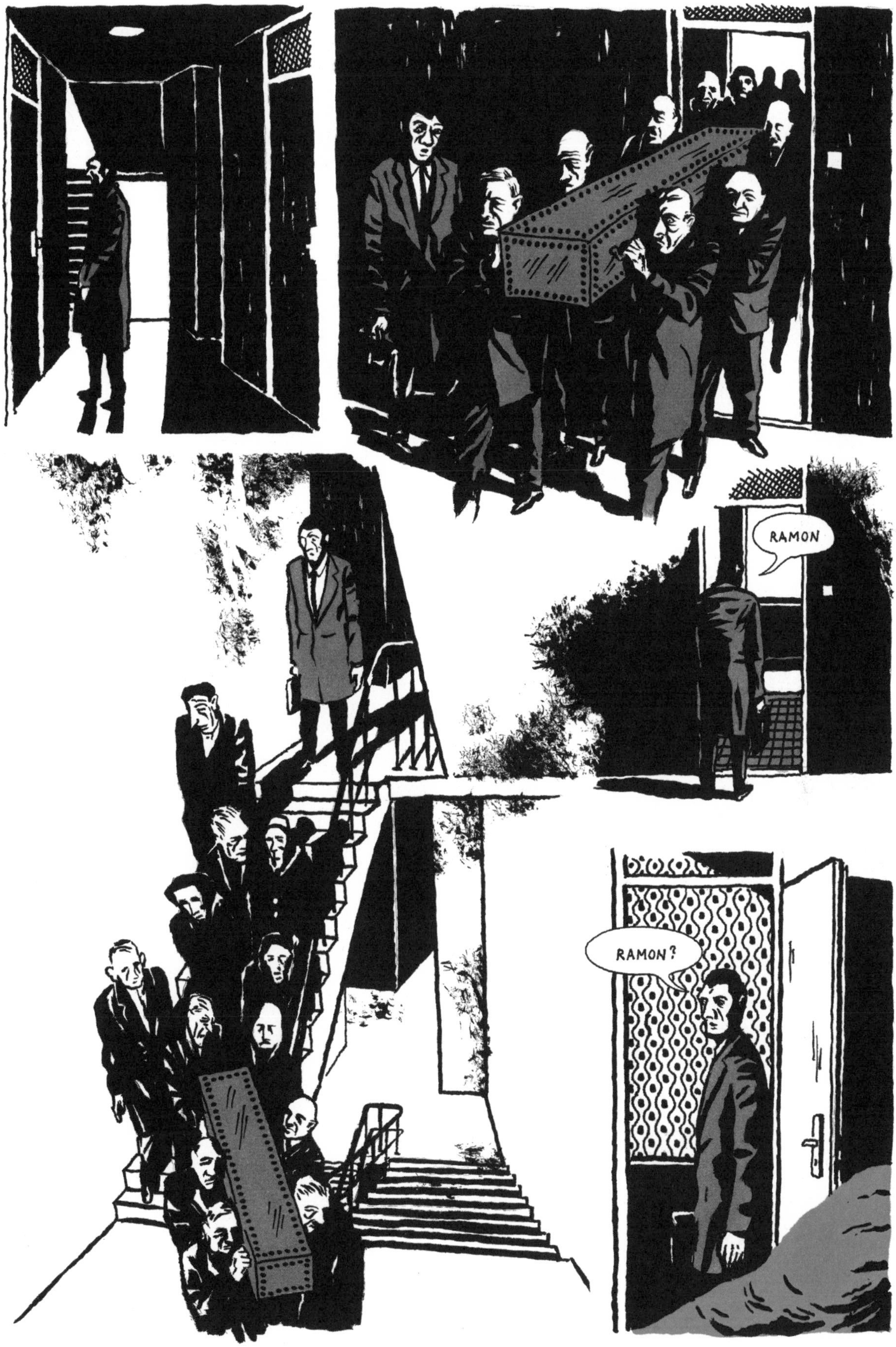
RAMON
RAMON?

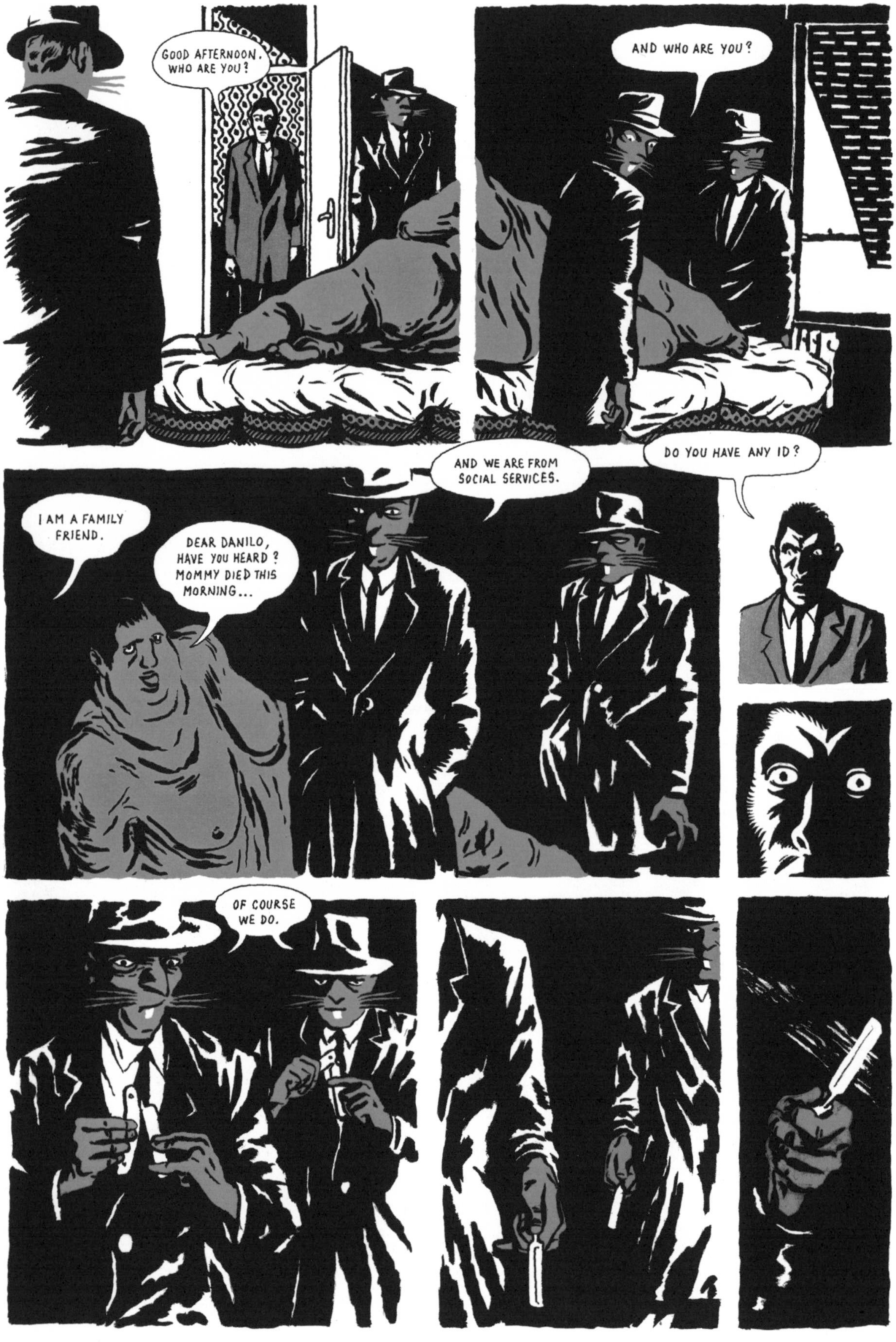
GOOD AFTERNOON, WHO ARE YOU?
AND WHO ARE YOU?
I AM A FAMILY FRIEND.
DEAR DANILO, HAVE YOU HEARD? MOMMY DIED THIS MORNING...
AND WE ARE FROM SOCIAL SERVICES.
DO YOU HAVE ANY ID?
OF COURSE WE DO.

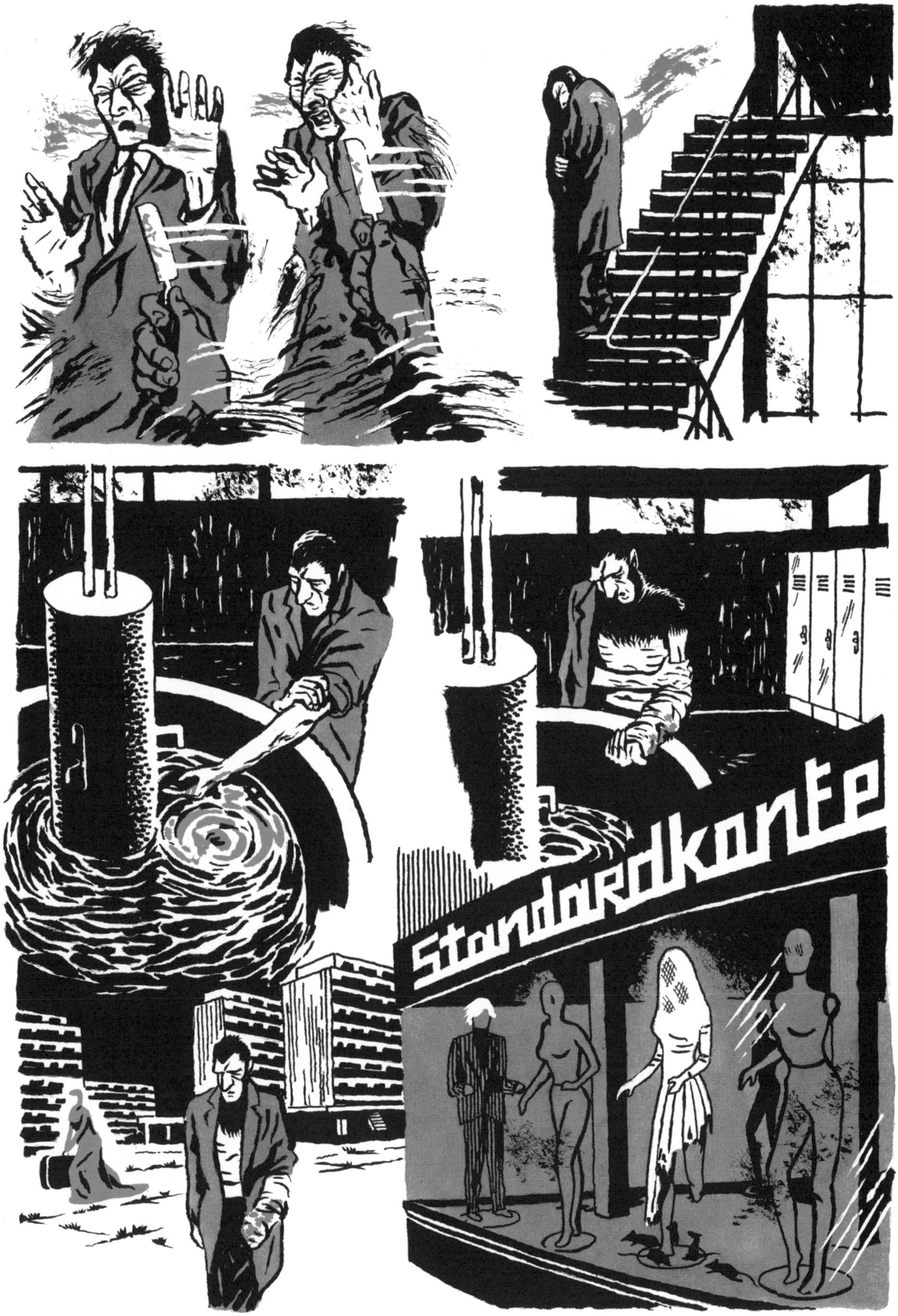
Standardkante

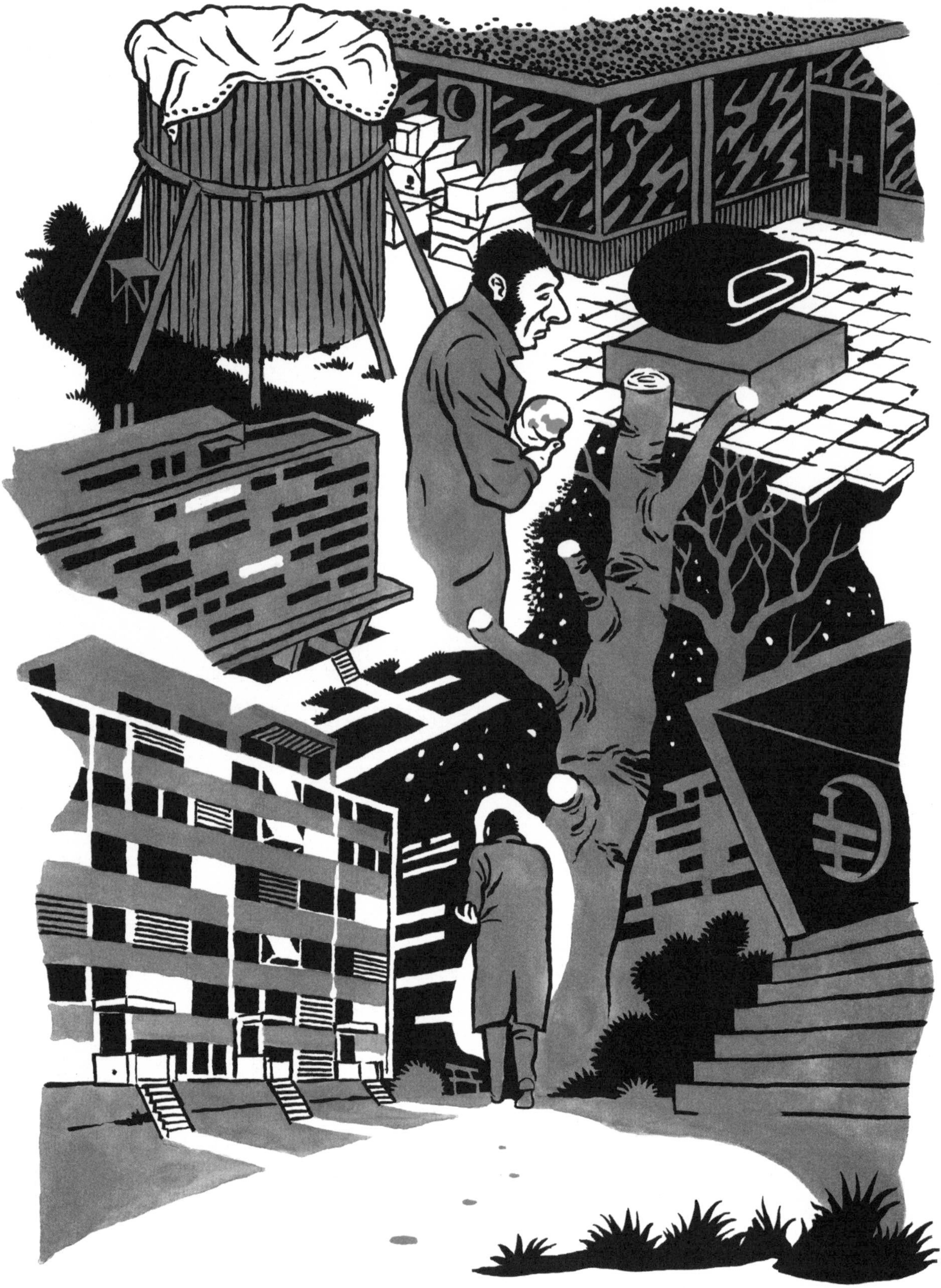

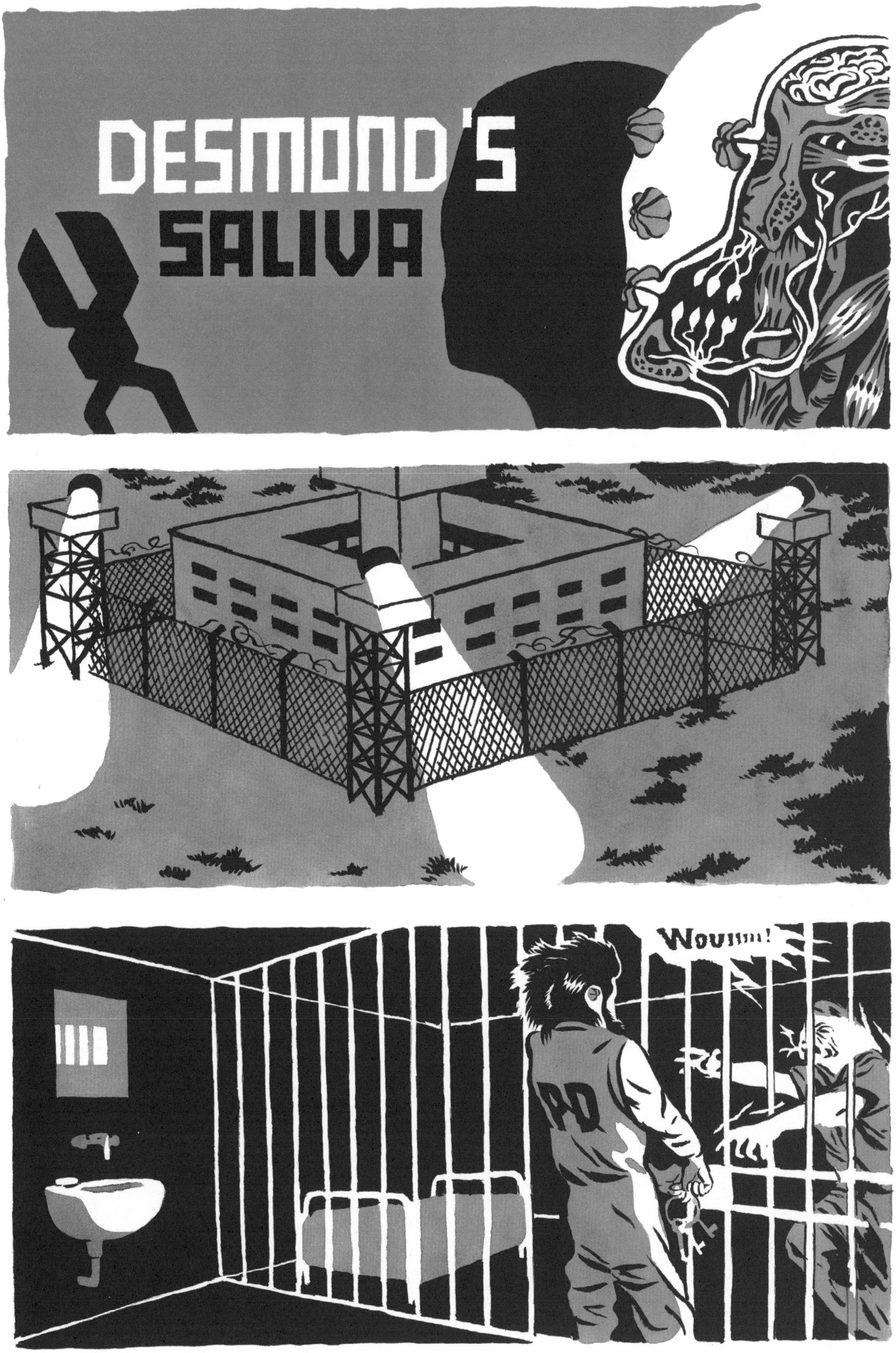
DESMOND'S
SALIVA
Wouuuu!
PD

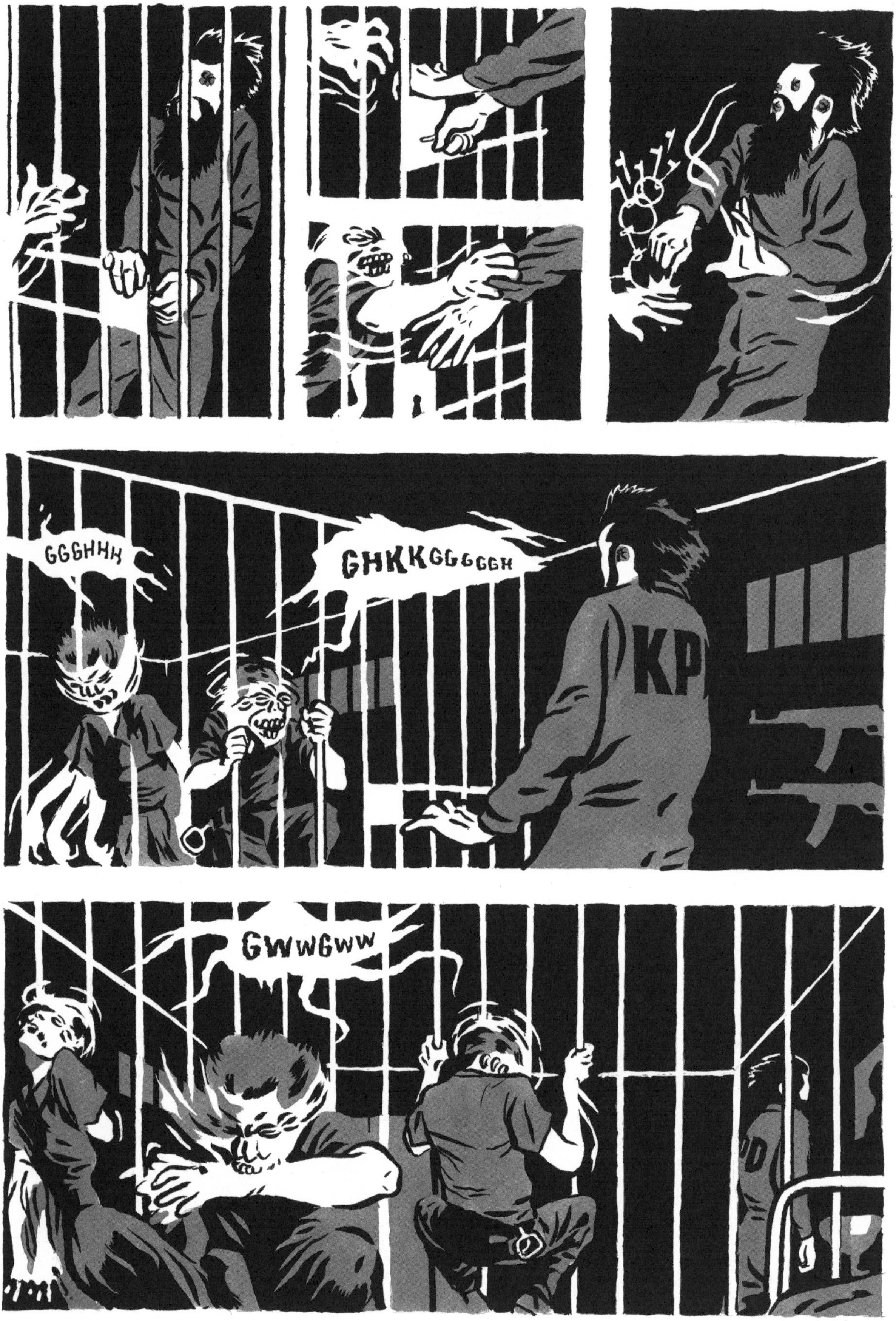
GGGHHH
GHKKGGGGGH
KP
GWWGWW

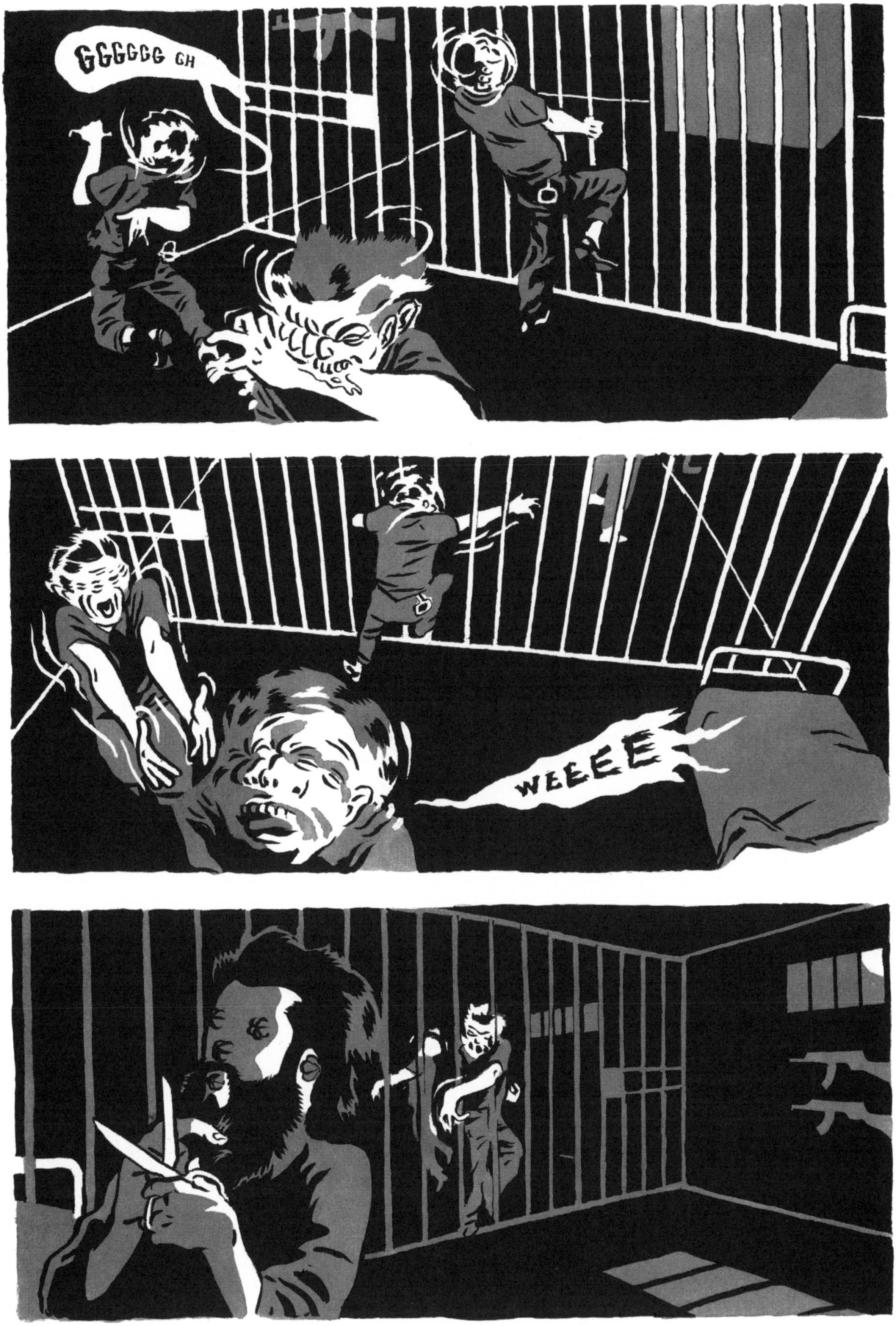
GGGGGG GH
WEEEE

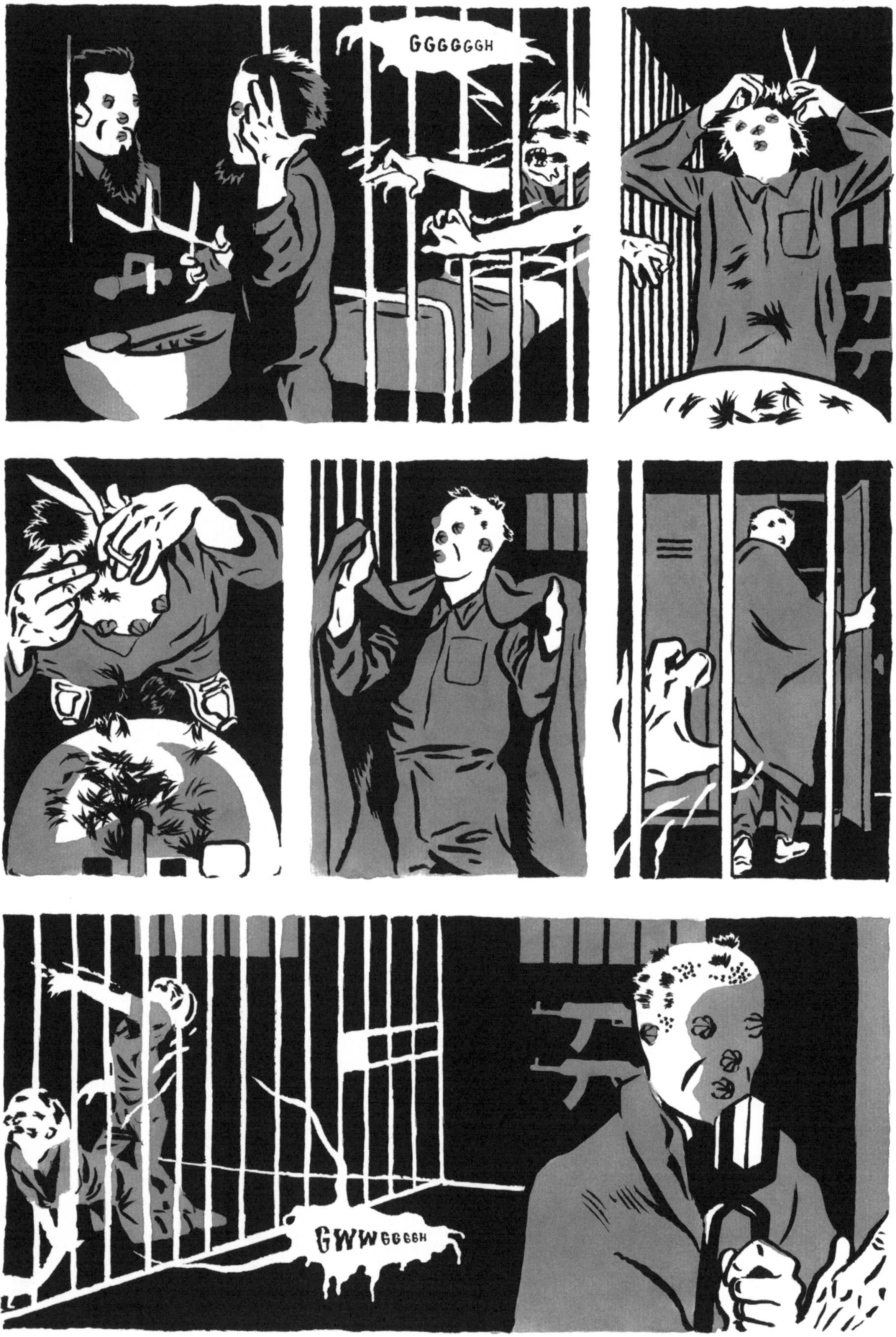
GGGGGGH
GWWGGGGH

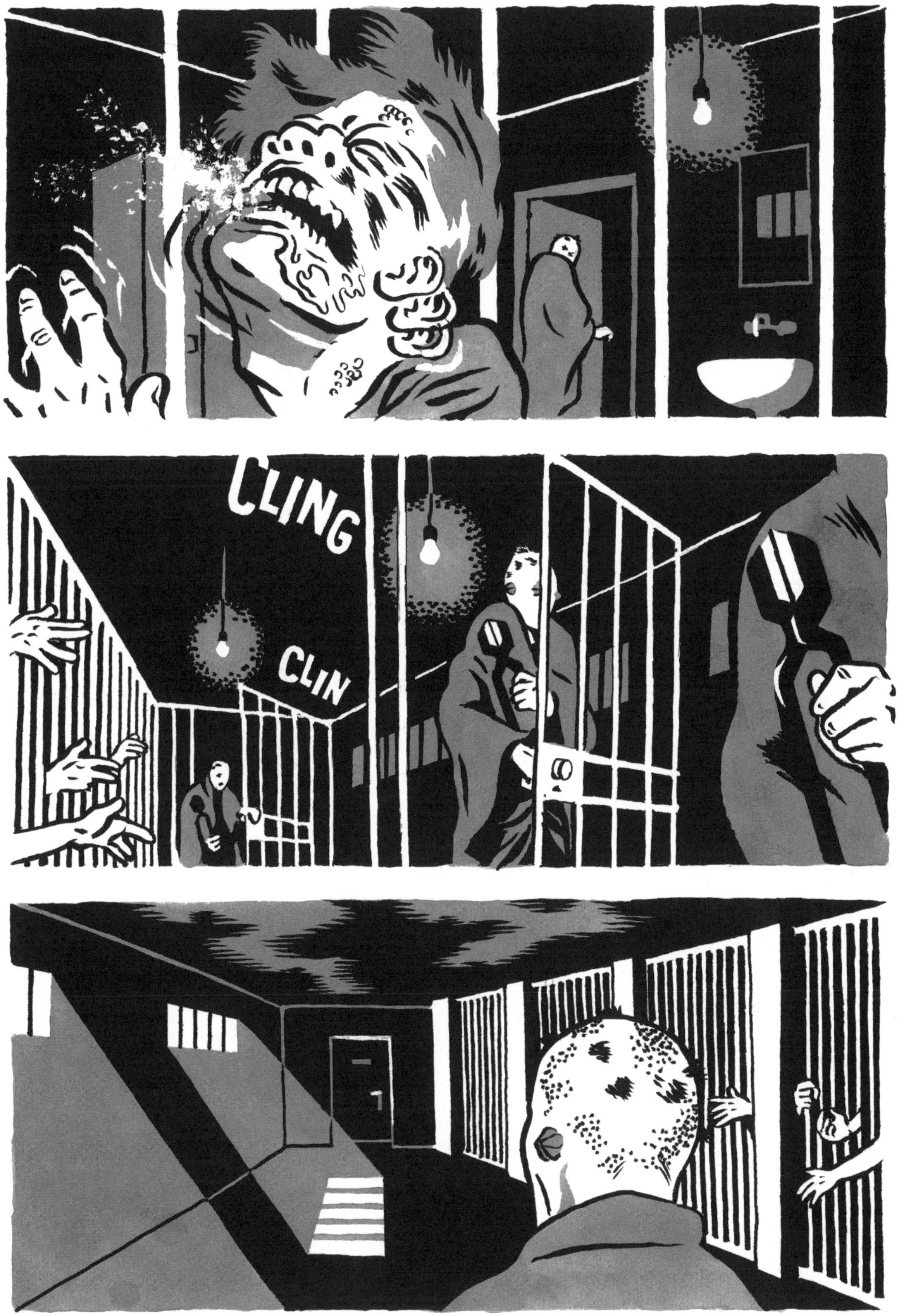
CLING
CLIN

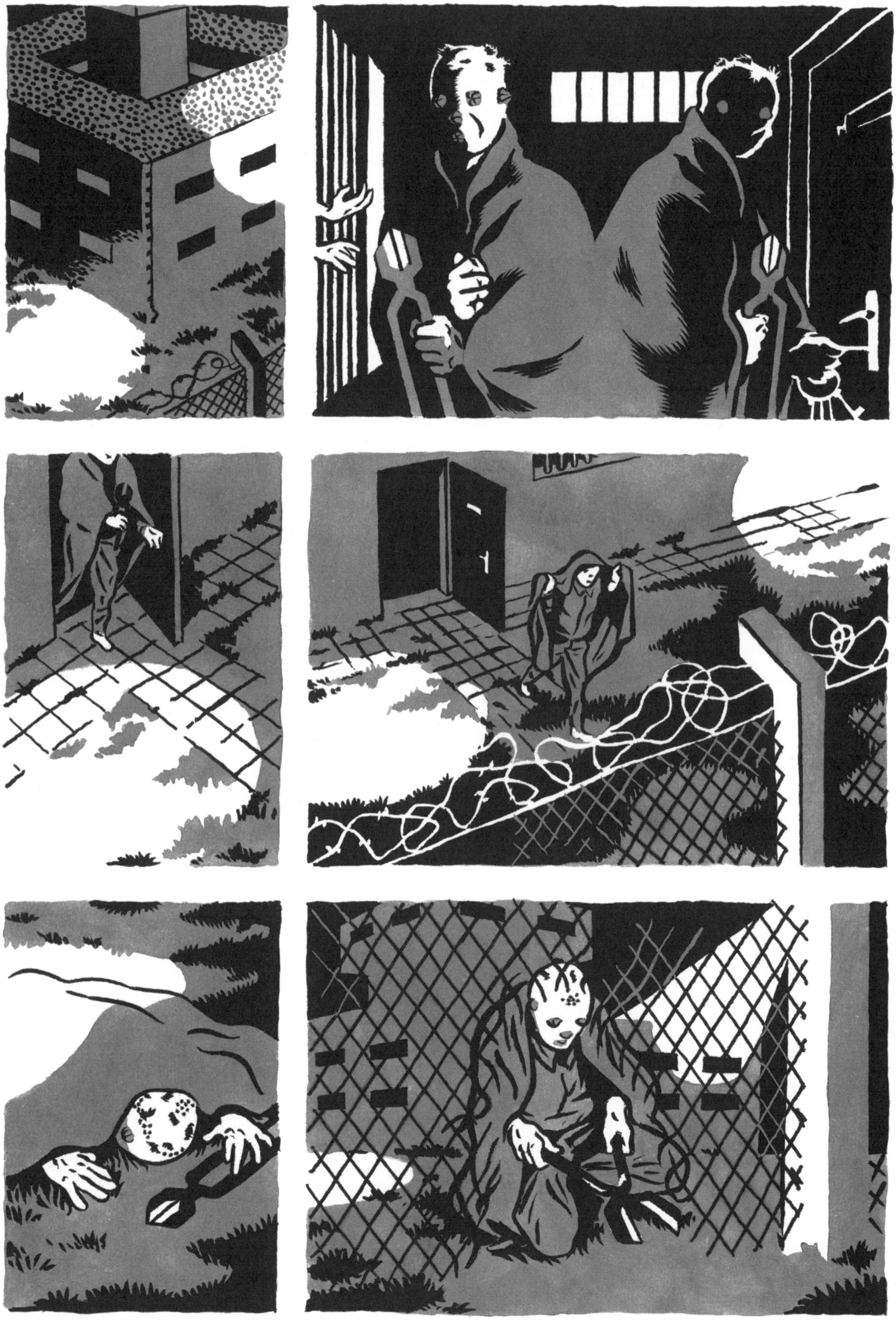

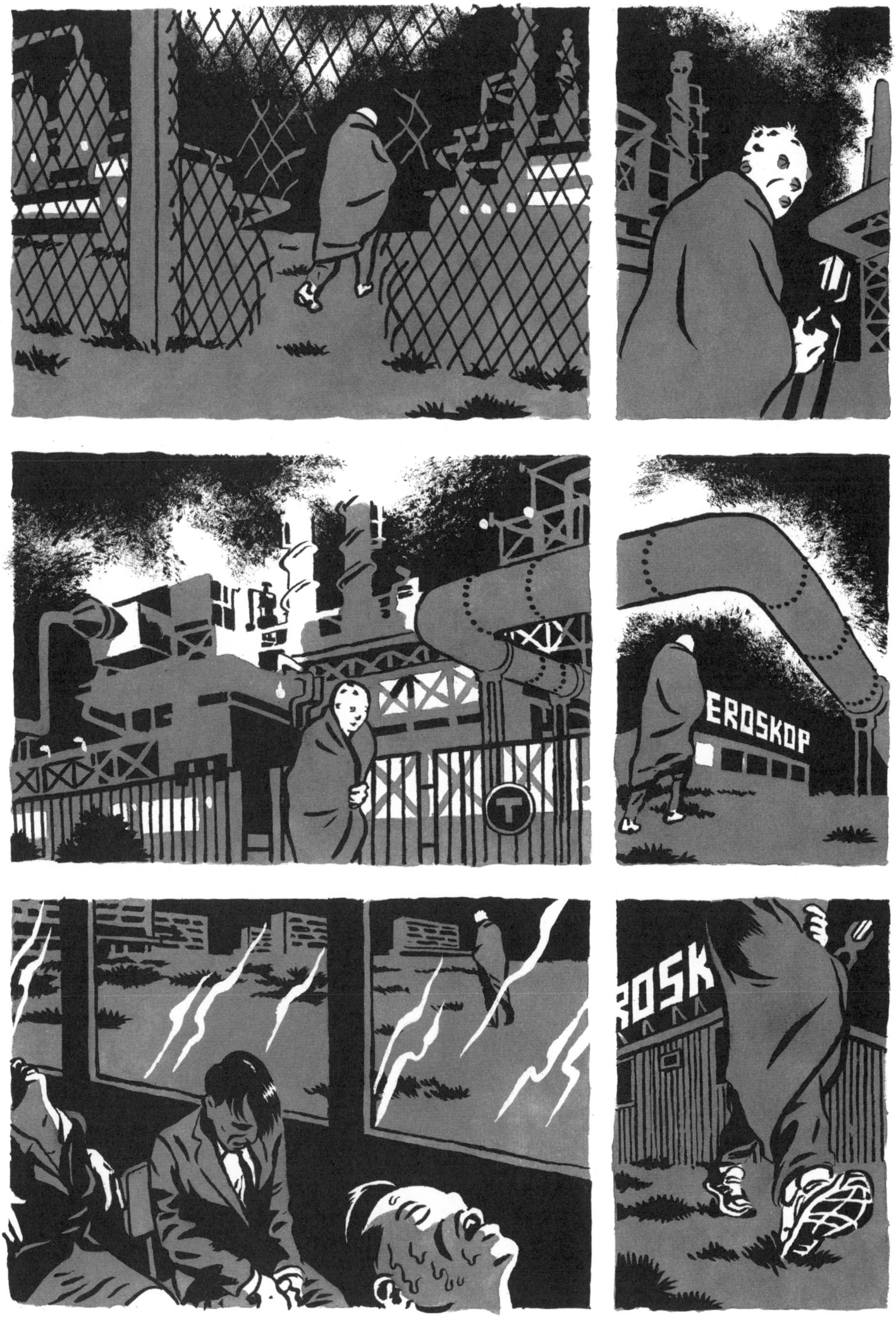
EROSKOP
ROSK

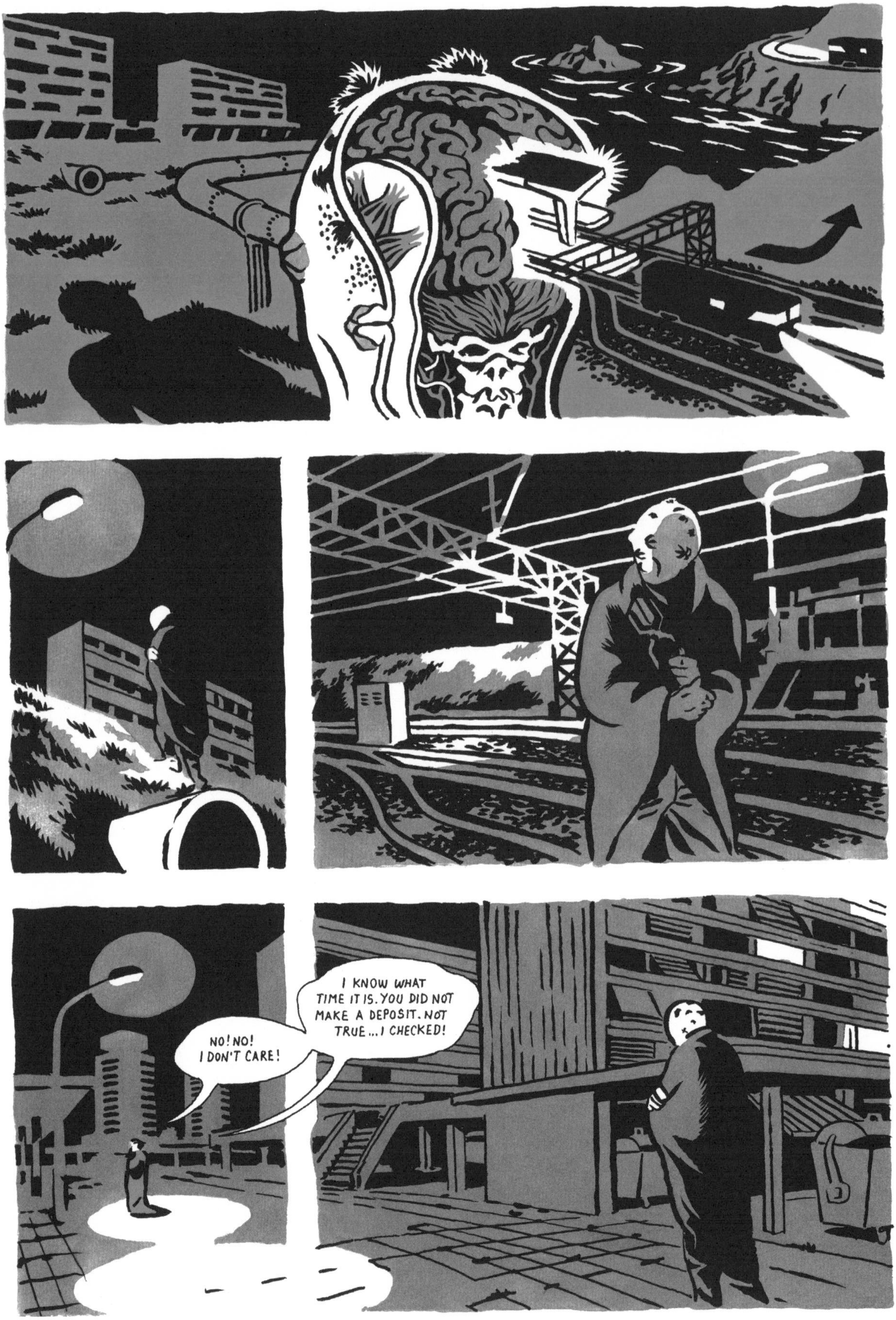
NO! NO! I DON'T CARE!
I KNOW WHAT TIME IT IS. YOU DID NOT MAKE A DEPOSIT. NOT TRUE... I CHECKED!

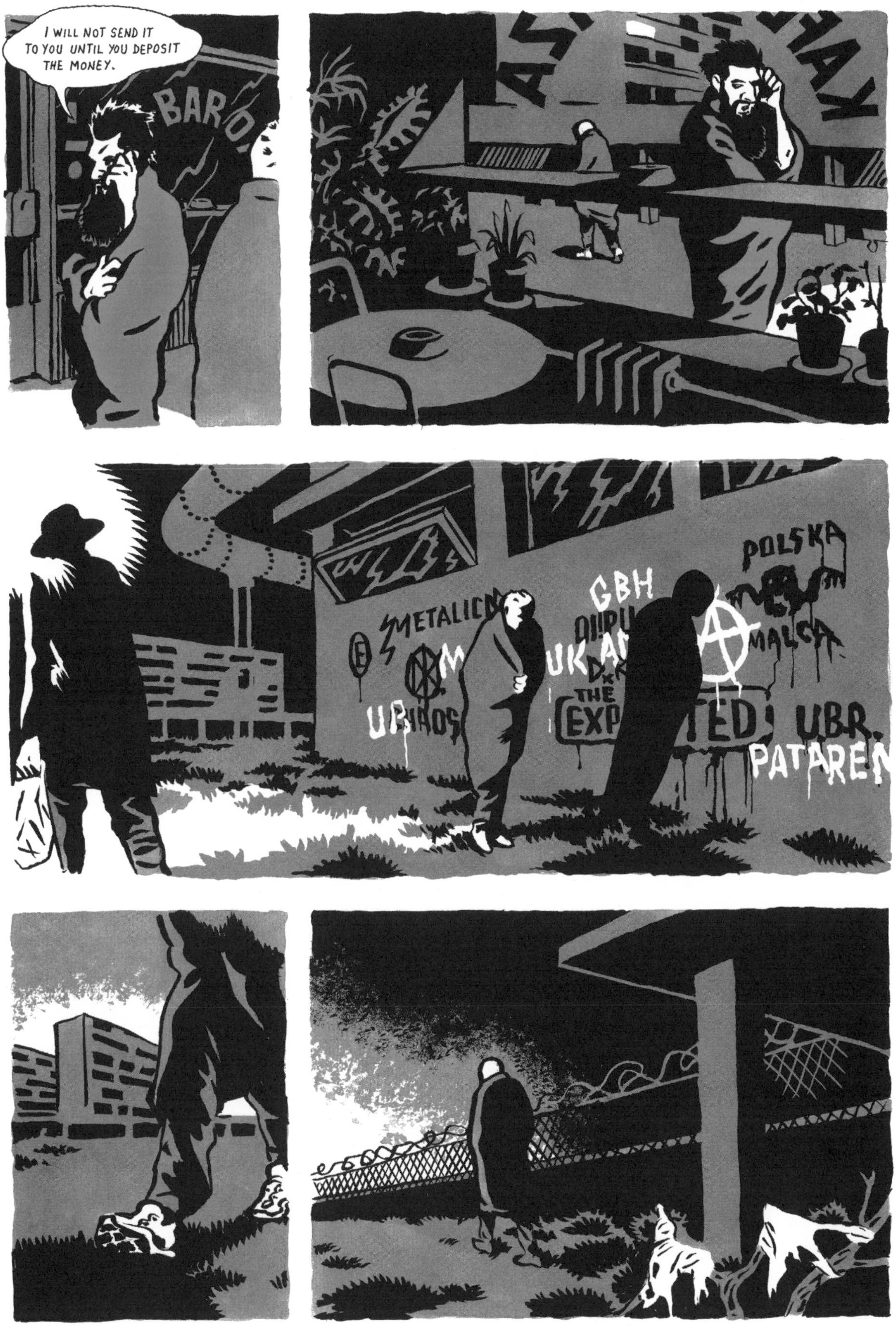
I WILL NOT SEND IT TO YOU UNTIL YOU DEPOSIT THE MONEY.
BAR
GBH
POLSKA
UBR.

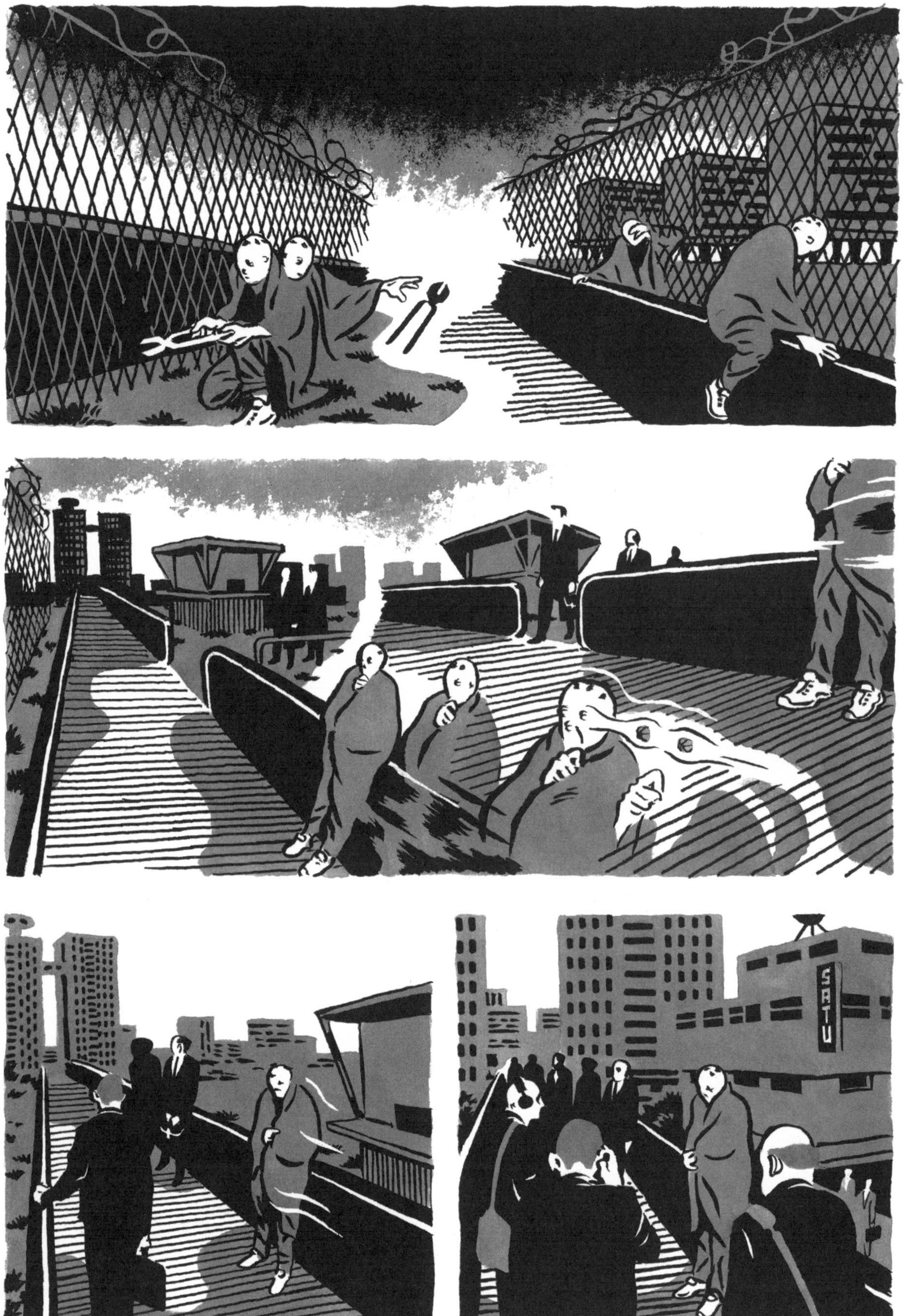
SATU

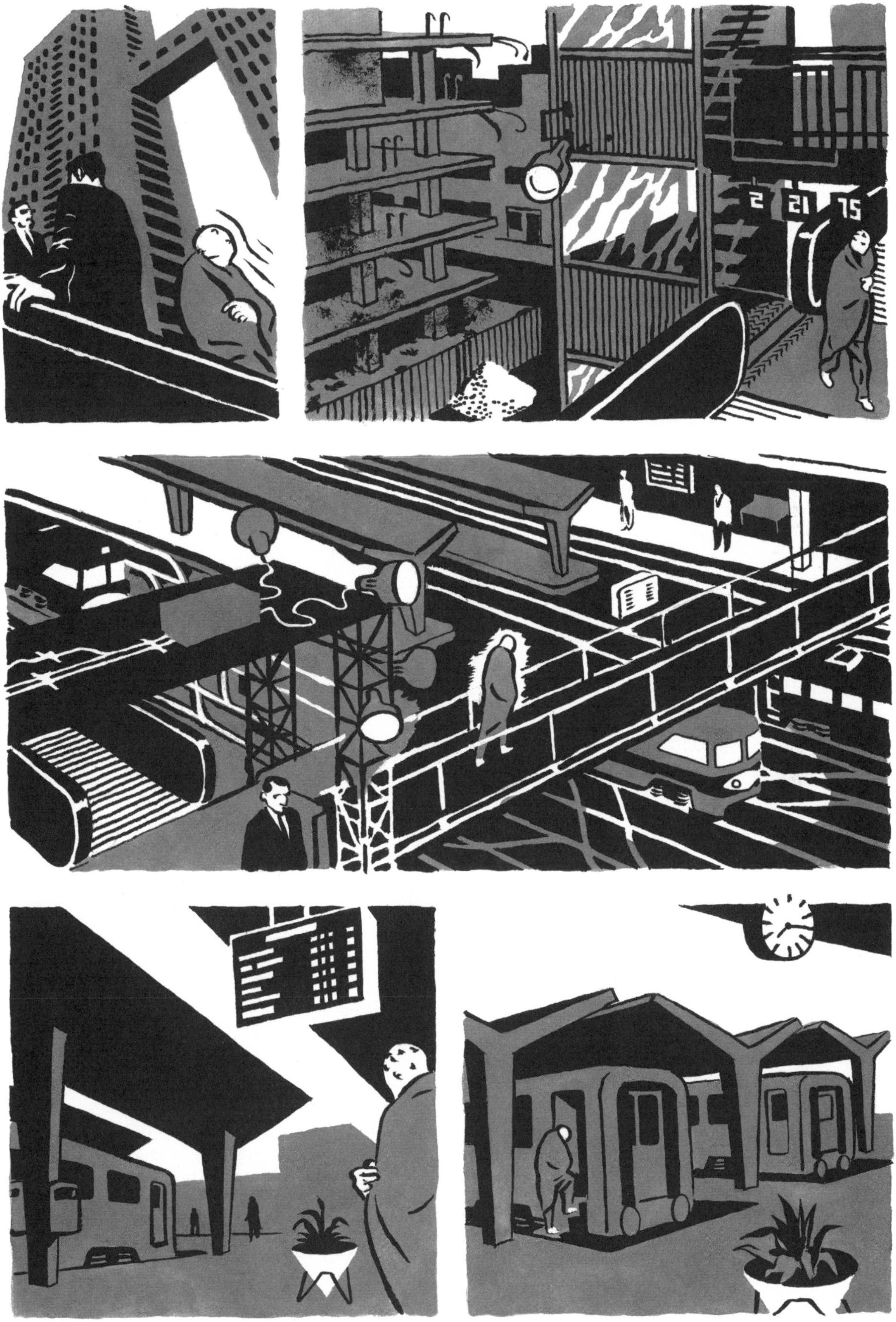
2
21
75

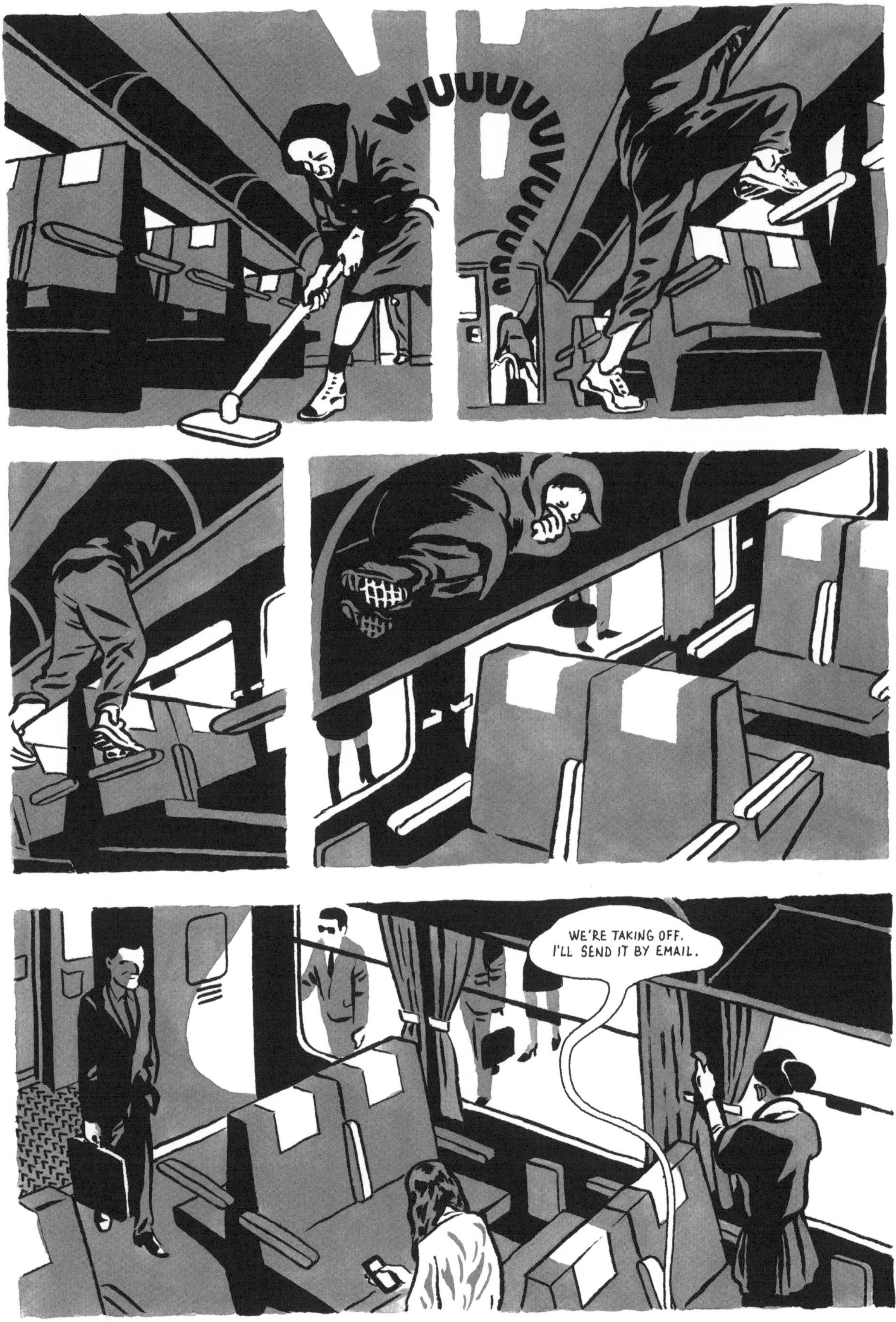
WUUUUUVUUUUU
WE'RE TAKING OFF. I'LL SEND IT BY EMAIL.

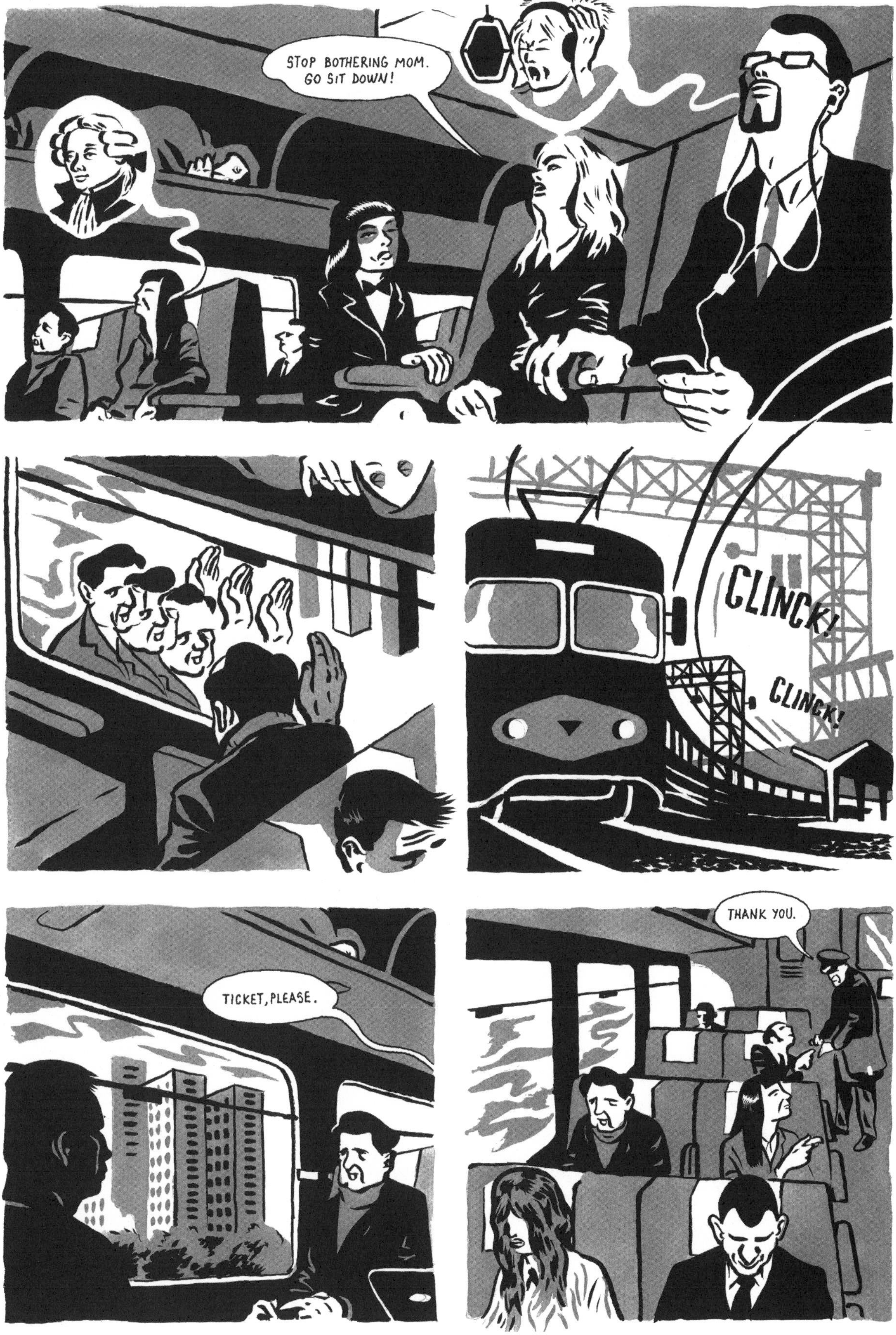
STOP BOTHERING MOM. GO SIT DOWN!
CLINCK!
CLINCK!
TICKET, PLEASE.
THANK YOU.

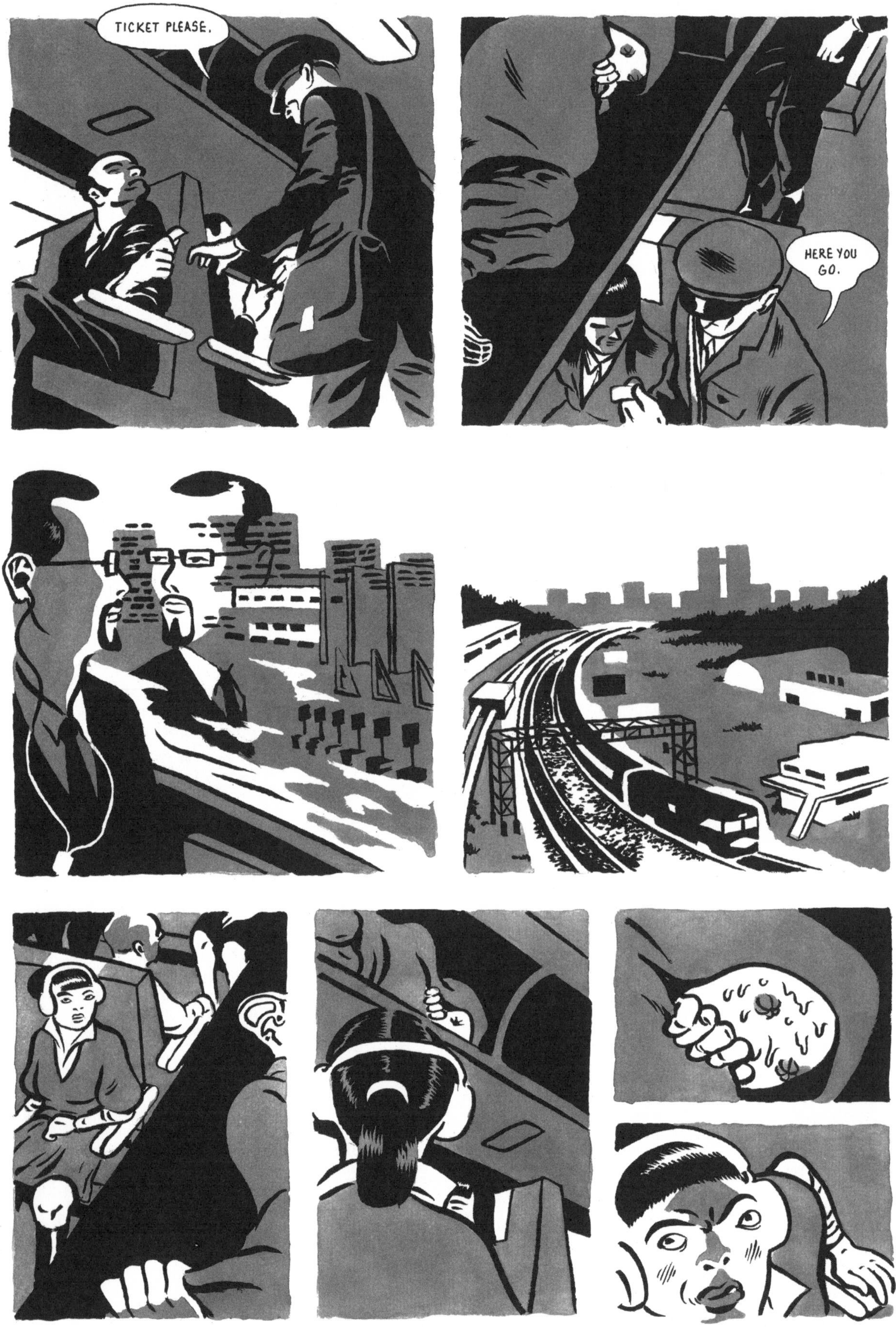
TICKET PLEASE.
HERE YOU GO.

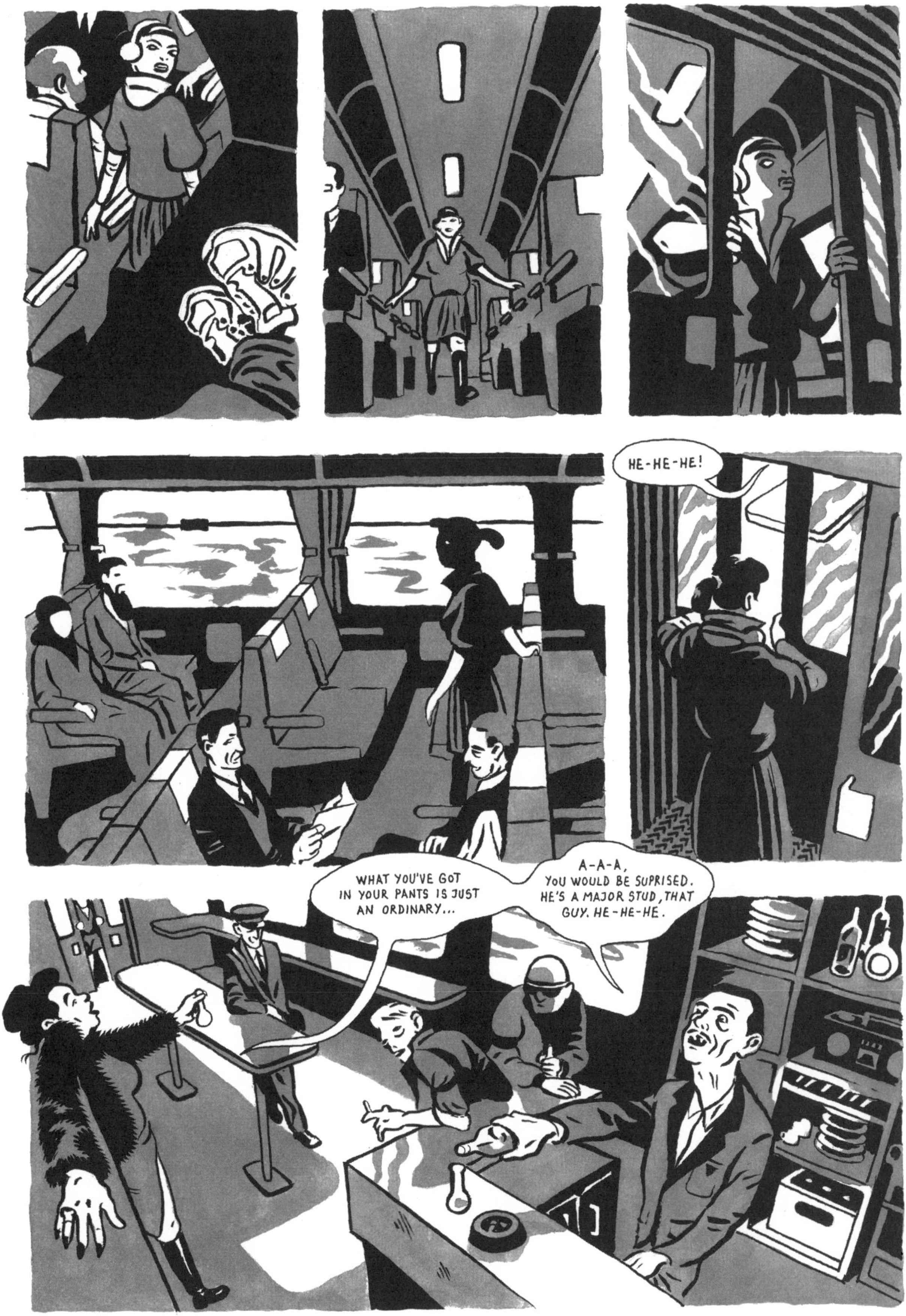
HE-HE-HE!
WHAT YOU'VE GOT IN YOUR PANTS IS JUST AN ORDINARY...
A-A-A, YOU WOULD BE SUPRISED. HE'S A MAJOR STUD, THAT GUY. HE-HE-HE.

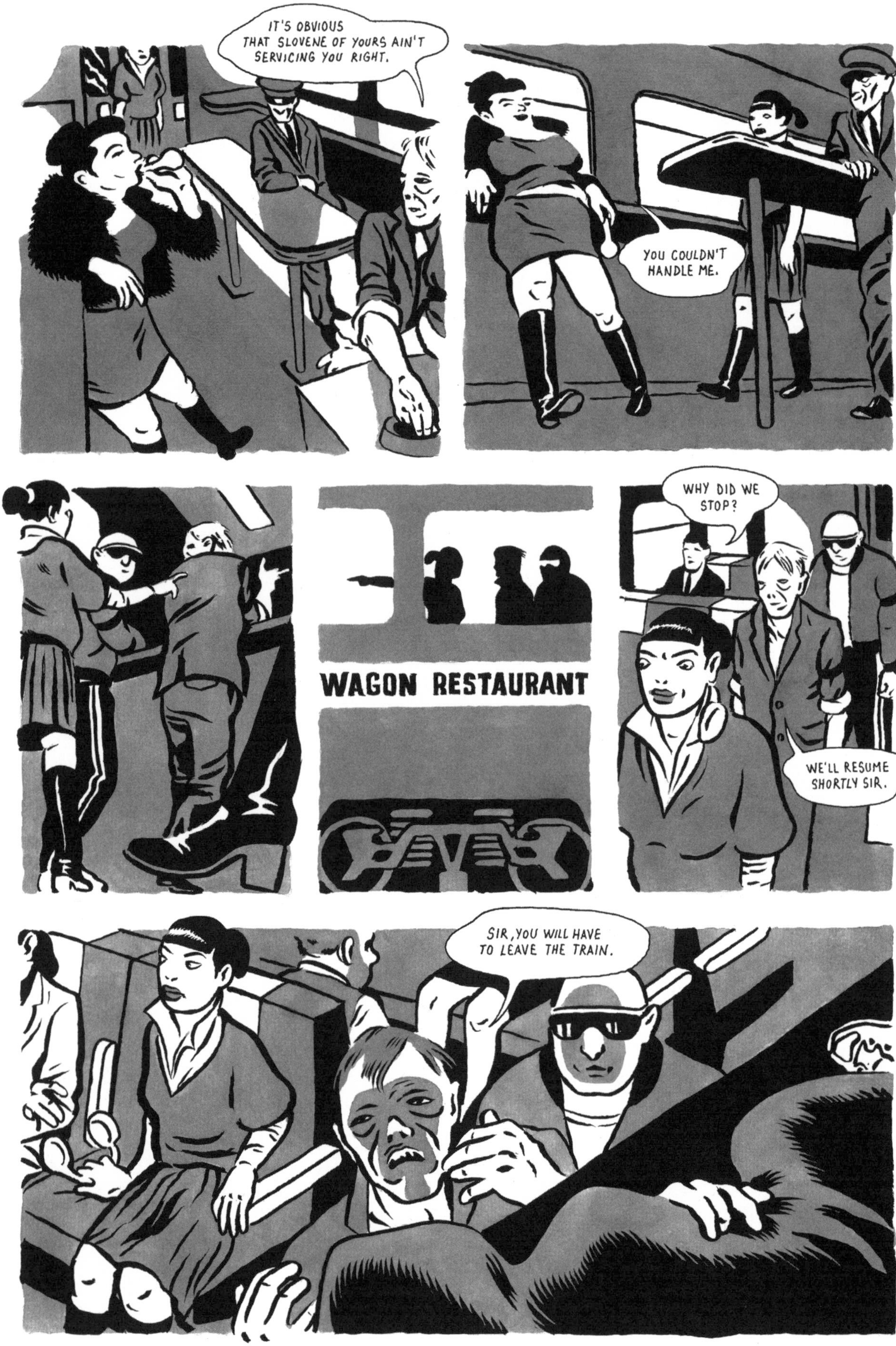
IT'S OBVIOUS THAT SLOVENE OF YOURS AIN'T SERVICING YOU RIGHT.
YOU COULDN'T HANDLE ME.
WAGON RESTAURANT
WHY DID WE STOP?
WE'LL RESUME SHORTLY SIR.
SIR, YOU WILL HAVE TO LEAVE THE TRAIN.

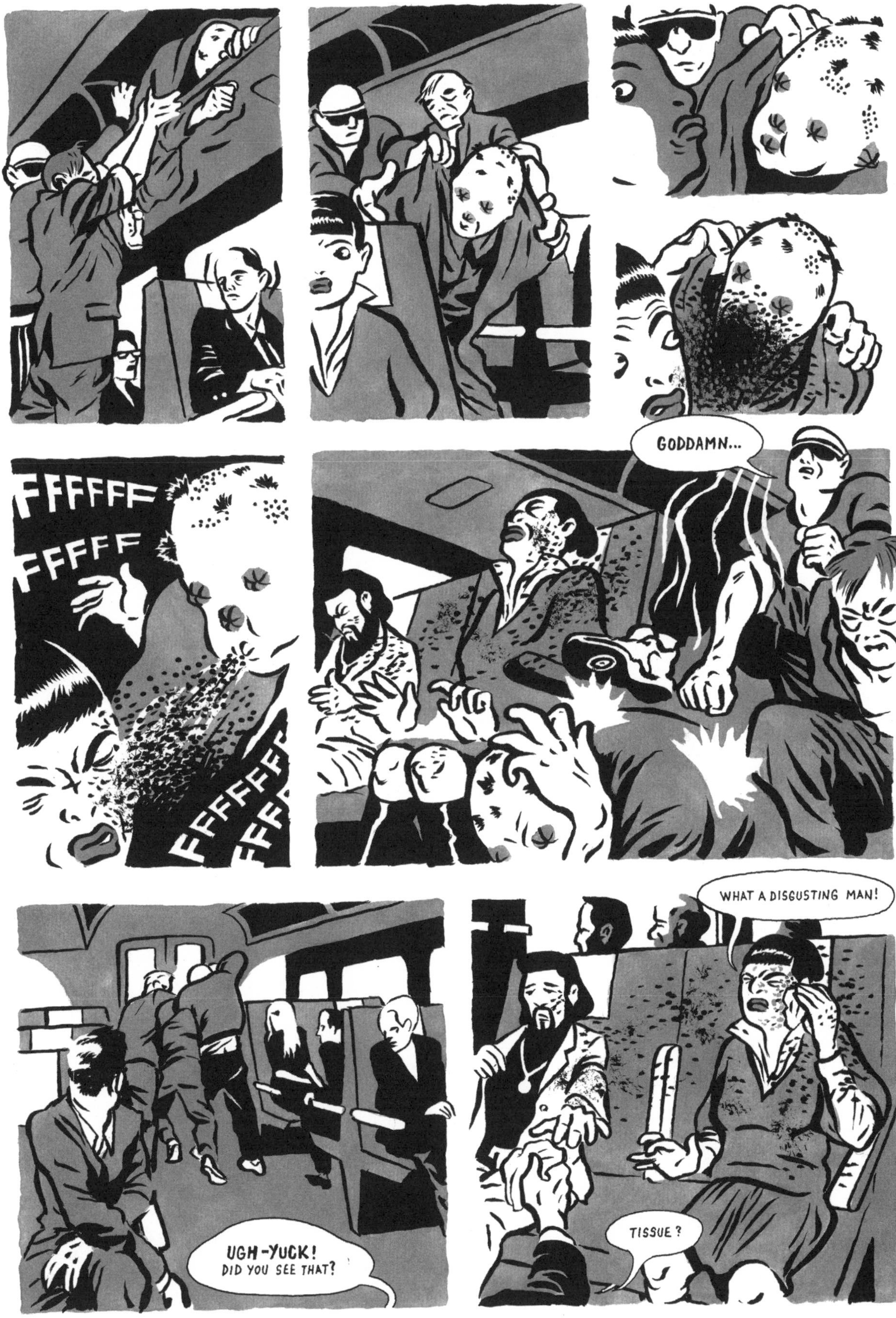
FFFFFF
FFFFF
FFFFFF
GODDAMN...
UGH-YUCK!
DID YOU SEE THAT?
WHAT A DISGUSTING MAN!
TISSUE?

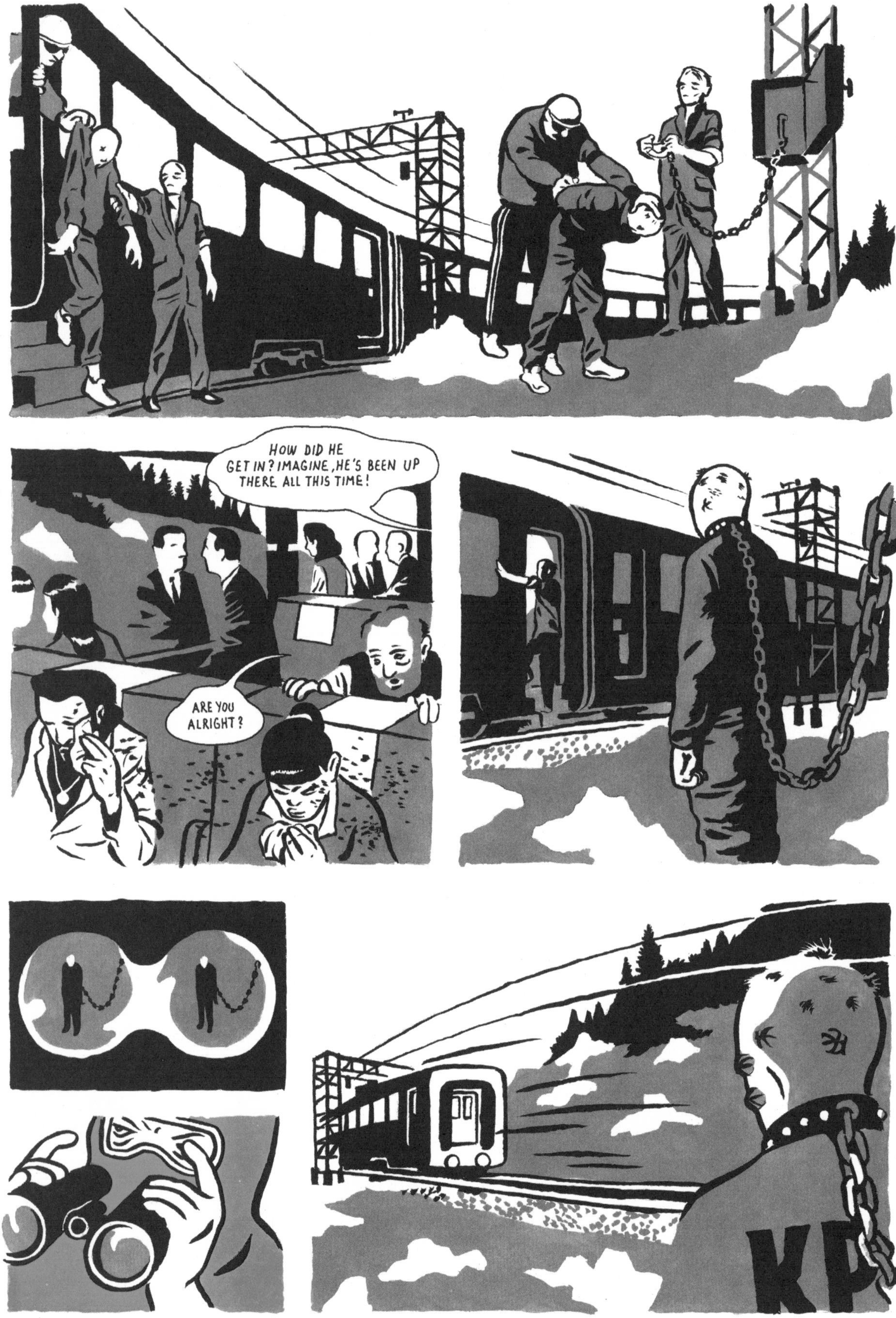
HOW DID HE GET IN? IMAGINE, HE'S BEEN UP THERE ALL THIS TIME!
ARE YOU ALRIGHT?
KP

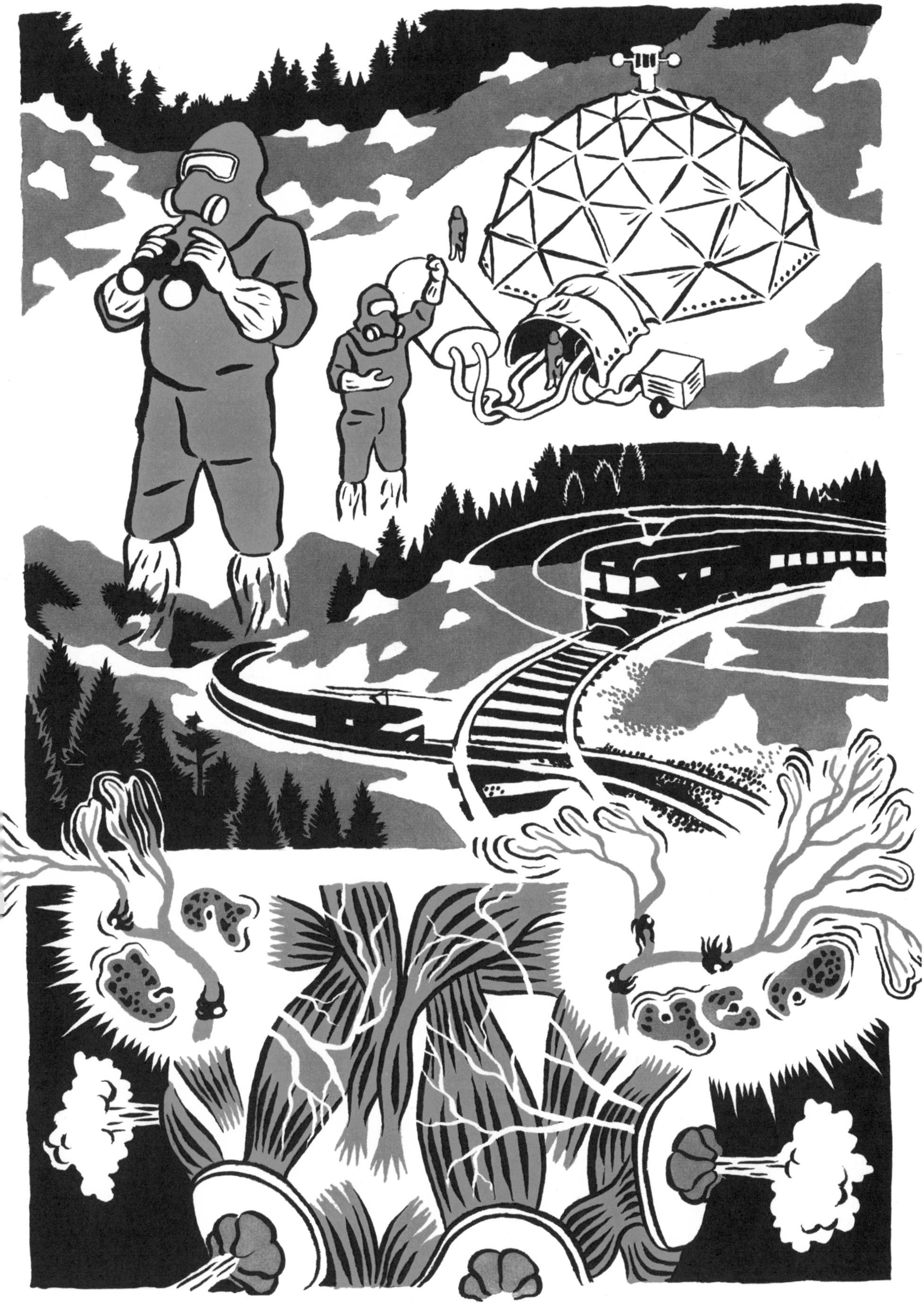

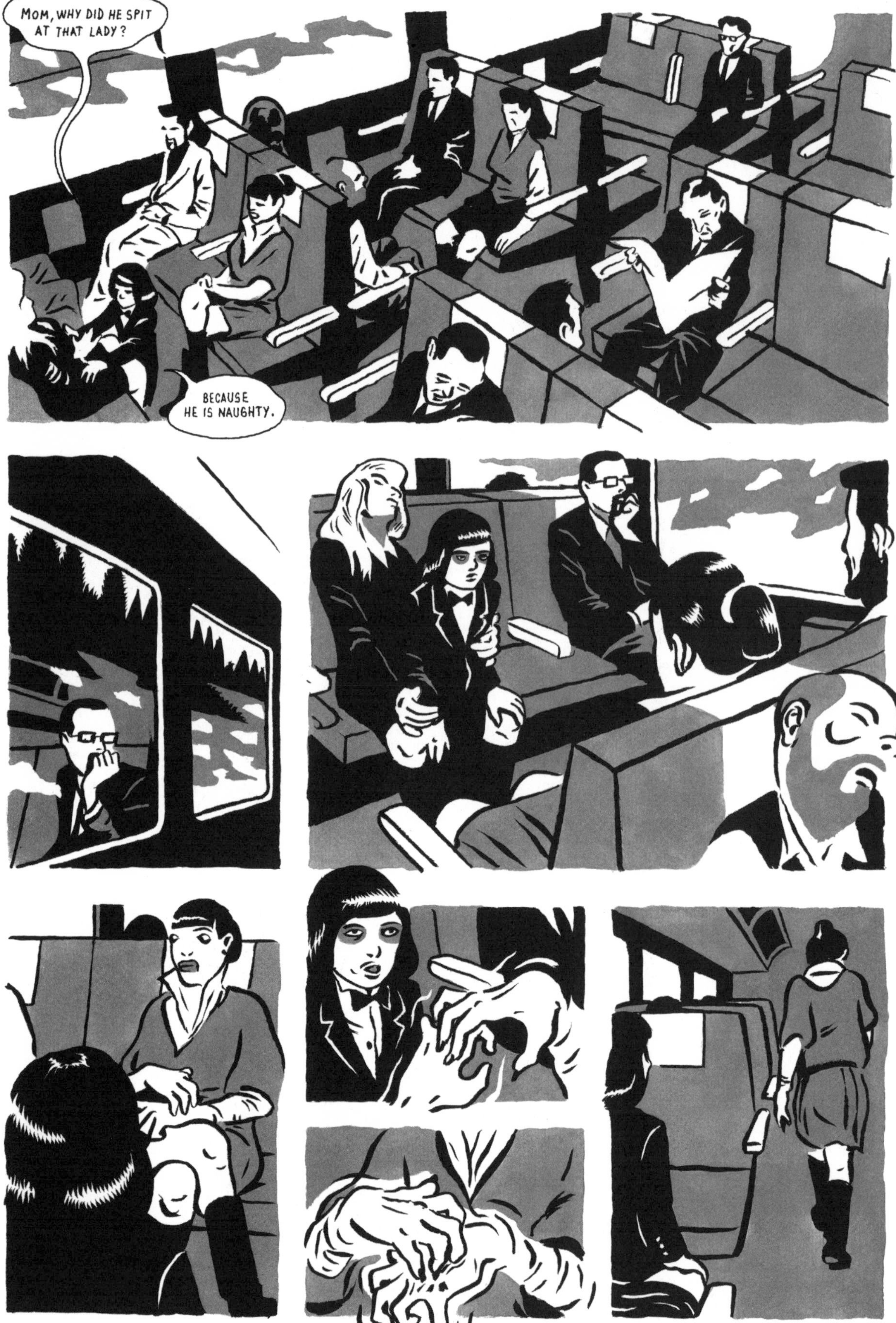
MOM, WHY DID HE SPIT AT THAT LADY?
BECAUSE HE IS NAUGHTY.

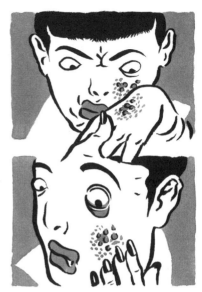

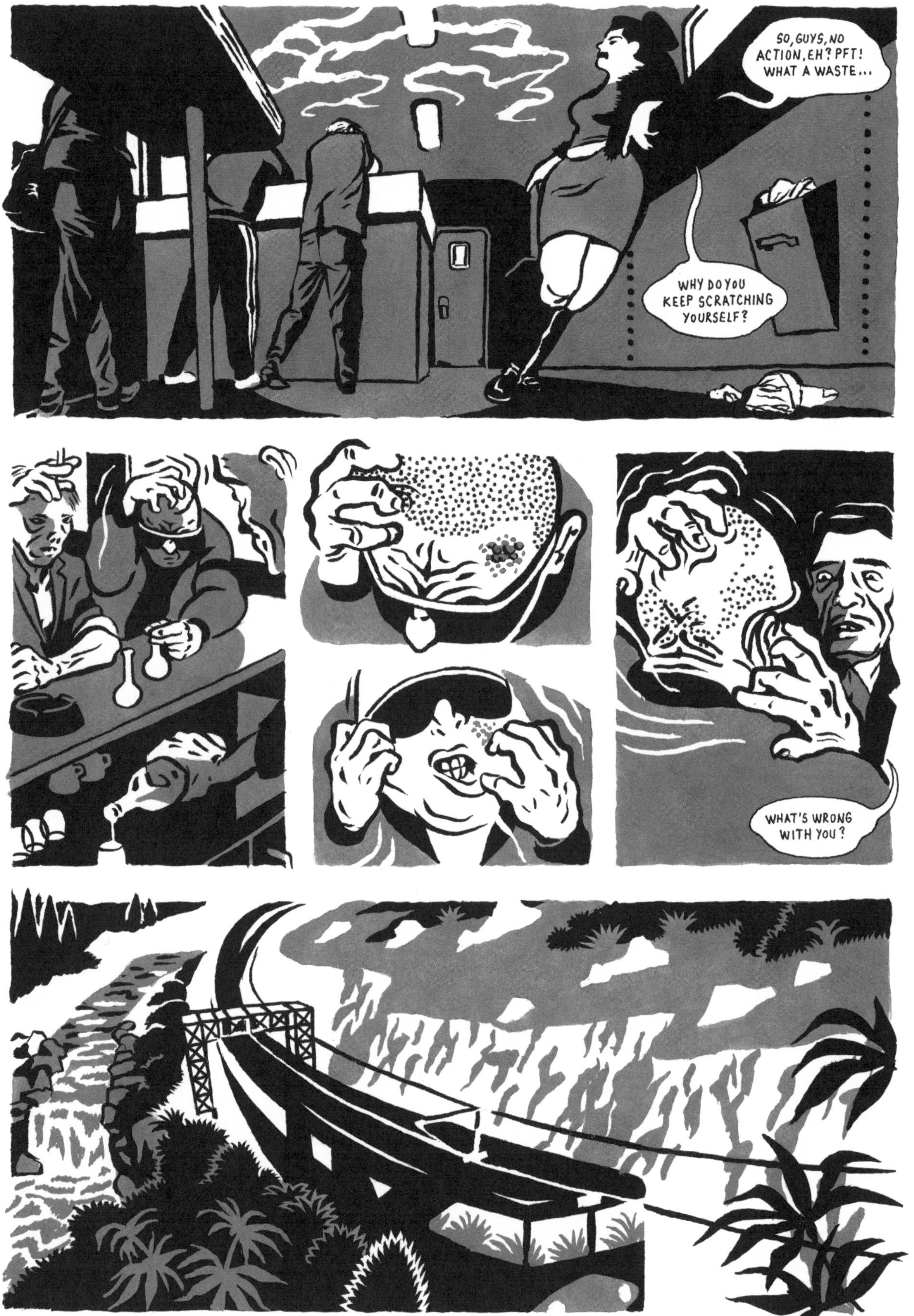
SO, GUYS, NO ACTION, EH? PFT! WHAT A WASTE...
WHY DO YOU KEEP SCRATCHING YOURSELF?
WHAT'S WRONG WITH YOU?

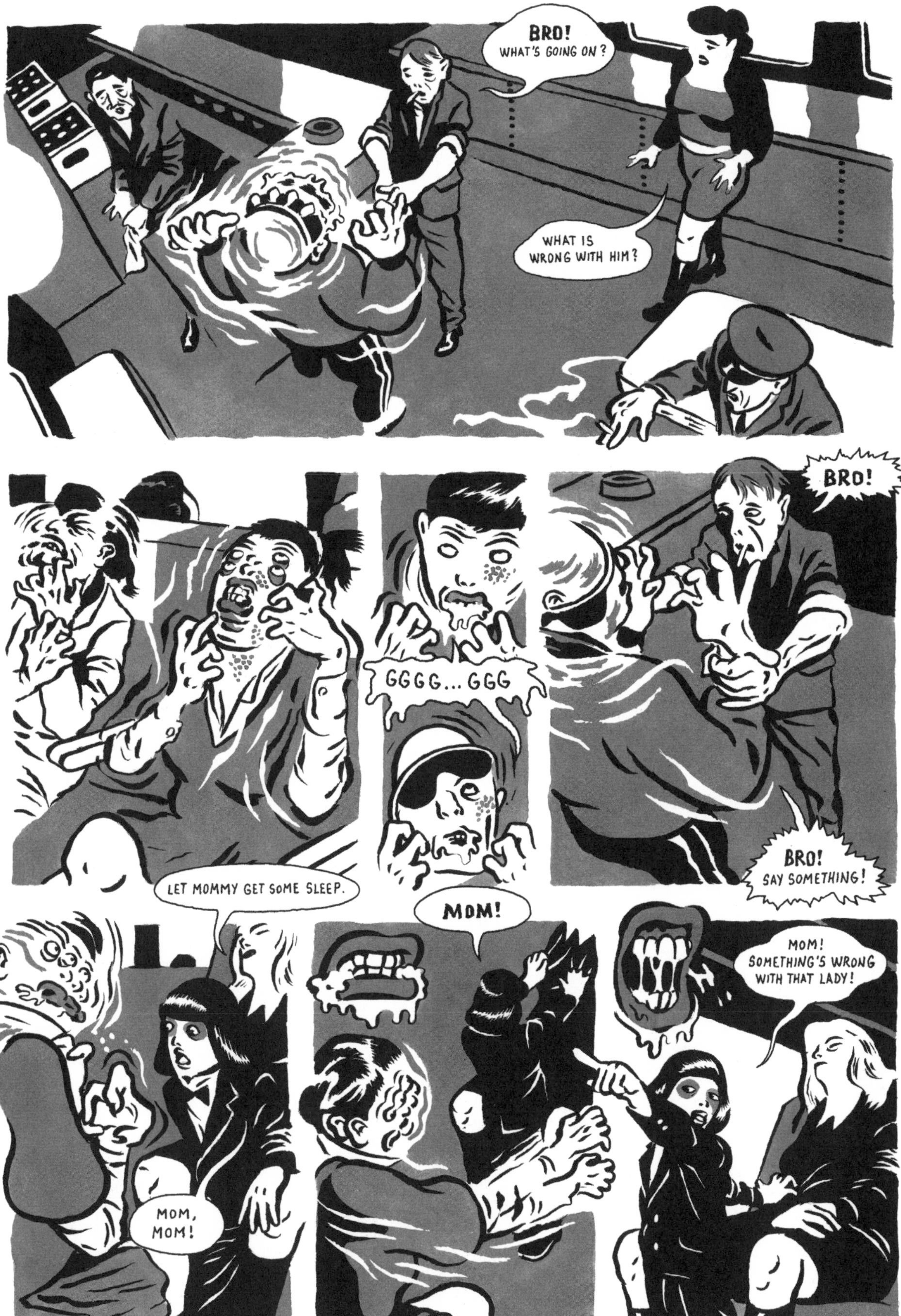
BRO! WHAT'S GOING ON?
WHAT IS WRONG WITH HIM?
GGGG... GGG
BRO!
BRO! SAY SOMETHING!
LET MOMMY GET SOME SLEEP.
MOM, MOM!
MOM!
MOM! SOMETHING'S WRONG WITH THAT LADY!

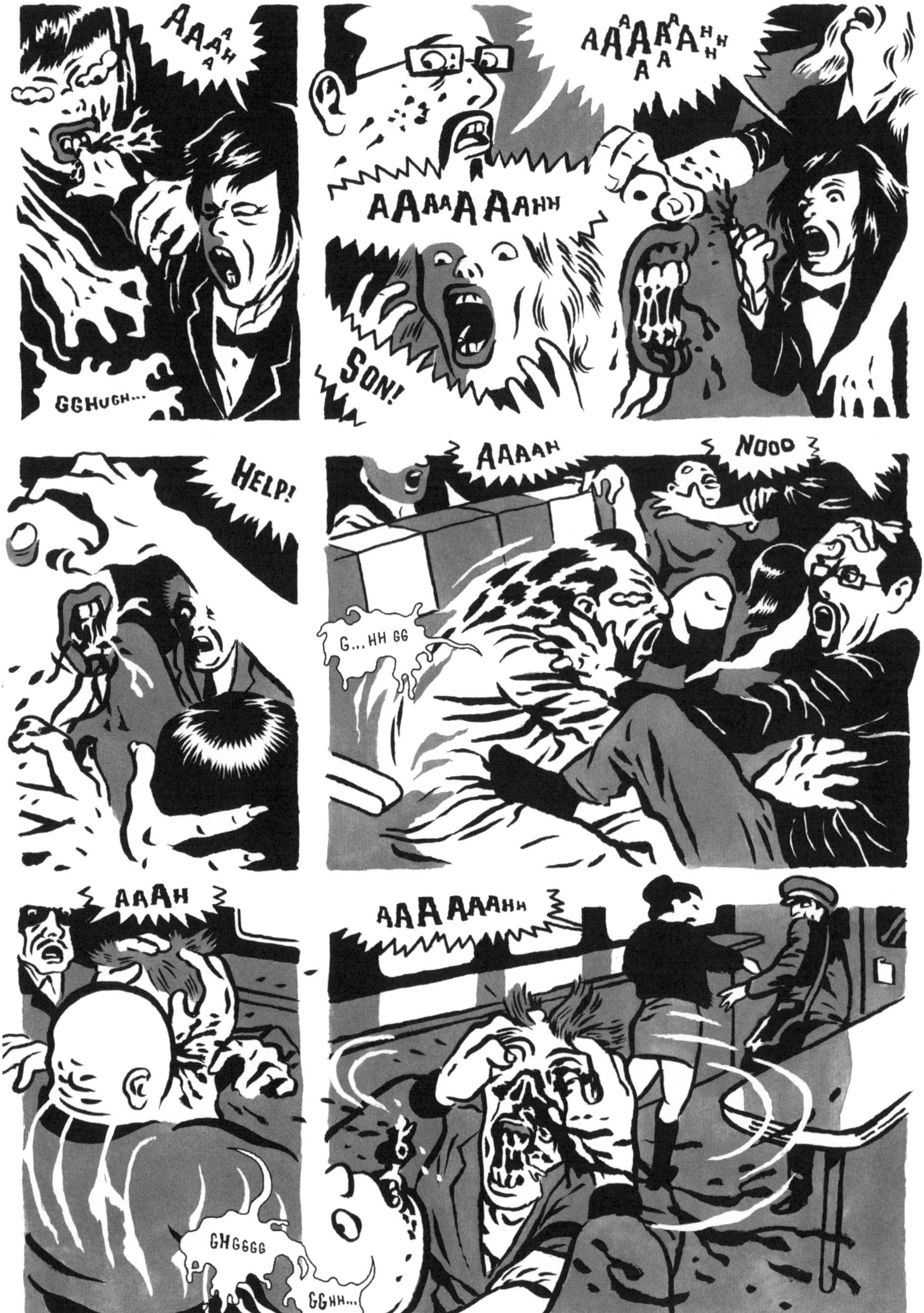

AAAAH
GGHUGH...
AAAAAAAHHH
AAAAAAAHH
SON!
HELP!
AAAAH
NOOO
G...HH GG
AAAH
AAAAAAAHH
GHGGGG
GGHH...

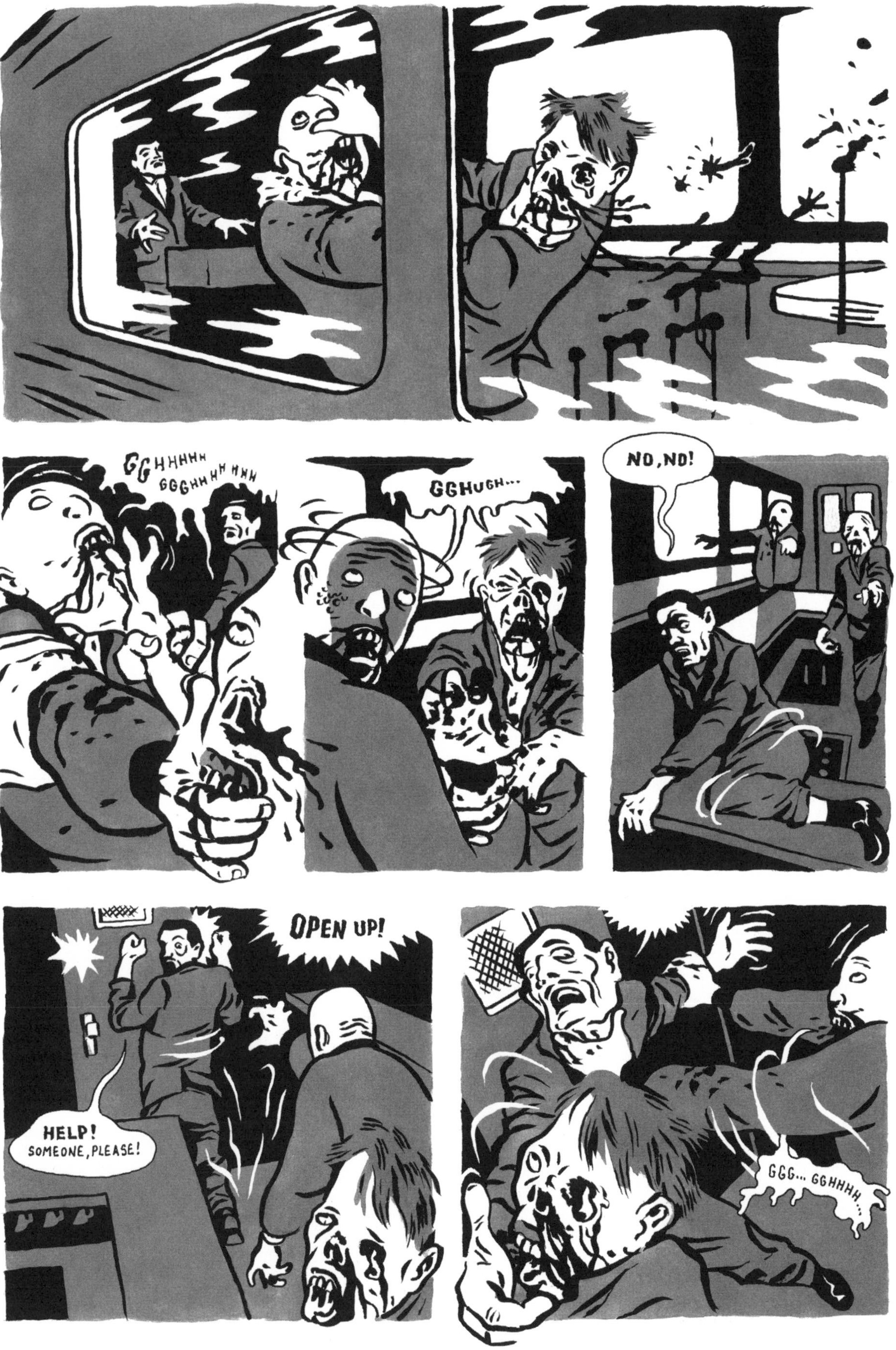
GGHHHHH GGGHHHHHHHH
GGHUGH...
NO, NO!
OPEN UP!
HELP! SOMEONE, PLEASE!
GGG... GGHHHH...

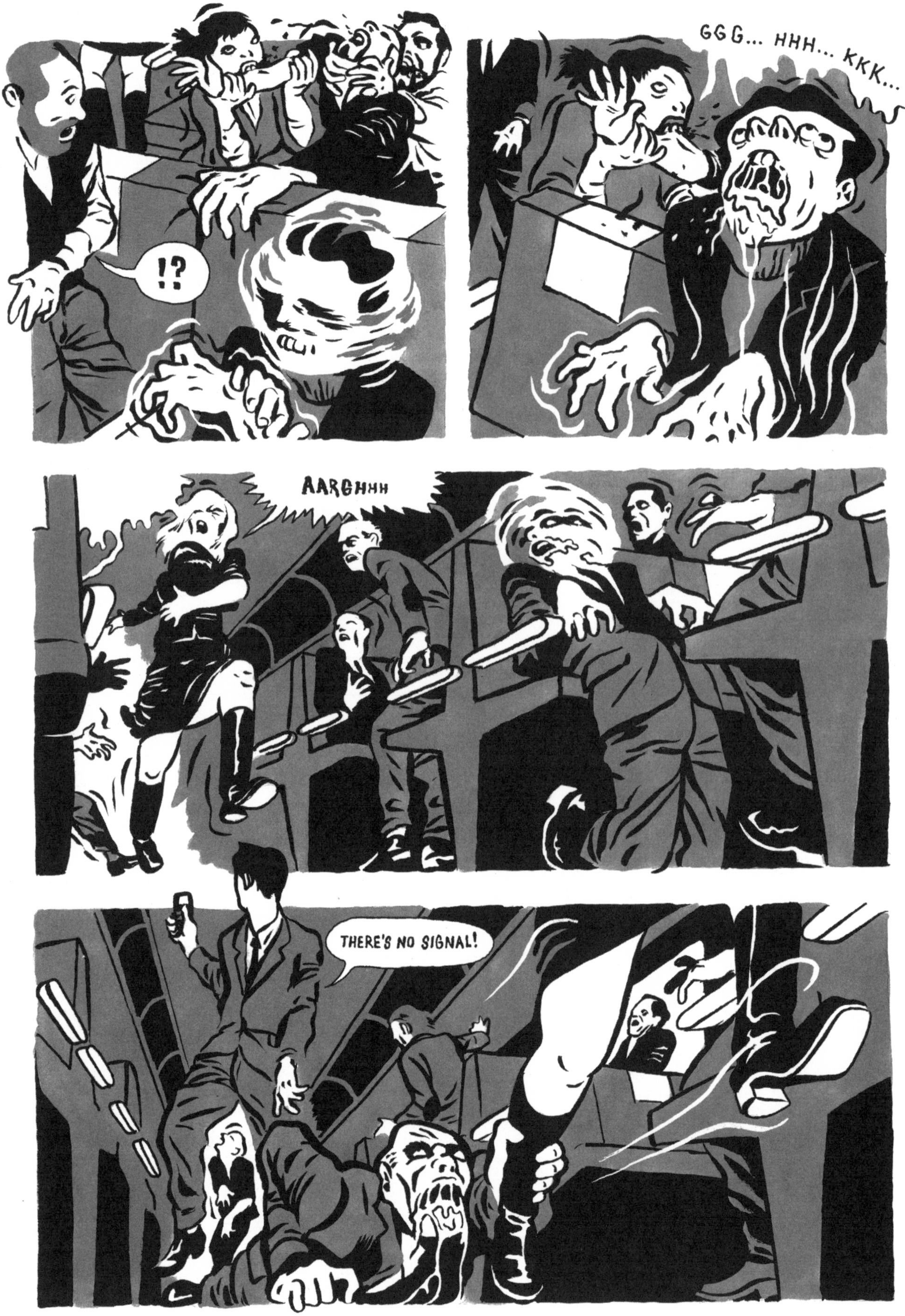
!?
GGG... HHH... KKK...
AARGHHH
THERE'S NO SIGNAL!

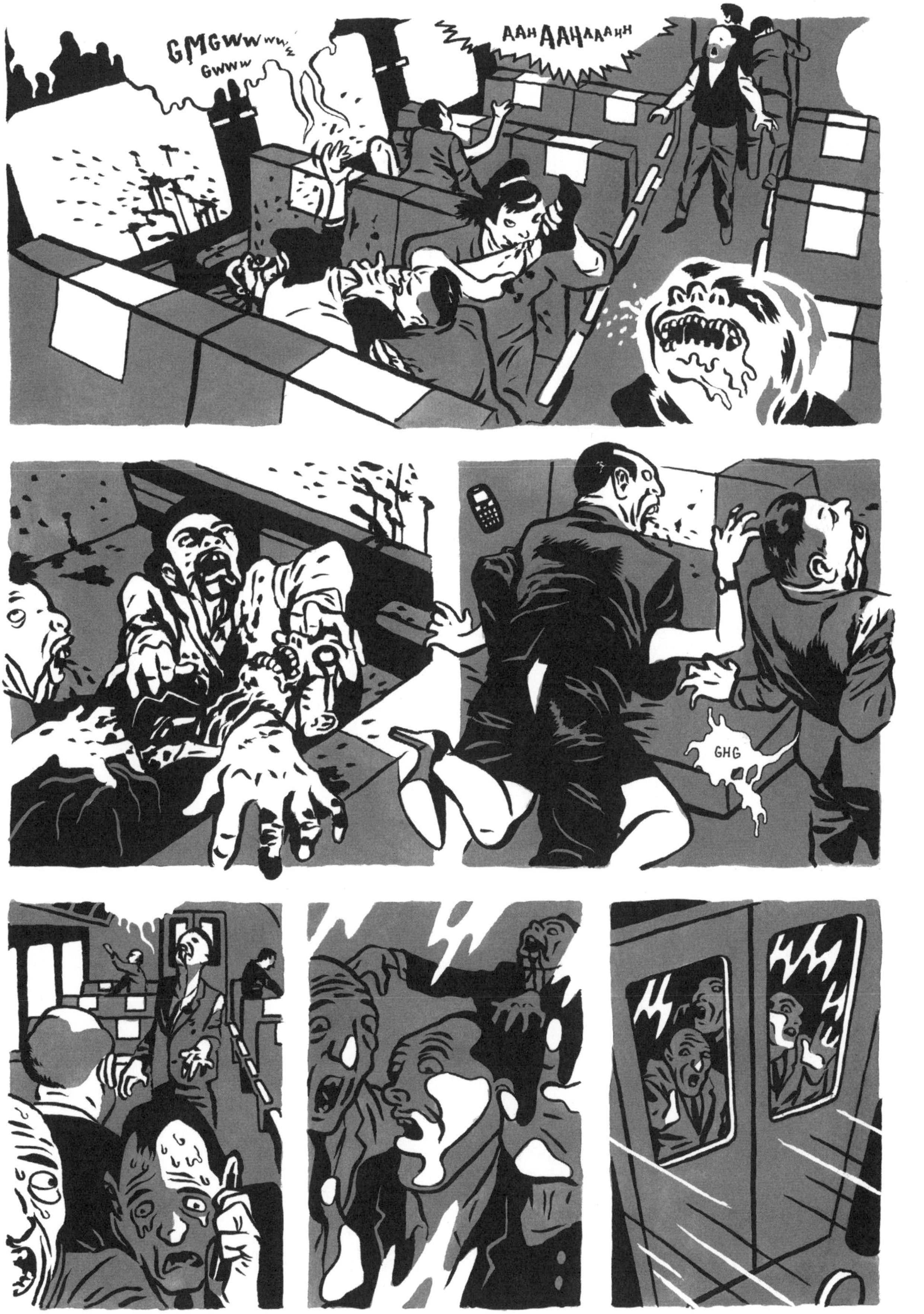
GMGWWwww
GWWW
AAHAAHAAAHH
GHG

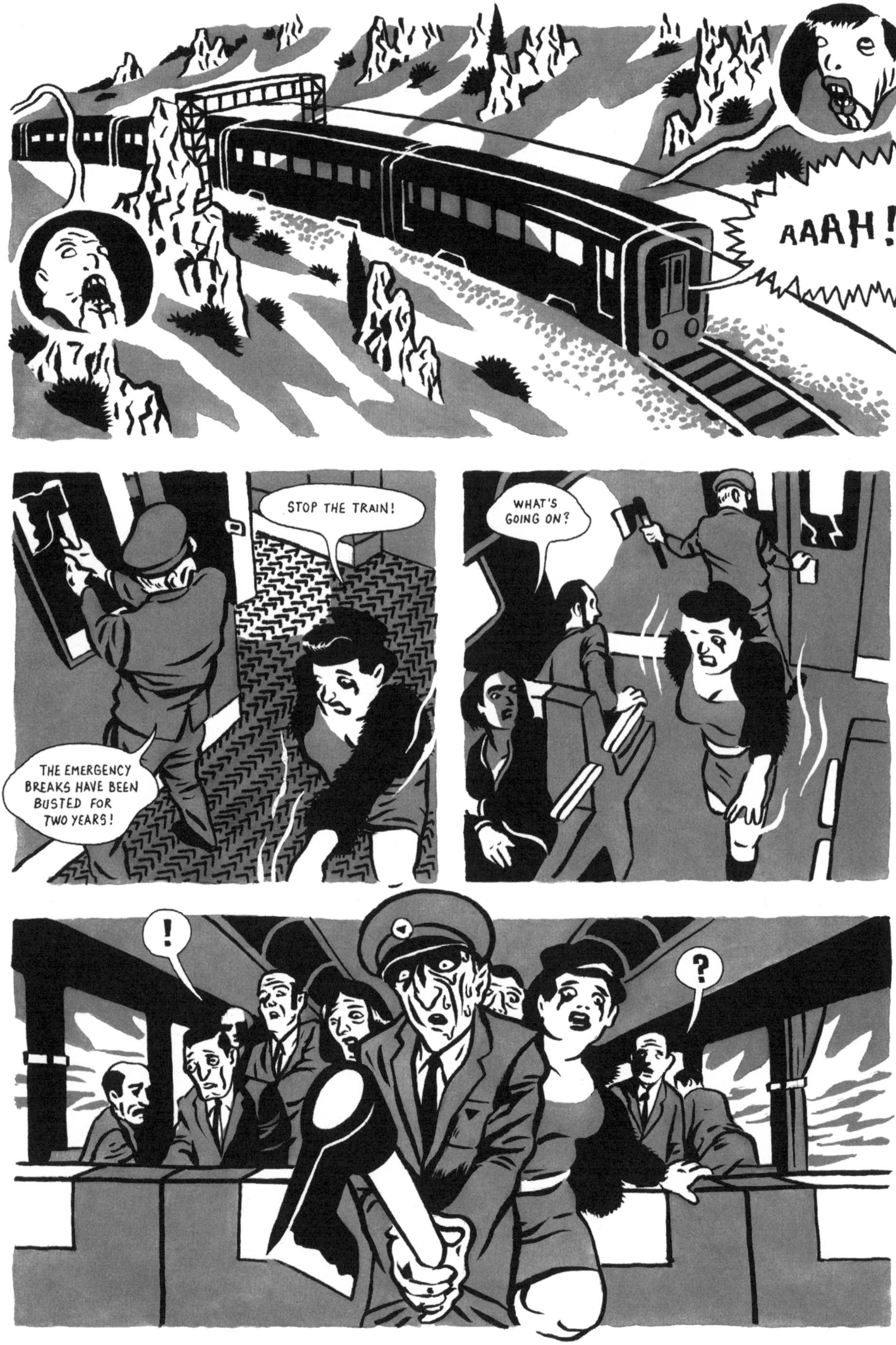
AAAH!
STOP THE TRAIN!
THE EMERGENCY BREAKS HAVE BEEN BUSTED FOR TWO YEARS!
WHAT'S GOING ON?
!
?

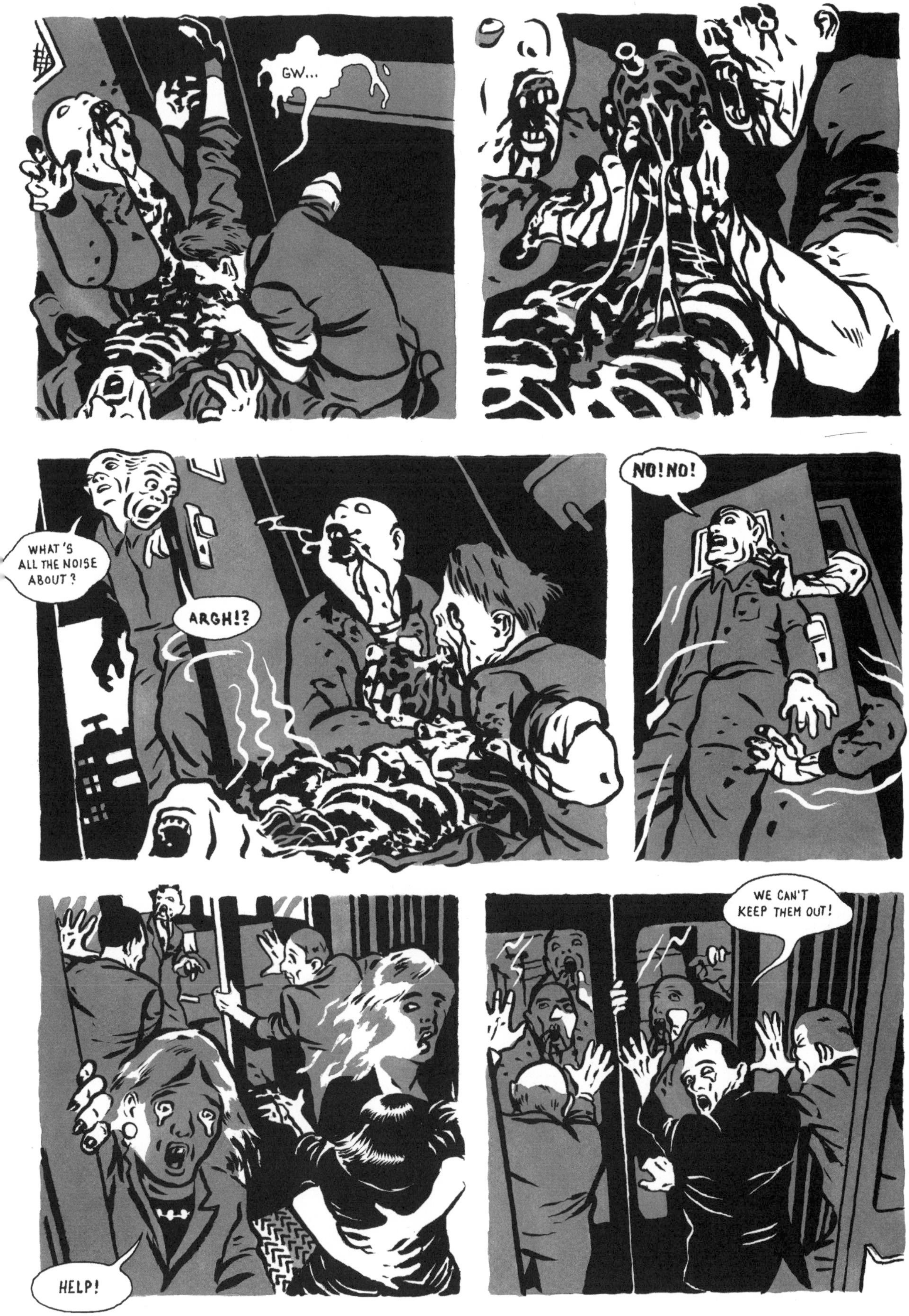
GW...
WHAT'S ALL THE NOISE ABOUT?
ARGH!?
NO! NO!
HELP!
WE CAN'T KEEP THEM OUT!

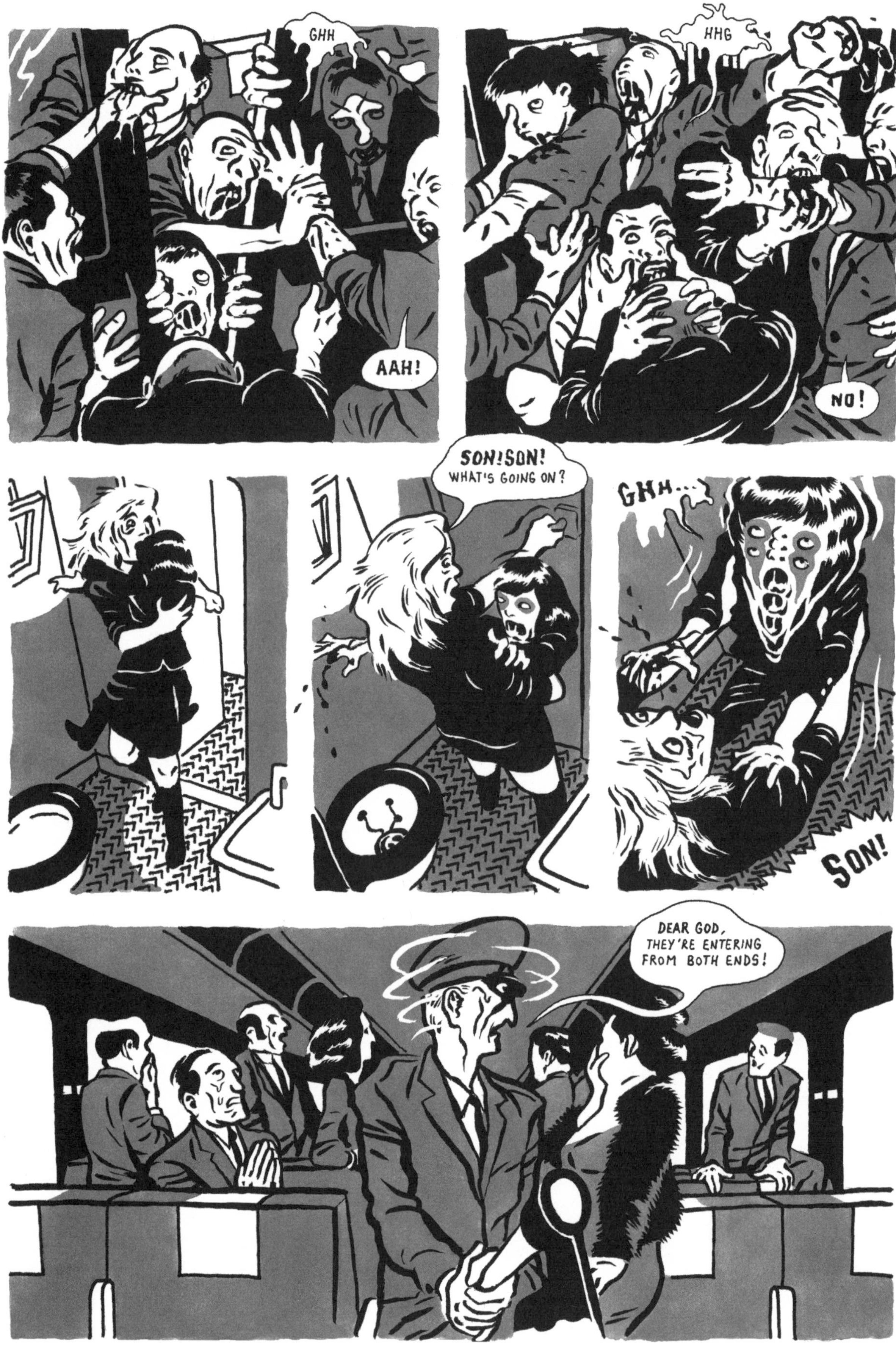
GHH
AAH!
HHG
NO!
SON! SON!
WHAT'S GOING ON?
GHH...
SON!
DEAR GOD, THEY'RE ENTERING FROM BOTH ENDS!

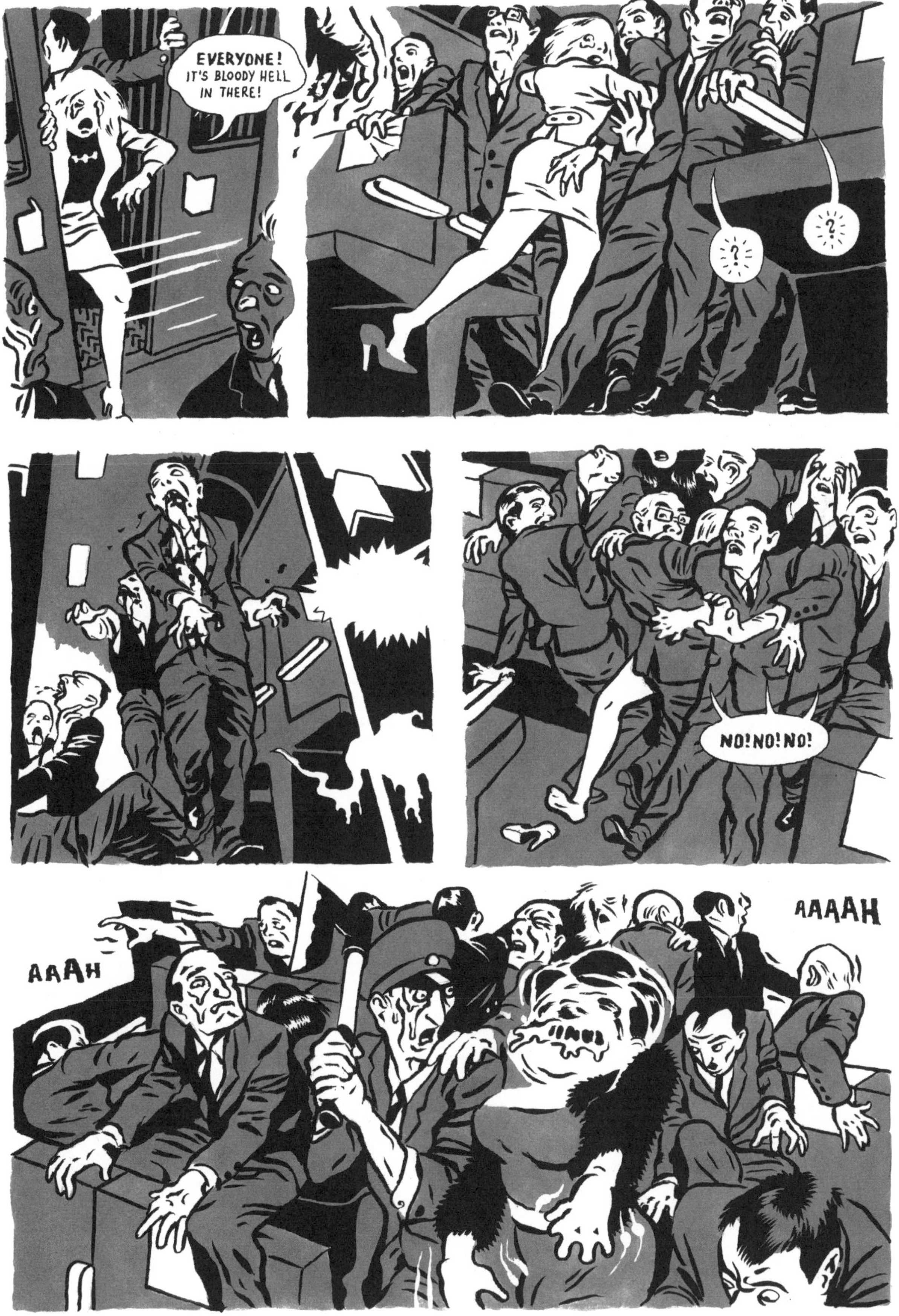
EVERYONE! IT'S BLOODY HELL IN THERE!
?
?
NO! NO! NO!
AAAH
AAAAH

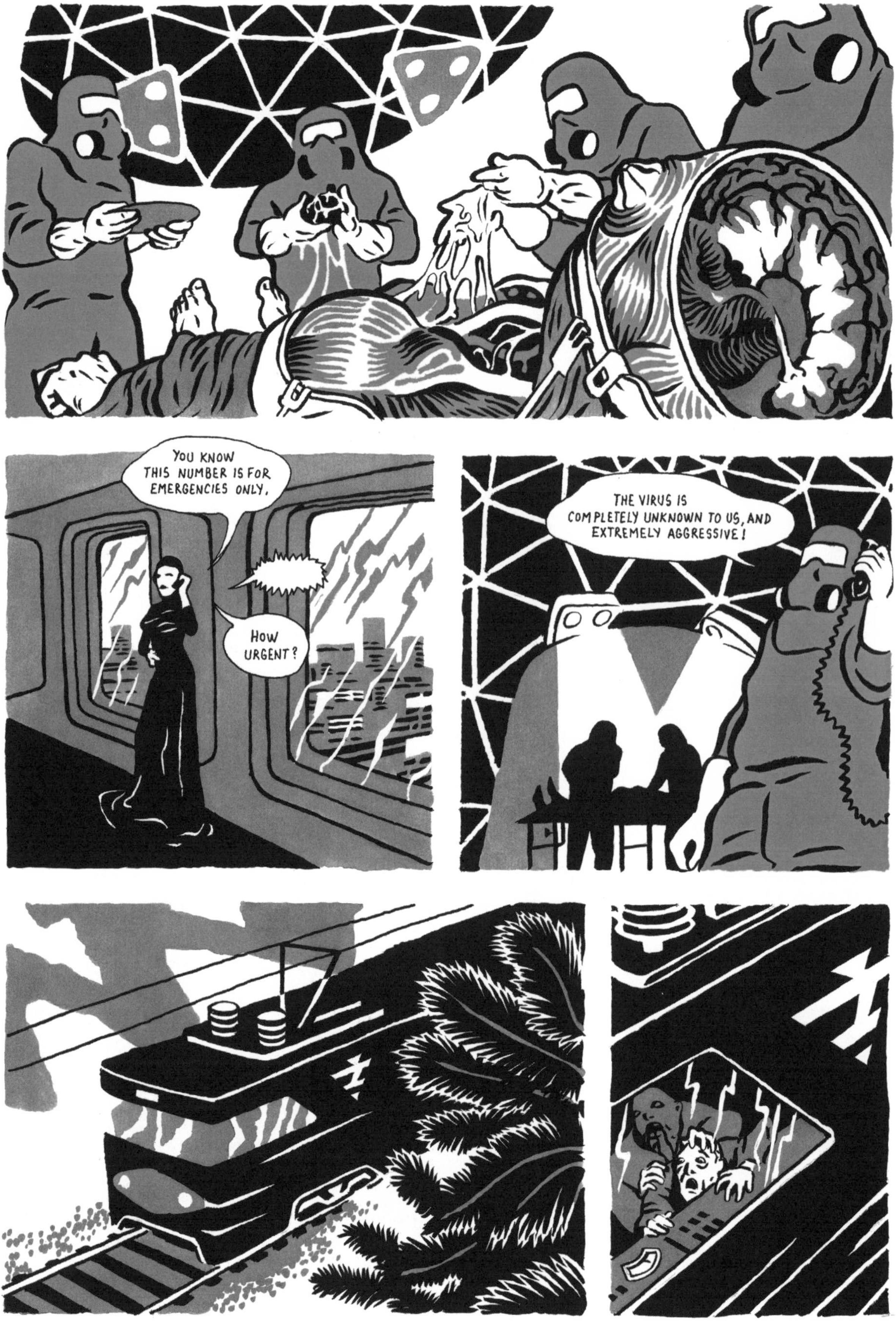
YOU KNOW THIS NUMBER IS FOR EMERGENCIES ONLY.
HOW URGENT?
THE VIRUS IS COMPLETELY UNKNOWN TO US, AND EXTREMELY AGGRESSIVE!

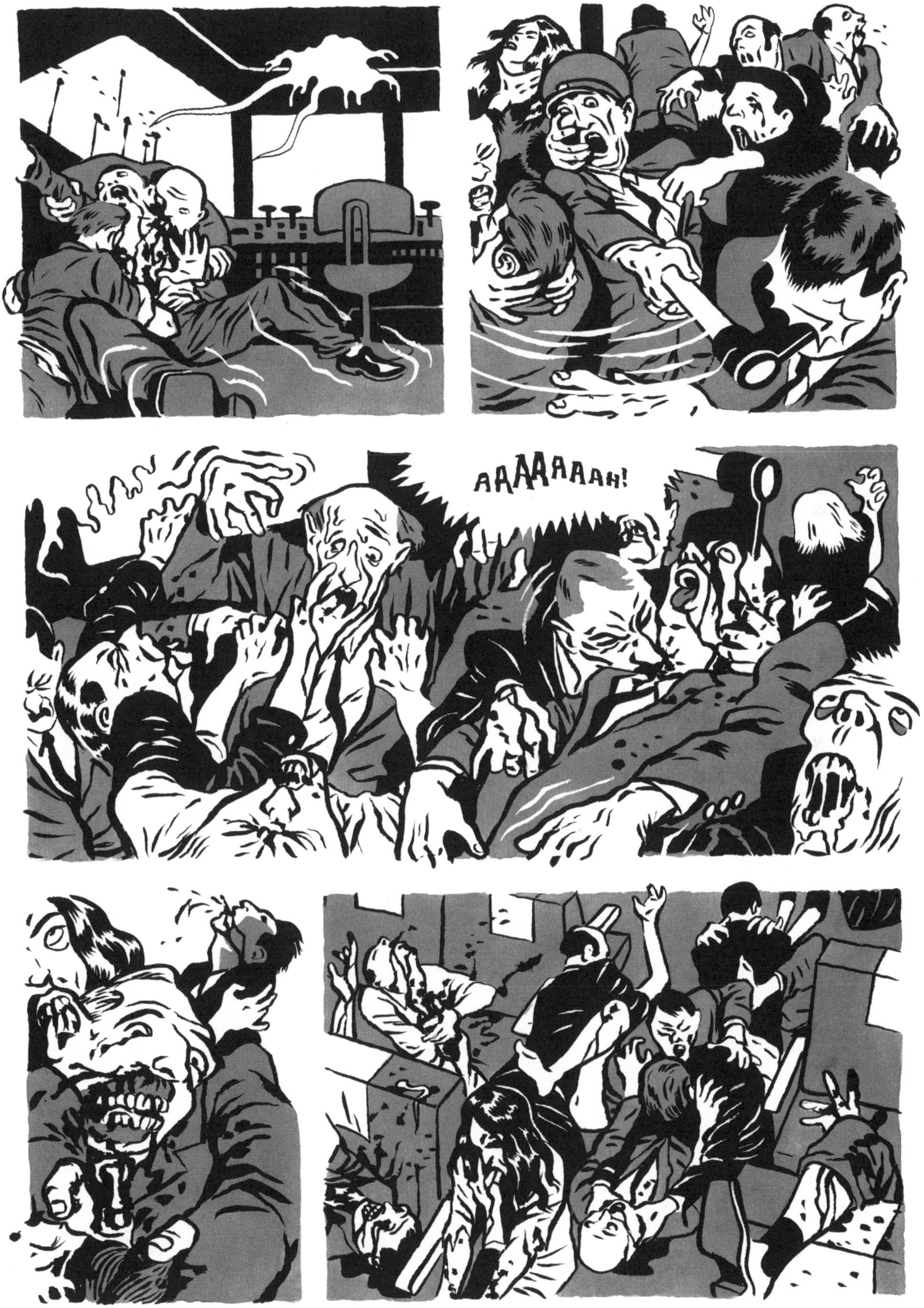
AAAAAAAH!

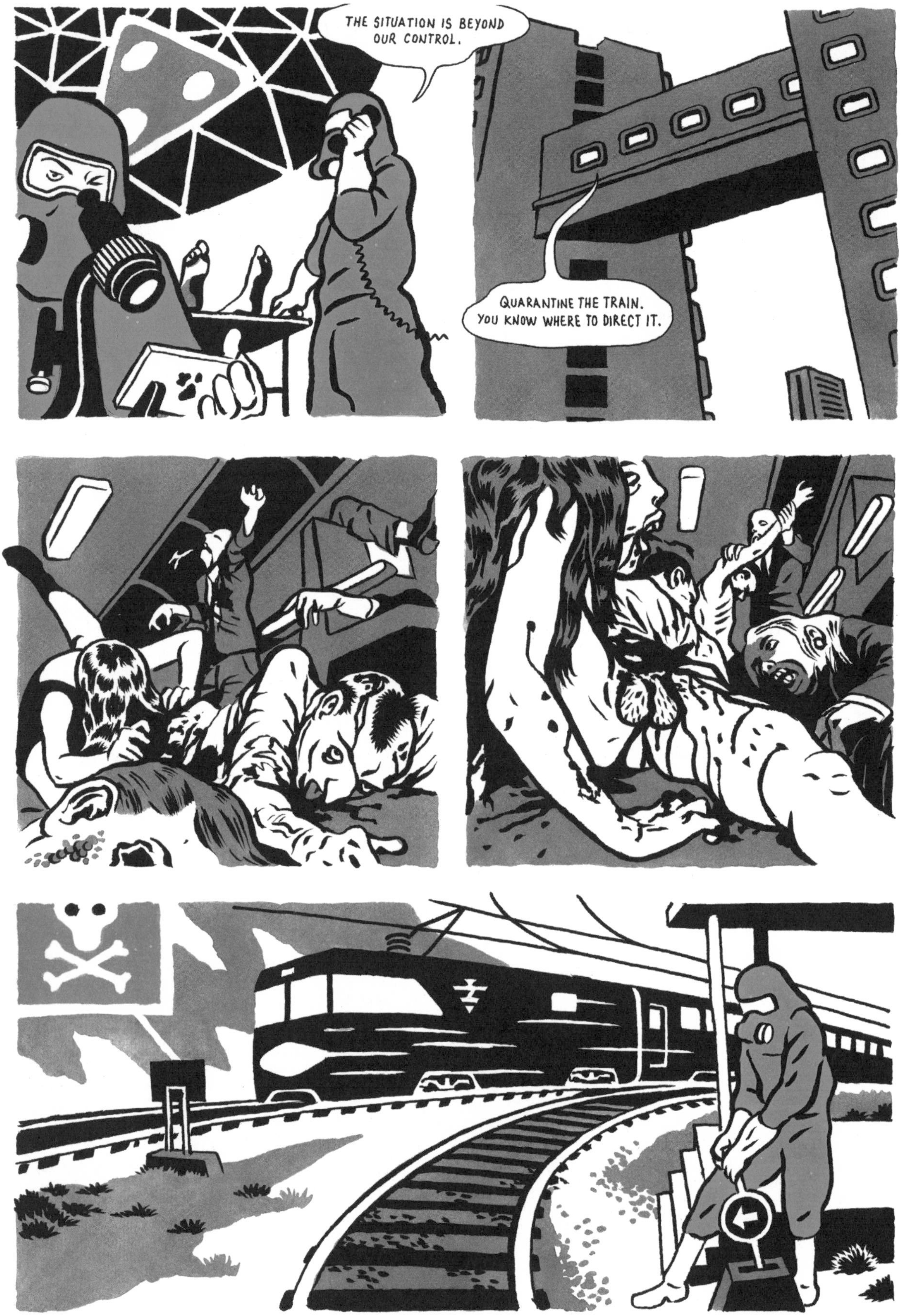
THE SITUATION IS BEYOND OUR CONTROL.
QUARANTINE THE TRAIN. YOU KNOW WHERE TO DIRECT IT.

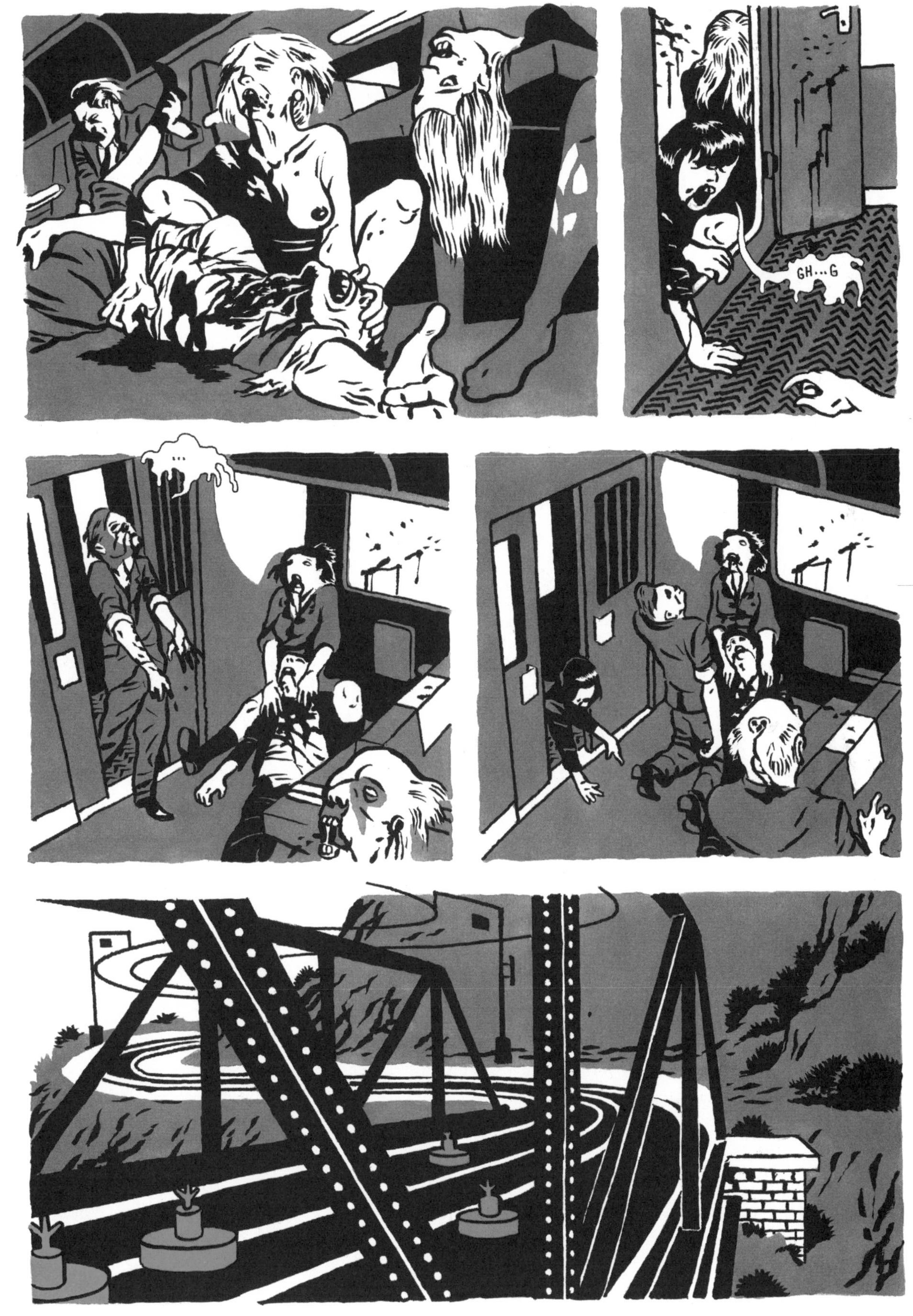
GH...G
...

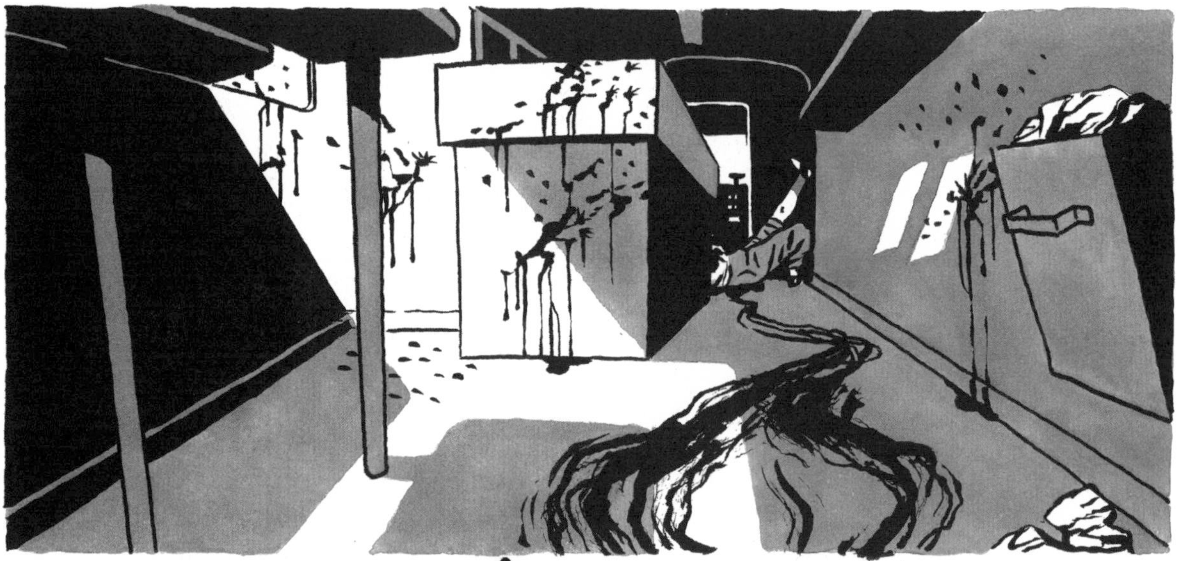

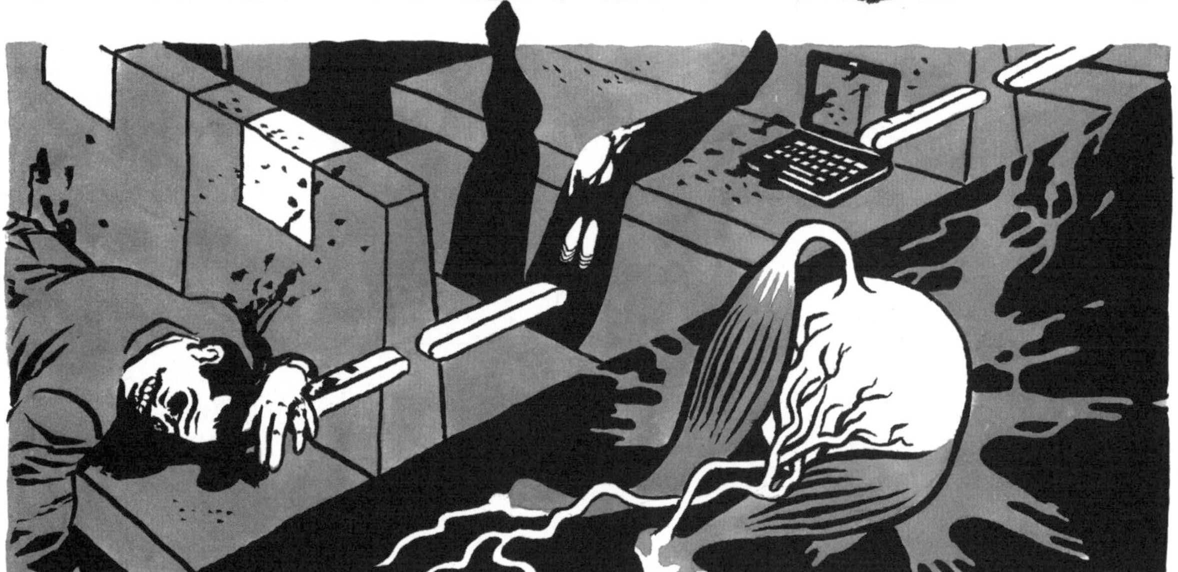

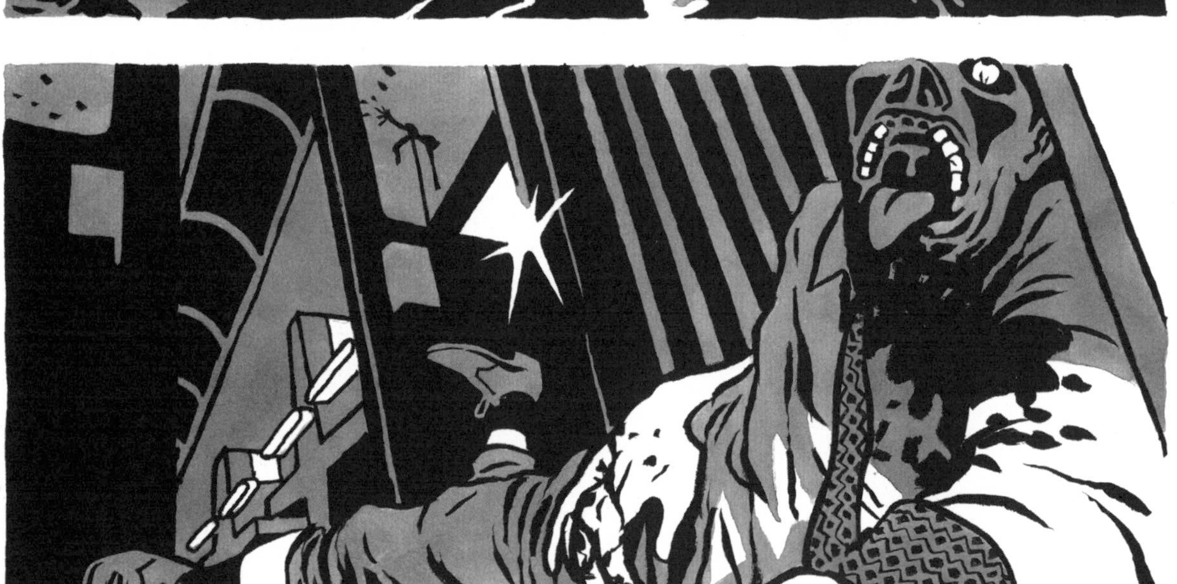

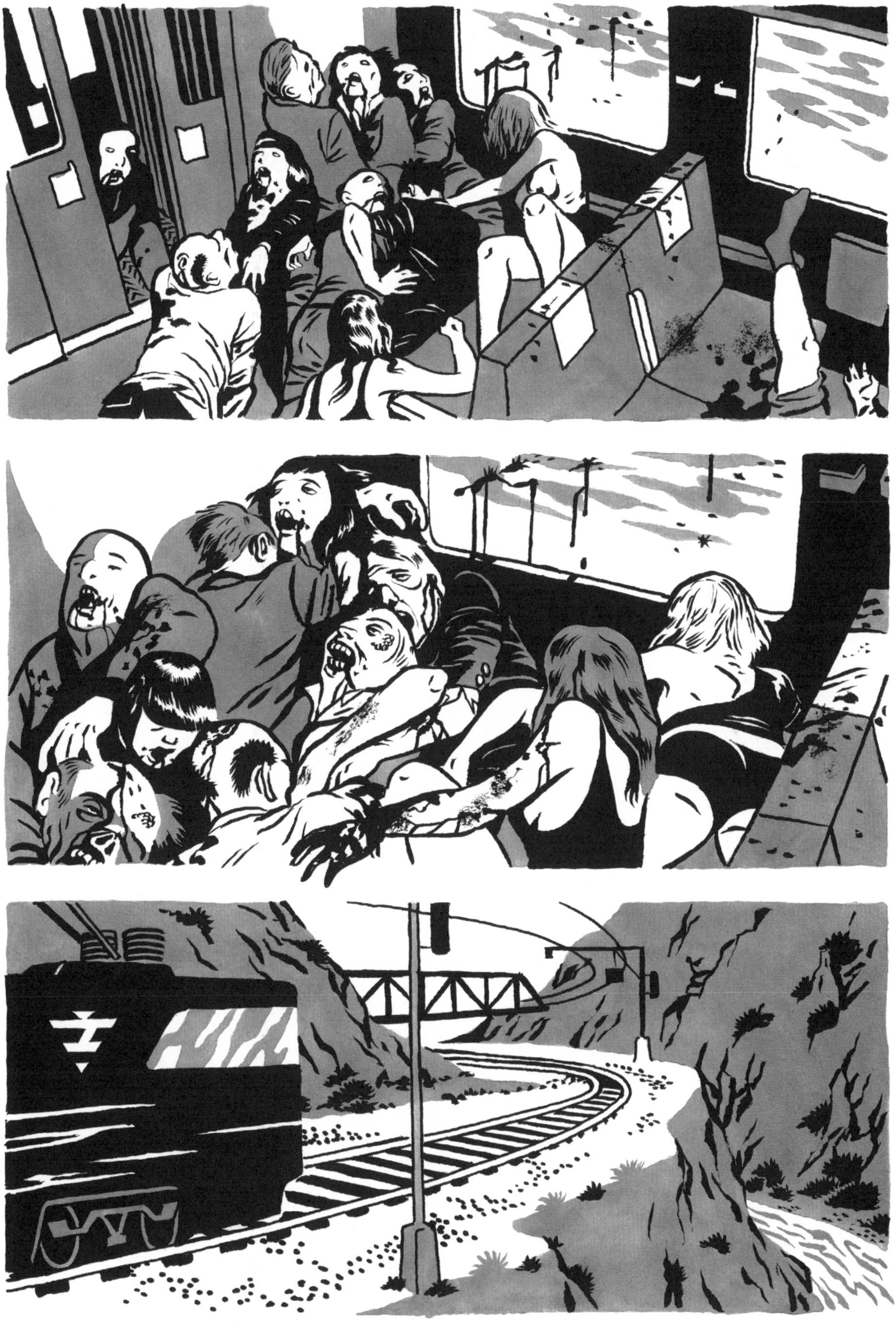

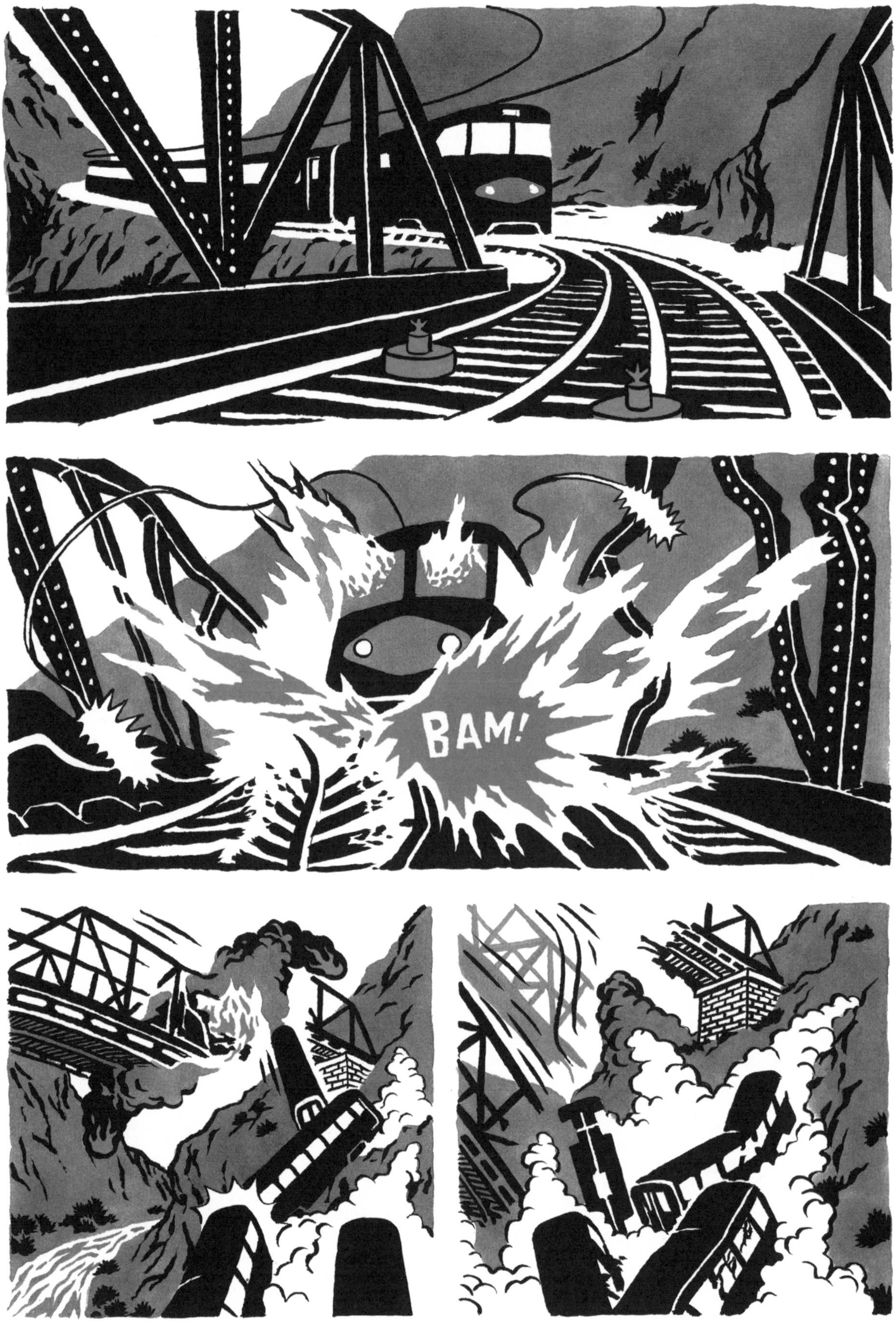
BAM!

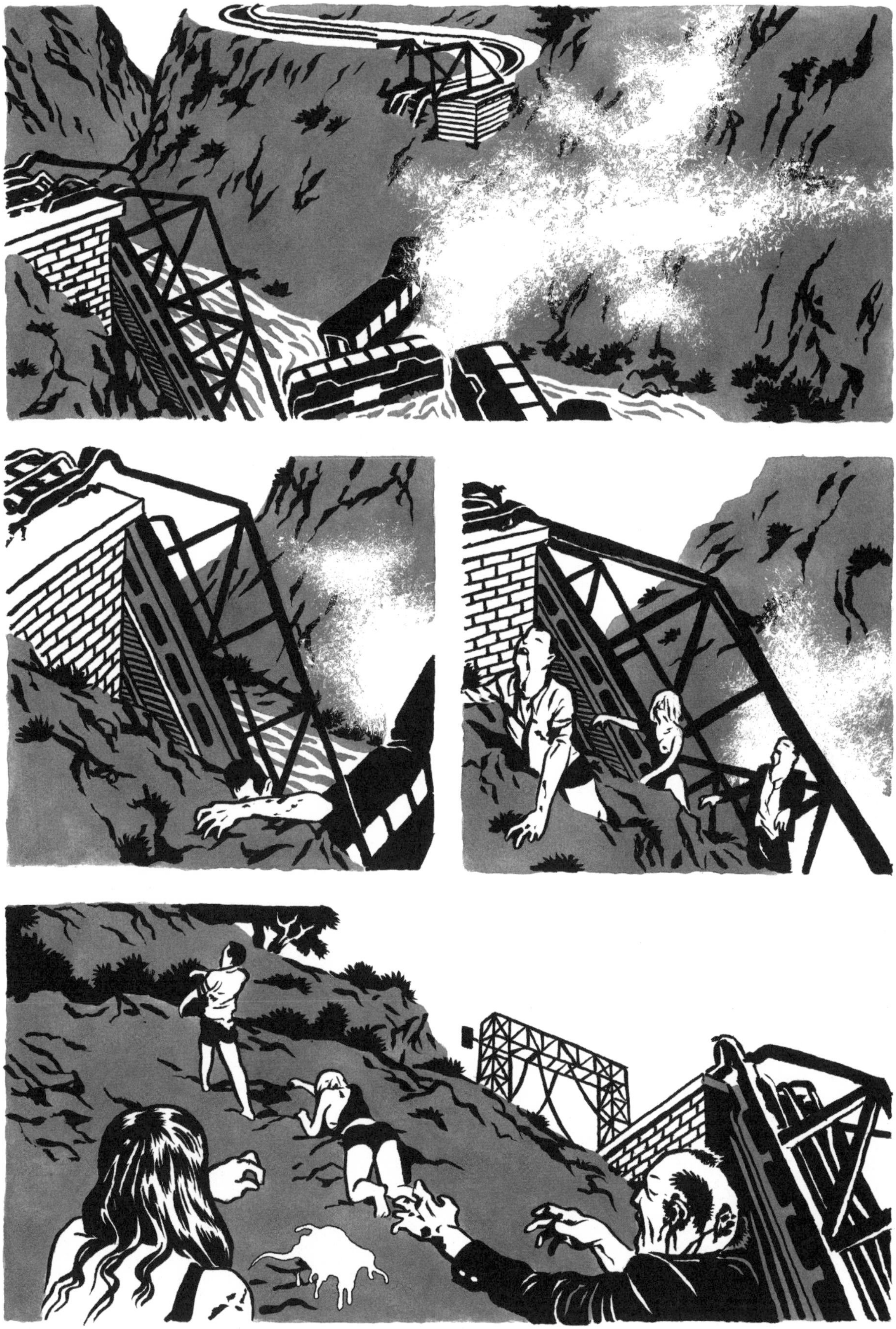

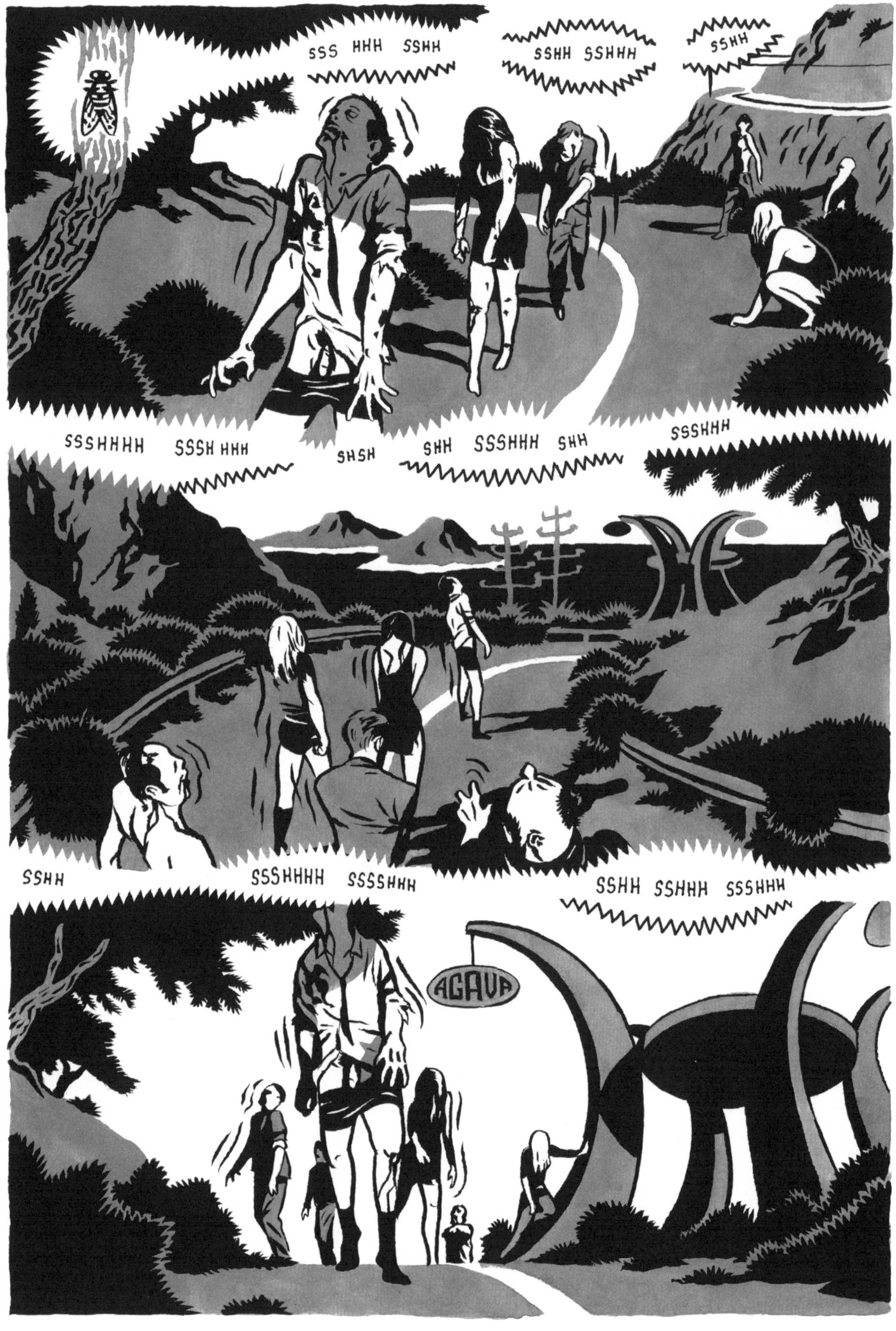
SSS HHH SSHH
SSHH SSHHH
SSHH
SSSHHHH SSSH HHH
SHSH
SHH SSSHHH SHH
SSSHHH
SSHH
SSSHHHH SSSSHHH
SSHH SSHHH SSSHHH
AGAVA

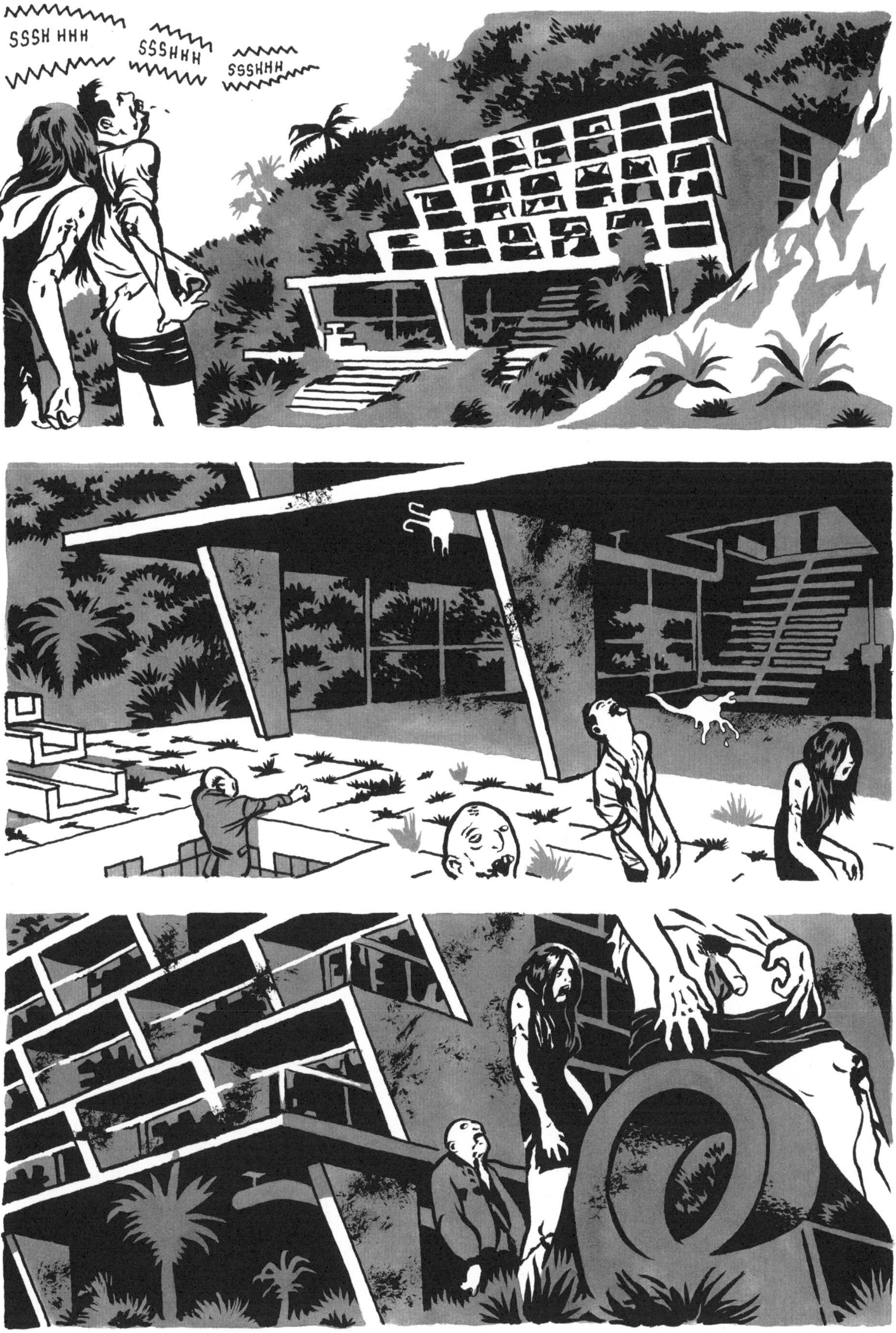
SSSH HHH
SSSHHH
SSSHHH

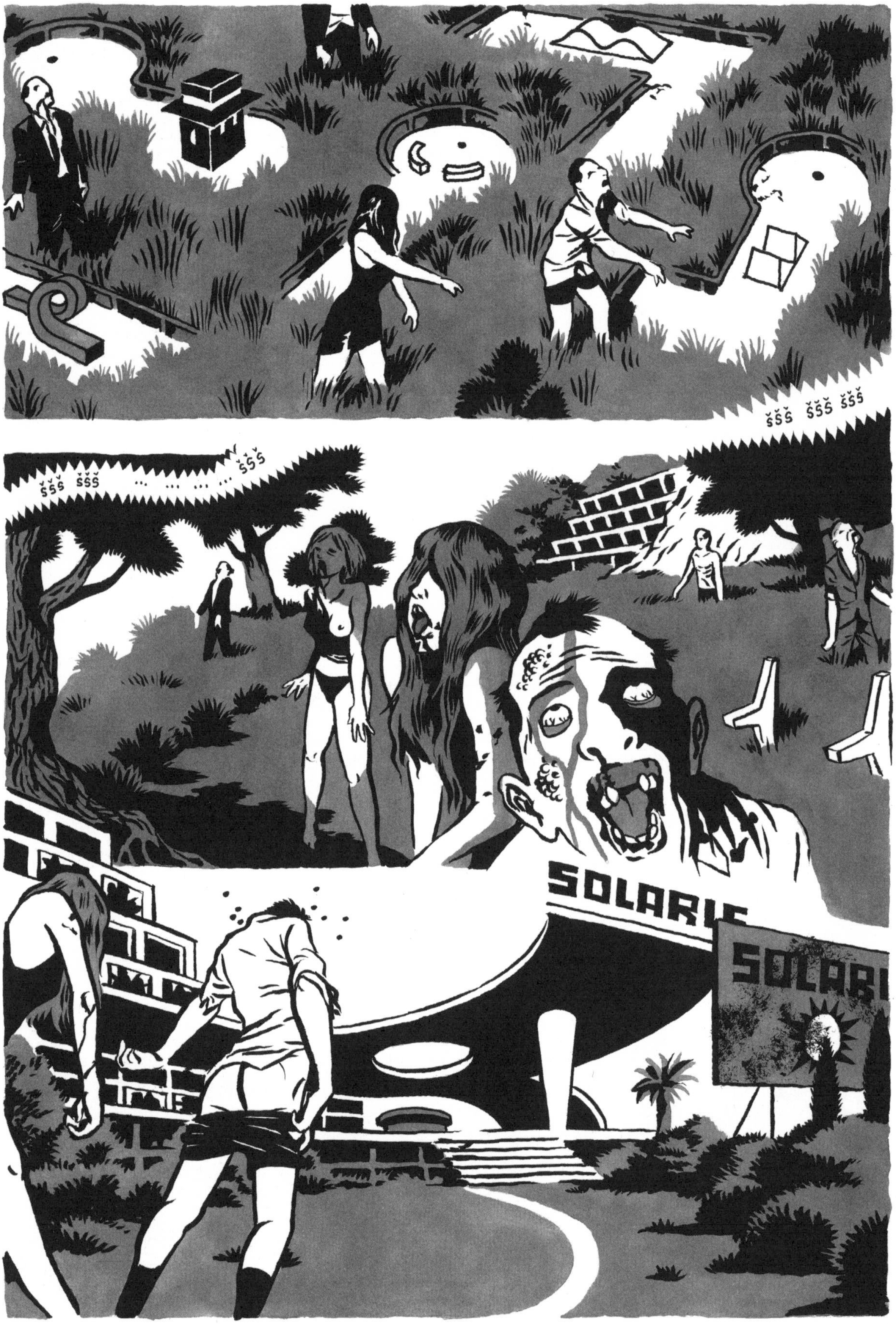
ŠŠŠ ŠŠŠ ŠŠŠ
ŠŠŠ ŠŠŠ ... ... ŠŠŠ

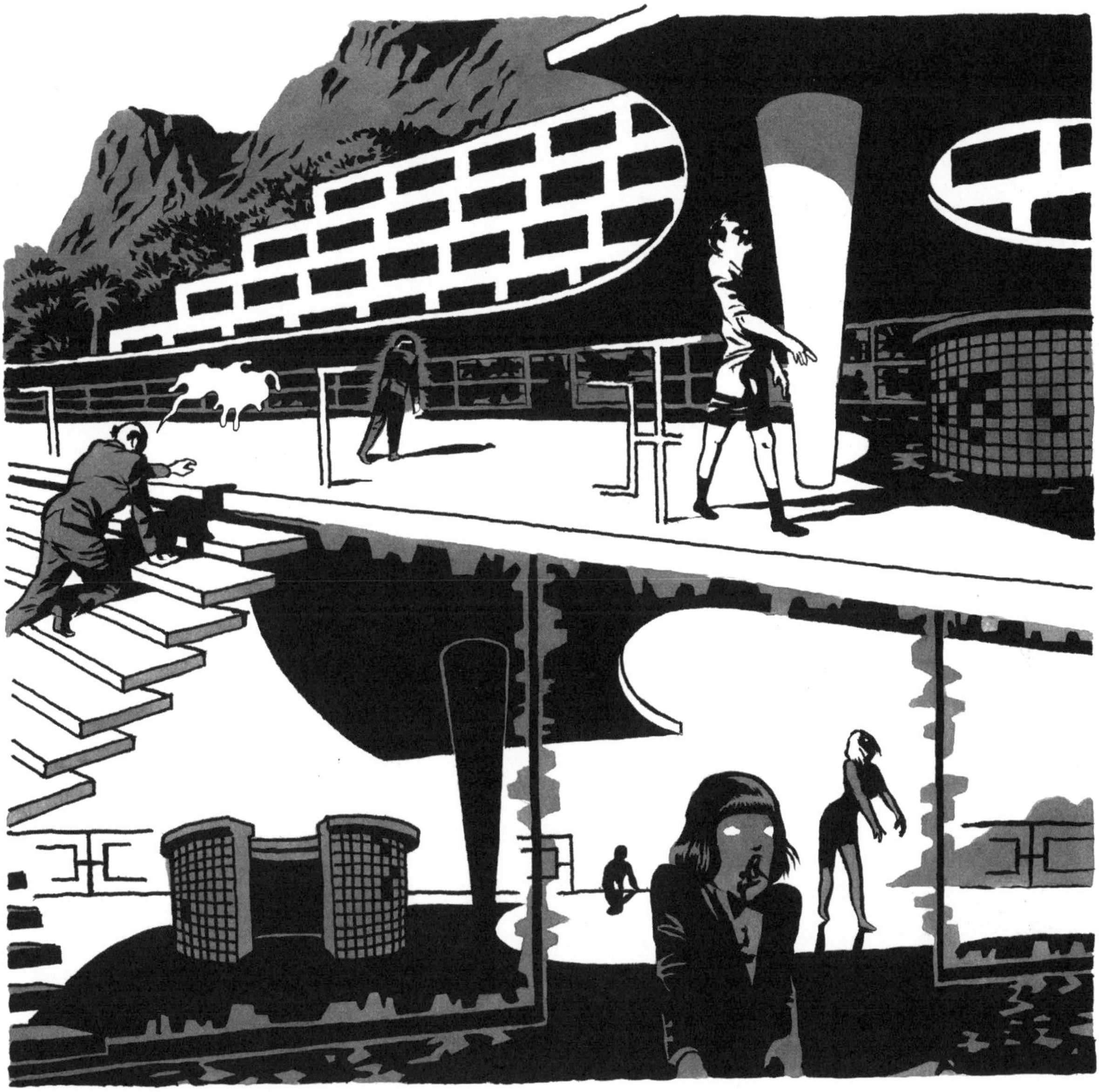

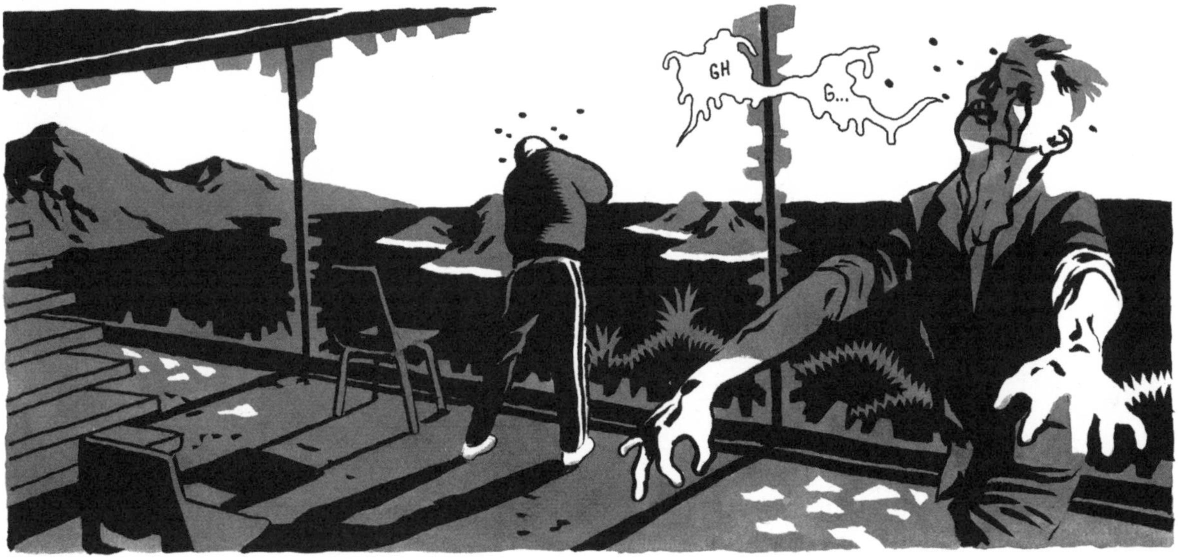
GH
G...

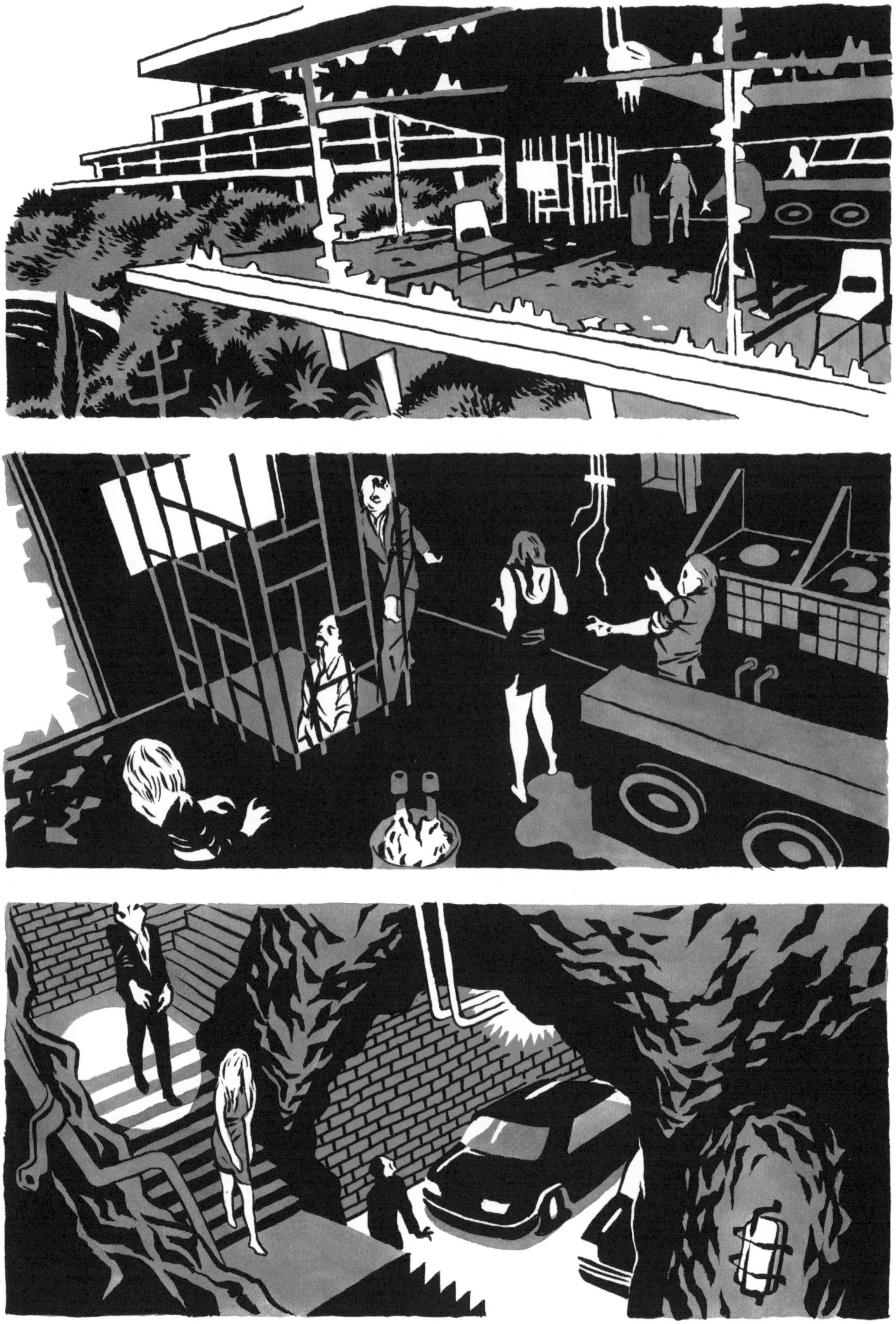

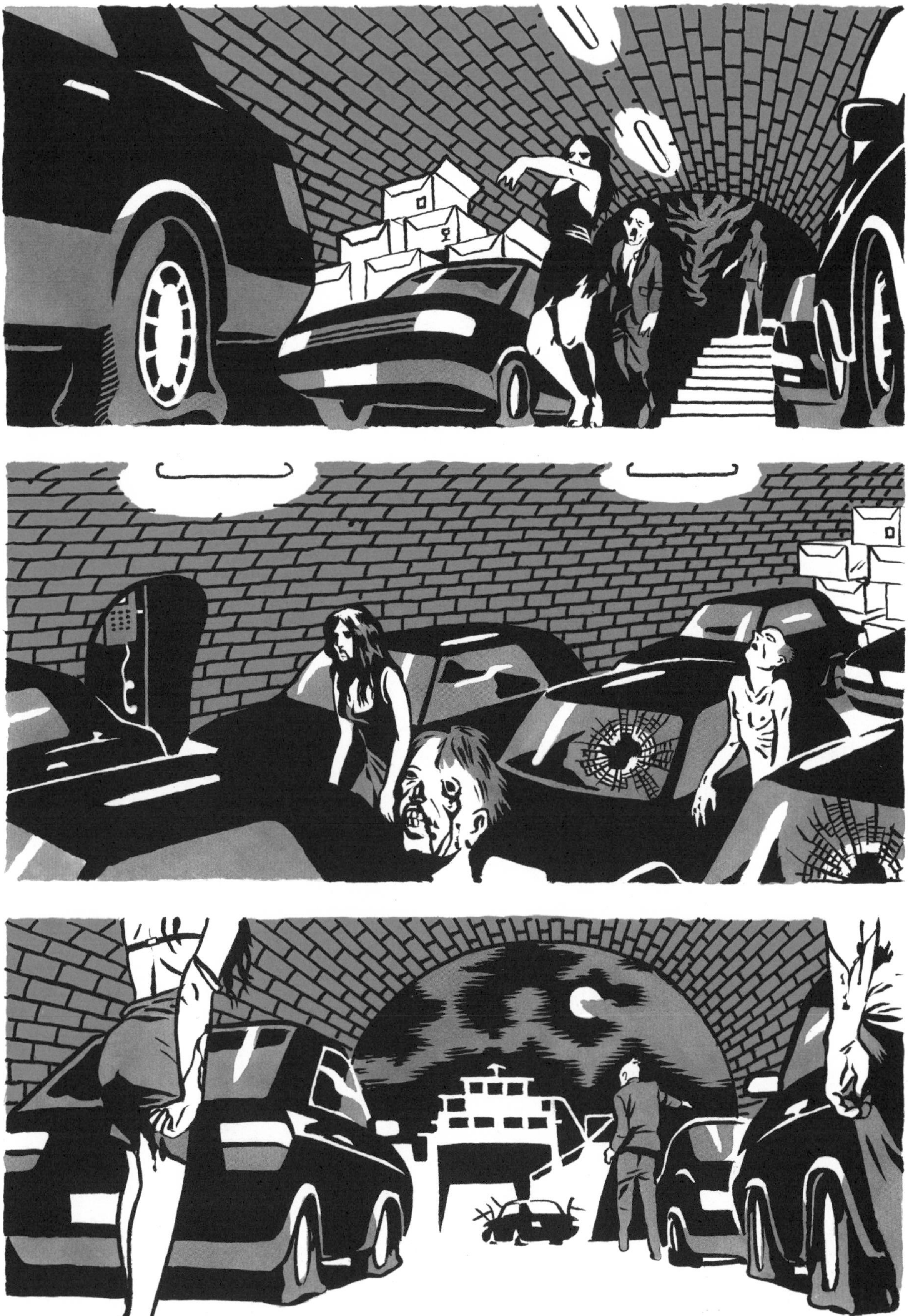

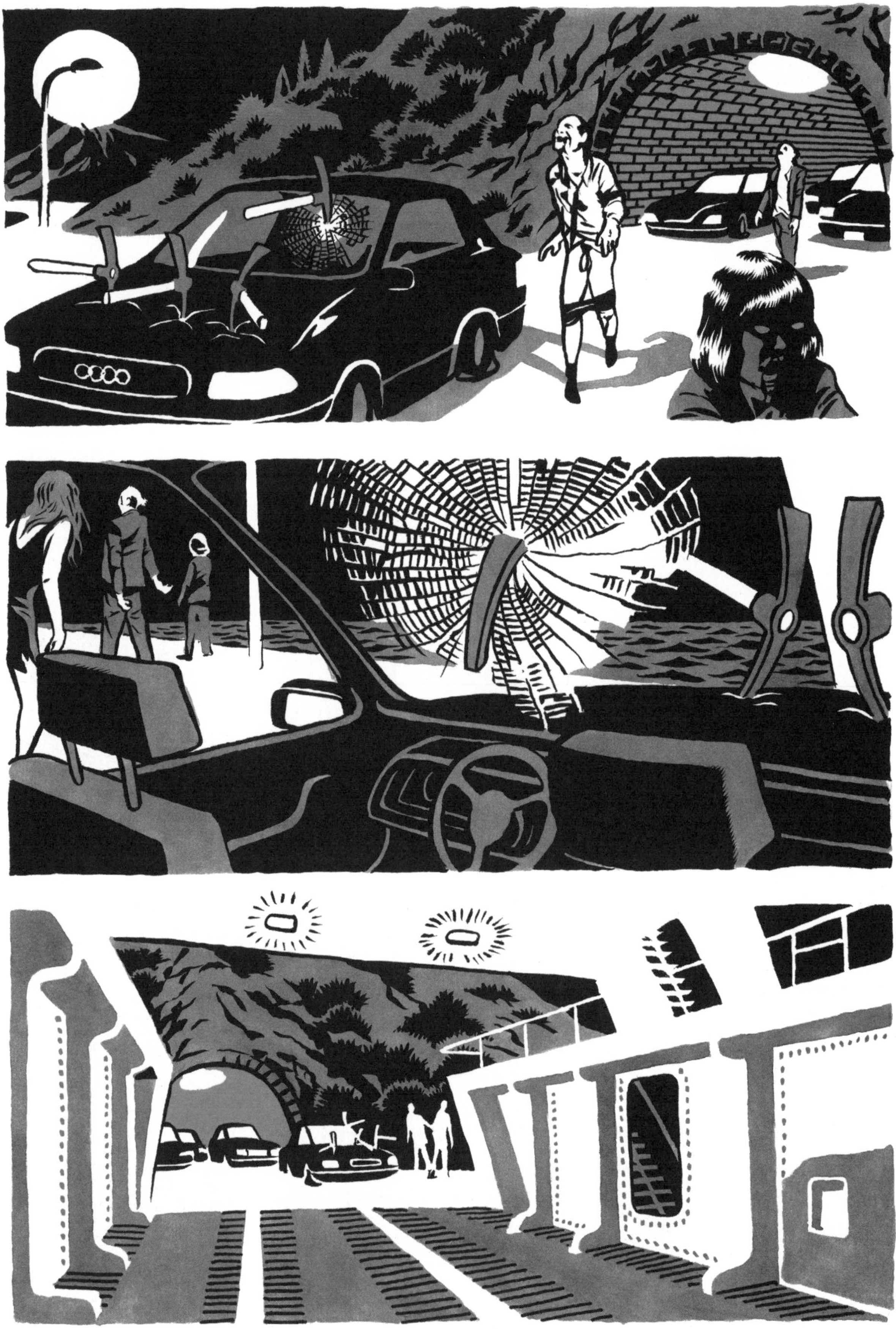

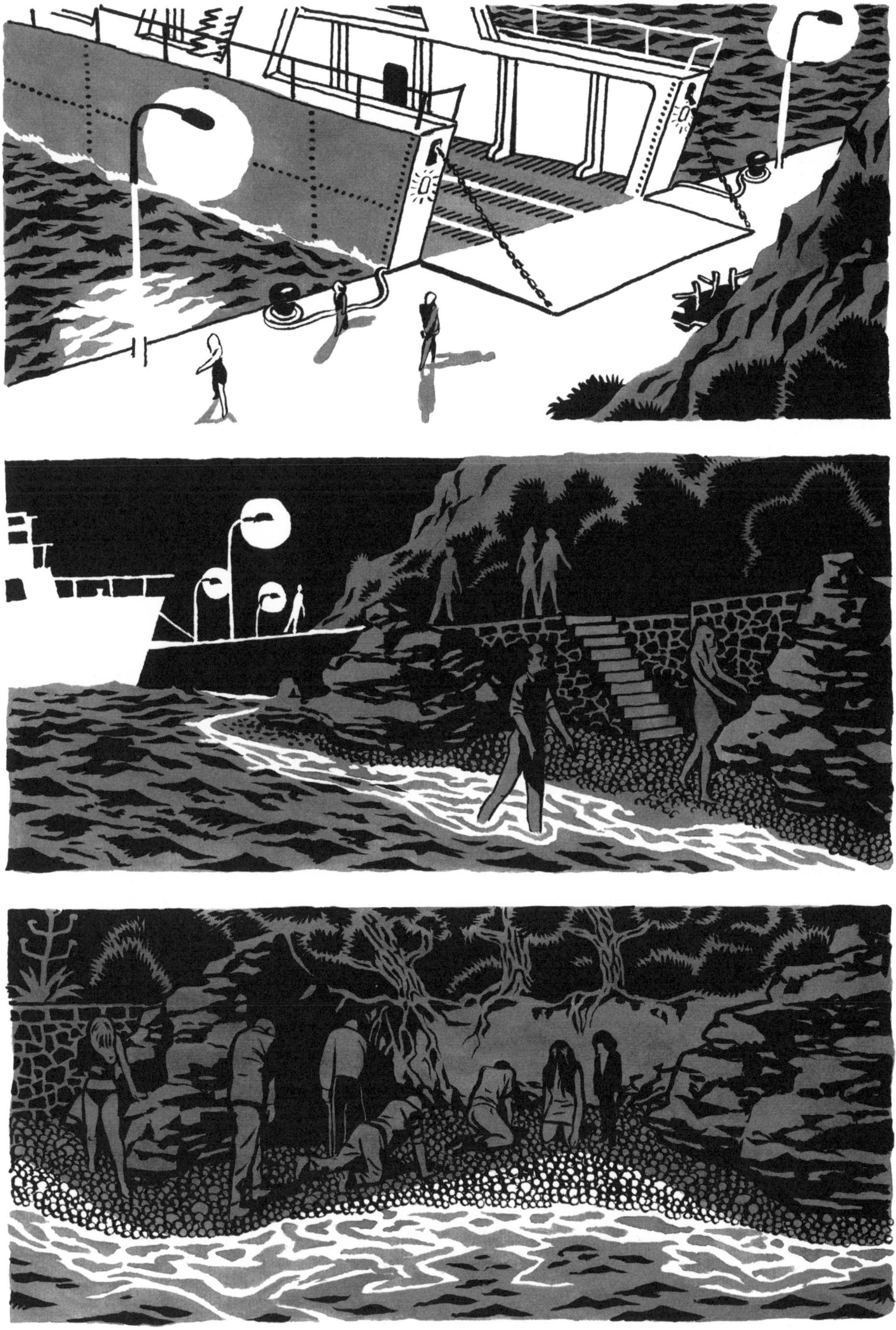

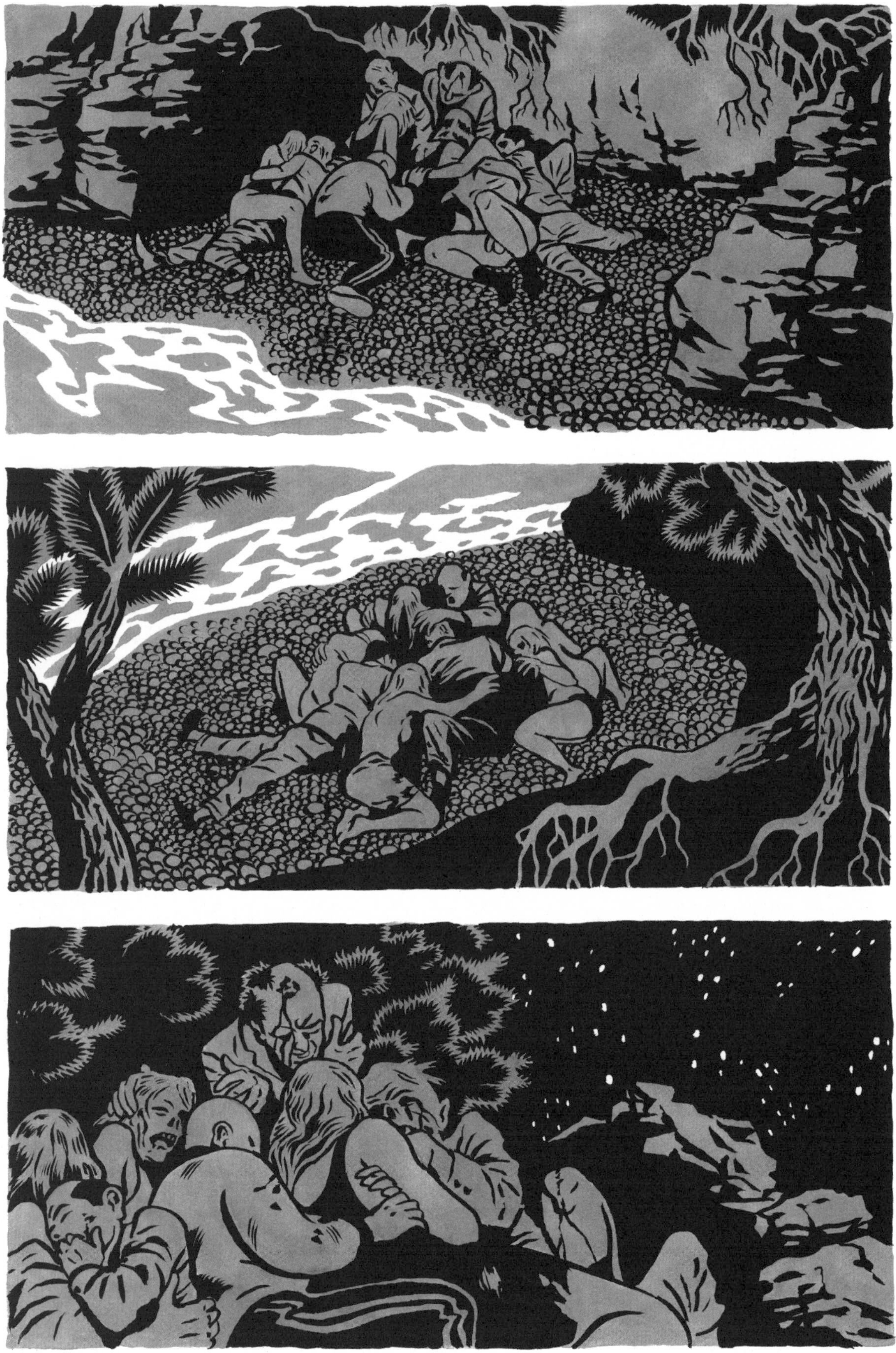

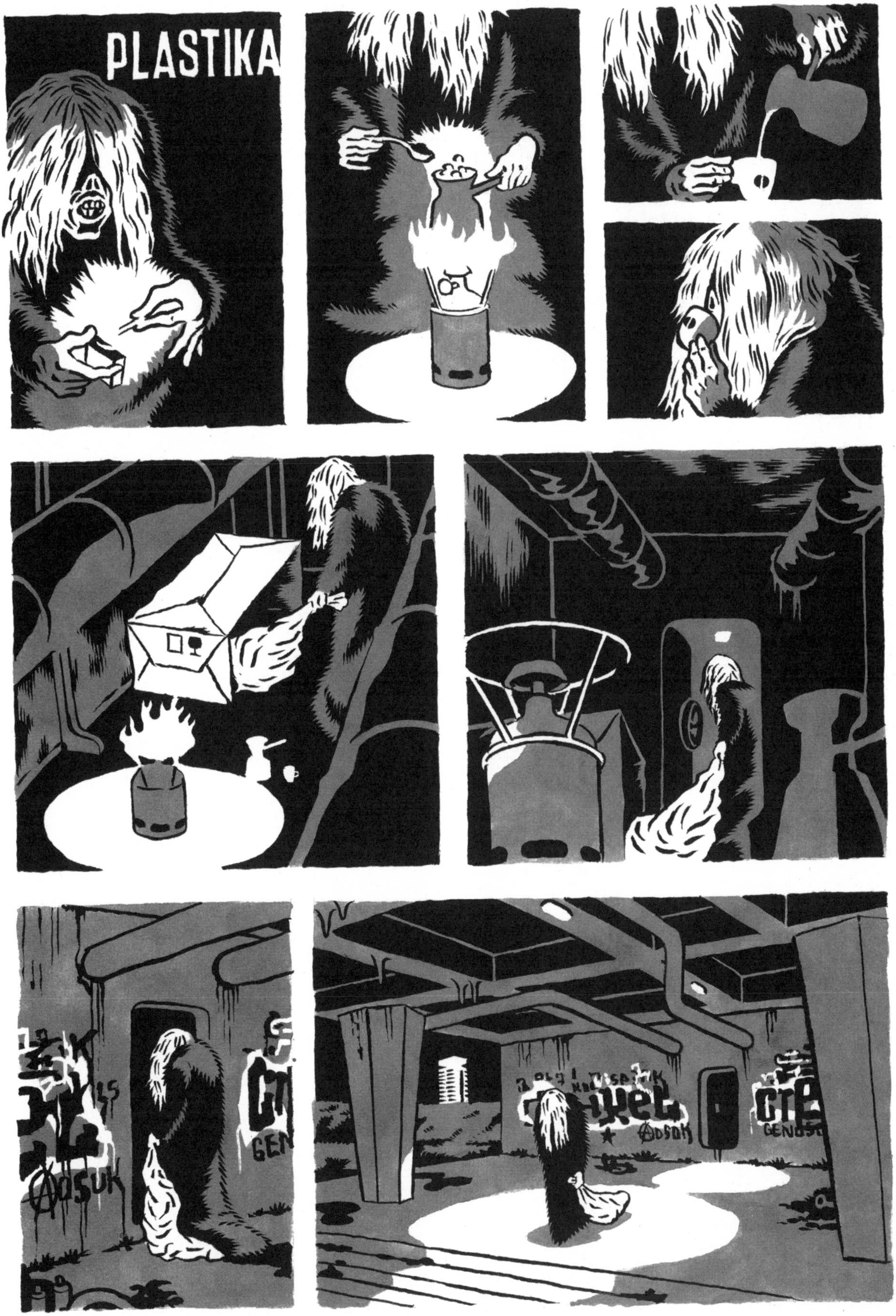
PLASTIKA

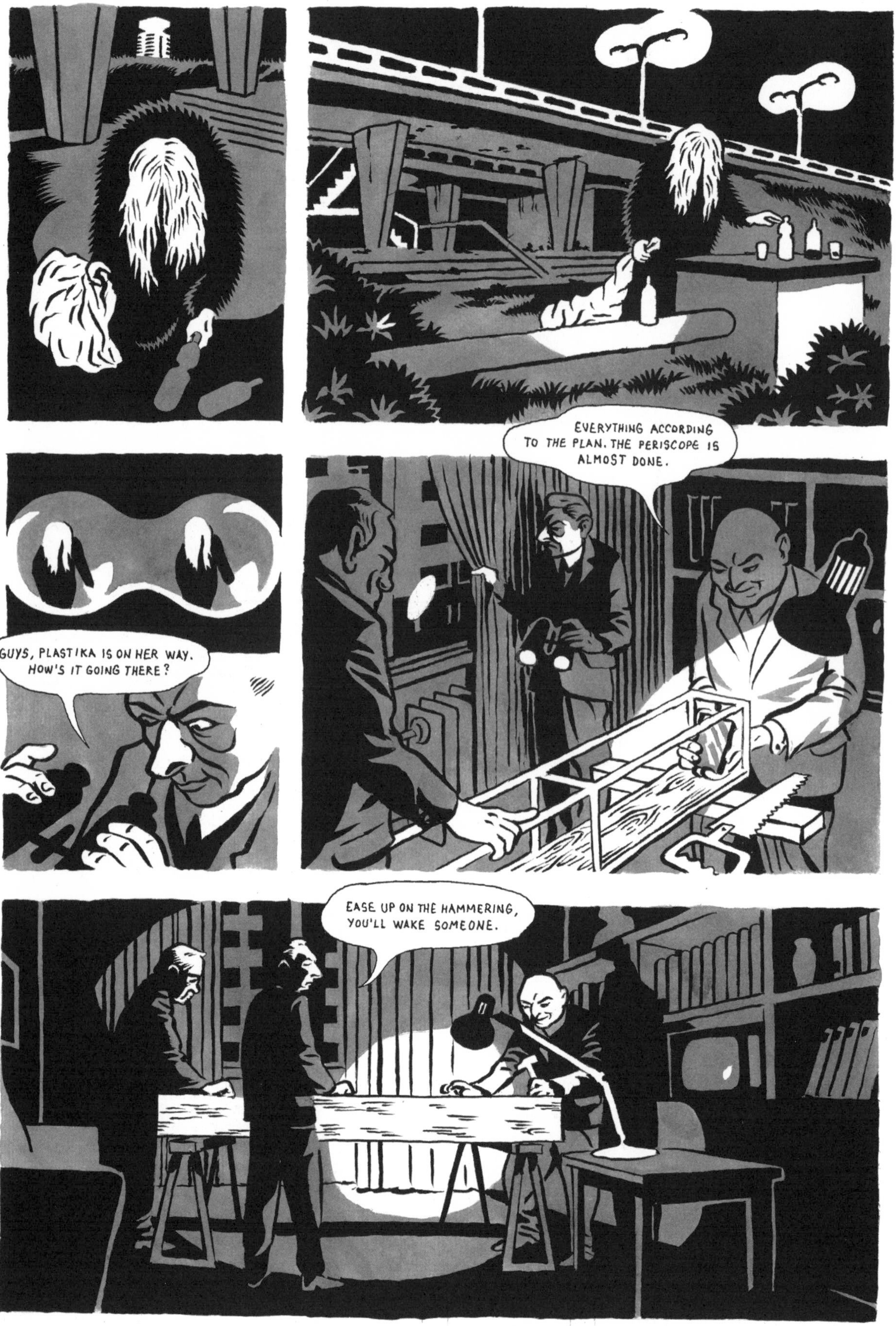
EVERYTHING ACCORDING TO THE PLAN. THE PERISCOPE IS ALMOST DONE.
GUYS, PLASTIKA IS ON HER WAY. HOW'S IT GOING THERE?
EASE UP ON THE HAMMERING, YOU'LL WAKE SOMEONE.

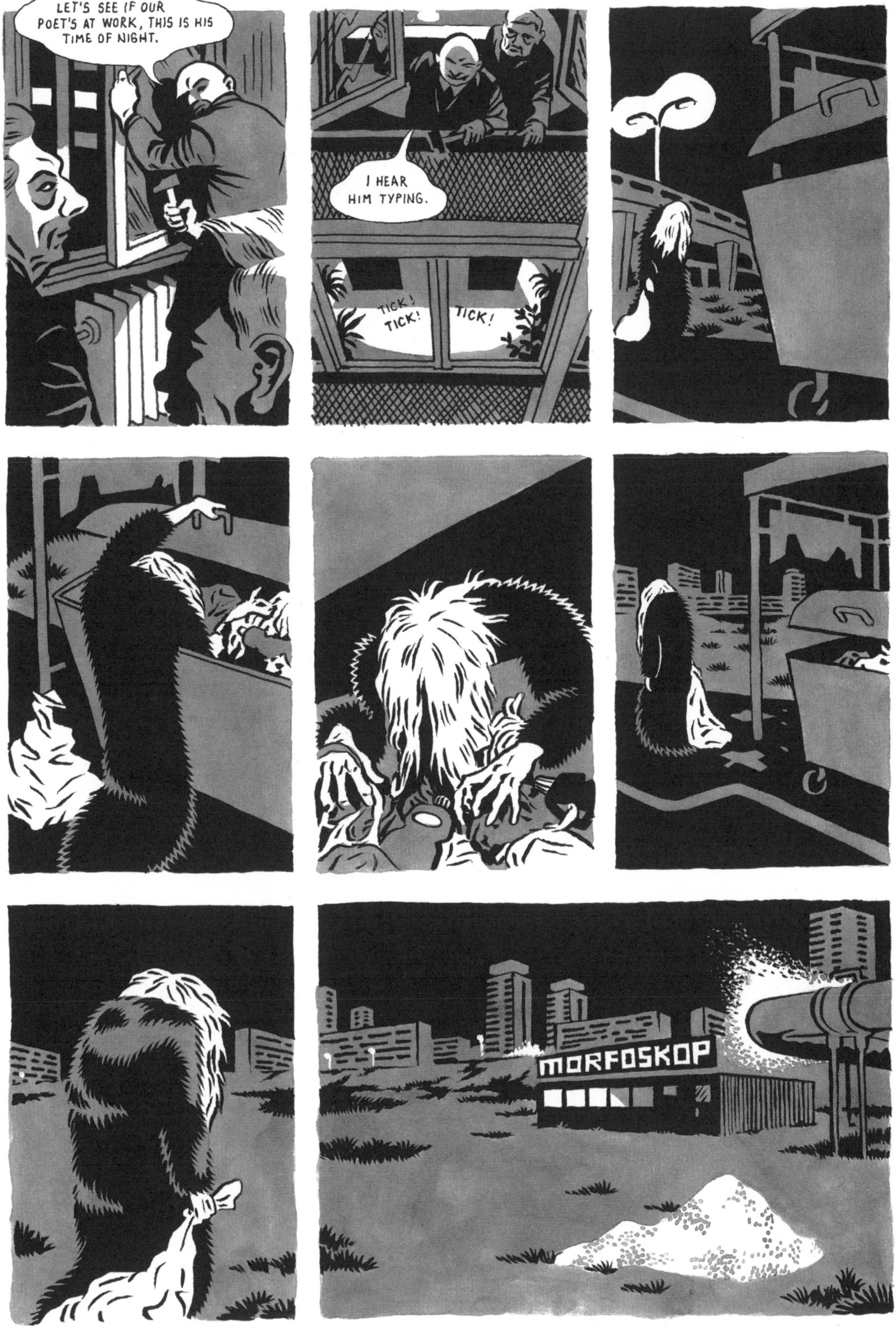
LET'S SEE IF OUR POET'S AT WORK, THIS IS HIS TIME OF NIGHT.
I HEAR HIM TYPING.
TICK! TICK!
TICK!
MORFOSKOP

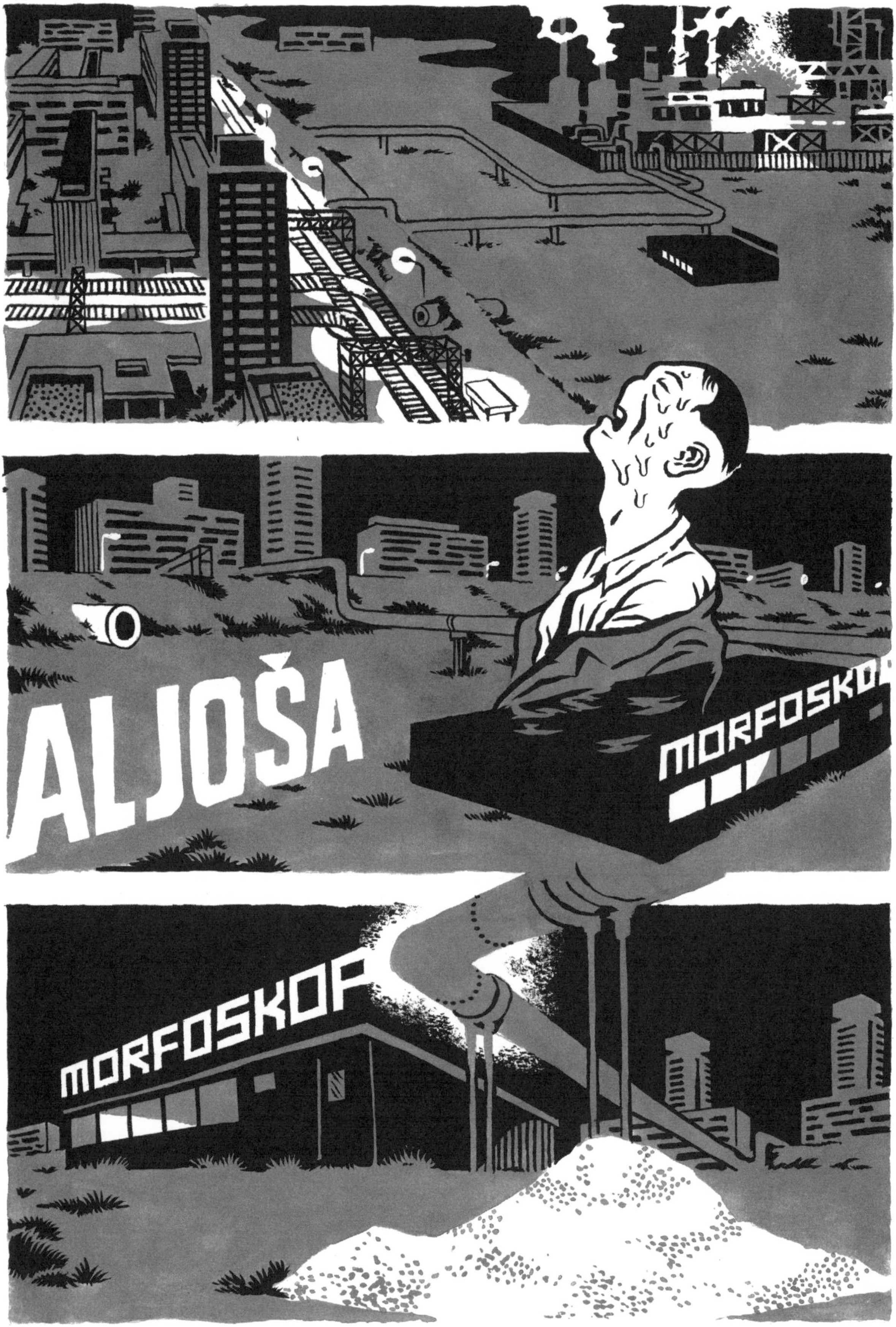
ALJOŠA
MORFOSKOP
MORFOSKOP

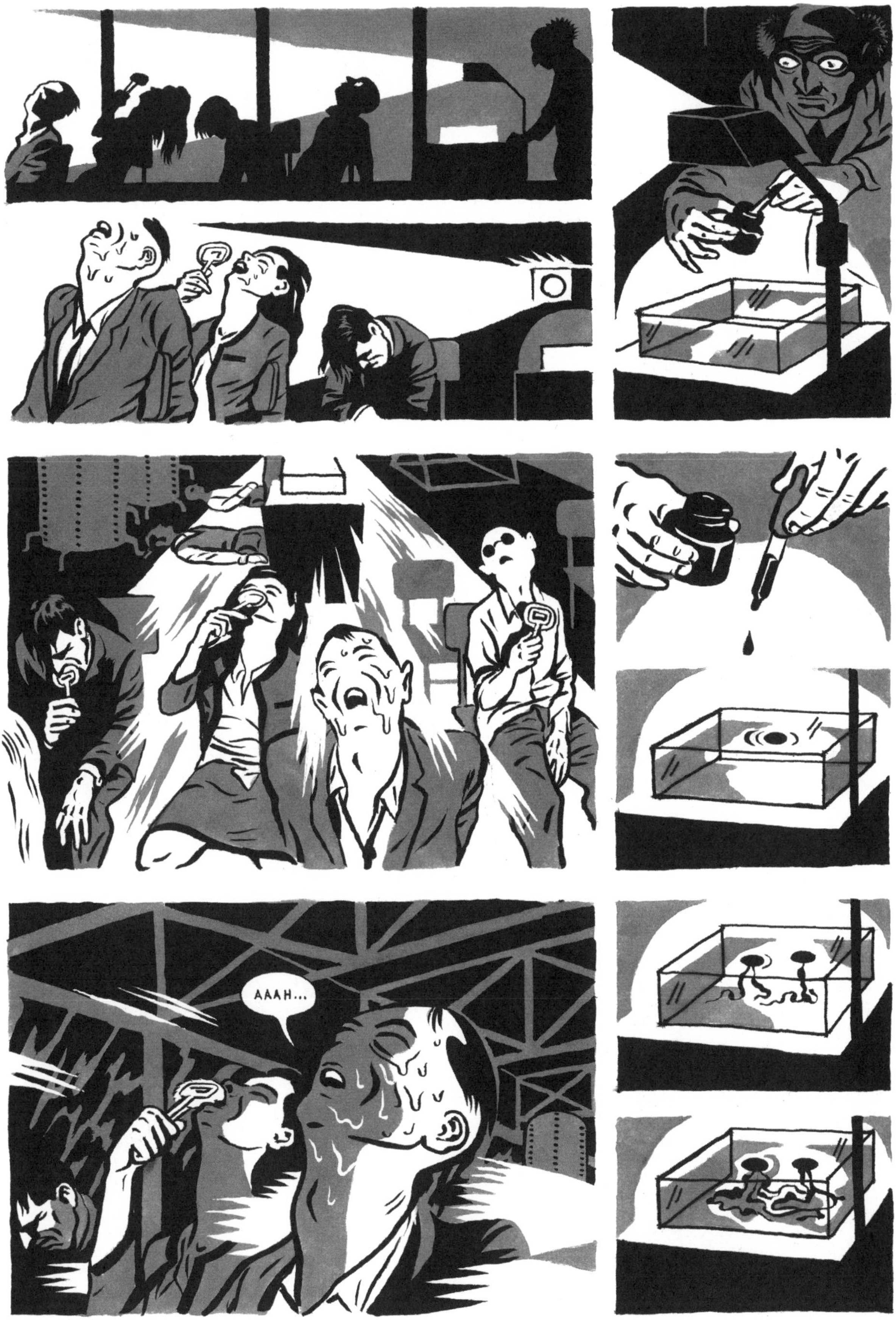
AAAH...

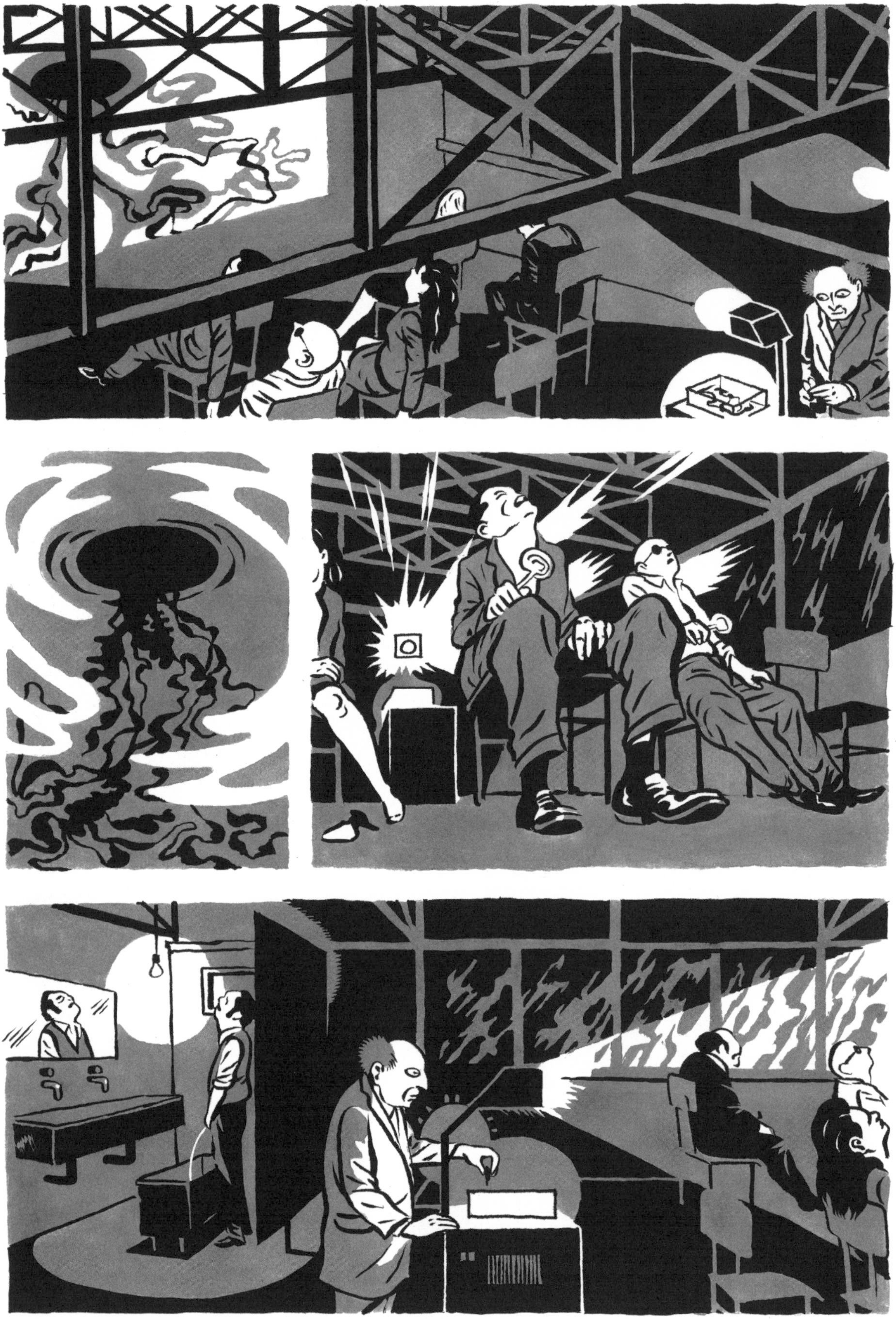

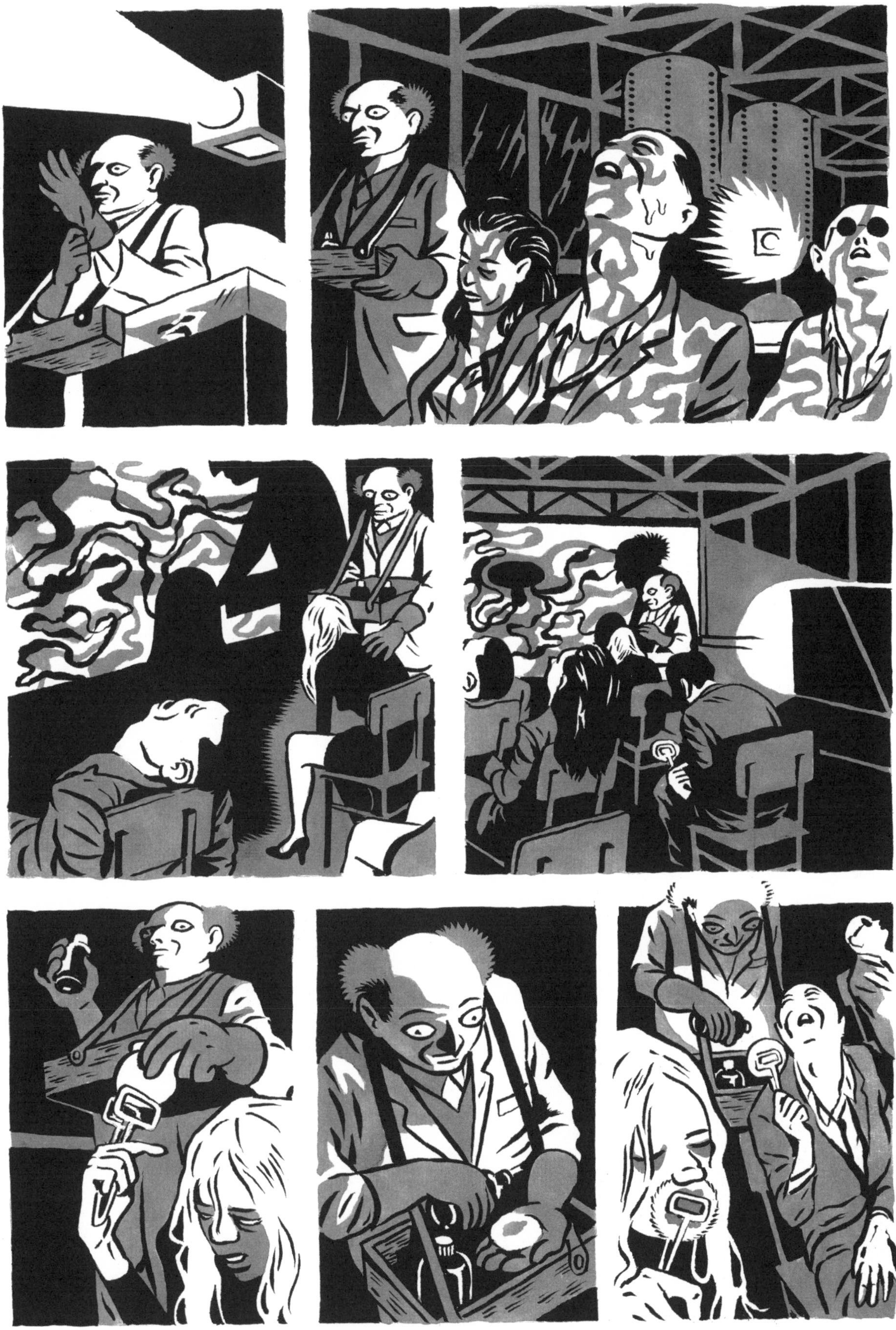

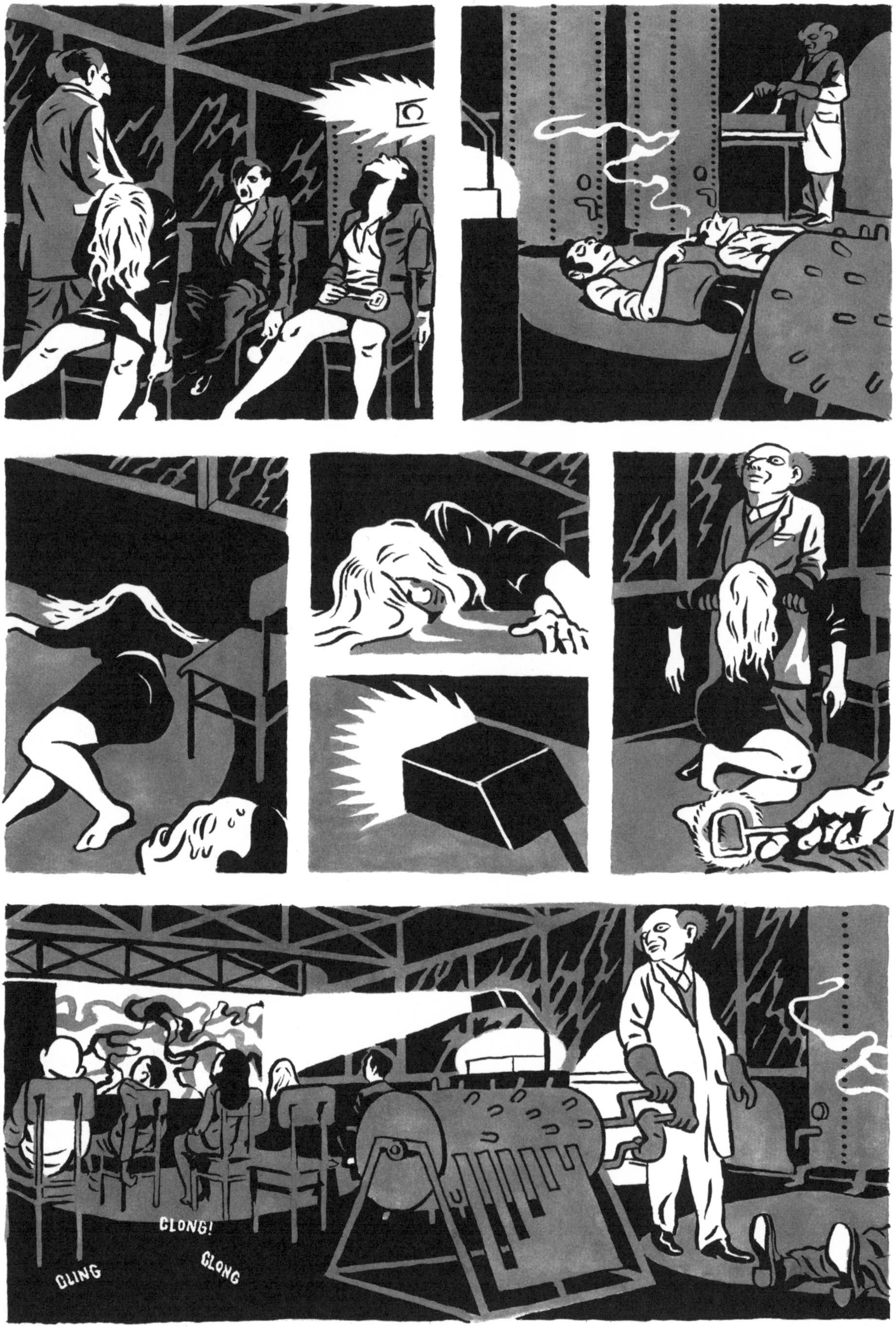
CLONG!
CLING
CLONG

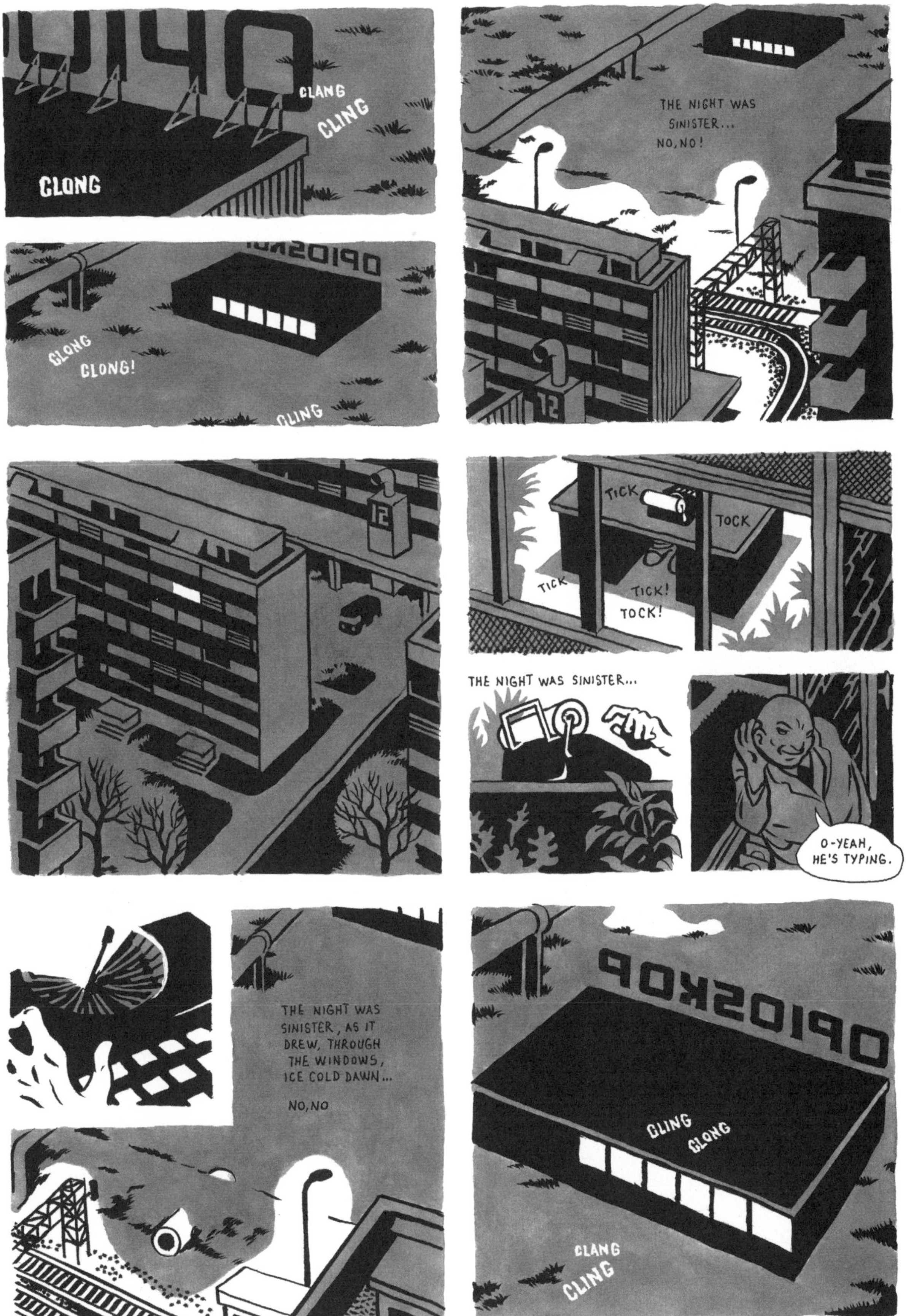
CLANG
CLING
CLONG
CLONG
CLONG!
CLING
THE NIGHT WAS
SINISTER...
NO, NO!
12
12
TICK
TOCK
TICK
TICK!
TOCK!
THE NIGHT WAS SINISTER...
O-YEAH,
HE'S TYPING.
THE NIGHT WAS
SINISTER, AS IT
DREW, THROUGH
THE WINDOWS,
ICE COLD DAWN...
NO, NO
OPIOSKOP
CLING
CLONG
CLANG
CLING

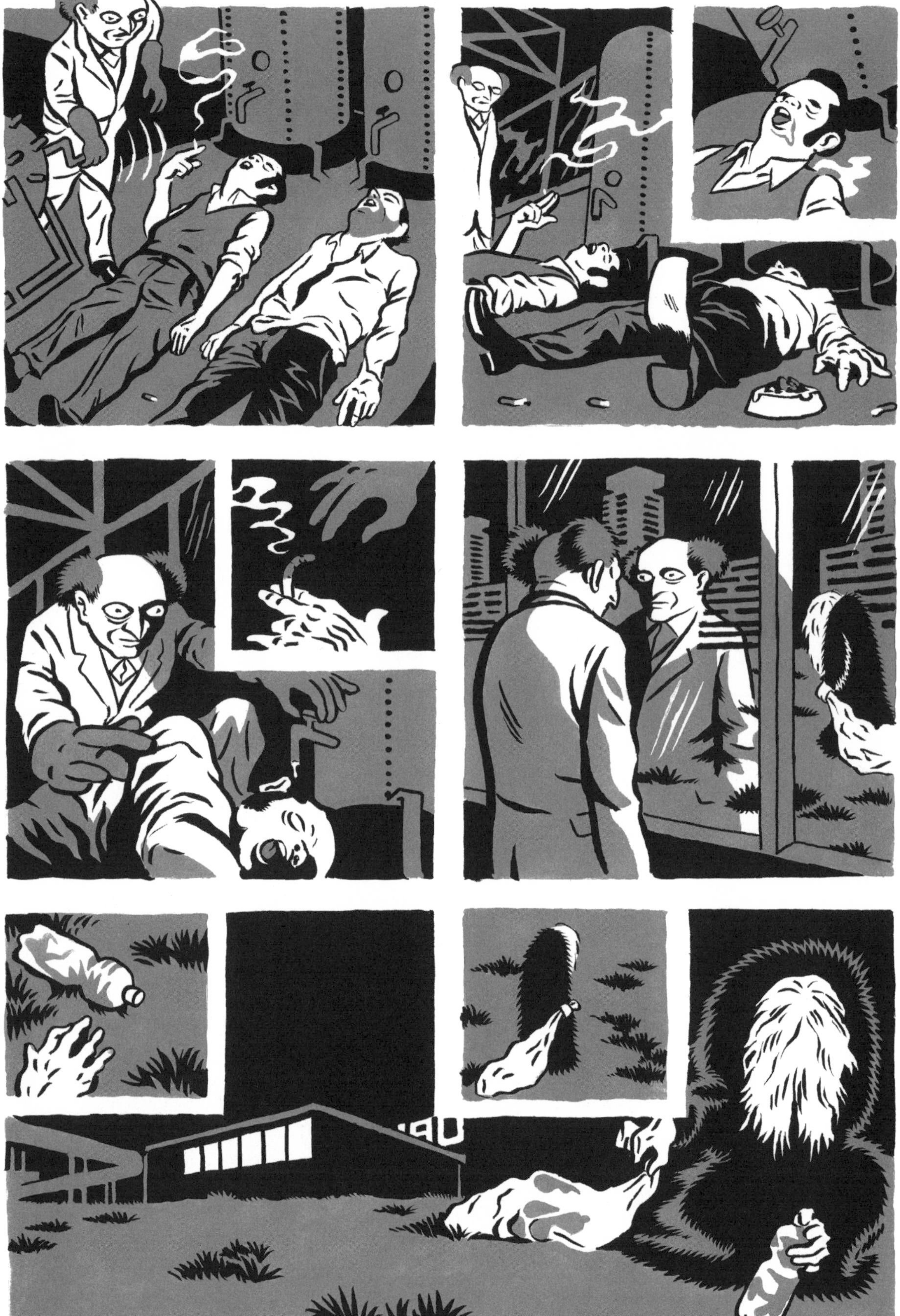

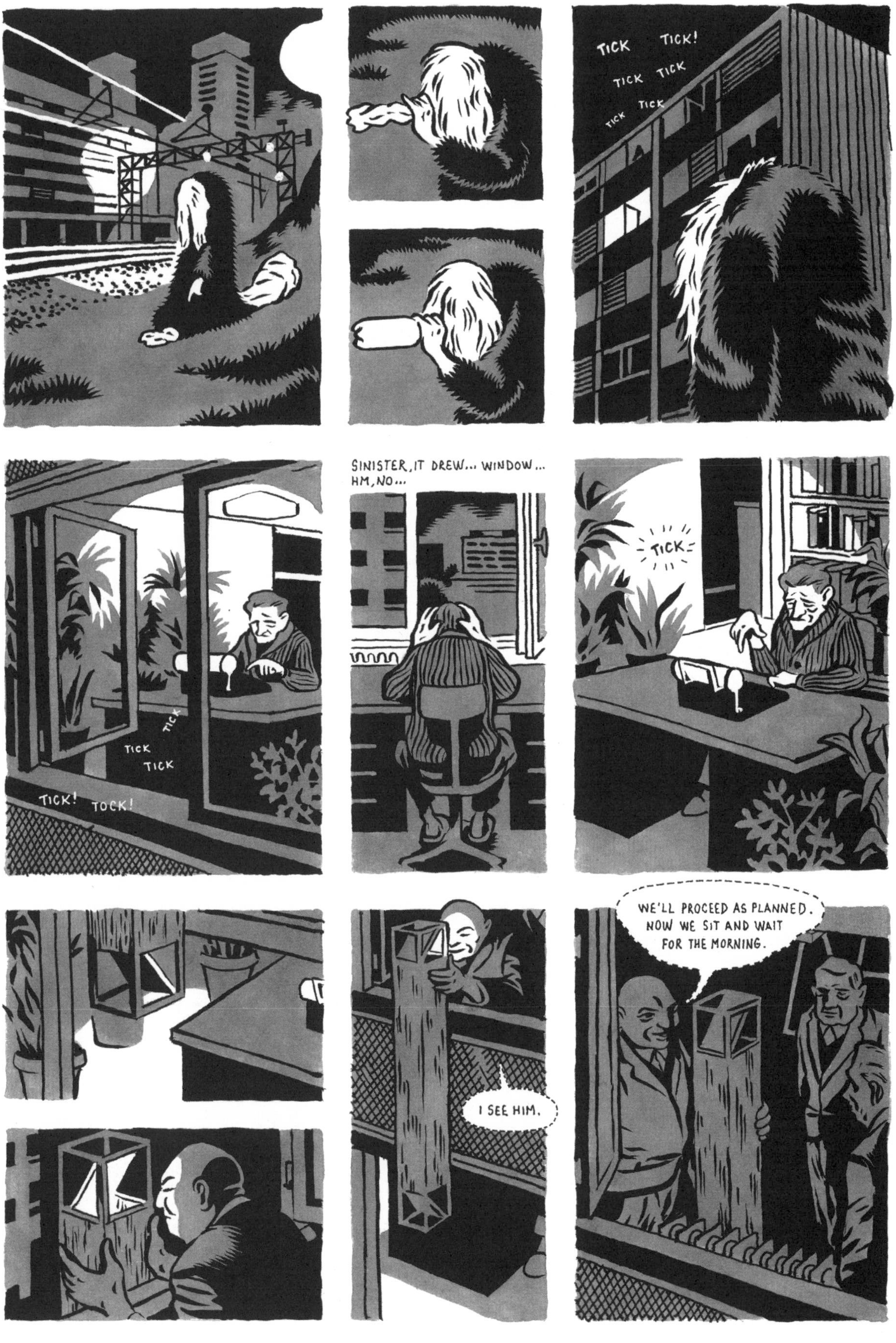
TICK TICK!
TICK TICK
TICK TICK
TICK
TICK
TICK
TICK! TOCK!
SINISTER, IT DREW... WINDOW... HM, NO...
TICK
I SEE HIM.
WE'LL PROCEED AS PLANNED. NOW WE SIT AND WAIT FOR THE MORNING.

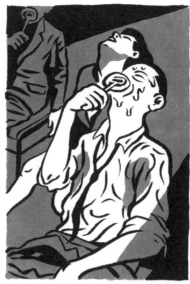

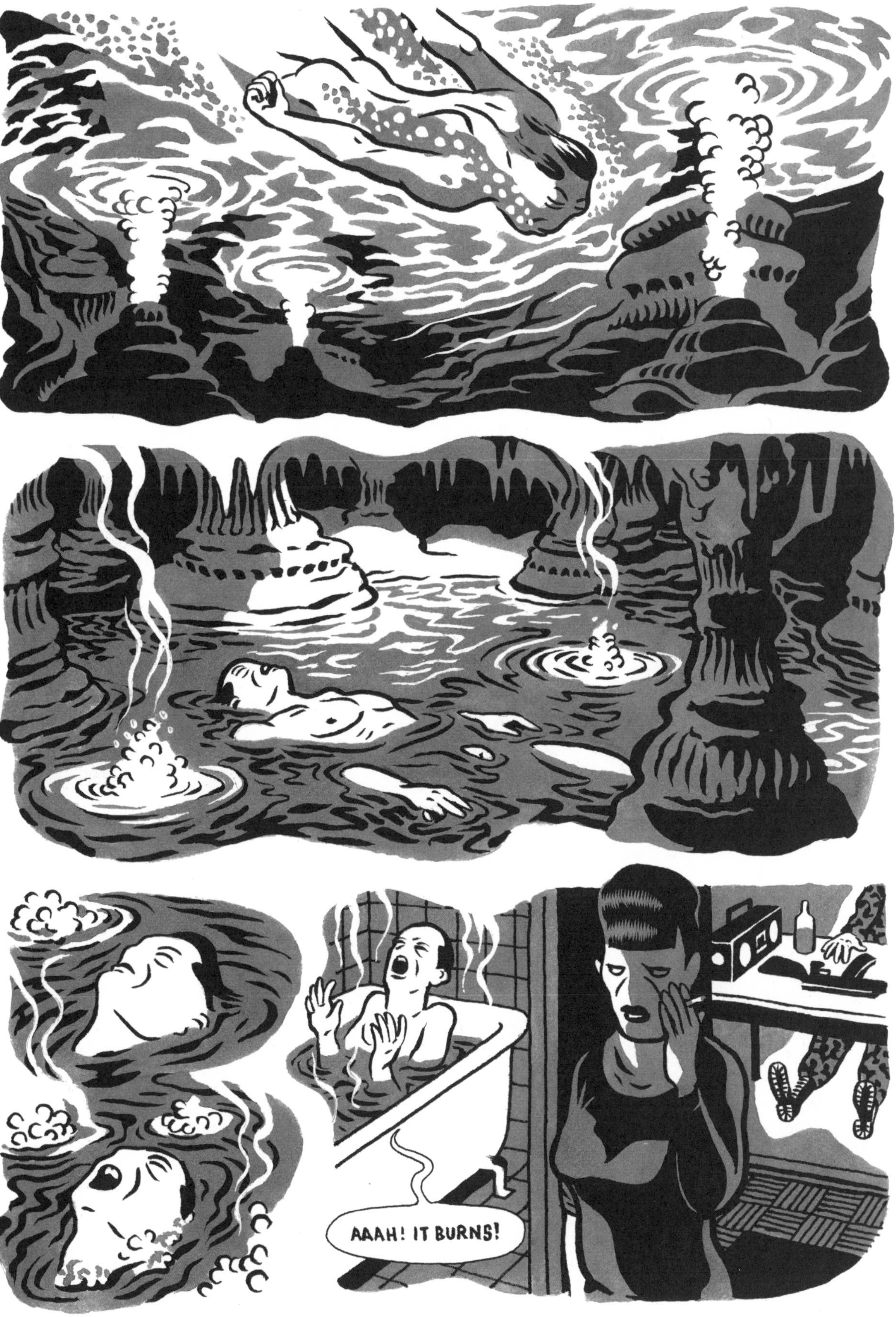
AAAH! IT BURNS!

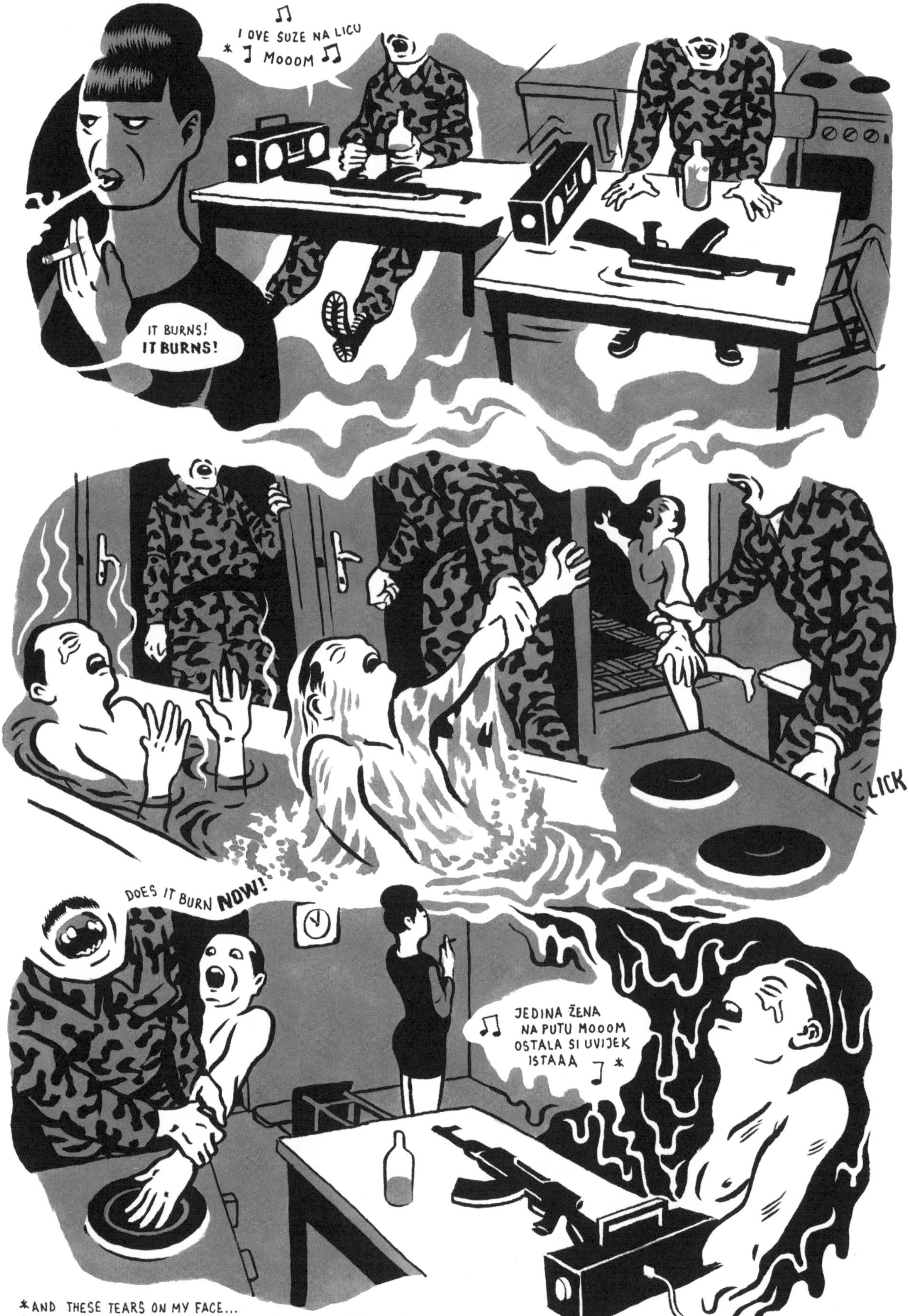
I OVE SUZE NA LICU * MOOOM
IT BURNS! IT BURNS!
CLICK
DOES IT BURN NOW!
JEDINA ŽENA NA PUTU MOOOM OSTALA SI UVIJEK ISTAAA *

*AND THESE TEARS ON MY FACE...
*THE ONLY WOMEN ON MY ROAD, YOU ALWAYS STAYED THE SAME...
(SONG "YOU ALWAYS STAYED THE SAME" BY MIŠO KOVAČ)

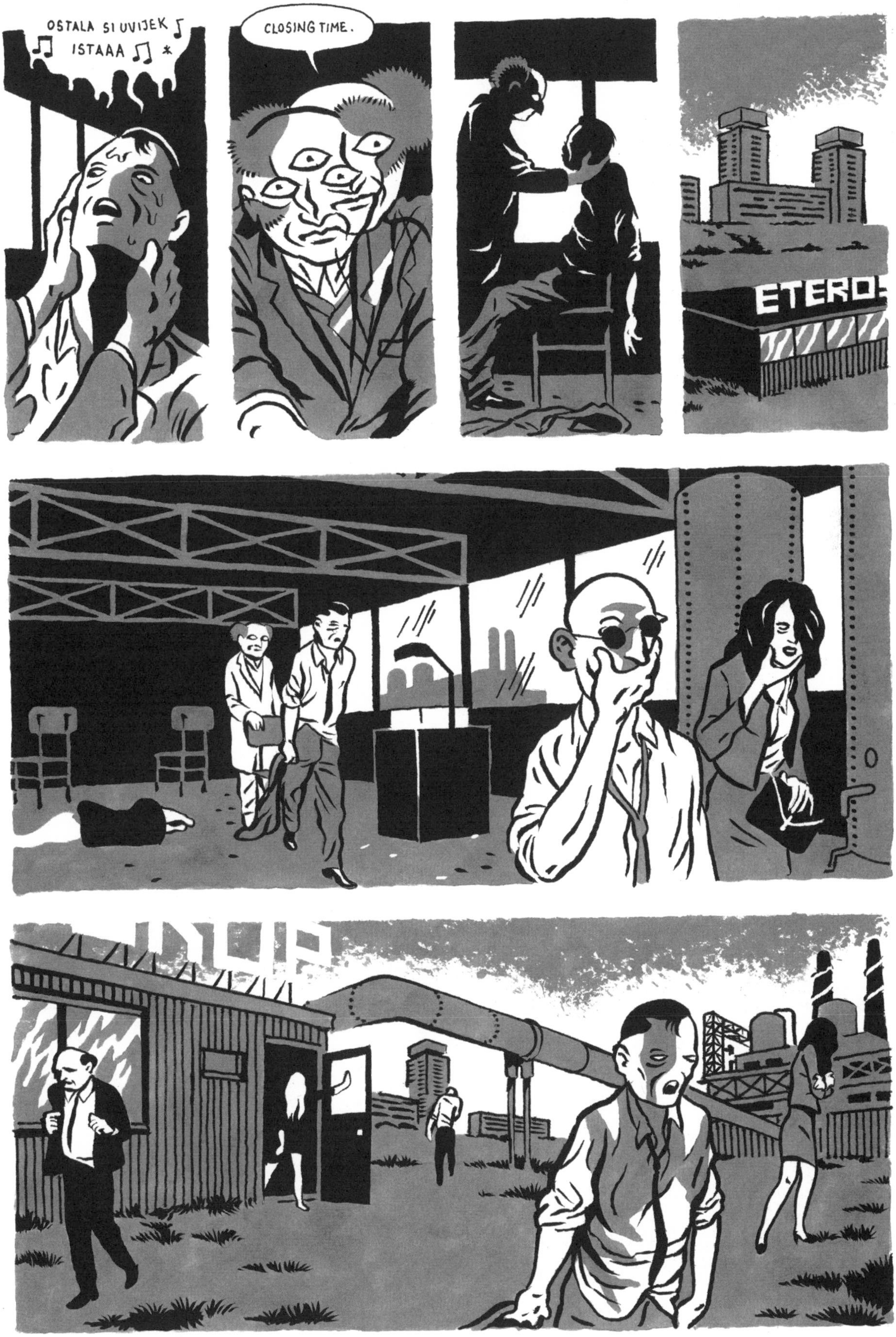
OSTALA SI UVIJEK ISTAAA *
CLOSING TIME.
ETERO

* YOU ALWAYS STAYED THE SAAAME!

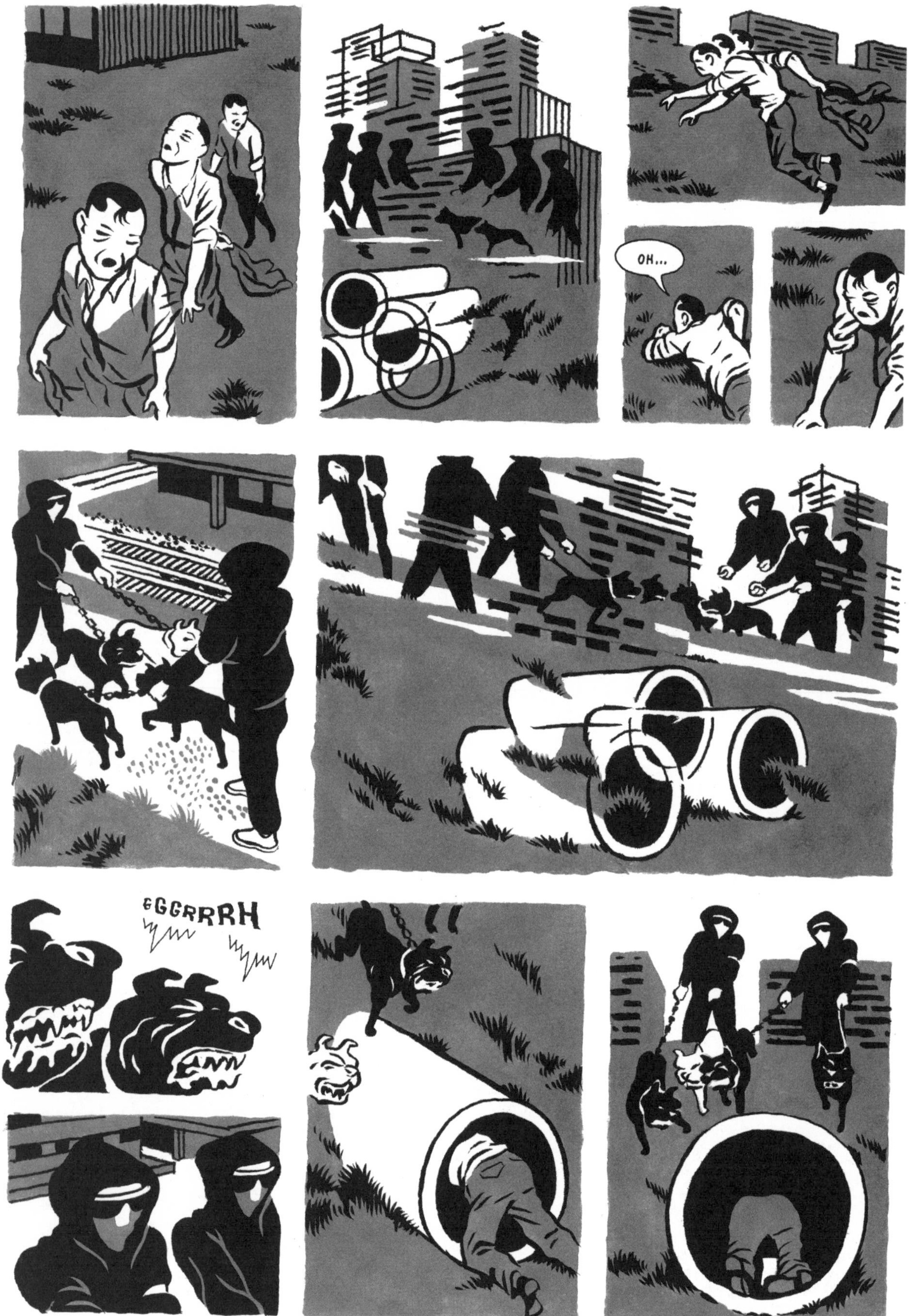
OH...
GGGRRRRH

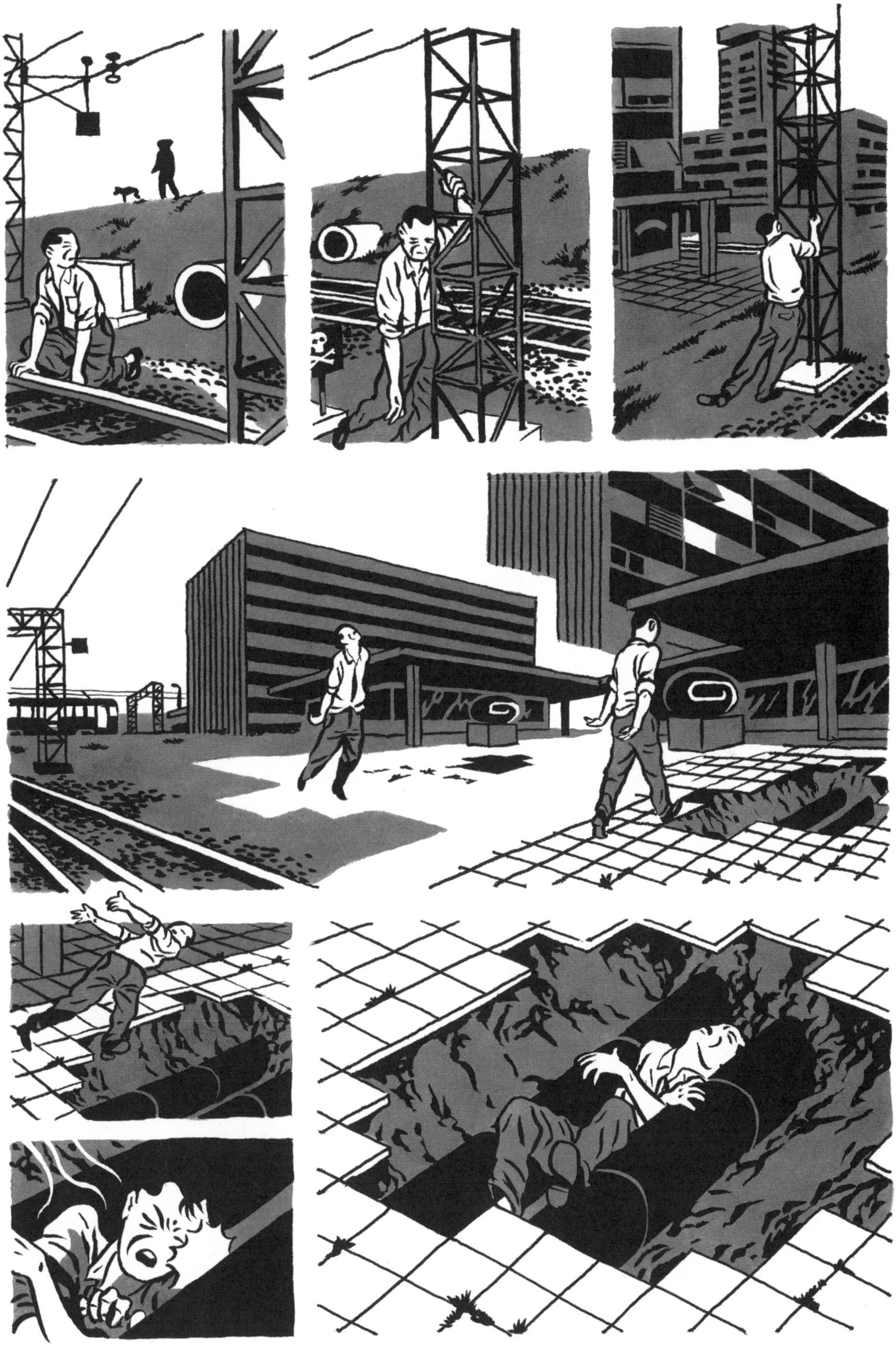

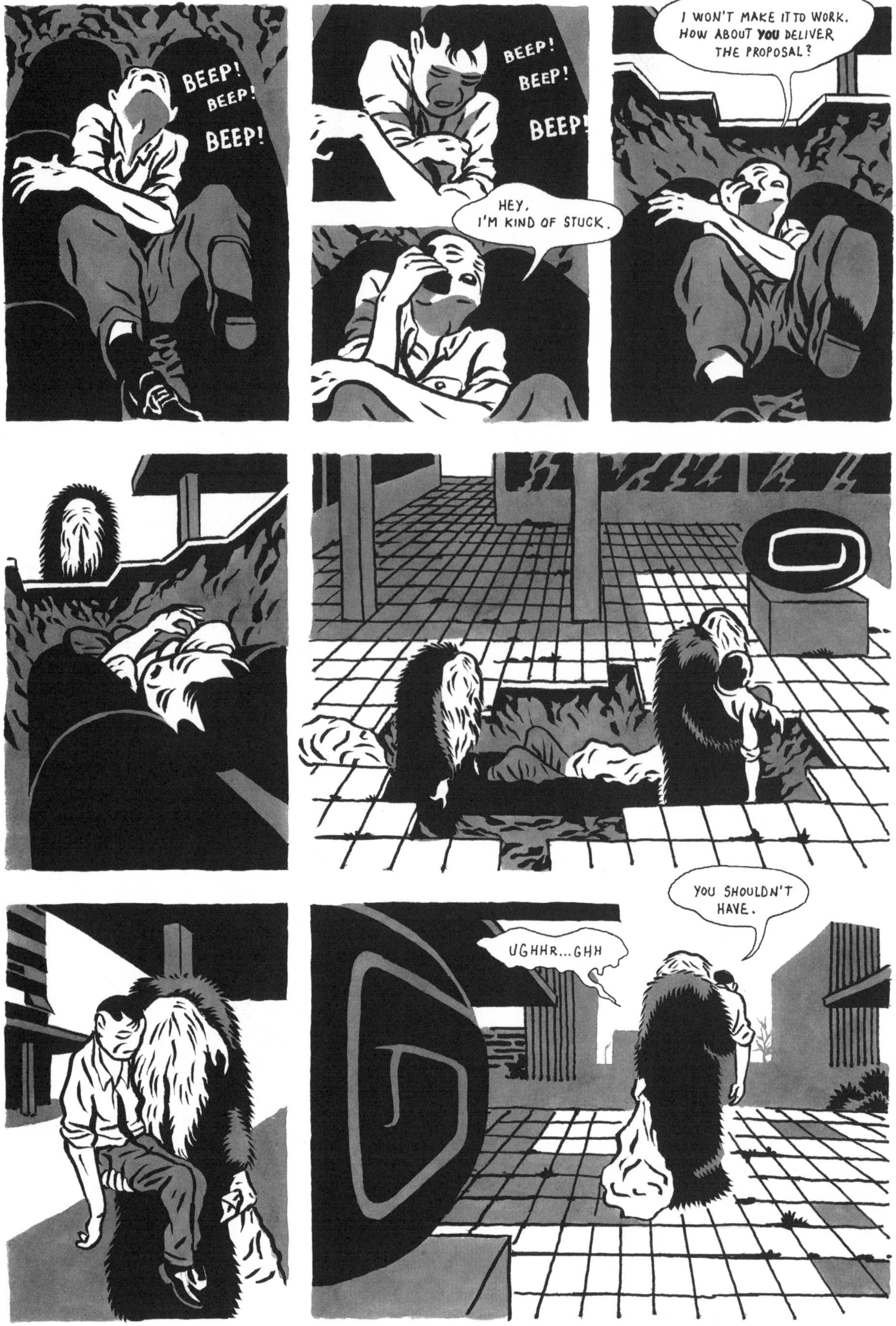
BEEP! BEEP! BEEP!
BEEP! BEEP! BEEP!
HEY, I'M KIND OF STUCK.
I WON'T MAKE IT TO WORK. HOW ABOUT YOU DELIVER THE PROPOSAL?
UGHHR...GHH
YOU SHOULDN'T HAVE.

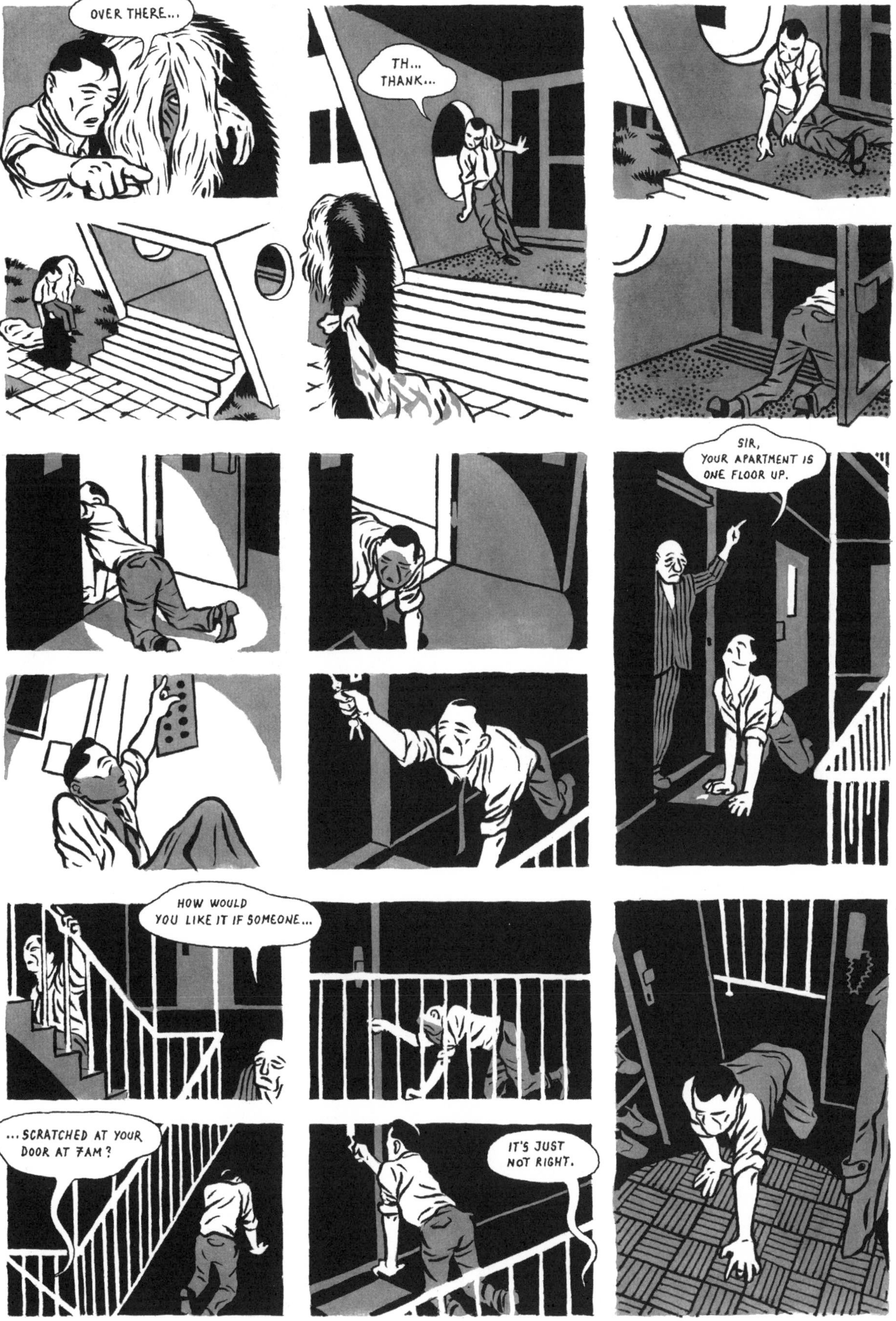
OVER THERE...
TH... THANK...
SIR, YOUR APARTMENT IS ONE FLOOR UP.
HOW WOULD YOU LIKE IT IF SOMEONE...
...SCRATCHED AT YOUR DOOR AT 7AM?
IT'S JUST NOT RIGHT.

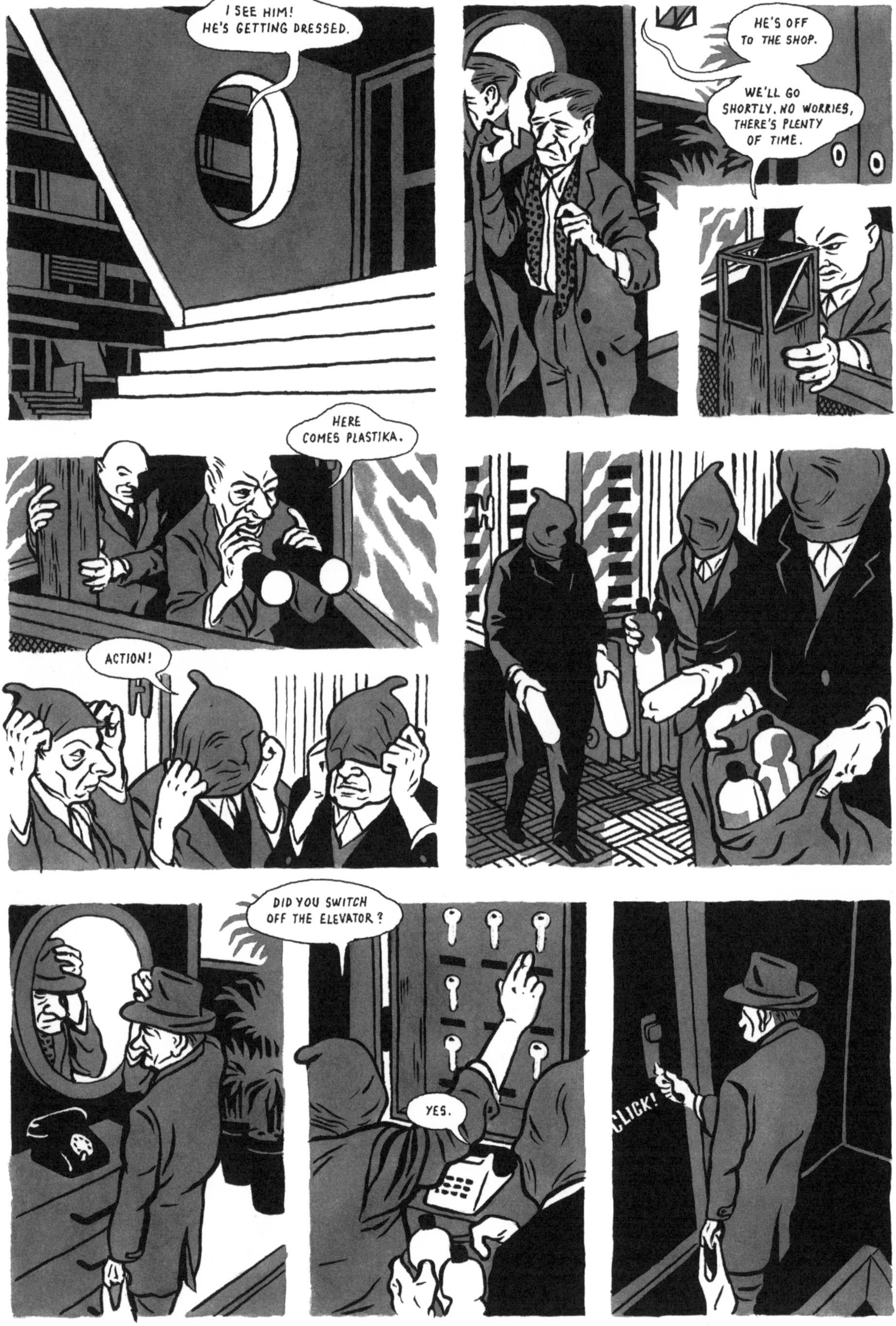
I SEE HIM!
HE'S GETTING DRESSED.
HE'S OFF TO THE SHOP.
WE'LL GO SHORTLY. NO WORRIES, THERE'S PLENTY OF TIME.
HERE COMES PLASTIKA.
ACTION!
DID YOU SWITCH OFF THE ELEVATOR ?
YES.
CLICK!

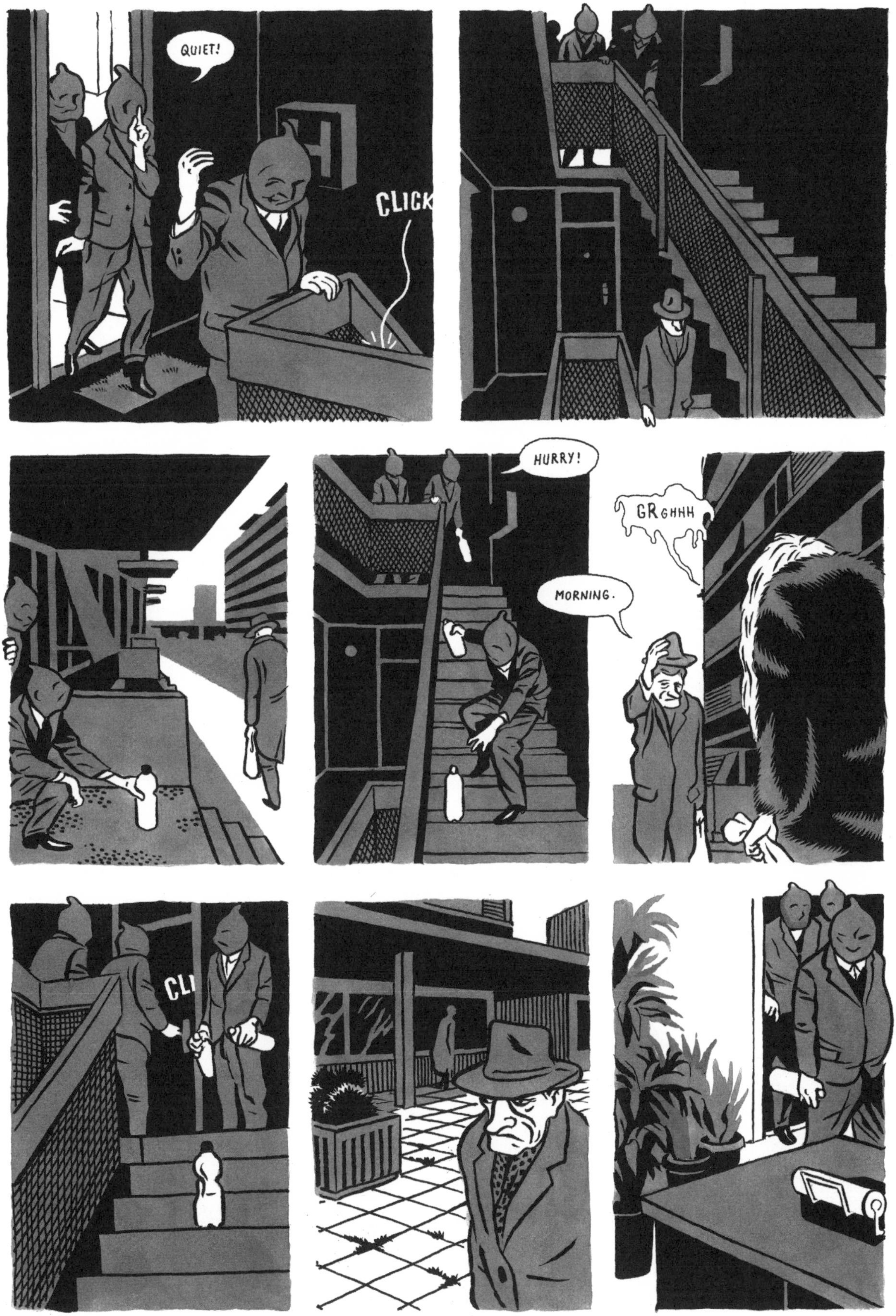
QUIET!
CLICK
HURRY!
GRGHHH
MORNING.
CLI

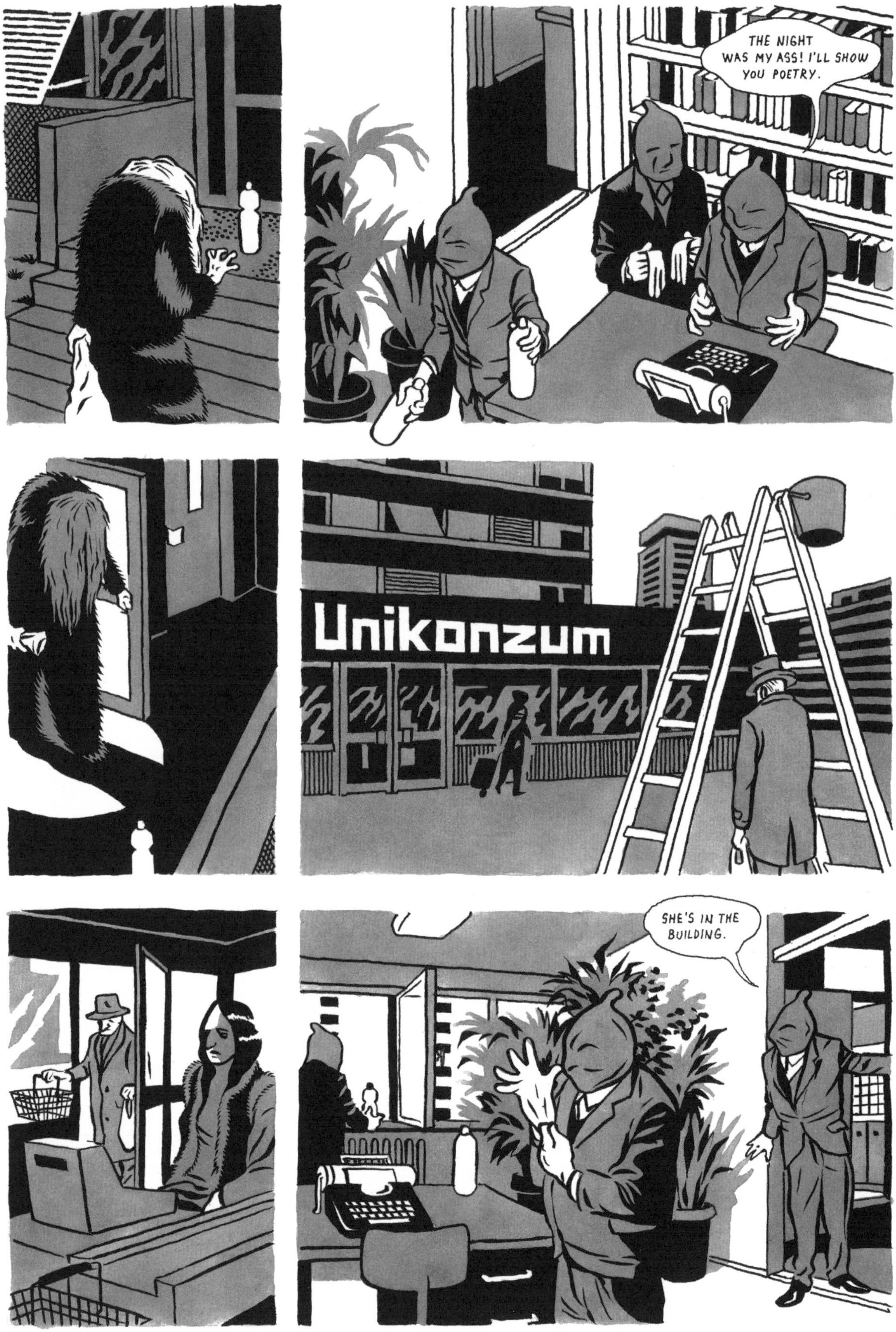
THE NIGHT WAS MY ASS! I'LL SHOW YOU POETRY.
Unikonzum
SHE'S IN THE BUILDING.

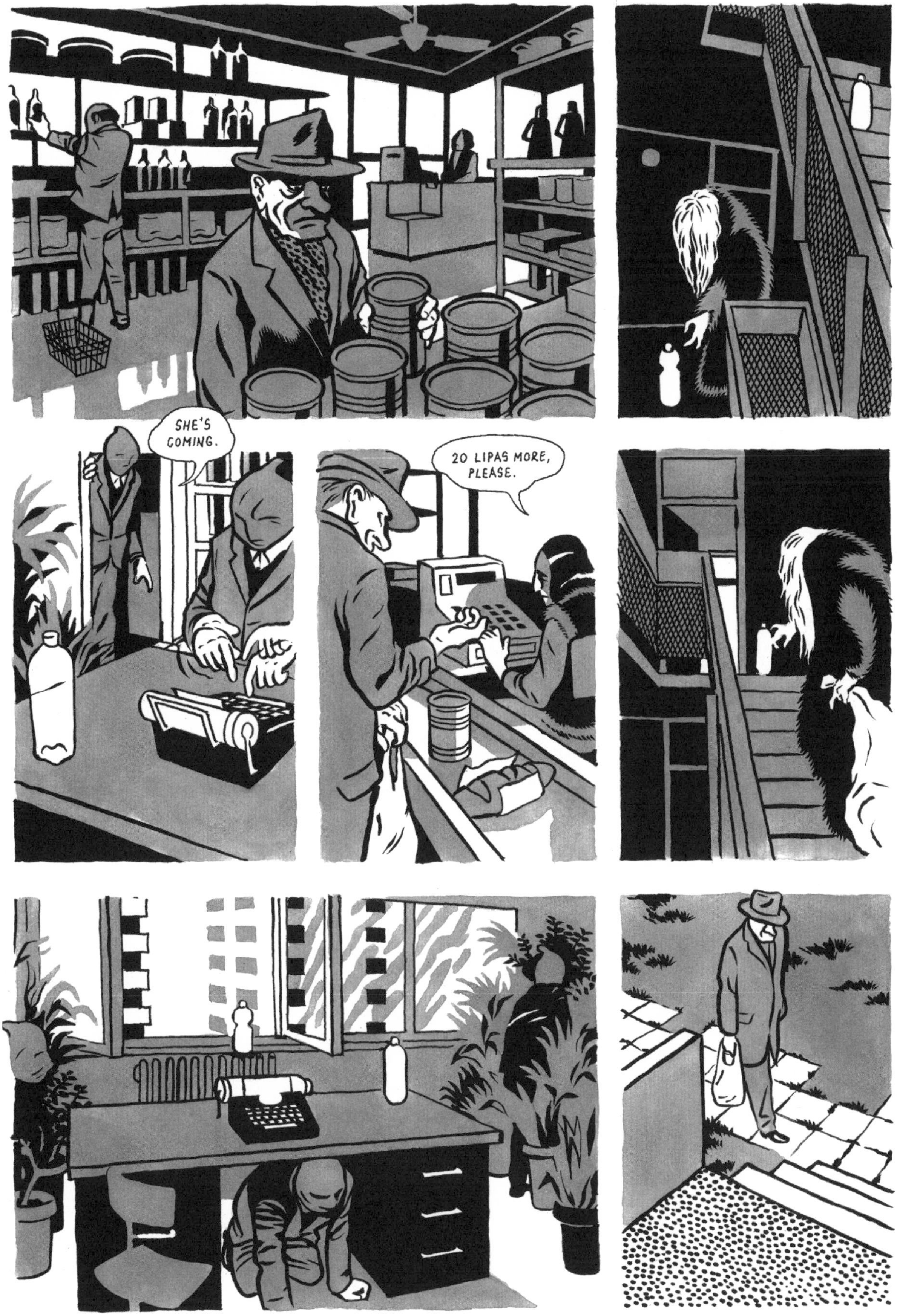
SHE'S COMING.
20 LIPAS MORE, PLEASE.

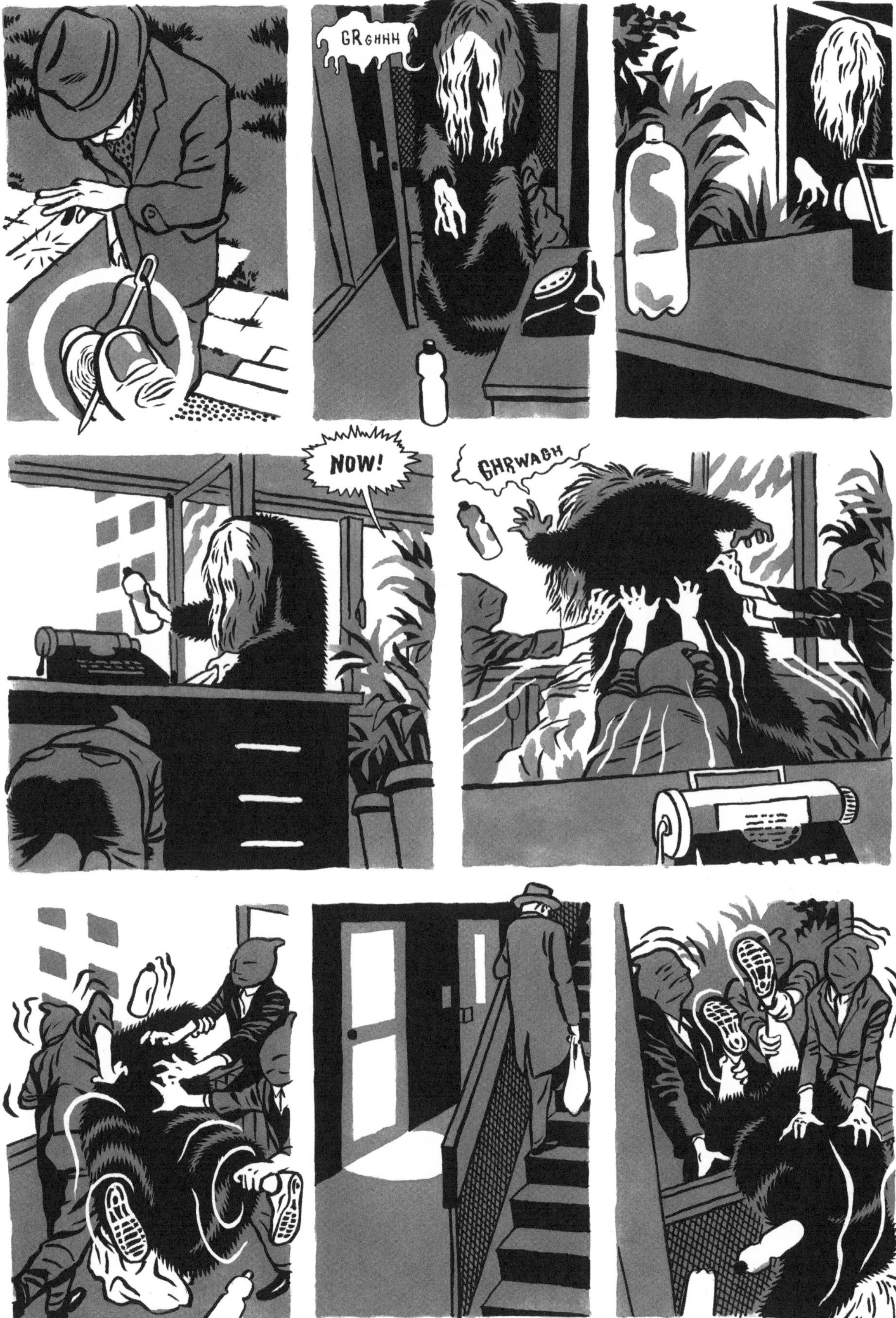
GRGHHH
NOW!
GHRWAGH

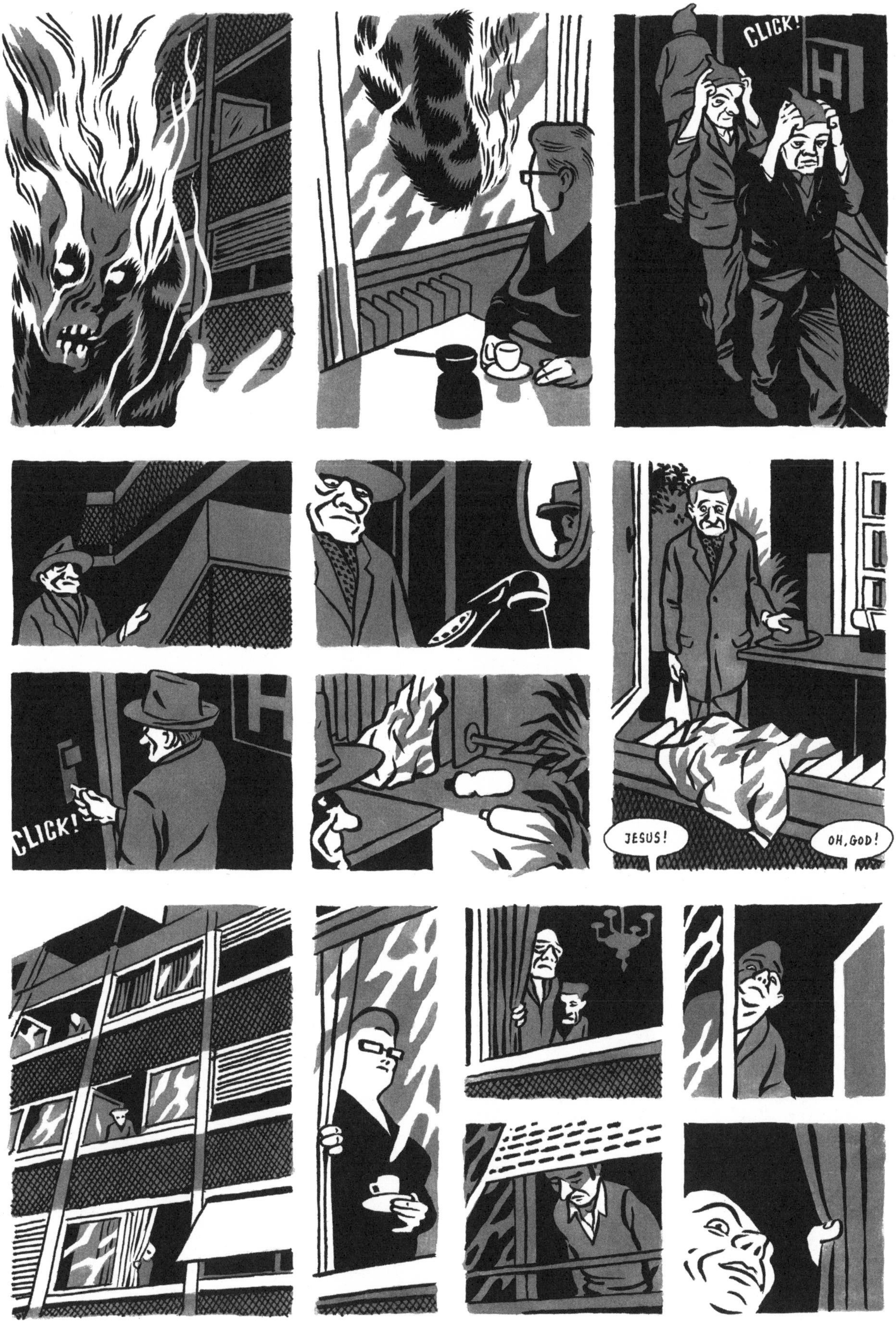
CLICK!
CLICK!
JESUS!
OH, GOD!

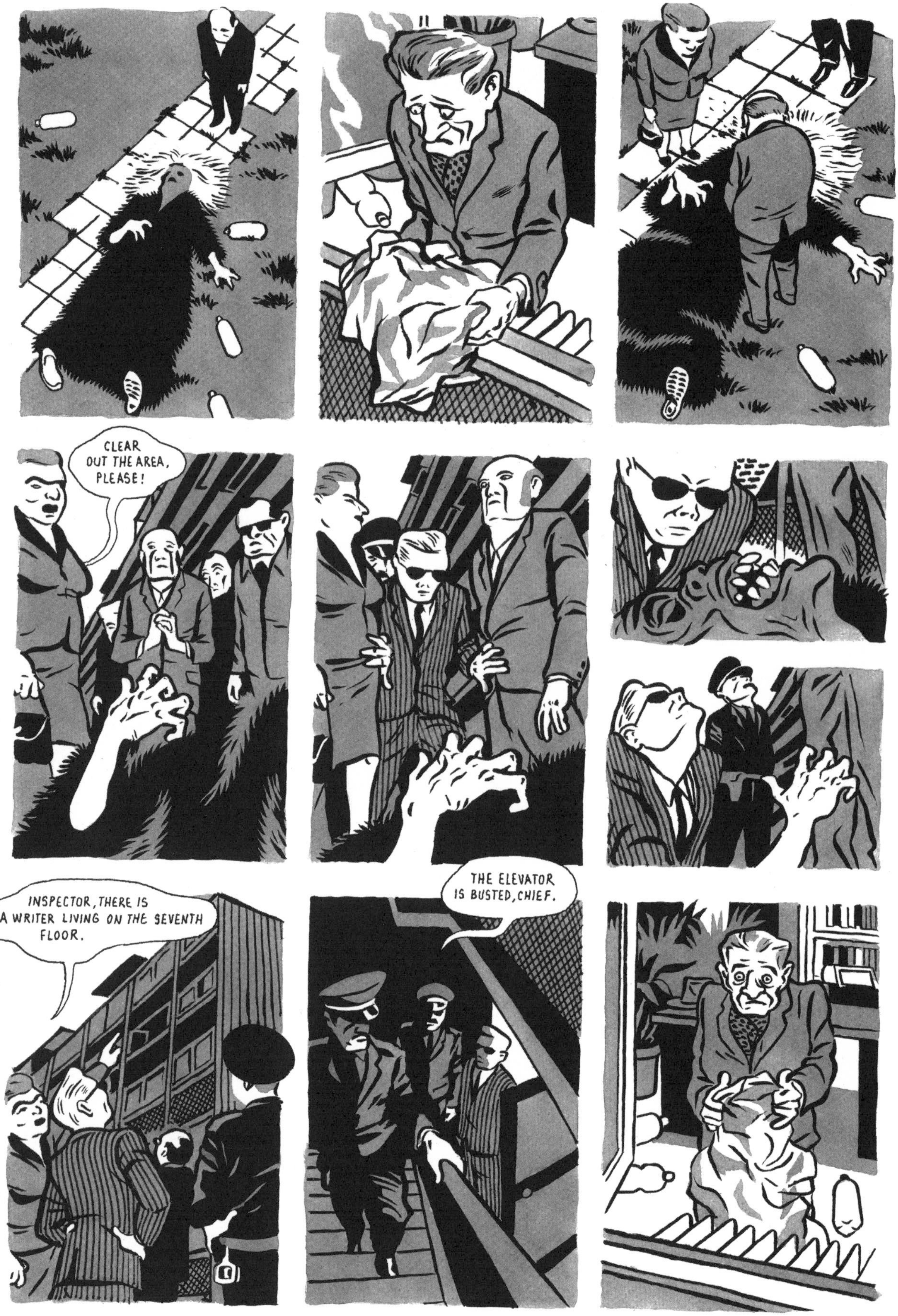
CLEAR OUT THE AREA, PLEASE!
INSPECTOR, THERE IS A WRITER LIVING ON THE SEVENTH FLOOR.
THE ELEVATOR IS BUSTED, CHIEF.

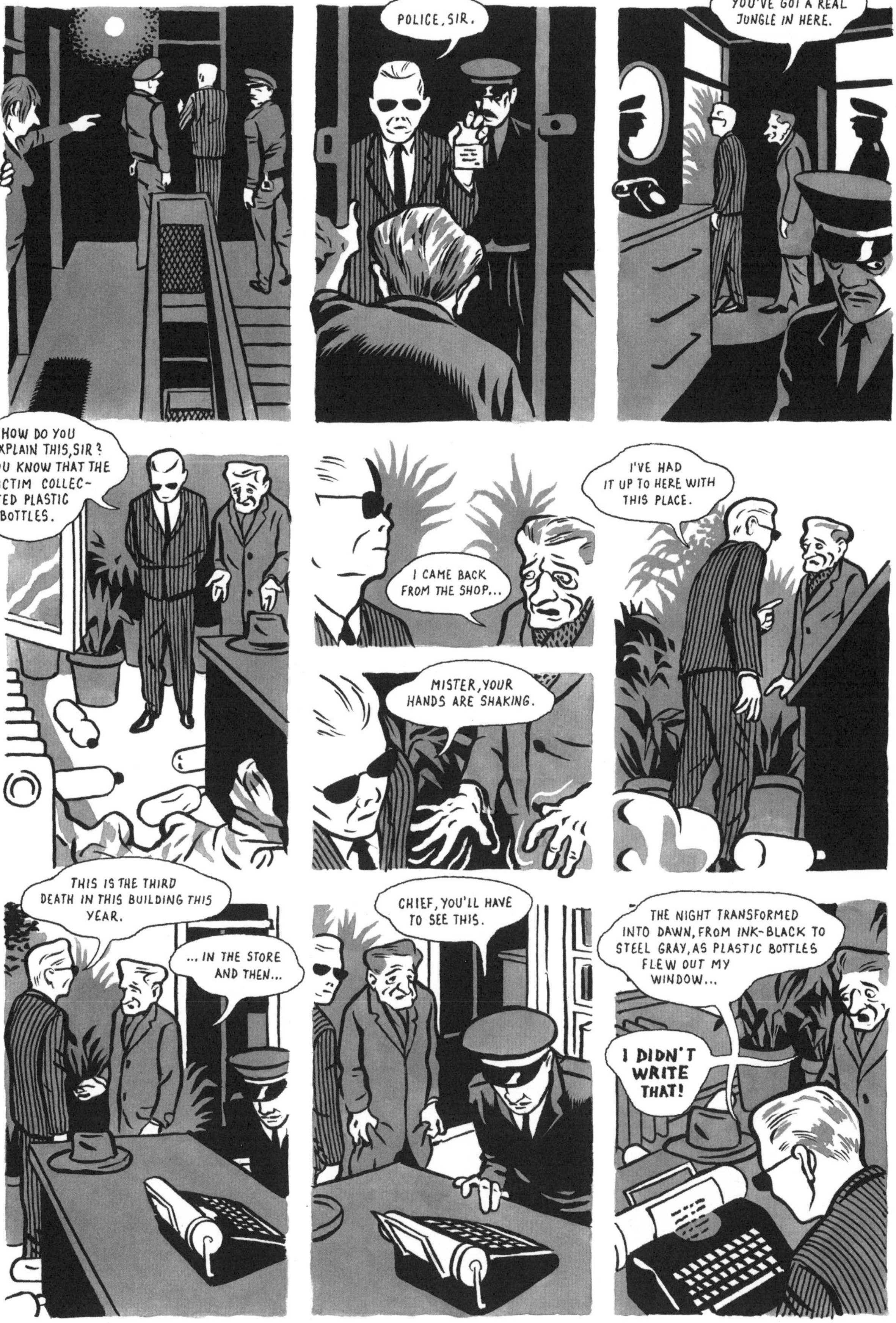
POLICE, SIR.
YOU'VE GOT A REAL JUNGLE IN HERE.
HOW DO YOU EXPLAIN THIS, SIR? YOU KNOW THAT THE VICTIM COLLECTED PLASTIC BOTTLES.
I CAME BACK FROM THE SHOP...
MISTER, YOUR HANDS ARE SHAKING.
I'VE HAD IT UP TO HERE WITH THIS PLACE.
THIS IS THE THIRD DEATH IN THIS BUILDING THIS YEAR.
... IN THE STORE AND THEN...
CHIEF, YOU'LL HAVE TO SEE THIS.
THE NIGHT TRANSFORMED INTO DAWN, FROM INK-BLACK TO STEEL GRAY, AS PLASTIC BOTTLES FLEW OUT MY WINDOW...
I DIDN'T WRITE THAT!

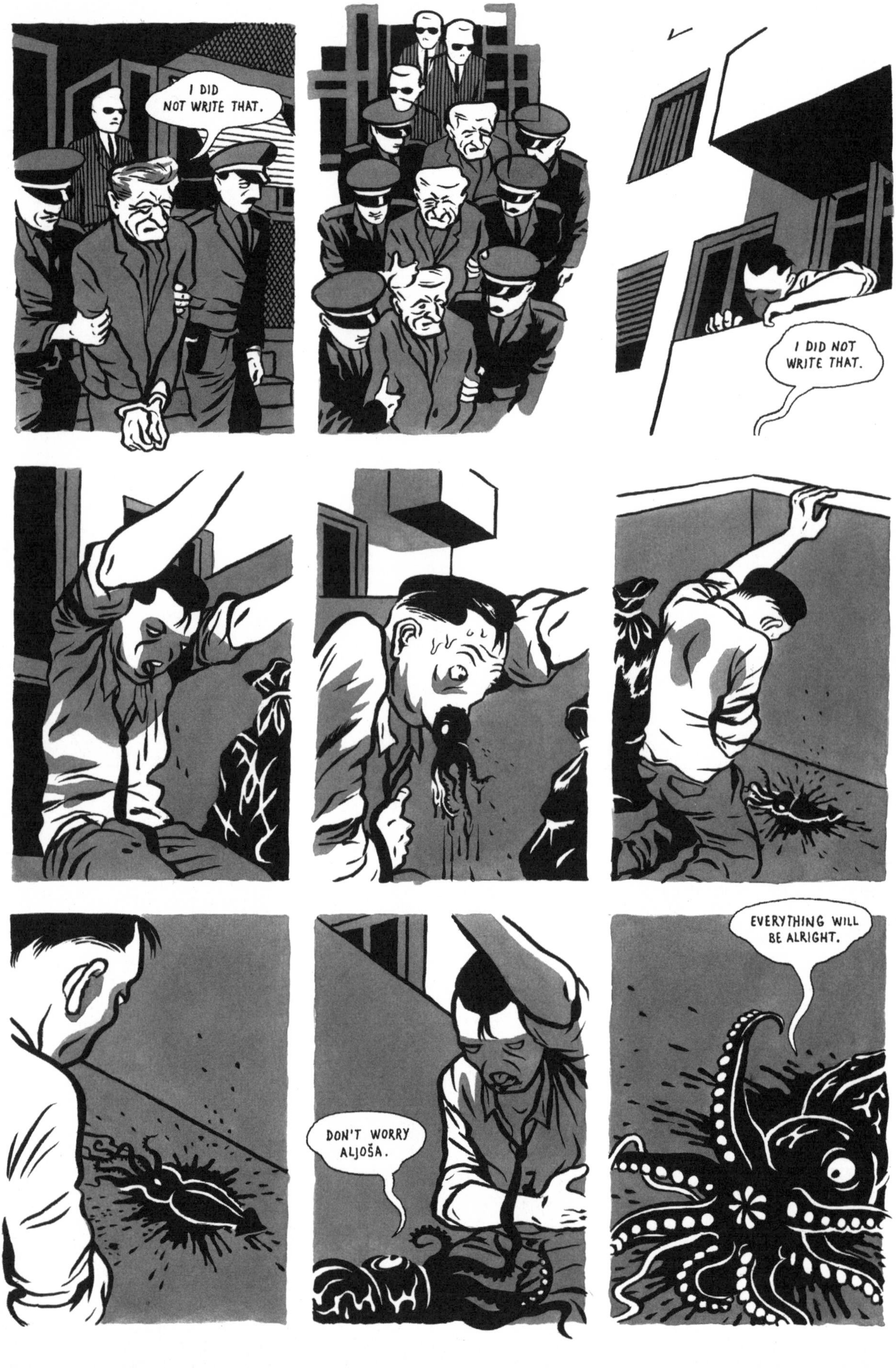
I DID NOT WRITE THAT.
I DID NOT WRITE THAT.
DON'T WORRY ALJOŠA.
EVERYTHING WILL BE ALRIGHT.

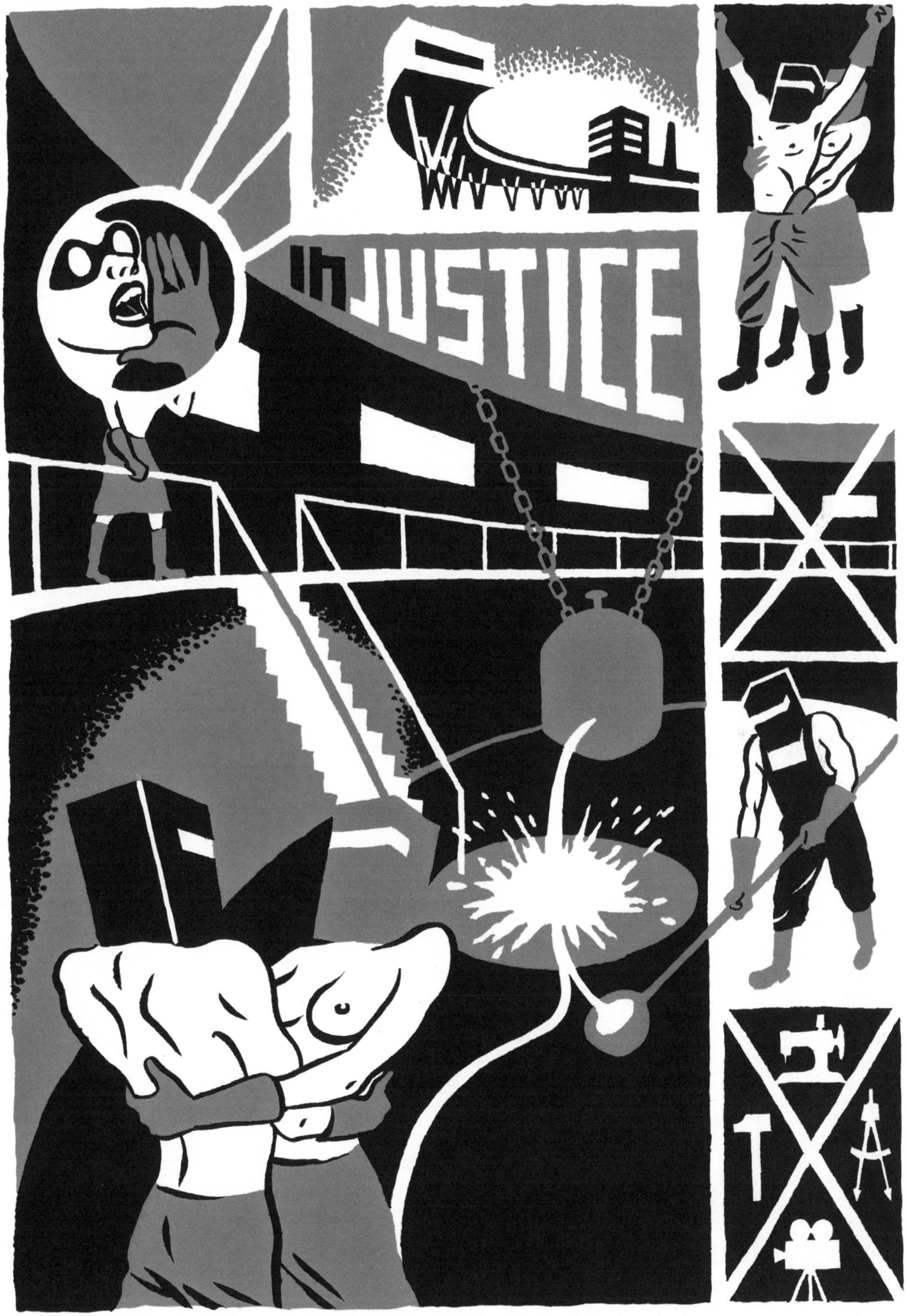
InJUSTICE

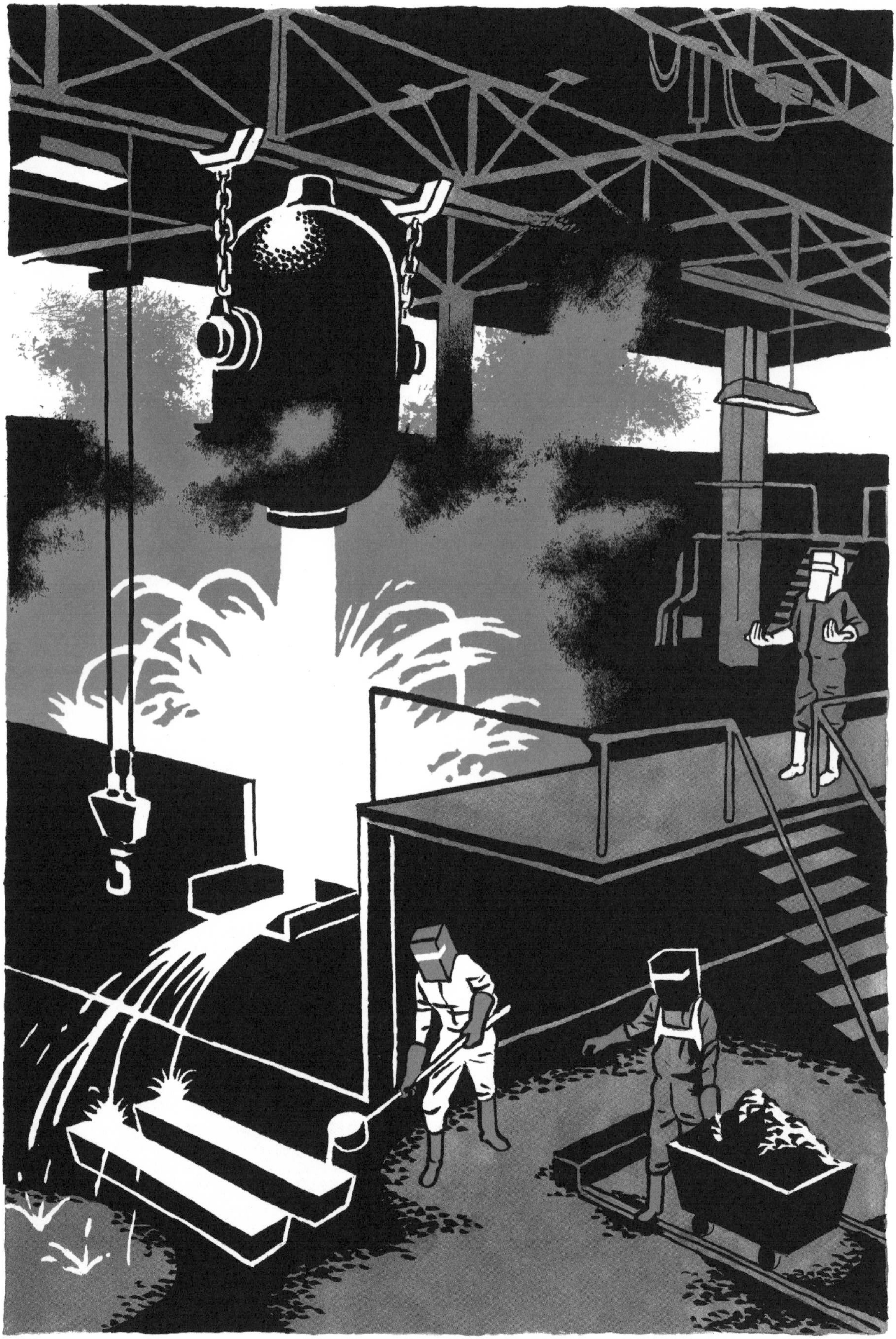

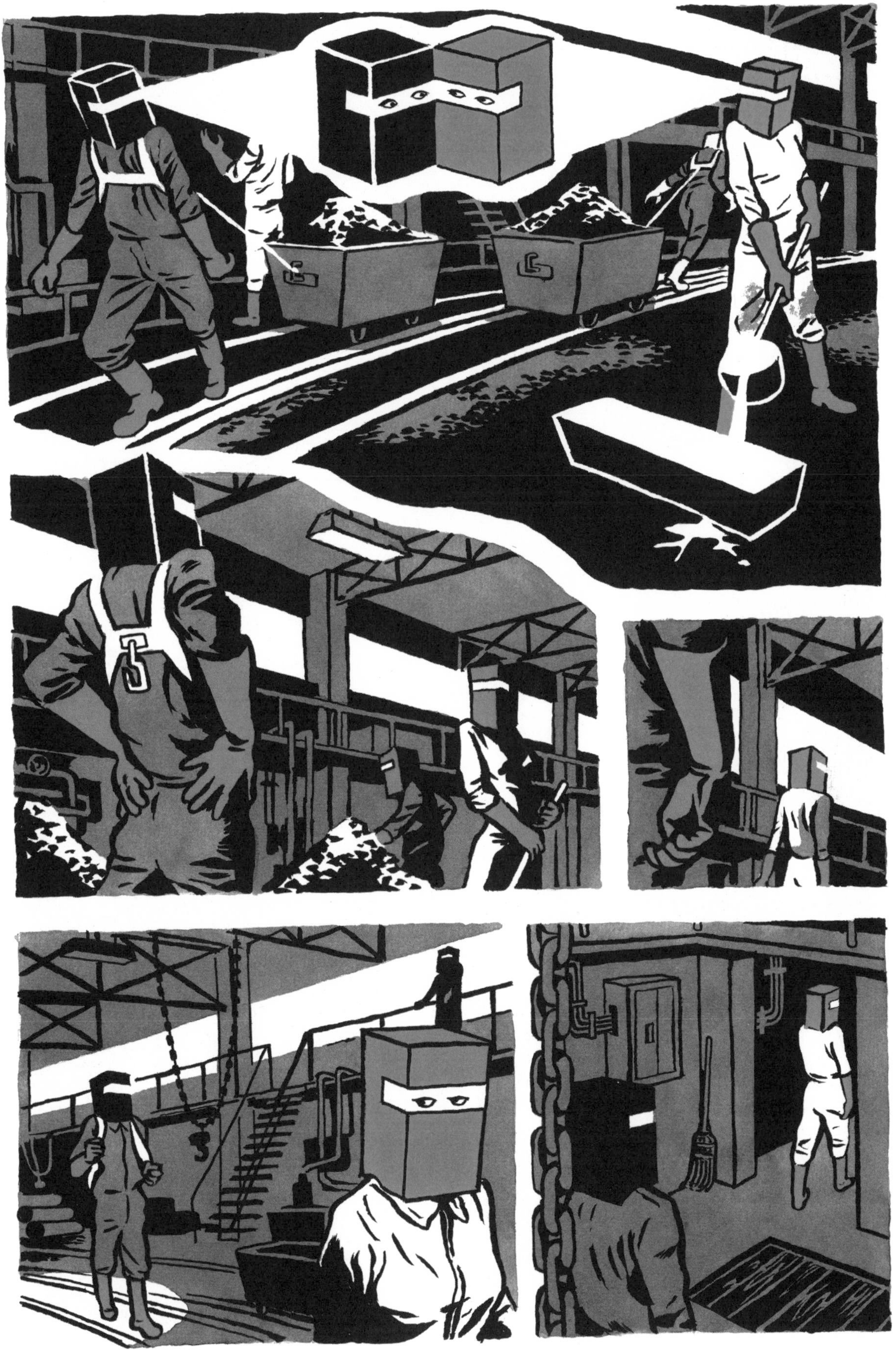

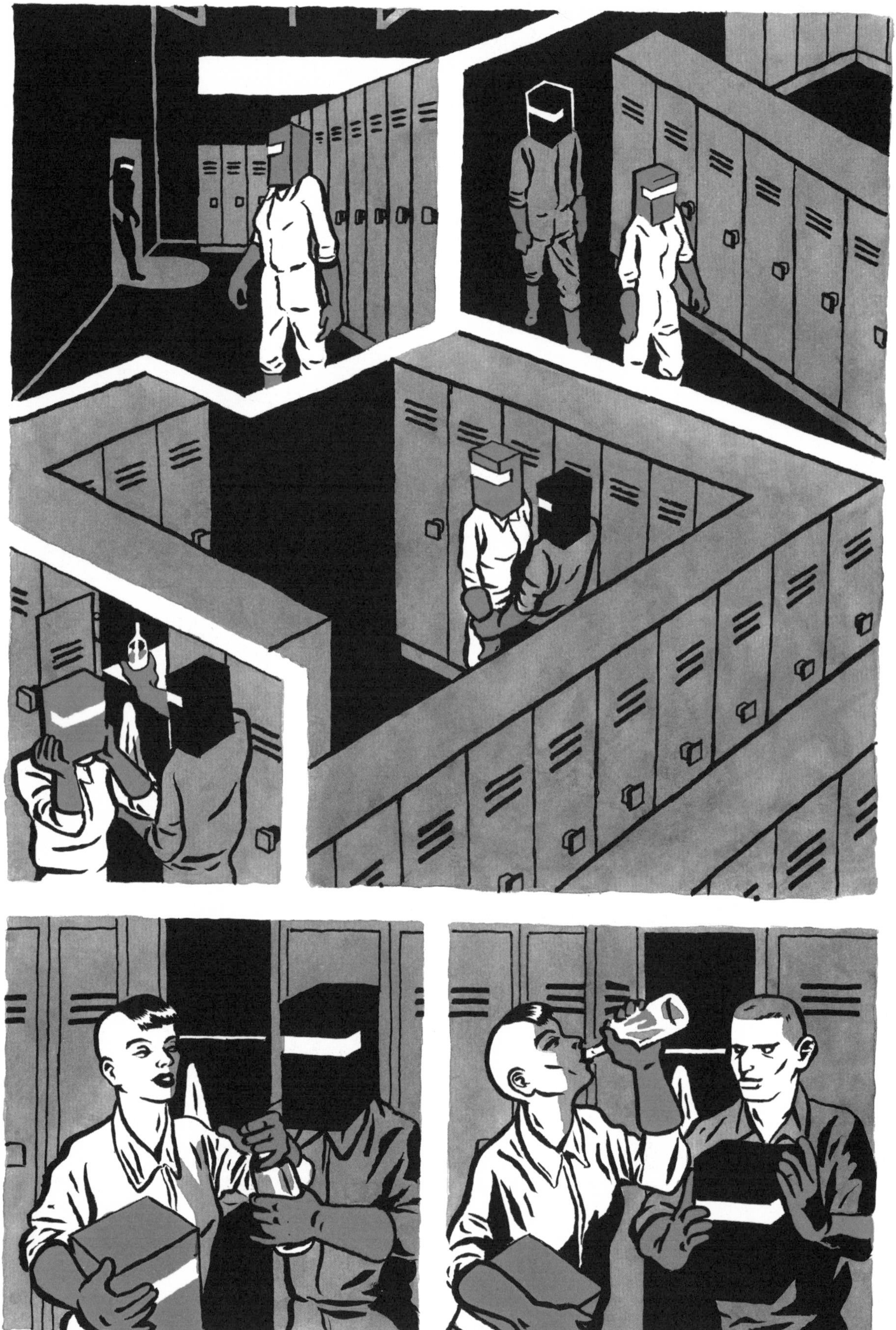

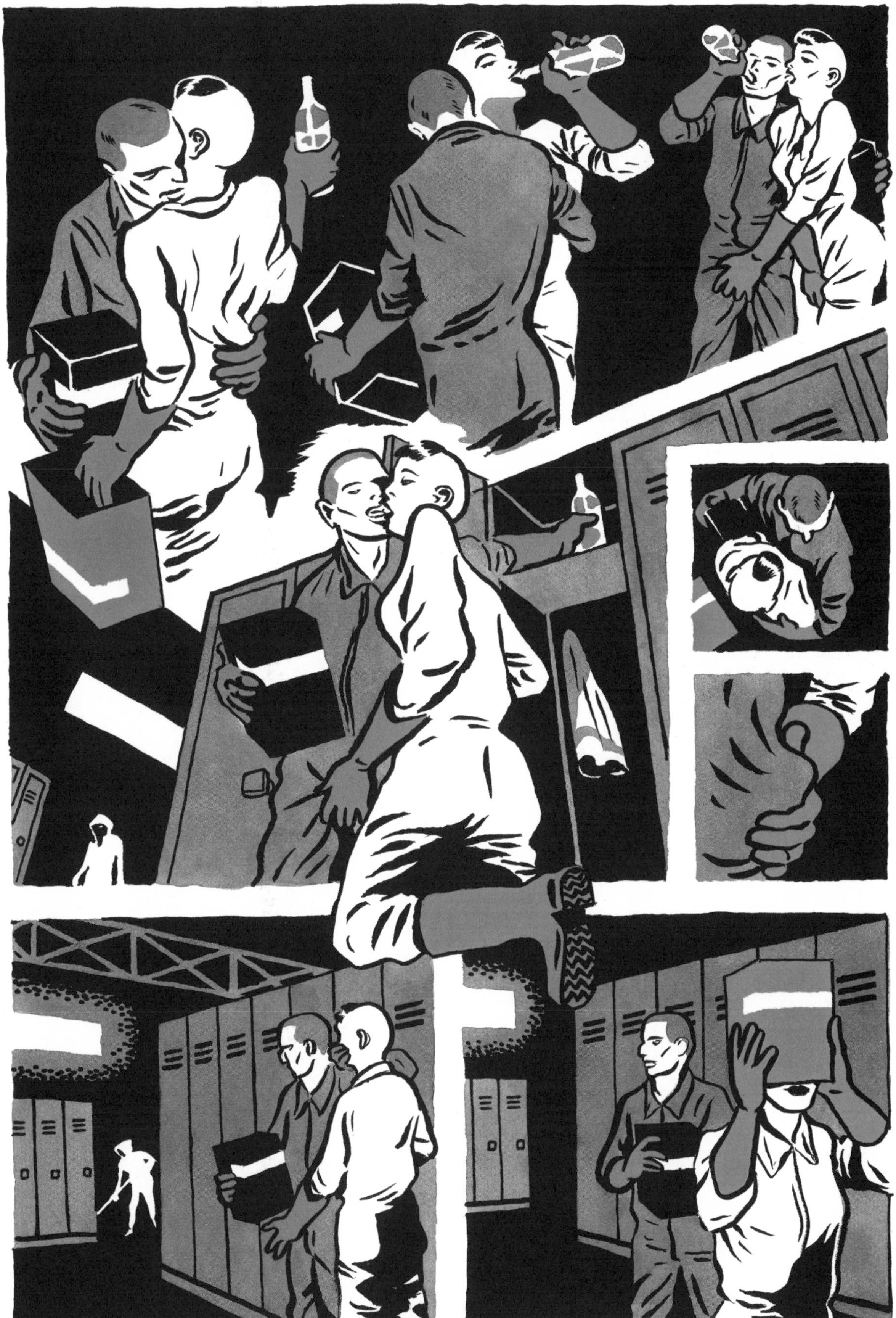

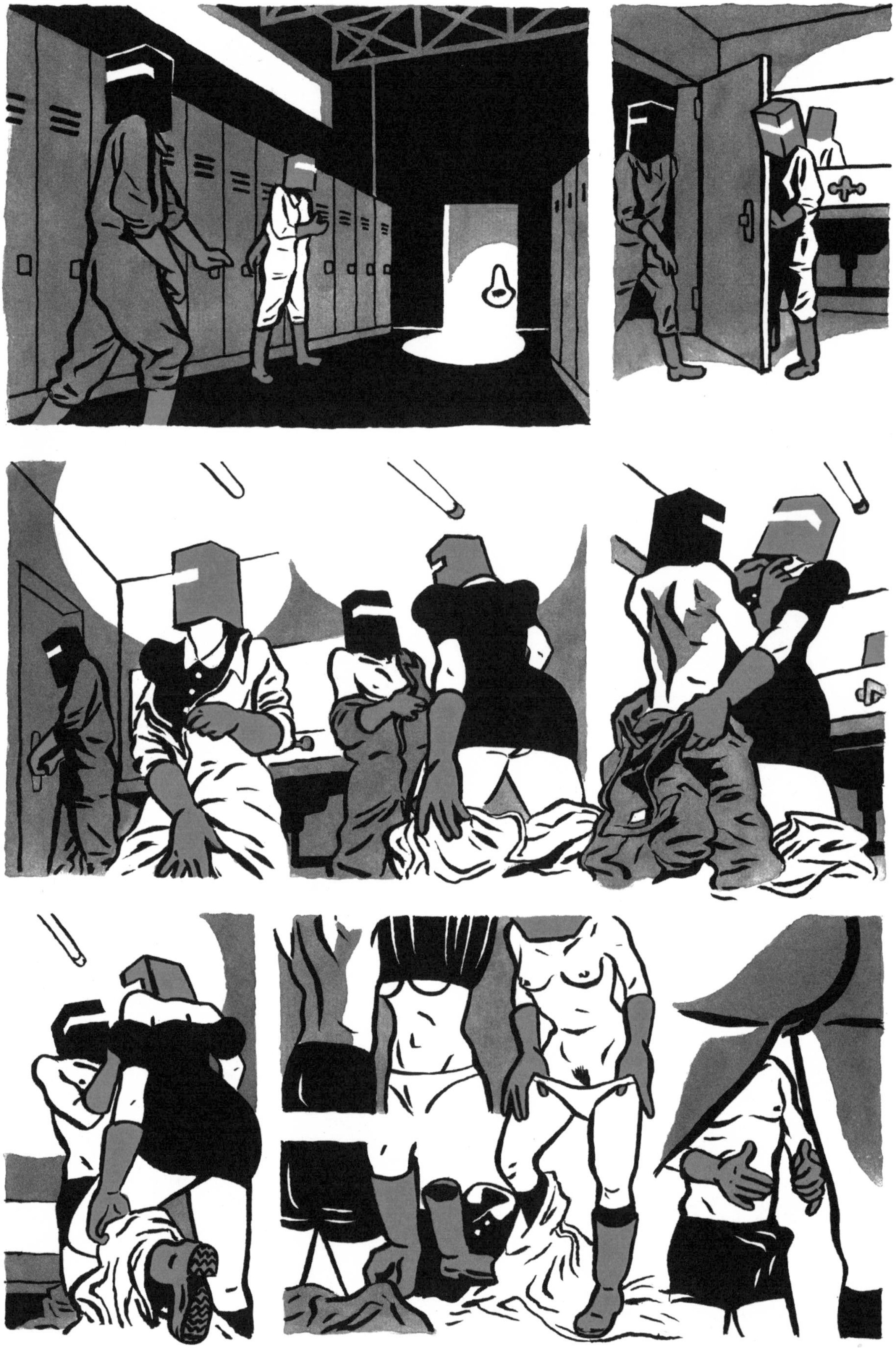

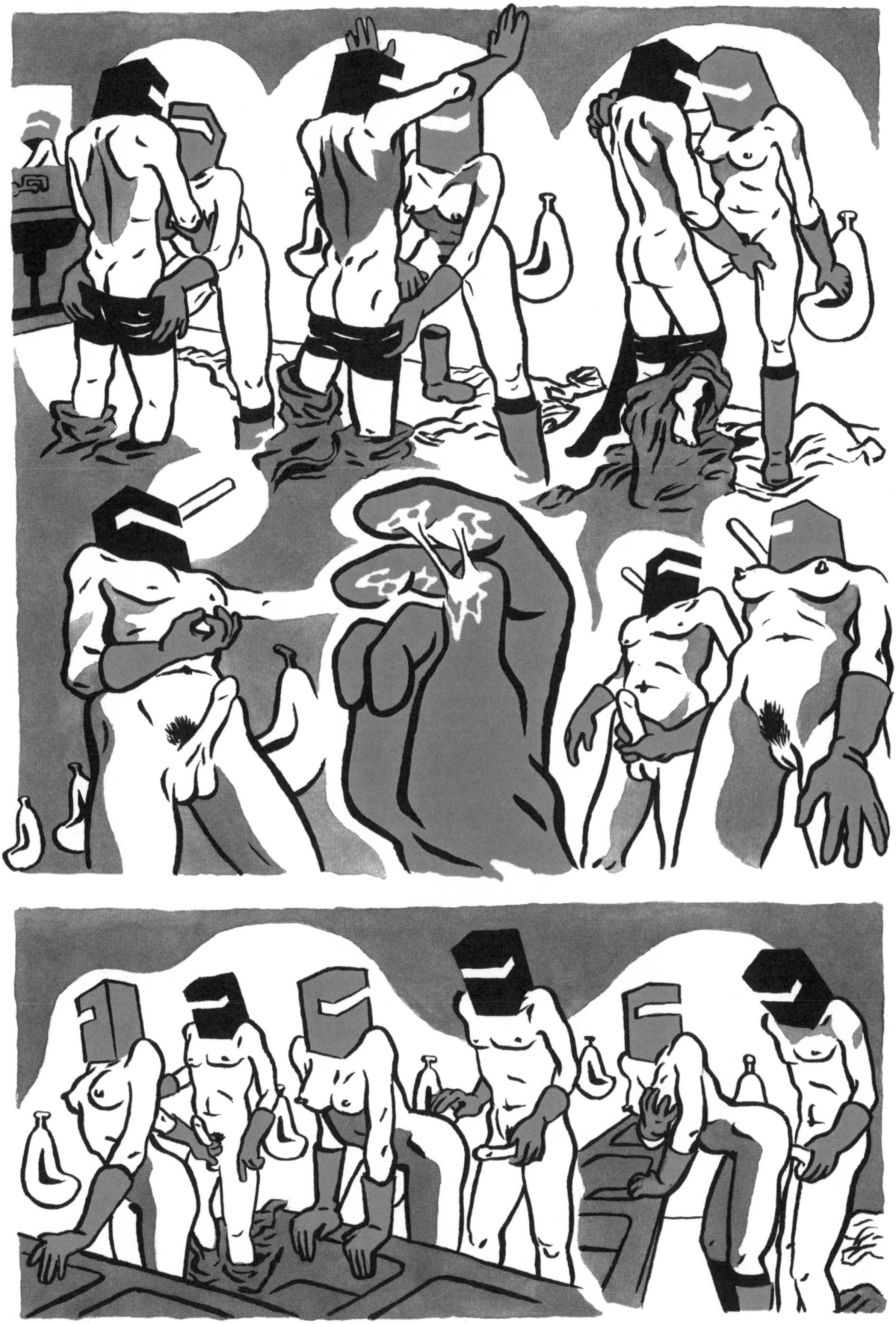

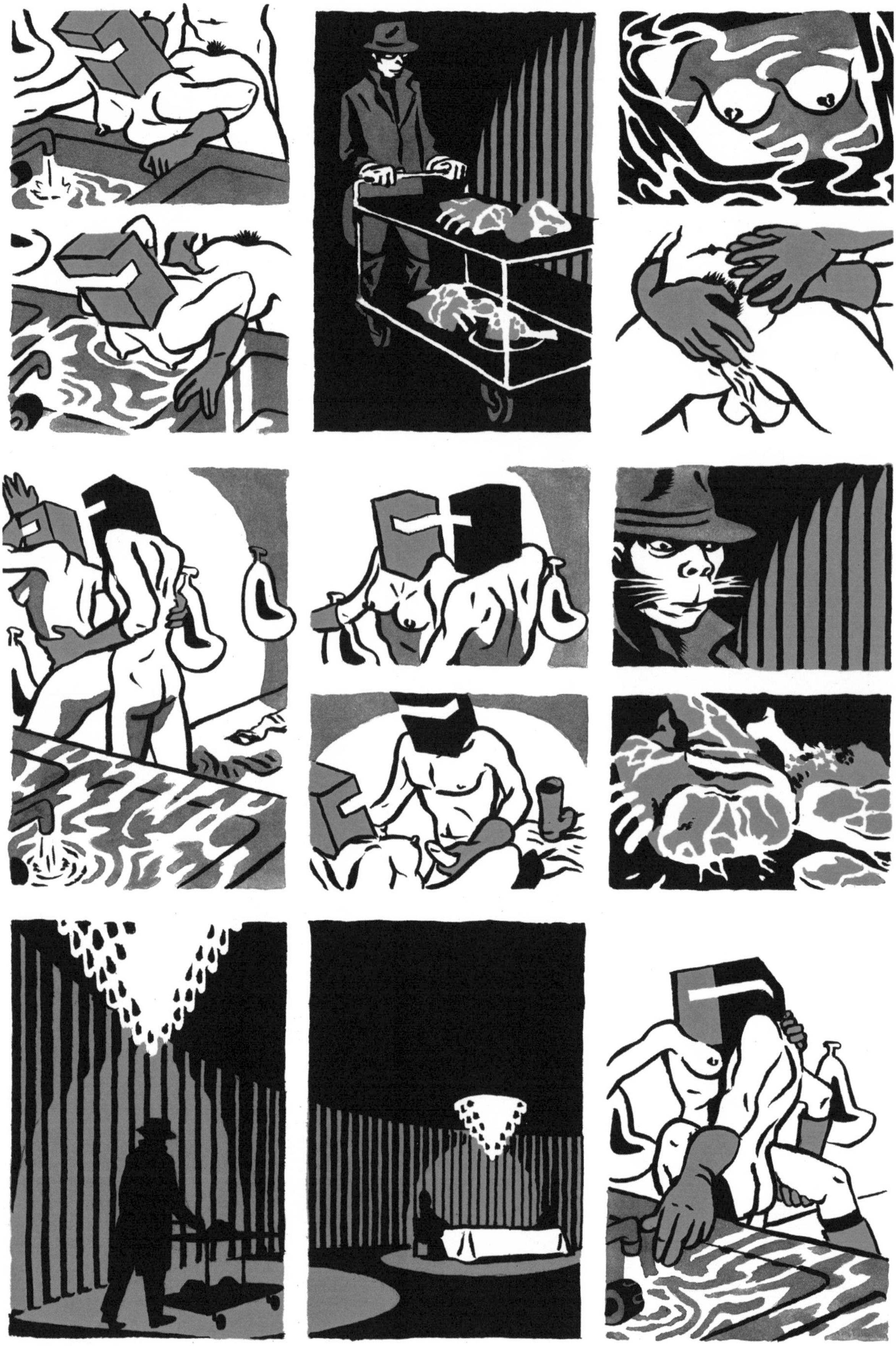

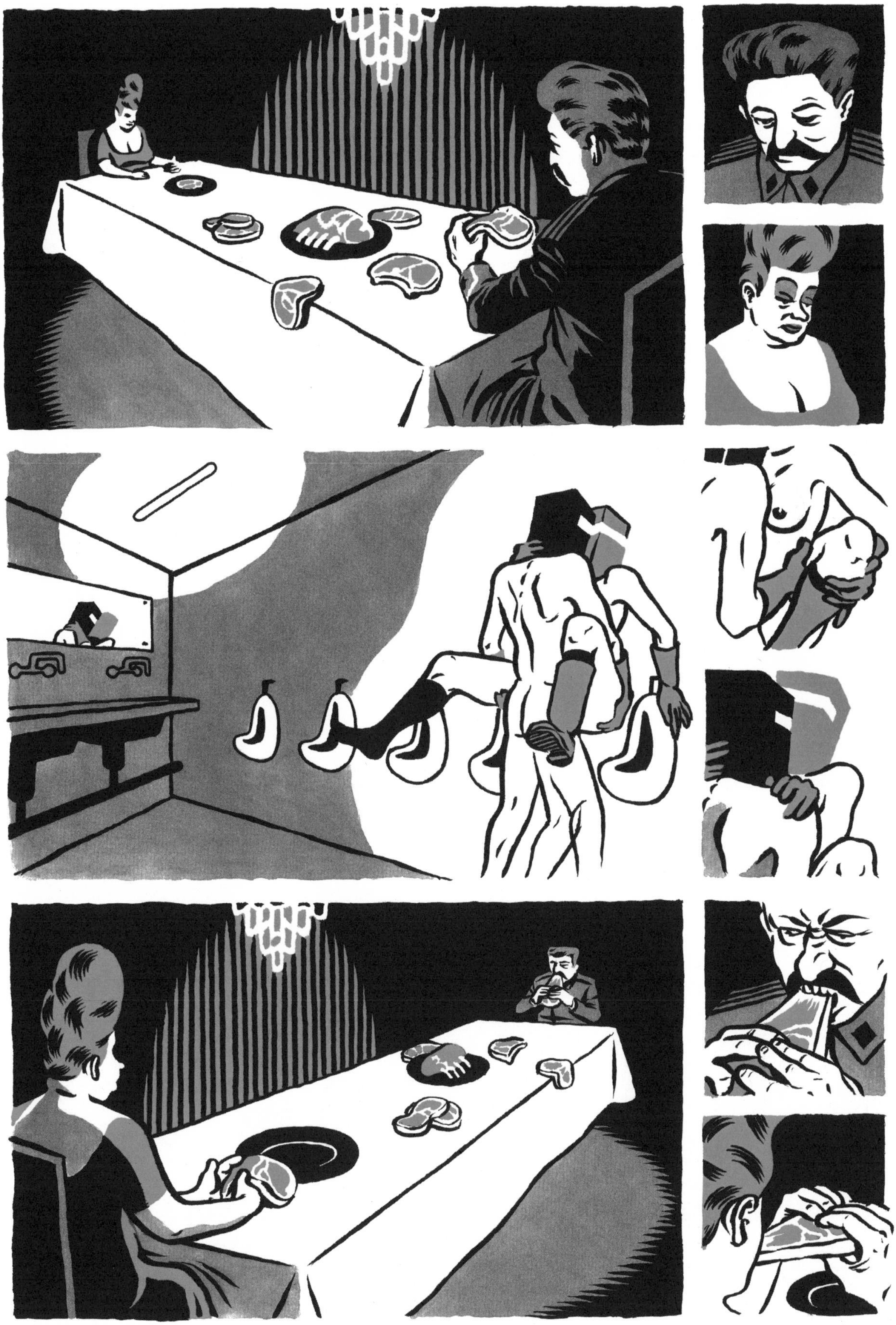

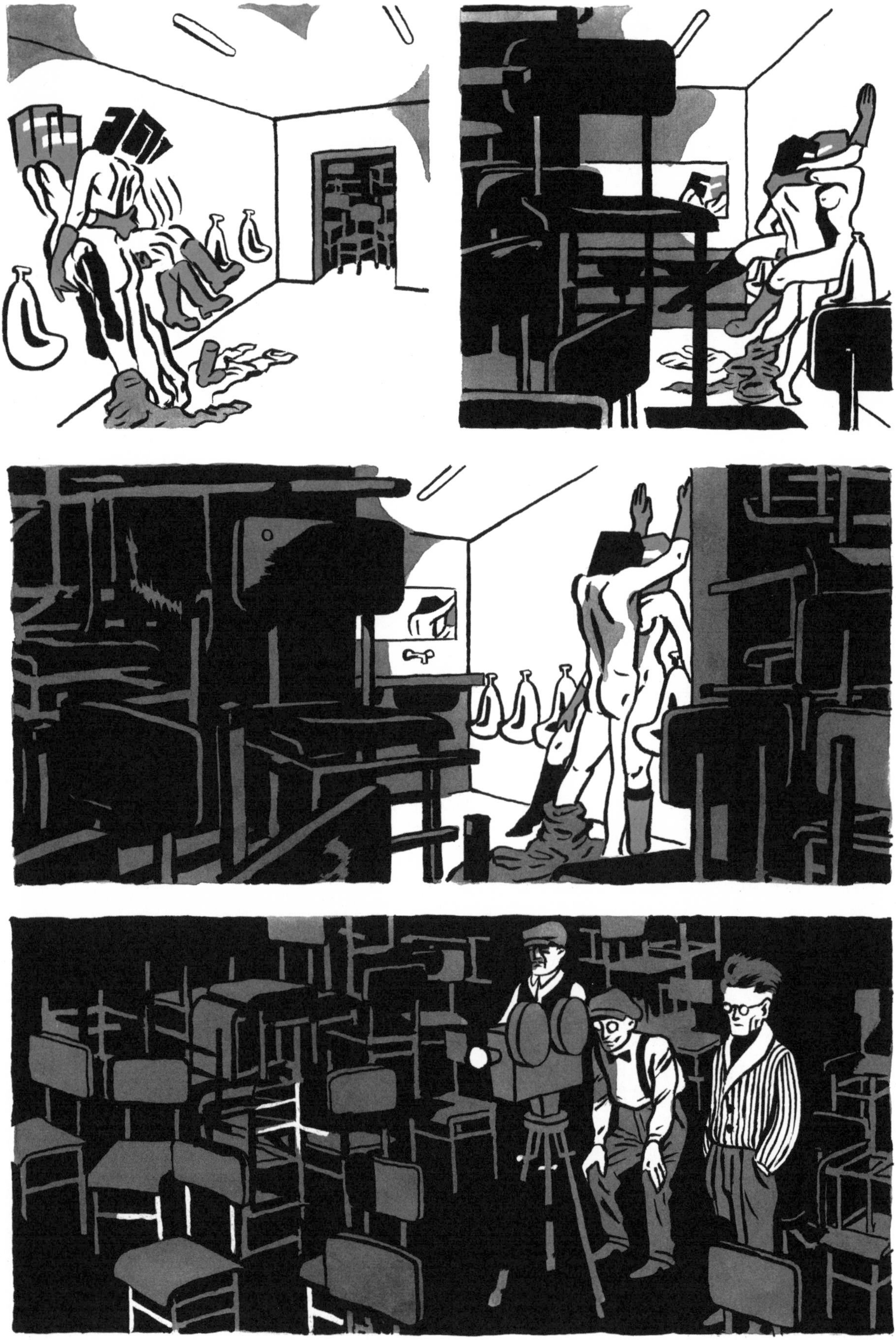

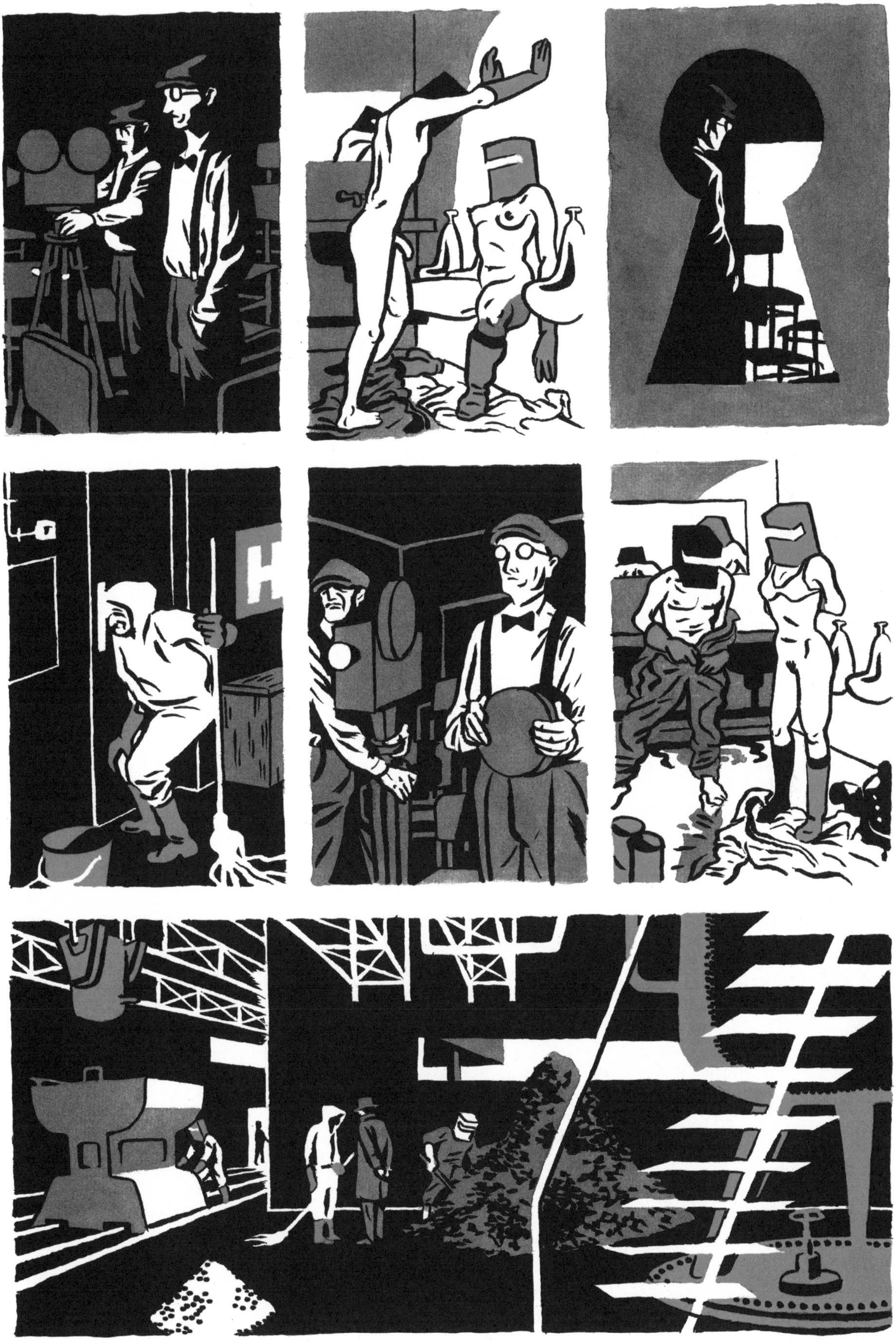

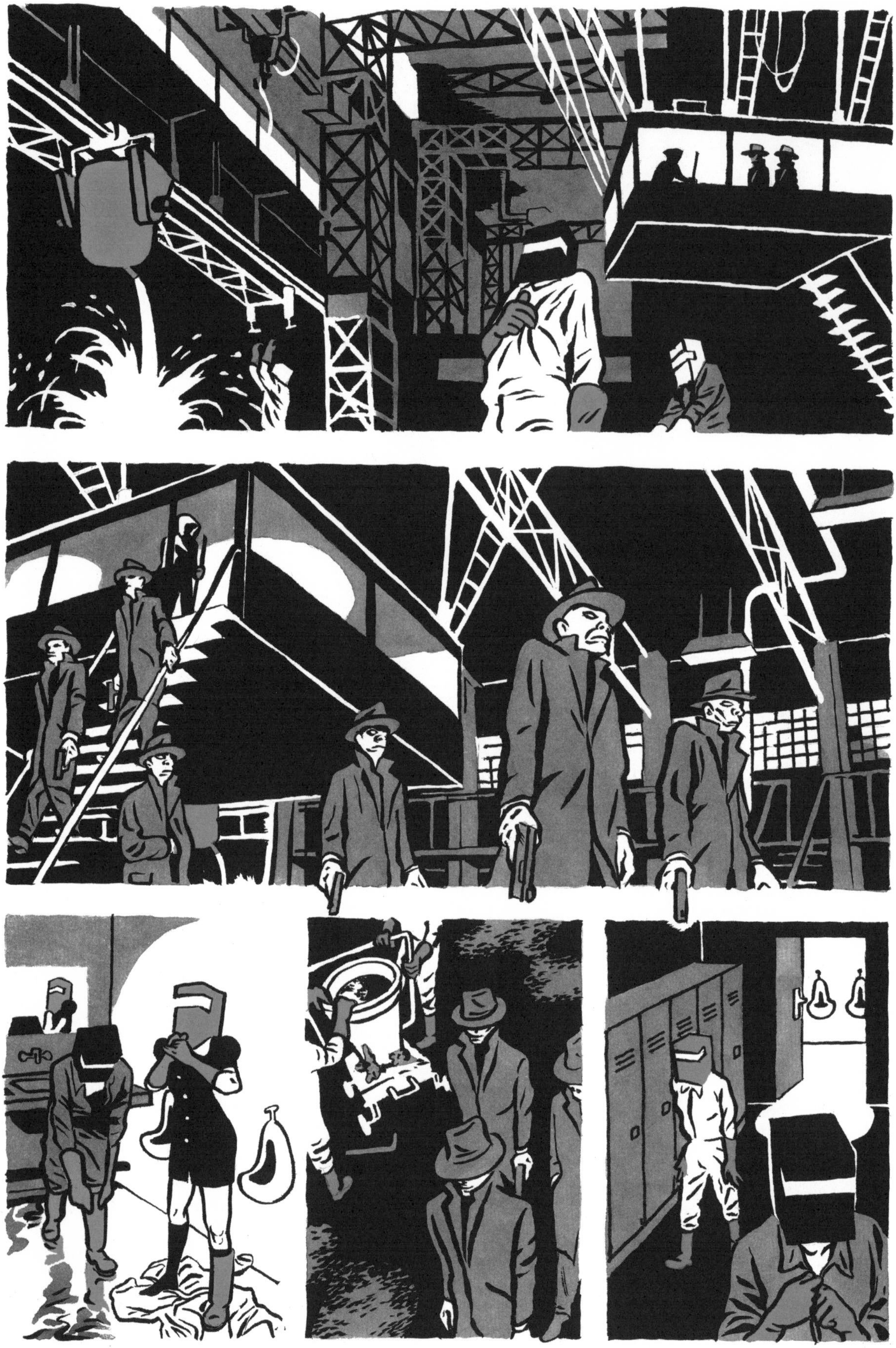

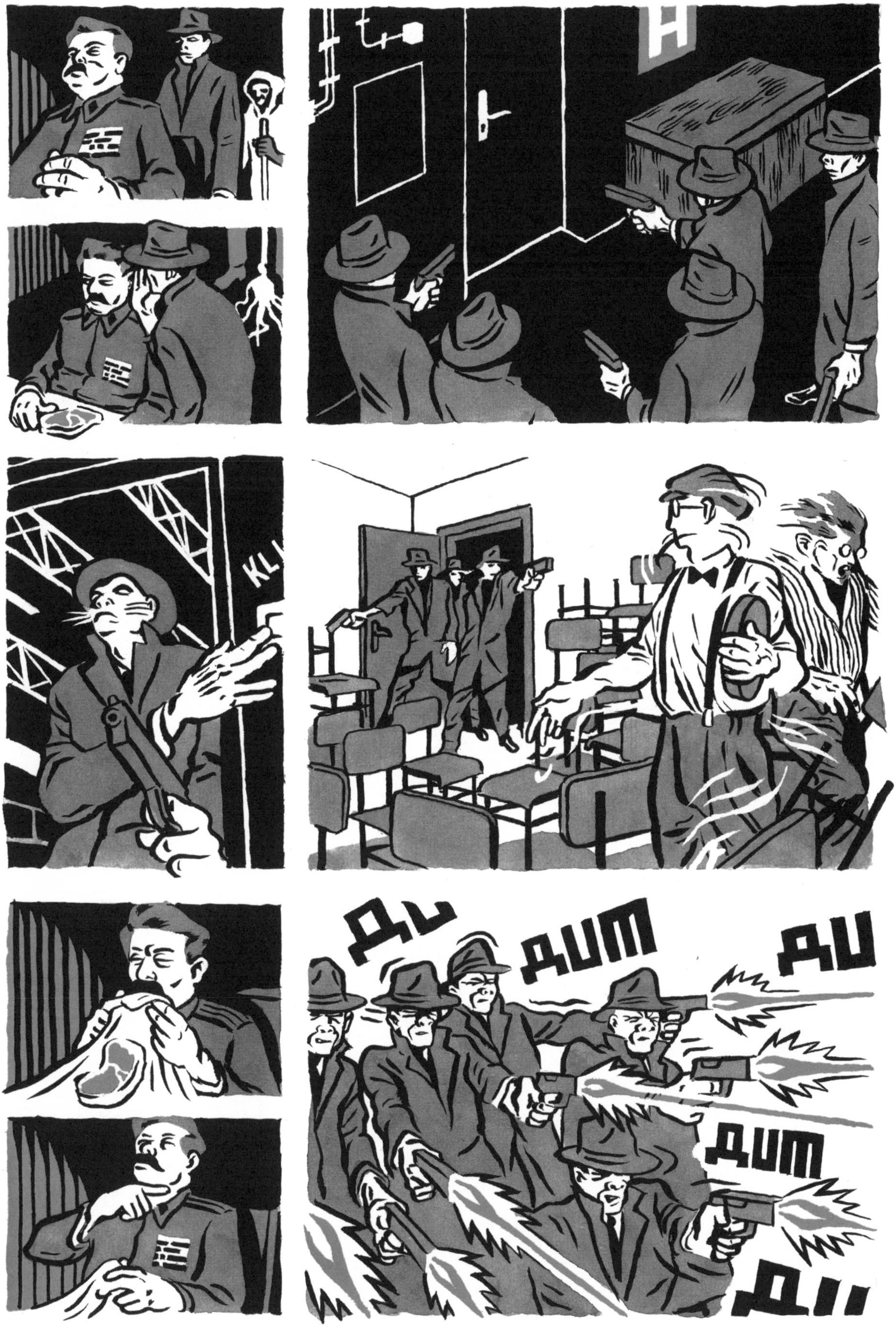
KL
ДИ
ДИМ
ДИ
ДИМ
ДИ

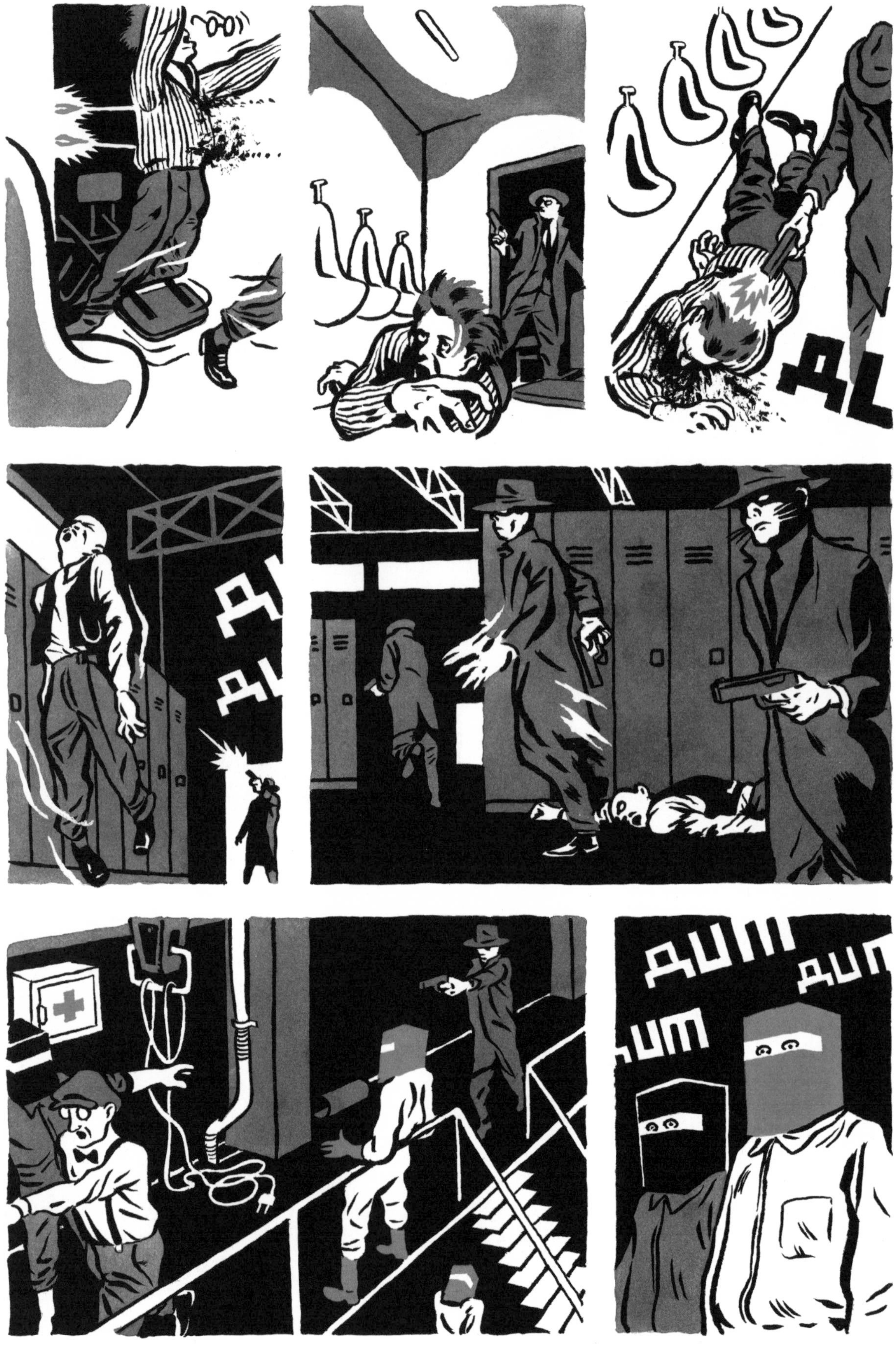

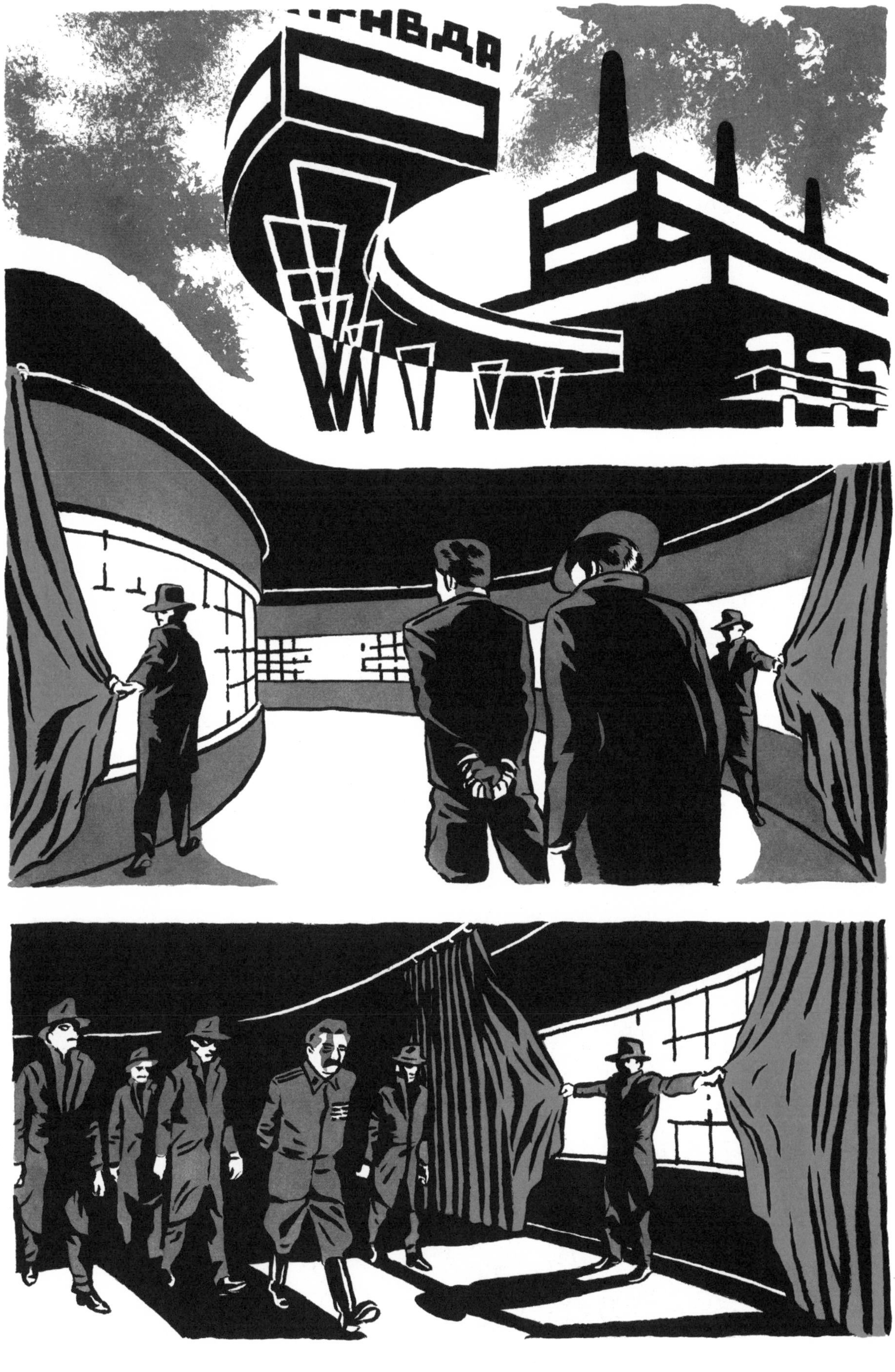

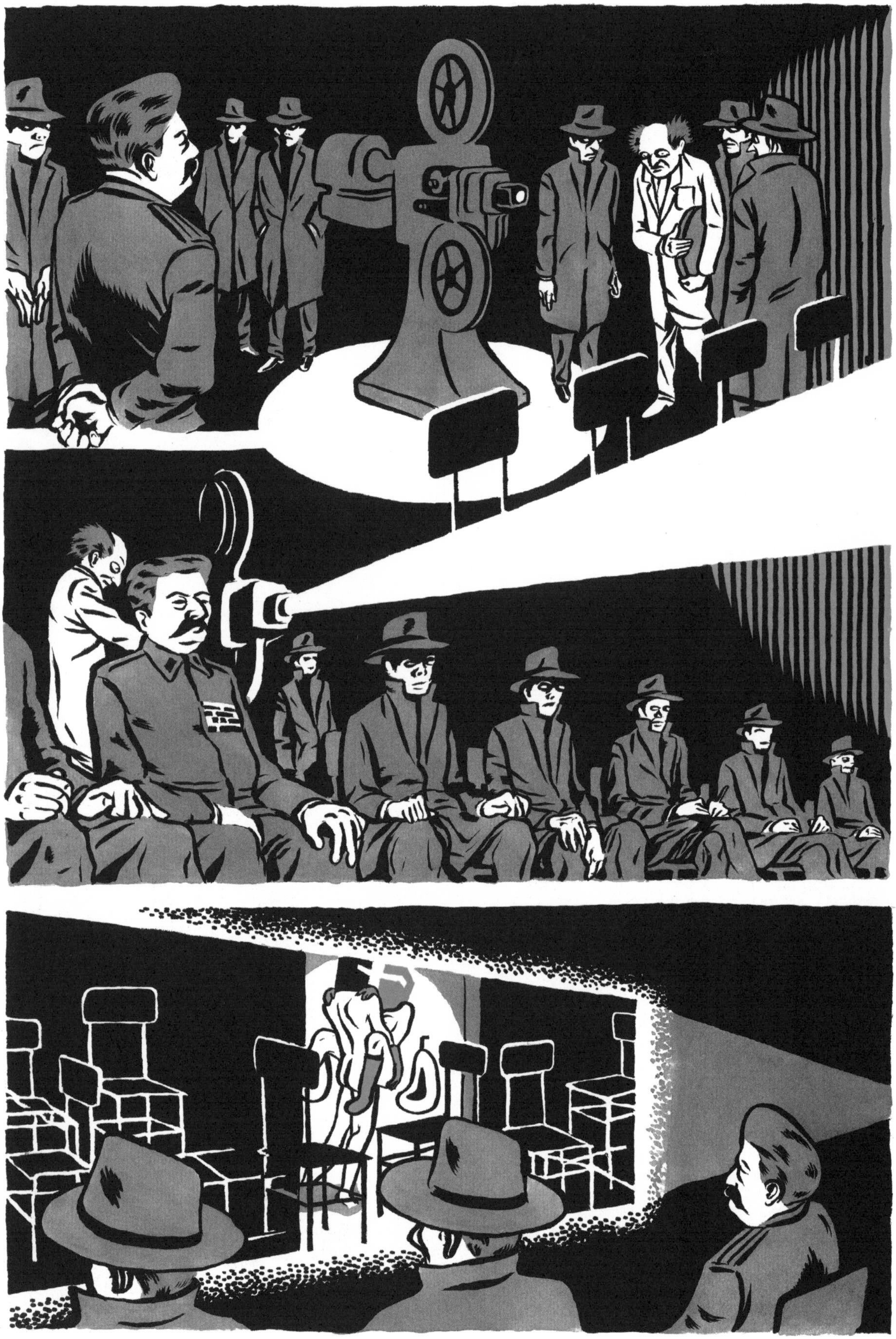

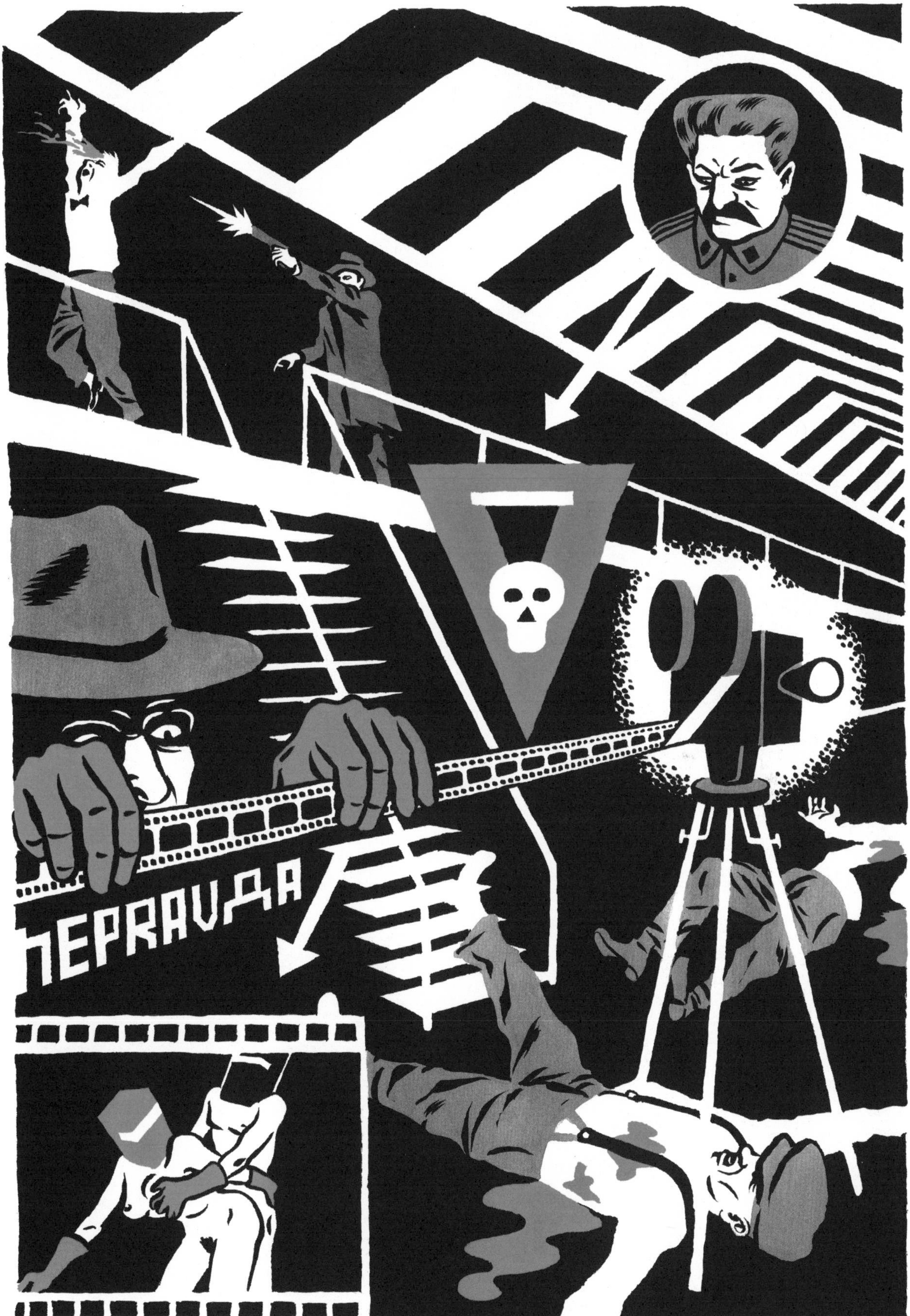
NEPRAVDA

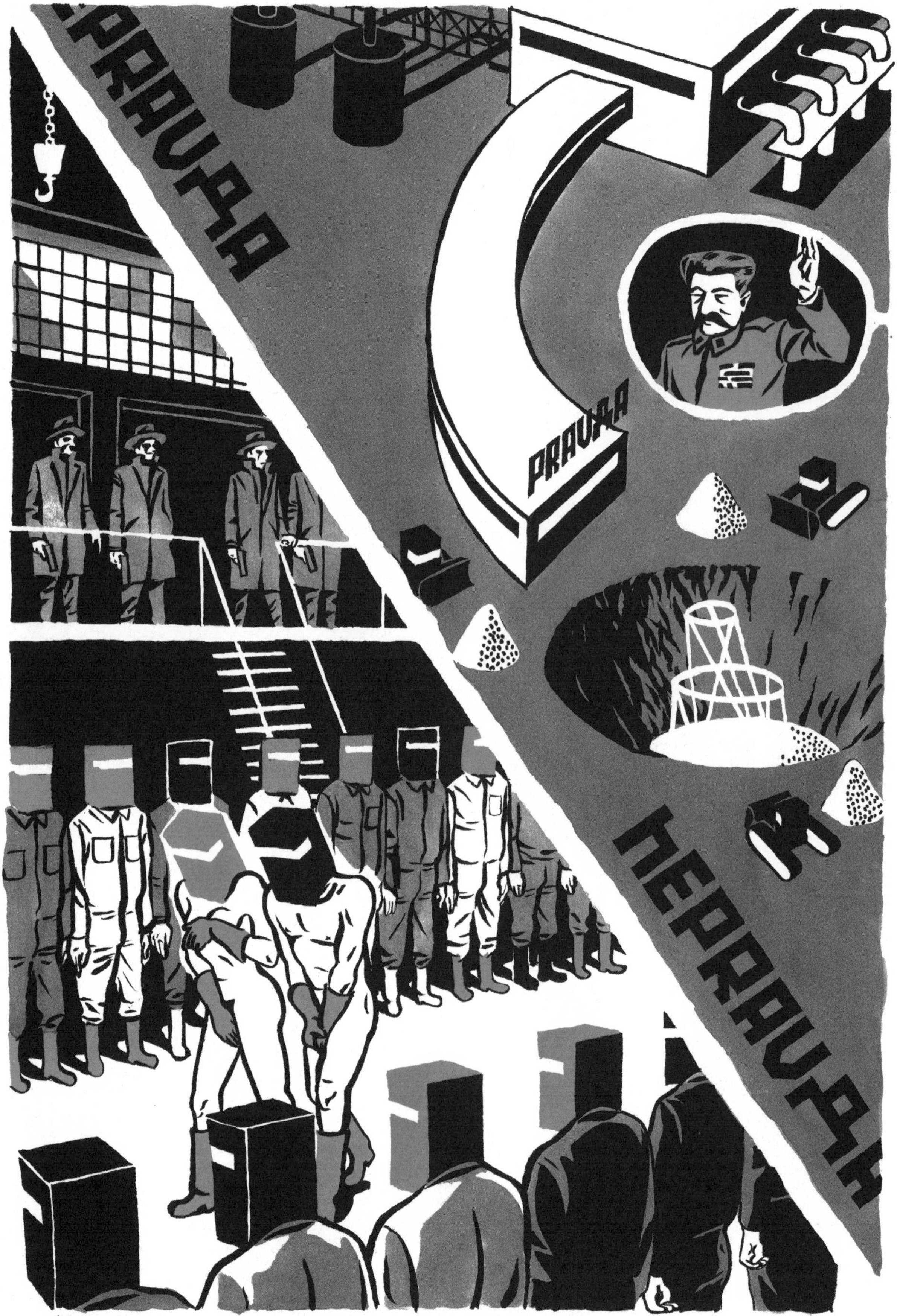
PRAVDA
PRAVDA
NEPRAVDA

* INJUSTICE – JUSTICE – INJUSTICE

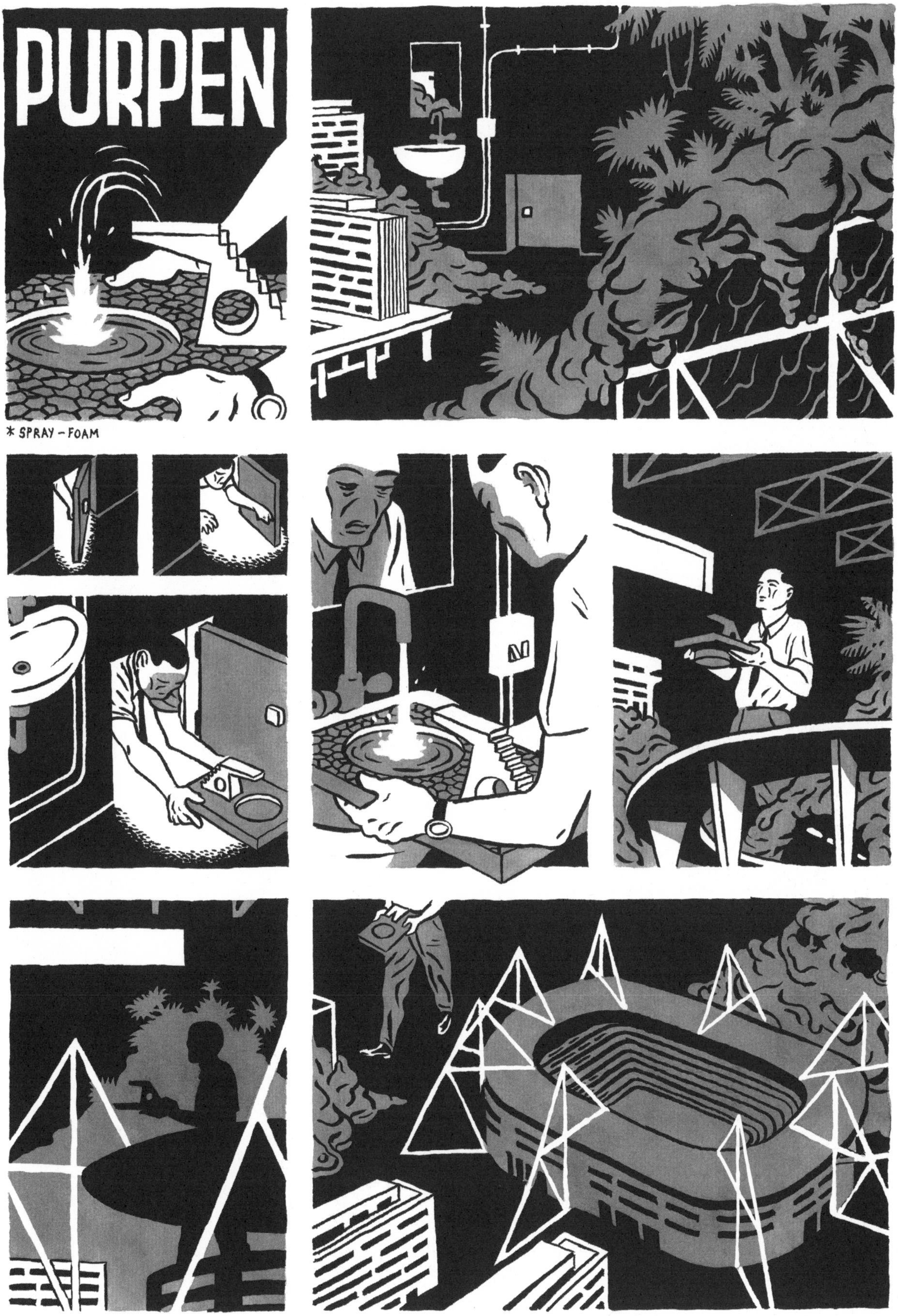
PURPEN
* SPRAY - FOAM

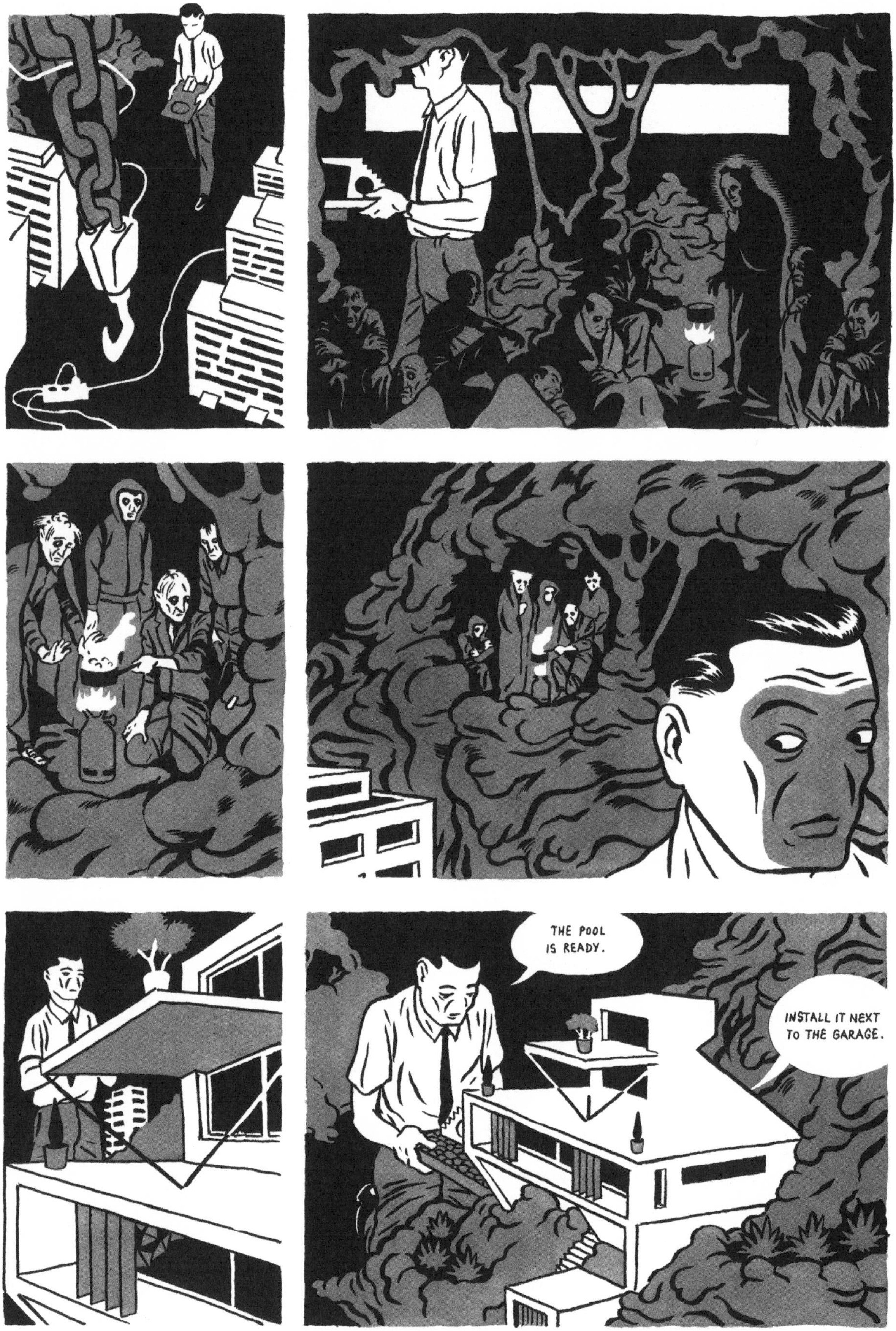
THE POOL IS READY.
INSTALL IT NEXT TO THE GARAGE.

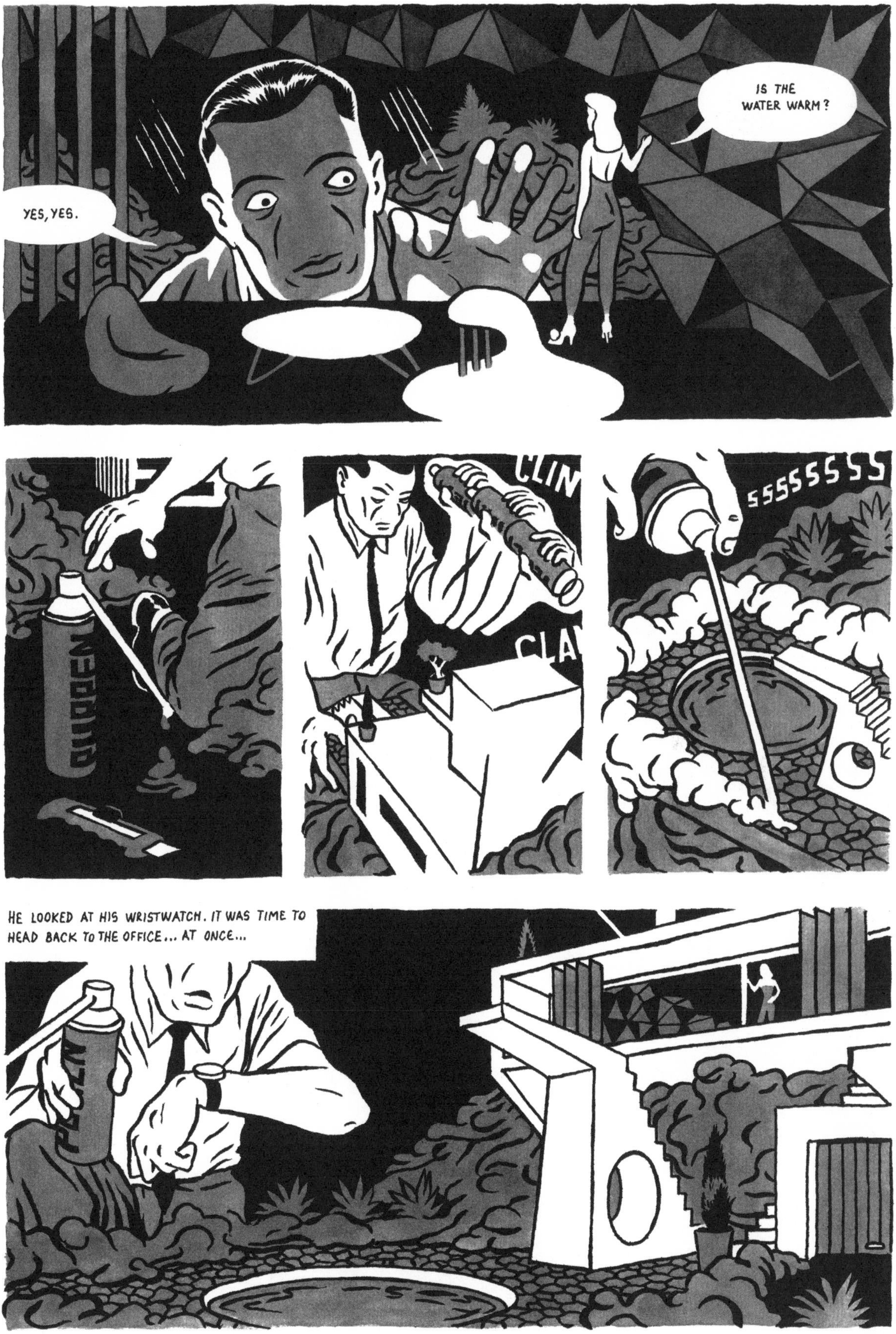
IS THE WATER WARM?
YES, YES.
SSSSSSSSS
HE LOOKED AT HIS WRISTWATCH. IT WAS TIME TO HEAD BACK TO THE OFFICE... AT ONCE...

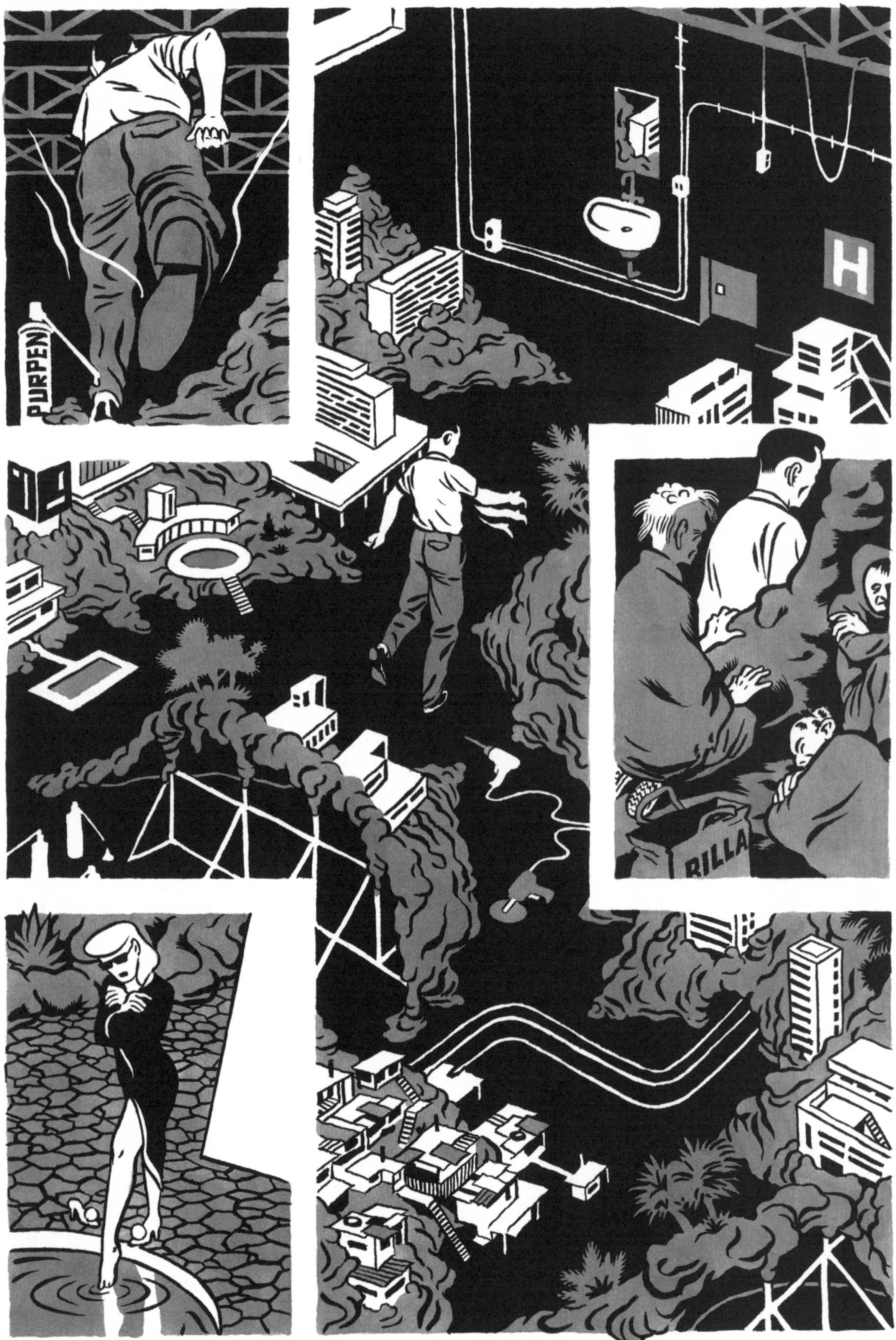
PURPEN
H
BILLA

OUTRO

GRGHHH

SSSSSSSSSSSSSSSSSSSS

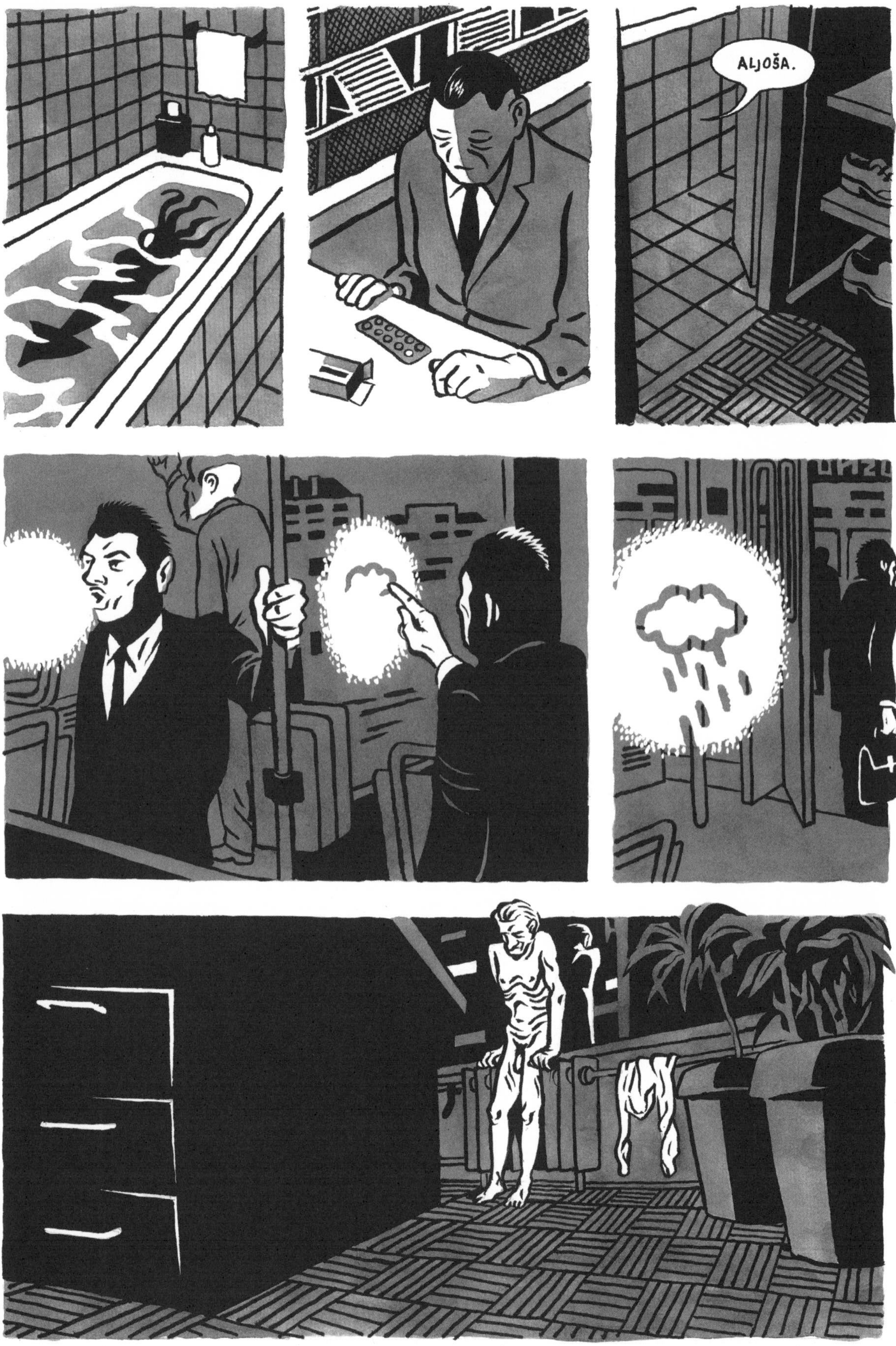
ALJOŠA.

THIS IS MY 1991 KEEPSAKE.

QUIT TAKING YOUR EYE OUT.

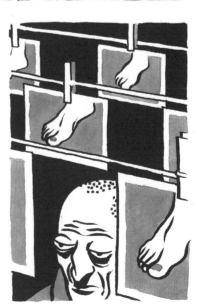

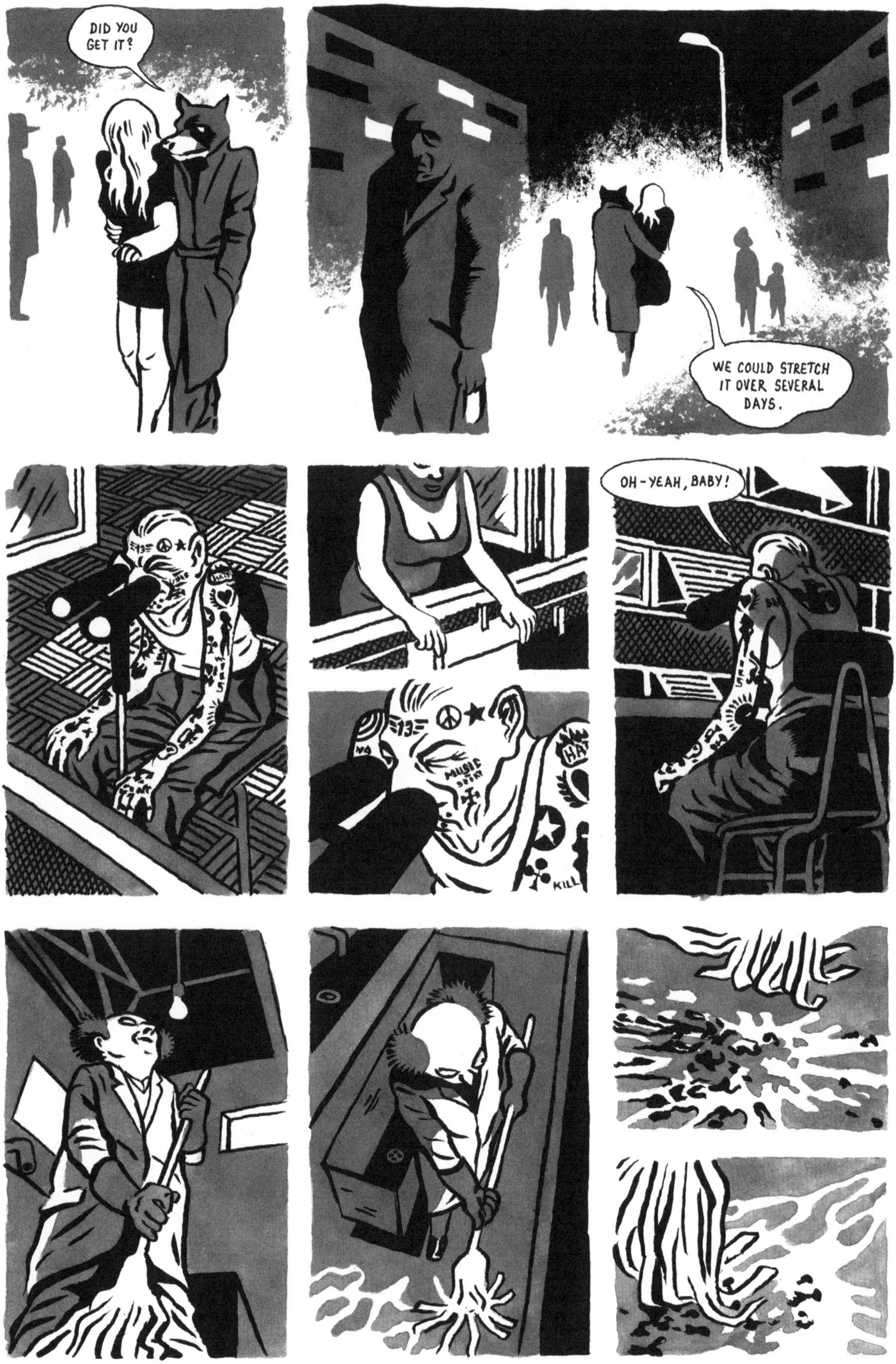
DID YOU GET IT?
WE COULD STRETCH IT OVER SEVERAL DAYS.
OH-YEAH, BABY!
KILL

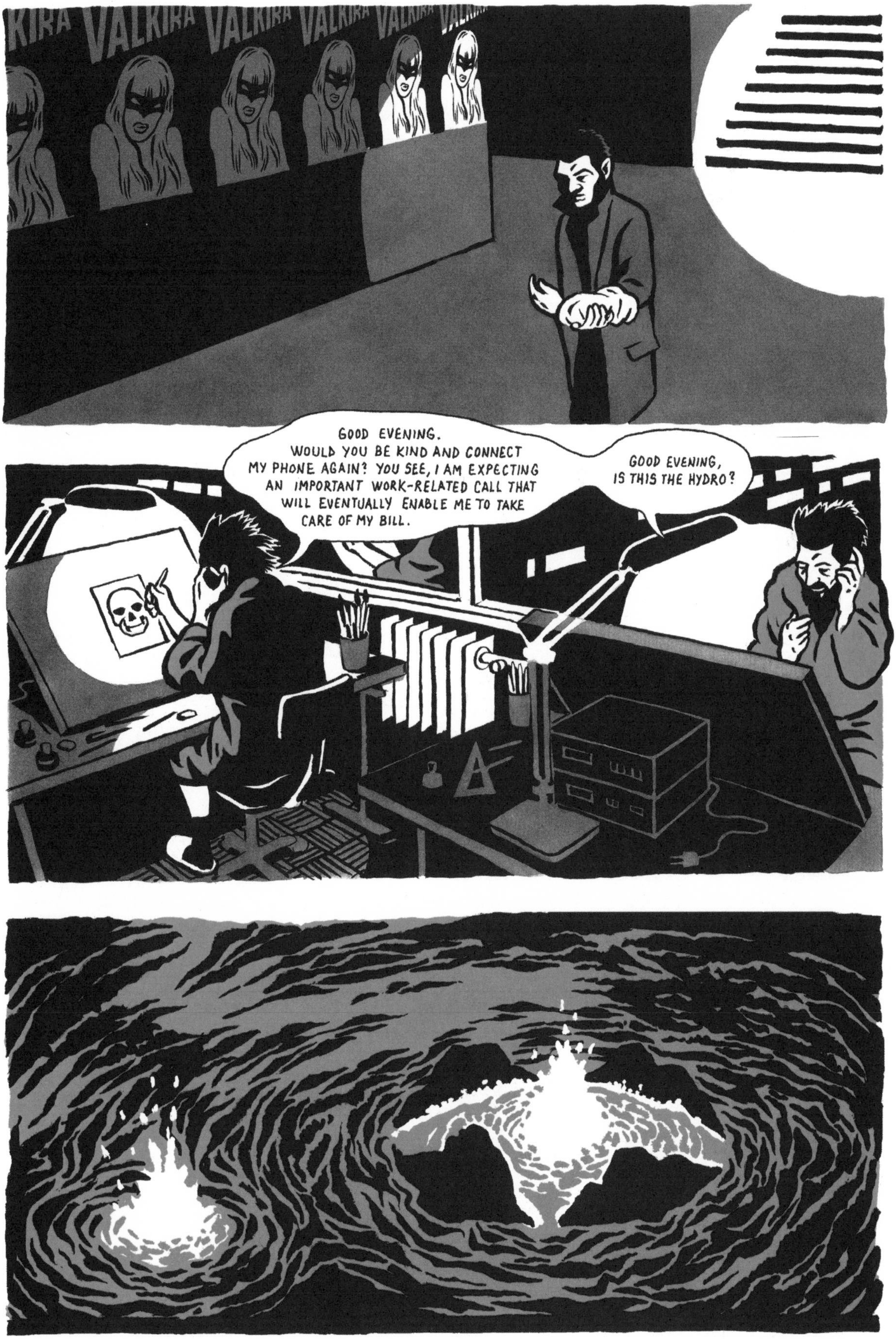

VALKIRA
VALKIRA
VALKIRA
VALKIRA
GOOD EVENING.
WOULD YOU BE KIND AND CONNECT MY PHONE AGAIN? YOU SEE, I AM EXPECTING AN IMPORTANT WORK-RELATED CALL THAT WILL EVENTUALLY ENABLE ME TO TAKE CARE OF MY BILL.
GOOD EVENING, IS THIS THE HYDRO?

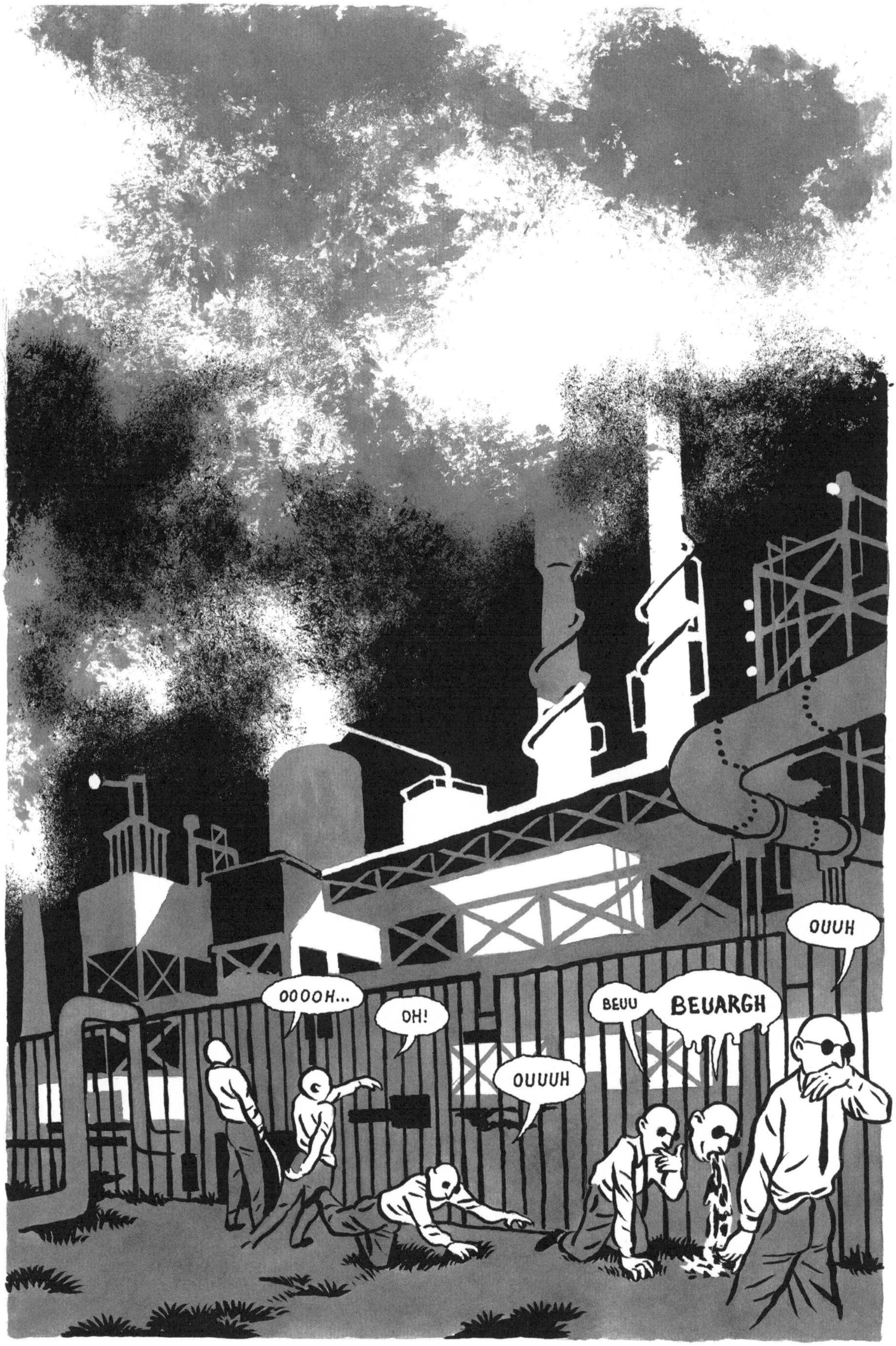
OOOOH...
OH!
OUUUH
BEUU
BEUARGH
OUUH

I first came across Igor's work in 2007 when, while visiting the old Croatian coast town of Dubrovnik, my travelling companion called to my attention a peculiar poster that promoted a certain 'Summer Culture Fever' festival. The poster was drawn entirely by hand, in brushstrokes reminiscent of the Soviet-era propaganda posters, yet the colour scheme reflected the careless summers often associated with popular youth culture of the 1960s socialist Yugoslavia. It depicted an odd sight, a crooning, tuxedo-clad lobster-man, attempting to seduce a glamorous woman. In the background one could see the seashore, and just around the bend the fortified outlines of the old city of Dubrovnik, complete with the imposing mountains directly behind. I had never seen anything like it. Despite the majestic glory of the medieval architecture I encountered at every turn, it was this image which would be synonymous with, and come to summarize, that entire trip.

It was my first visit to the region since I had left the country formerly known as Yugoslavia. I left in 1990, shortly before the onset of war and the consequent dissolution of the union. I hadn't bothered visiting for seventeen years. There was no one and nothing left to visit. Besides, according to the western media outlets available at the time, nothing but nationalistic rhetoric had been heard coming from the region for a long time. If there were any liberal voices left, they seemed eerily silent or somehow filtered out. Occasional exceptions would arise, such as the works of the Croatian author Dubravka Ugresic, or the Serbian feminist author Jasmina Tesanovic, both of whom were forced into exile. Voices of my generation were disturbingly absent, and I often wondered how they were coping. The answer, or part of the answer, would soon come to me through the body of work of Serbian cartoonists, especially Aleksandar Zograf, collected and published in 2006 by Top Shelf as *Regards From Serbia*. It was thanks to Aleksandar's invitation to visit his home town of Pancevo that I had found myself on that pleasurable detour in Dubrovnik, and back in the bosom of the old country again. What Aleksandar had inadvertently done, was change my life profoundly, simply by introducing me to the Serbian branch of the Balkan underground comics scene.

I soon found out that most of those liberal voices had moved out of their respective countries and into exile or had retreated into the underground. Those who dared express the opposing opinion in public would often find themselves vilified by the call-out culture of the politically biased media, or targets of special interest groups. In a region so heavily burdened by ethnic hatred and painful memories of the most recent war, I found an oasis of free thought, a tribe of cultural *unitarians*, the Balkan comics underground.

And although the countries occupied by this elusive tribe - Serbia, Croatia, Slovenia – still, to this day, continuously engage in the political game of one-upmanship and demonization of the other, their underground network continues to grow, as it did during the 1990s, despite war and mainstream politics. Magazines like *Stripburger,* based in Slovenia, were known to publish work by artists regardless of nationality all throughout the 1990s. Komikaze collective and magazine based in Zagreb still continues this mission, as does Novo Doba festival in Belgrade. Inspired by this model, countless other magazines and festivals have sprouted across the region.

It was through the Komikaze anthology that I first learned of Igor Hofbauer's work, and was able to put a name to the poster that had mesmerised me back in Dubrovnik. As it turned out, his comics were, and still are, regarded as the shining example of the Balkan comics underground.

Why am I writing all this? Because without providing the context I feel like I am denying the western audience the opportunity to fully comprehend the importance of Igor's work. If the fall of Yugoslavia presented an eerie foreshadowing of the political turmoil we are witnessing globally today, the Balkan underground offers a model of creative reflection, and an example of positive and unifying forces from which we can all learn and draw inspiration. It will also make you appreciate the communal effort behind the idea to bring this book before you. Johanna Marcadé-Mot, the co-founder of Novo Doba has graciously volunteered her services as letterer and designer, as she had previously done for the French edition of this book. This tendency to collaborate is deeply rooted in the culture of the Balkan underground, driven by the continuous need to reach out and connect. This is in opposition to the surface cultures which often venerate separateness and tend to emphasise differences.

In conclusion, nothing comes as close to bringing to life the shadows of the surface cultures like the comics of Igor Hofbauer. This book embodies the demons that have plagued this region for the past three decades, told in a familiar noir style, reminiscent of the old Twilight Zone episodes; except, in this case, the terror is real, and lived by millions. There is nothing else I can say about Igor's work, except that this book is meant to be held, leafed through, experienced, and ultimately praised. I have waited a long time to see his work brought to the North American public, and I thank Andy Brown for making this happen.

— Nina Bunjevac

Translation from the original Croatian by Nina Bunjevac
Design and lettering by Johanna Marcadé-Mot

Library and Archives Canada Cataloguing in Publication
Hofbauer, Igor
[Mister Morgen. English]
Mister Morgen / Igor Hofbauer ; Nina Bunjevac, translator.
Translation of: Mister Morgen.
ISBN 978-1-77262-013-9 (softcover)

1. Comics (Graphic works). I. Bunjevac, Nina, translator
II. Title. III. Title: Mister Morgen. English

PN6790 C873 H6713 2017 741.5'94972 C2017-900275-9

#8 in the Conundrum International Imprint edited by Andy Brown
First English language edition

Printed in Korea by TWP America, Inc

Conundrum Press
Wolfville, Nova Scotia, Canada
www.conundrumpress.com

Distribution in Canada: Litdistco
Distribution in UK: Turnaround
Distribution in US: Consortium

Conundrum Press acknowledges the financial support of the Canada Council for the Arts, the government of Canada through the Canada Book Fund, and the Province of Nova Scotia's Creative Industries Fund toward its publishing activities.

Canada
Canada Council for the Arts
Conseil des Arts du Canada
NOVA SCOTIA